Expanding Ecuador's Exports

PRAEGER SPECIAL STUDIES IN INTERNATIONAL ECONOMICS AND DEVELOPMENT

Expanding Ecuador's Exports

A COMMODITY-BY-COMMODITY STUDY WITH PROJECTIONS TO 1973

Ralph J. Watkins

Prepared by
Surveys & Research Corporation

FREDERICK A. PRAEGER, Publishers
New York · Washington · London

The purpose of the Praeger Special Studies is to make specialized research monographs in U.S. and international economics and politics available to the academic, business, and government communities. For further information, write to the Special Projects Division, Frederick A. Praeger, Publishers, 111 Fourth Avenue, New York, N.Y. 10003.

FREDERICK A. PRAEGER, PUBLISHERS
111 Fourth Avenue, New York, N.Y. 10003, U.S.A.
77-79 Charlotte Street, London W.1, England

Published in the United States of America in 1967
by Frederick A. Praeger, Inc., Publishers

Library of Congress Catalog Card Number: 66-15451

Printed in the United States of America

PREFACE

This study was undertaken by Surveys & Research Corporation for the National Economic Planning and Coordination Board of the Government of Ecuador.

Dr. Ralph J. Watkins, Vice President of Surveys & Research Corporation, directed the project and participated in the extensive field work conducted by the three principal specialists who served as consultants — Mr. Roger F. Burdette, agricultural economist; Dr. Amihud Kramer, processing industry specialist and Professor of Food Technology at the University of Maryland; and Mr. Joseph A. Sinclair, foreign trade specialist and head of the International Division, Commerce and Industry Association of New York. Miss Gizella Huber, a senior economist on the staff of Surveys & Research Corporation, was in charge of home office research, documentation, and tabulations of basic data and was responsible for the projections of Ecuador's exports. Mr. Alexander Ganz, Research Associate with the Harvard-M. I. T. Joint Center for Urban Studies, served as consultant on the projections of Ecuador's over-all economic targets.

In Ecuador extensive interviews were held with government officials, including officials and staff of the Planning Board, the Central Bank of Ecuador, the Development Bank of Ecuador, the Ministry of Investment Promotion, the Ministry of Economy, the Directorate of Agriculture, and the Ecuadorian office of the Latin American Free Trade Association (LAFTA). Similarly, interviews were held with officials of the American Embassy, AID Ecuador, other embassies, the Food and Agriculture group (FAO), the United Nations Special Fund's Fisheries Institute, the Reconversion Center for the provinces of Azuay, Canar, and Morona Santiago in Cuenca, the Pichilingue Agricultural Experiment Station, and provincial and municipal officials. In field visits to practically all sections of the country, discussions were held with Ecuadorian trade associations, producers' organizations, crop farmers, beef and dairy cattle producers, timber growers and distributors, fishing outfits, processors of farm, forest, and fishery products, and large and small manufacturers and distributors.

v

In the course of their work in Ecuador, Mr. Burdette and Dr. Kramer were given access by the Planning Board to drafts of many of the preliminary reports prepared for the Board by the Italconsult Mission under a program financed by the Organization of American States.

Many sources supplied basic trade statistics and commodity information--the U. S. Departments of Agriculture, Commerce, and Interior, the Organization of American States, the Pan American Union, the Food and Agriculture Organization, the United Nations, the World Bank, the Monetary Fund, and others.

To all who contributed to this study, Surveys & Research Corporation wishes to express its indebtedness and sincere thanks.

Ralph J. Watkins
Vice President
Surveys & Research Corporation

CONTENTS

LIST OF TABLES

Expanding Ecuador's Exports

CHAPTER **1** ECUADOR'S
EXPORT
TRADE

The pattern of export trade of Ecuador is that of a primarily agricultural economy with major reliance on the United States market. Products of Ecuador's farms, forests, and fisheries accounted in 1961 for about 98 percent of the value of her exports, and manufactures and minerals for about 2 percent. Of the 98 percent share, fisheries products accounted for about 4 percent and forestry products less than 1 percent, farm products thus accounting for around 94 percent. For 1962, total exports amounted to $143 million, or about $32 per capita.

The outstanding feature of Ecuador's export trade during the past decade has been the continued sharp increase in banana exports and the domination of the trade by three products— bananas, coffee, and cacao as will be seen from the table on the following page.

The "big three" have accounted on the average for almost 90 percent of annual export earnings, although dropping to around 85 percent over the past two years. Within this triumvirate, some important shifts have occurred during the past five years. Not only have banana exports continued to increase significantly, from an annual average of $56.6 million in 1953-57 to $83.0 million in 1958-62, but their relative importance in total exports has also risen substantially—from 49 percent in the first half of the decade to 60 percent in the past five years.

One of the great success stories in the postwar world of international trade has been Ecuador's capture of first place in banana exports, rising dramatically from less than 2 percent of the world market in 1935-39 and only 4 percent in 1945-49 to 25.6 percent in 1958-61. A crucial element in that

1

VALUE OF PRINCIPAL EXPORT PRODUCTS AND
THEIR SHARE IN TOTAL EXPORTS
(In Millions of Dollars)

	Total Value	Bananas[a]	Cacao	Coffee	Rice	Other	Combined Value Big Three[b]
1958	$133.9	$72.9	$20.4	$26.3	$3.5	$10.9	$119.6
1959	142.4	89.7	21.8	17.5	2.3	11.2	129.0
1960	146.2	88.9	21.4	21.9	3.7	10.2	132.2
1961	127.5	80.9	15.6	14.3	2.6	14.0	110.8
1962	142.9	82.9	15.7	20.9	0.6	22.8	119.5
Avg. 1953-57	115.0	56.6	20.9	25.7	3.7	8.1	103.2
Avg. 1958-62	138.6	83.1	19.0	20.2	2.5	13.8	122.2
Percent Distribution of Exports							
1958	100.0	54.4	15.2	19.6	2.6	8.2	89.3
1959	100.0	63.0	15.3	12.3	1.6	7.9	90.6
1960	100.0	60.8	14.6	15.0	2.5	7.0	90.4
1961	100.0	63.4	12.2	11.2	2.1	11.0	86.9
1962	100.0	58.0	11.0	14.6	0.4	16.0	83.6
Avg. 1953-57	100.0	49.2	18.2	22.3	3.2	7.0	89.7
Avg. 1958-62	100.0	60.0	13.7	14.5	1.8	10.0	88.2

a. Adjusted value of banana exports to reflect estimated true f.o.b. price, as distinct from export receipts surrendered to Central Bank.

b. Bananas, cacao, and coffee.

Sources: Boletin del Banco Central del Ecuador, September-December, 1962; Memoria del Gerente General del Banco Central, 1961; U. S. Department of State, Foreign Service Dispatches.

success story has been an equally dramatic marshaling of
the world-wide resources of disease specialists in tropical
agriculture, manufacturers of spraying machinery, the
chemical and petroleum industries, and commercial aviation
in a successful campaign against sigatoka, a leaf blight which
took its name from an infected district in the Fiji Islands.

Coffee and cacao have suffered sharp losses in their relative shares of total exports, coffee dropping from 22.3 percent in the earlier period to 14.5 percent in 1958-62 and cacao
from 18 percent to 13.7 percent. And their combined aggregate value in 1958-62 was $43 million below their 1953-57
total.

The product which has experienced the sharpest decline,
however, both in absolute value and in share of the trade,
has been rice. In 1953, rice exports totaled over $6 million
and accounted for 6.6 percent of total exports; in 1962, they
had dropped to little more than half a million dollars and
represented about 0.5 percent of total exports.

Other products for which Ecuador has been a traditional exporter include fisheries products, sugar, castor beans, balsa
wood, pharmaceutical products, toquilla straw ("Panama")
hats, pyrethrum, kapok, tagua nuts or "vegetable ivory," and
others of lesser importance. In the aggregate these other
exports doubled their share of total exports over the past five
years, from 8.1 percent in 1958 to 16.0 percent in 1962. The
increase from the 1953-57 period to 1958-62 was from 7 percent to 10 percent of total exports. Fisheries products and
sugar have accounted for the major share of the gains. In
dollar terms these other exports have increased over the past
five years from $11 million to a little under $23 million.

Ecuador's aggregate exports have gained in value over the
past decade, but the gain has been due primarily to the large
increases in banana exports. As the table of Aggregate Export
Earnings indicates, the gain in banana exports was greater
than the gain in total exports. Banana exports for 1958-62
were $132 million above the previous five-year total, whereas

aggregate exports showed an increase of only $117 million.
Calculated on an annual basis, banana exports averaged a
yearly gain of 8. 0 percent; aggregate exports only 2. 3 percent. Cacao export earnings in 1958-62 averaged 1. 8 percent annually less than in the preceding five years and coffee,
4. 5 percent less. Other exports registered an average annual
gain of 11. 4 percent.

AGGREGATE EXPORT EARNINGS
1953-57 and 1958-62
(In Millions of Dollars)

	Total	Bananas	Cacao	Coffee	Rice	Other
1953-57	$575. 1	$283. 2	$104. 4	$128. 8	$18. 4	$40. 4
1958-62	692. 9	415. 3	94. 9	100. 9	12. 7	69. 1
	+$117. 8	+$132. 1	-$ 9. 5	-$ 27. 9	-$ 5. 7	+$28. 7
Aggregate percent change 1958-62 over 1953-57	+20. 5	+46. 6	-9. 0	-21. 7	-31. 0	+71. 0
Average annual percent change	+2. 3	+8. 0	-1. 8	- 4. 5	-7. 7	+11. 4

The sharp loss in export earnings from both coffee and
cacao was attributable not to decreased tonnages but to sharp
declines in prices. As the table on the following page shows,
shipments of both coffee and cacao averaged substantially
higher in the 1958-62 period than in the five years previously,
but the average export value of cacao had dropped from 35. 5
cents per pound to 28. 5 cents; for coffee, the comparable
values were 49. 9 cents and 32. 2 cents per pound. Banana
exports showed a very slight decline in average value per

TOTAL EXPORT VALUE, VOLUME, AND UNIT VALUE
OF BANANAS, CACAO, AND COFFEE
(In Millions of Dollars)

	Bananas			Cacao			Coffee		
	Total Value	Volume (1,000 stems)	Value per stem	Total Value	Volume (mil. lbs.)	Value per lb. (cents)	Total Value	Volume (1,000 bags)	Value per lb. (cents)
1958	72.9	28.9	2.52	20.4	49.5	41.2	26.3	500.5	39.7
1959	89.7	34.8	2.58	21.8	62.9	34.7	17.5	395.6	33.4
1960	88.9	35.9	2.48	21.4	80.3	26.7	21.9	524.2	31.6
1961	80.9	32.7	2.47	15.6	71.7	21.8	14.3	391.6	27.6
1962	82.9	34.3	2.42	15.7	69.3	22.7	20.9	551.1	28.7
Avg. 1953-57	56.6	21.5	2.63	20.9	58.8	35.5	25.7	389.7	49.9
Avg. 1958-62	83.1	33.3	2.50	19.0	66.7	28.5	20.1	472.6	32.2

5

stem between the two 5-year periods, but the number of stems
exported increased by almost 55 percent.

During the past five years, the United States has absorbed
an average of roughly two-thirds of Ecuador's total banana
and coffee exports and over half of its cacao exports. Western
Europe averaged around 20 percent of banana exports, 30 percent of cacao, and 35 percent of coffee exports, with Germany
being a major market for all three products, although France
and Italy topped German purchases of Ecuadorian coffee. In
Latin America, Chile has been a steady market for Ecuadorian
bananas, and Colombia has been a major purchaser of cacao.
More recently, Japan has developed into a growing market for
Ecuador's bananas and cacao.

Of Ecuador's total exports over the years 1958-62, averaging $139. 8 million, the United States took 59. 3 percent;
Europe, 30. 0 percent; Latin America, 9. 0 percent; Asia,
1. 4 percent. Very small amounts went to Africa and Oceania;
and a similarly small amount directly to Canada, most of
Canada's purchases of Ecuadorian products being transshipped
from the United States.

These essential features of Ecuador's export trade point up
the need for diversification of the export base, regarding both
products and markets.

World demand for Ecuadorian bananas can be expected to
increase in the aggregate as standards of well-being rise, but
the relative rate of growth in major areas may level off. This
is particularly true of Western Europe, where per capita consumption in a number of countries is already approaching
United States levels and where Latin American exports will
be facing increasing difficulties in maintaining their markets
in the face of preferential treatment accorded to exports of
the European Economic Community's Associated Territories.

In the United States, while no radical shift in present
sources of banana supply is indicated, per capita consumption
has shown essentially no change over the past decade. This

leveling off suggests that the future rates of growth in banana imports may be dependent primarily on population growth.

There are favorable prospects for Ecuador of significant expansion of banana exports to Japan. For the first half of 1963 Japan replaced Germany in second place among importers of Ecuadorian bananas, and prospects for further sharp increases appear excellent.

Prior to late in 1962 Japan had restricted her banana purchases to Taiwan, but that small island, with its own program of both agricultural and industrial diversification, is no longer able to meet the demands of the Japanese market. Those demands are rising sharply as living standards move up in the booming economy of Japan. A planned reduction of the ad valorem duty on bananas from 70 to 30 percent within two years should bring a reduction in price and a further rise in consumption. Whether this distant market can be retained beyond the next seven to ten years will depend on the degree of success of current efforts by a consortium to develop banana production in North Borneo or other areas in the Far East.

For coffee, the limiting factor will be quota restrictions. Under the International Coffee Agreement, which has been ratified by the producing and importing member countries and became effective October 1, 1963, Ecuador has been allotted an annual quota of 552,000 bags for the coming three years. This level provides little scope for export expansion, since 1962 exports were already at this level—totaling slightly over 551,000 bags. Increased earnings from coffee exports, therefore, will be dependent on the price rises that may come from the stabilizing effects of the Agreement, or from other supply-demand changes, or from the establishment of markets outside the importing member countries of the Agreement. Presumably, future increases in world consumption will be prorated on the basis of the present proportionate shares of the exporting countries.

For cacao, the outlook appears improved, as a result of the agreement reached at the March, 1963, meeting of the

Cocoa Study Group to exempt Ecuador and other producers of
flavor cacao from the quota restrictions called for under the
impending international agreement. This exemption will not,
of course, guarantee increases in Ecuador's exports but will
at least assure freedom for Ecuadorian producers to ship the
maximum amount that they can market. Demand for flavor
cacao has not kept pace with aggregate cacao consumption:
global cacao exports in the past five years averaged 863,180
metric tons, an increase of more than 23 percent over the
1952-56 average, whereas flavor cacao exports increased
only 3.8 percent. The stabilizing effects on cacao prices of
the pending international agreement—if it is finally ratified—
may turn the tide in favor of a return to increased uses of
flavor cacao.

Over-all growth in export earnings will depend in part on
prospects for the "big three," in part on the prospects for
the present marginal exports, and in part on the development
of new export products and new markets which, in turn, will
depend on the availability of financial backing for new industries and on intensified marketing activities. These possibilities are explored in detail in the succeeding chapters.

CHAPTER **2** PRODUCTION BASE
FOR EXPORTS

Ecuador consists of three major regions or zones: the
coastal region, called the Costa; the two Andean ranges and
their intermountain basins or valleys, called the Sierra; and
the region lying east of the Andes, called the Oriente. All the
present major export products except part of the coffee crop
are produced in the Costa. The Sierra with its more agree-
able climate supports more than half of the population of the
country but relatively few exports. The Sierra's export potential lies in the area of temperate zone crops and products.
The Oriente with almost half of the area of the country (the
Costa and the Sierra each cover about one-fourth of the area)
is undeveloped and largely uninhabited apart from small
numbers of primitive Indians.

Somewhat more than 600,000 hectares of Ecuadorian soil
are presently devoted to the cultivation of bananas, cacao,
coffee, rice, and sugar—the traditionally important export
crops that have accounted for around 90 percent of Ecuador's
exports by value. There are ample lands of good quality and
accessible to the sea to support a production volume of each
of these products several times its present export volume. In
the rich volcanic and alluvial soils of the Guayas, Daule, and
Esmeraldas river basins and the San Lorenzo area alone there
are undeveloped lands around four times as large in area as
the present hectarage now producing these products. In addition to these undeveloped lands on the western side of the
Andes Mountains, in the Costa, Ecuador has still larger areas
on the eastern side of the Andes, the Oriente. These undeveloped lands to the east of the Andes will not be used over the
near future for producing export crops heavy and bulky in relation to their value, such as bananas and rice, for transport
costs would be prohibitive. On the other hand, crops of high
value in relation to their bulk, such as coffee and cacao, can
ultimately be produced for export economically in this area.

In the succeeding sections of this chapter the production
base for each of Ecuador's present more significant exports
will be examined.   The purpose of that examination will be
to determine the adequacy of the resource base, to appraise
the effectiveness of production, to identify barriers to more
effective performance, and generally to analyze the prospects
for continued or enhanced export volume.

BANANA PRODUCTION

For more than a decade bananas have constituted Ecuador's
number one export, accounting in 1962 for $82.9 million out
of her total export earnings of $142.9 million or 58 percent.
Yet this major export industry in Ecuador is relatively young;
it was not until 1946 that Ecuador shipped more than a million
stems.   Ecuador ranks number one in the world in banana
exports, accounting for a little over one-fourth of world exports over the past five years, compared with only 4 percent
in 1945-49 and less than 2 percent in 1935-39.

This industry is based fundamentally on an abundant supply
of fertile volcanic and alluvial soils in the coastal region of
Ecuador within easy reach of tidewater and on low labor costs.
These twin factors have enabled Ecuador to capture first place
in the world banana market.   It is possible that nowhere else
in the world can the large and flavorful Gros Michel banana be
produced as economically as in Ecuador.   And probably no
other banana-producing area has so much unused and fertile
soil, permitting extensive shifts in the areas under cultivation
as disease control or other conditions have required.

Still another major factor in Ecuador's capture of first
place in the world banana market has been a successful campaign against the leaf blight called sigatoka, which has
ravaged many other banana-producing areas over the period
of Ecuador's rise.   Financed by a modest tax on each stem
exported, an energetic Campaign in Defense of the Banana
has been carried out by the government through the National
Association of Banana Growers of Ecuador (Asociacion
Nacional de Bananeros Ecuatorianos or ANBE), involving

among other things comprehensive spraying and restricting
export of bananas to banana plantations inscribed under the
control program.

The spraying program is highly effective in keeping insect
damage and sigatoka under control, but it is not effective
against the root fungus known as "mal de Panama, " or Panama disease. No effective controls have been developed for
Panama disease. Certain controls are partially effective in
reducing the spread of the disease but the infested area must
be abandoned. Panama disease is always a serious potential
threat, but up to date it has not been a serious deterrent to
output. It has appeared from time to time, requiring abandonment of banana plantings and the shift of production to other
areas. Fortunately for Ecuador, the long dry season, occupy-
ing most of the second half of the year, helps notably to prevent the spread of this fungus disease; and the abundance of
fertile lands in the Costa provides the basis for shifts to new
areas. Clearly, however, the potential threat calls for a
major research effort to seek to discover control methods.

Production Levels and Trends

Bananas under cultivation in Ecuador in 1961 accounted for
151, 000 hectares out of a total hectarage of about 610, 000 devoted to the five principal export crops. The indications are
that total acreage devoted to bananas has changed very little
over the past decade, although both production and exports
have increased sharply. The 1954 Census reported total acreage planted at 159, 980 hectares of which 115, 080 hectares
were harvested. (The Junta de Planificacion estimate of
151, 000 hectares may not have included plantings that were
used for shade for coffee and cacao, from which production
was probably inconsequential.) Meantime production increased from 62 million stems in 1954 to 78 million in 1961;
and exports rose over the same period from 19 million stems
to 33 million.

Although total acreage planted has changed little, there
have been major shifts among the provinces within Ecuador,
as the following table makes clear.

BANANA PRODUCTION BY PROVINCE, 1961, 1954
(In Hectares)

| Province | 1961* | | 1954** | | |
	Plantings	Production (Stems)	Plantings	Area Harvested	Production (Stems)
Los Rios	60,000	30,000,000	28,170	20,320	9,848,000
El Oro	25,000	15,000,000	13,610	9,400	5,139,000
Guayas	19,000	9,500,000	33,450	22,920	11,721,000
Esmeraldas	16,000	8,000,000	36,320	25,250	10,369,000
Pinchincha	13,000	6,500,000	8,270	7,200	3,583,000
Cotopaxi	10,000	5,000,000	1,130	920	457,000
Manabi	3,000	2,500,000	27,450	19,500	14,595,000
Canar	2,000	1,000,000	2,810	1,890	343,000
Bolivar	1,000	500,000	2,290	2,150	1,254,000
Others	-	-	6,480	5,530	4,776,000
Total	149,000	78,000,000	159,980	115,080	62,085,000

* Source: Junta de Planificacion.

** Source: Primer Census, Agropecuario Nacional 1954, Republica del Ecuador.

12

These shifts have doubtless reflected the energetic search for the most suitable lands for banana production during the period of zooming banana exports, although part of the reason has doubtless been the abandonment of disease-infested areas and the move to more suitable areas. Still another reason has probably been the shift to areas more accessible to ports.

The dramatic rise in exports can be seen from the following table:

BANANA EXPORTS, 1944-62

Year	Number of Stems Exported (In Thousands)
1944	541
1945	694
1946	1,301
1947	2,687
1948	3,895
1949	5,378
1950	6,610
1951	9,605
1952	16,755
1953	15,836
1954	19,225
1955	23,900
1956	22,600
1957	26,100
1958	27,900
1959	34,500
1960	34,900
1961	33,000
1962	34,258

Source: Banco Central del Ecuador.

The table also makes clear that exports leveled off after 1958 at approximately 34 million stems. For the first seven months of 1963 banana exports (preliminary data) were 19 percent above those in the same period of 1962, and with the sharp rise of exports to Japan, it is probable that 1963 total exports may run to 38-40 million stems.

The increases in production can be attributed primarily to the disease-control program. The hectares inscribed under that control program since 1956-57 have been as follows:

Crop Year	Hectares Inscribed under the Control Program
1956-57	610
1957-58	34,173
1958-59	52,538
1959-60	79,343
1960-61	101,879
1961-62	91,454

Unless a grower is inscribed in the disease-control program, exporters will not buy his bananas. However, being in the program and following the spray program faithfully does not assure a grower that he will find an export market for his entire production. Most growers discard part of the harvested stems at the farm, and rejects at the ports frequently run as high as 20 percent of a grower's total shipments. These rejects are not a complete loss as they are used locally for animal feed, for processing, and for sale in the domestic market as fresh bananas, but prices paid for local consumption and processing are far below those paid by the exporters, generally ranging from one to three sucres a stem.

The leveling off of exports over the past four years has been due to factors other than production potentials. There were only about 100,000 hectares inscribed in the disease-control program in 1960-61 and somewhat less in 1961-62, averaging two-thirds of the total acreage. If properly cultivated one hectare should yield about 500 stems of exportable quality bananas annually. This would give about 45 to 50

million stems of exportable quality from the acreages under
the disease-control program. If all acreages planted had been
under the control program and well cultivated, about 75 million
stems would have been available for export.

It is clear that there is no production barrier to increased
exports; if markets can be found the production base is more
than adequate, not merely in present planted acreage but in
fertile lands highly suitable for new plantings. The leveling
off of exports beginning in 1959 does not mean that Ecuador
can expect no further export increases. The export demand
situation in Japan is highly favorable for further increases,
and per capita consumption in Western Europe is rising although competition from the EEC Associated Territories is a
major threat. The continued increase in population in the
United States will permit some increases even though United
States per capita consumption has shown little change for a
decade, at about twenty-one pounds a year. To bring about
these increases the country will need to take steps to promote
the sale of bananas and continue to meet the competition of
other exporting countries. If proper measures for sales promotion, quality control, and governmental programs to promote banana exports are taken, exports can still be increased
considerably above the present levels. It is reasonable to
expect that exports of fresh bananas can be expanded to at
least 50 million stems by 1973 and possibly to 55 to 60 million.

Banana Production Methods

The farmers producing bananas in Ecuador can be placed
in three general groups based primarily upon size of plantings
and cultivation methods as follows:

Peasant Farmers

These normally have less than ten hectares planted to
bananas. They use only family labor and generally have cacao
or coffee or both interplanted among the bananas. They give
little if any attention to disease control, and for various
reasons sometimes do not bother to harvest the bananas for
market. Most of the acreage outside the banana disease-control

program, about one-third of the total, is planted by this group.

Small and Medium-Size Producers

These usually have from ten hectares to fifty hectares.
They depend upon family labor for part of the planting and
cultivation practices, but also hire some additional labor.
They frequently sell to a buyer who does the harvesting. They
can generally be expected to be inscribed under the disease-
control program but must depend upon the government-sponsor-
ed program to provide the spraying services. This group will
normally have other crops under cultivation, such as cacao,
coffee, and rice. Some also have pastures for the grazing of
cattle.

Large Producers

These have more than fifty hectares planted to bananas and
will generally depend upon bananas as the major source of
their income. They utilize hired labor for nearly all the work
of planting, weeding, and harvesting of the crop. For this
group the export price of bananas is a very important consideration as to whether they will continue in the banana enterprise.
If prices fall below certain levels they cannot continue to produce at a profit and will abandon the banana production and
shift to some other crop. In this group there are about 500
producers, of whom about 16 are in the category of company
or industrial farms, having 500 hectares or more each under
banana production.

The small and medium-size farmers account for about 20
percent of the acreage planted for the export markets and the
large farmers about 72 percent. The very large farmers—
those having 500 hectares or more in bananas—control about
20 percent of the exportable production of the country.

Quality Standards and Trends

No international standards have been developed for bananas.
This makes it difficult to get any data that will realistically
indicate quality trends. In general, Ecuadorian bananas enjoy

an excellent reputation for quality in the world markets. All
exports are of the Gros Michel variety, which ships well in
the green state and ripens to a good flavor upon arrival in the
foreign markets. The fact that exporters reject up to as much
as 20 percent of each shipment arriving at the ports is a
practice that causes bitter complaints by growers, but it has
doubtless been a factor helping to keep the standards of quality
for export high. The disease-control program of ANBE is
another factor that has resulted in a consistently high quality
standard for exports. The recent trend to ship more boxed
bananas will result in still higher quality standards, provided
that strict inspection procedures are followed.

Marketing Methods in Use

The small and medium-size growers may harvest their
bananas with their own labor crews or they may sell to a local
buyer who does the harvesting. The bananas are cut and carried
to the roadside or river landing, which is the first assembly
point. At this point a number of stems are rejected and only the
larger stems with well-filled fingers are selected for shipment
to the ports of export. Those selected for export are wrapped
in banana stalks to cushion the stems and prevent damage from
bruising during the haul to the ports. The rejects are used for
animal feed or processing or sold to buyers who haul them to
local markets for internal consumption.

The larger growers follow much the same procedures in the
handling of their bananas except they will do their own harvesting and shipping to the ports, whereas most small growers sell
at the farm to a local buyer who does the hauling to market.
The larger growers are reported to select much more carefully for quality and therefore have fewer rejects at the ports
of export.

Some ten to fifteen years ago nearly all the bananas arrived
at the ports by small river barges and boats, but today a high
percentage arrives by truck. This change in transport methods
has come about with the building of roads into the banana-producing regions. The farmers along the navigable rivers continue to ship by boat and barge, and there is some transshipment

from truck to barge at river ports. Trucking rates are considerably higher than boat and barge rates, but trucking is
more rapid, flexible, and dependable.

When the bananas reach the ports of export, they are graded
by the exporter. All stems that fail to meet the quality or size
standards of the exporter are rejected. Then they are washed
to remove dust, insects, and spray residues and are prepared
for loading aboard the oceangoing ships. Most exporters are
still enclosing each stem in a plastic bag and then loading
aboard ship by hanging each stem individually from an over-
head rail. Recently some of the exporters have started to use
shipping boxes, packing them with the hands of bananas removed from the stem; but boxed shipments still account for
less than one-tenth of total shipments. Boxing is more costly
at the shipping point but it is a much more efficient shipping
method and the boxed bananas can be delivered to the retail
stores when the bananas reach the markets in the importing
country, thereby minimizing handling costs.

The stems rejected by the export graders are sold for local
consumption, for processing, or for animal feed, generally
priced from one to three sucres per stem, a price that covers
only a fraction of the trucking costs of five or six sucres from
the farm to the port of export. The stem may be sold for as
much as four or five sucres if it is of extra quality and bought
for shipment to other areas of Ecuador for local consumption.

Production Costs, Price Levels, and Trends

No adequate farm management studies have been conducted
in Ecuador to determine production costs. Such production
cost studies as are available were made by budgetary types of
analysis, in which someone who is familiar with production
methods merely adds up the normal costs of performing each
cultural operation. After arriving at a cost per hectare in this
manner, a yield per hectare is arbitrarily set and the cost of
producing a stem of bananas is estimated. Most of the studies
of this type place the cost of bringing a hectare of virgin land
into production, including the first harvest, at about 3,500

sucres and that for succeeding years at 2,500 sucres to 3,000 sucres. A yield of about 600 stems per hectare is then esti-mated with a farm value of 10 sucres to arrive at the following profits per hectare:

Yield of 600 stems at 10 sucres gives gross income of S/6,000
Less costs 1st year   3,500
   Net profit to farmer 1st year   2,500

Yield of 600 stems at 10 sucres gives gross income of   6,000
Less costs for 2nd and each succeeding year   2,500
   Net profit to farmer 2nd and each succeeding year   3,500

Yield of 600 stems at 10 sucres gives gross income of   6,000
Less costs 2nd and each succeeding year   3,000
   Net profit to farmer 2nd and each succeeding year   3,000

Some inquiries among individual producers while on a field trip in the Santo Domingo de los Colorados area regarding costs, income, and profits revealed considerable variation from one grower to another as follows:

Grower A

Sale of 500 stems to local buyer at farm at 11 sucres   S/5,500
Sale of 120 stems to local buyers of rejects at 2 sucres   240
Used on farm 130 stems for animal feed valued
   at 1 sucre   130
Total income from one hectare   5,870
Less production costs of   2,500
   Net profit per hectare   3,370

Grower B

Sale of 500 stems to local buyer who did the
   harvesting at 5 sucres   S/2,500
Rejects of 150 stems were lost for lack of a buyer   000
Total income from one hectare   2,500
Less production costs, cleaning and weeding only   800
   Net profit per hectare   1,700

Grower C

Sale of 100 stems to exporter at port at 22 sucres   S/2, 200
Loss of 500 stems for lack of a buyer at port of export   000
Total income from one hectare   2, 200
Less costs:
   Production costs, weeding, cleaning,
      spraying, and harvesting   S/1, 600
   Hauling to port 600 stems at 2 sucres
      (in own truck)   1, 200   2, 800
      Net loss per hectare   600

Grower D

No sales for lack of buyers, fed 650 stems to
   livestock at estimated value of 1 sucre   S/   650
Less production costs of   1, 500
   Net loss per hectare   850

It is obvious that those interviewed were not representative, but the results are of interest as showing instances of the variation in actual conditions encountered.

The evidence is inadequate and conflicting, but the studies available plus the interviews held with a small number of banana farmers indicate that production costs at the farm will average about 5 sucres per stem. The costs of transporting from the farm to the ports of export will average approximately another 5 or 6 sucres per stem, bringing total production and marketing costs at the port of export to an average of about 10 to 11 sucres per stem. The f.o.b. price on bananas going to the United States is about 23 sucres per stem. But these stems have incurred various taxes and fees which will absorb much of the excess over the grower's production and shipping costs. The bananas exported to Europe and Japan are priced f.o.b. port of export at about 19 sucres per stem, and those to South American ports up to 14 sucres. These prices also include the extra costs added through export taxes and levies.

The exporter sells in a foreign country and is paid in the currency of that country or in United States dollars. He will

consider his f.o.b. costs at the dollar costs of exchange for
the sucres he must buy to pay farmers and his Ecuadorian
operating costs. Under Ecuadorian law the Central Bank of
Ecuador requires the exporter to turn over to the Bank foreign
exchange earnings in the amount currently of $1.80 per stem
exported, for which he receives sucres at the official rate of
18 to the dollar (actually 17.82, the buying rate) in contrast to
the free market rate, currently at 19 and a fraction sucres to
the dollar but for the year ended June 30, 1963, having ranged
from 23.27 in July, 1962, to 21.23 in June. For balance-of-
payments purposes, the Central Bank assumes that the exporters sell their bananas at the world price, which the Bank
estimates currently at $2.60 per stem. The exporter's ex-
cess, then, over the amount of foreign exchange for which he
received sucres at the official rate, is 80 cents, which amount
he can sell at the free market rate.

The revenue to Ecuador from the export of bananas is
computed by the Central Bank on the basis of this world price.
Thus, the 1962 exports of a little over 34 million stems brought
an estimated foreign exchange revenue of approximately $83
million or an average value for that year of about $2.45 a stem.

CACAO PRODUCTION

Prior to 1900, Ecuador was the world's largest exporter of
cacao. In 1850 Ecuadorian exports were 5,500 short tons.
They increased slowly until about 1900, when they were averaging slightly above 20,000 tons. Between 1900 and 1930 there
was a rapid increase in world demand, and world exports expanded from about 50,000 tons to 500,000 tons annually.
Ecuador was able to expand its exports from an average of
20,000 tons in 1900 to 49,000 tons in 1916, but by 1933 her
exports had fallen to less than 12,000 tons. Between 1950 and
1960 considerable recovery was made, and Ecuador has averaged about 33,500 metric tons of exports during the past three
years. In the meantime world exports have expanded to slightly over 1 million tons annually.

The decrease in Ecuadorian exports between the late 1920's
and the late 1940's is attributed in large part to an infestation
of diseases, primarily "Witches'-broom" and "Monilia Pod
Rot, " but another factor was undoubtedly the sharply lowered
prices that prevailed from 1921 through 1946. The New York
price per pound fell from an average of almost 16 cents in 1920
to less than 8 cents in 1921 and except for 1928 and 1929 did
not rise above 10 cents until 1947, barely exceeding 4 cents in
the 1930's. The 1947 average of more than 25 cents, from a
level of 9 cents in 1946, initiated a period of relatively favorable prices.

Cacao Production Methods

Cacao is produced by both large haciendas and small farmers
in Ecuador. But the methods followed by both the small and the
large producers are substantially the same. Both use large
amounts of hand labor and very little mechanized equipment.
The large producers who must hire the labor they use will
abandon their plantings sooner than the peasant-type farmer
if prices are low or if another crop, such as bananas, gives
a higher net return. In most cacao-producing areas of
Ecuador, cacao and bananas are frequently interplanted, with
the bananas serving as shade for the cacao. In the establishment of a new cacao planting, the banana gives an immediate
return during the first few years before the cacao starts to
yield a crop. This interplanting system makes it easy for the
small or peasant-type farmer to become established in the
cacao enterprise. A large percentage of the recent cacao
plantings has been made by the small and medium-size farmers
using the interplanting system.

Production Levels and Trends

Since the establishment of the Pichilinque Experiment
Station in 1943, considerable work has been done to introduce
new high-producing plants and varieties resistant to diseases.
This has been followed by a number of new plantings which are
giving yields that exceed those of the older plantings which
were infested with diseases. When Fowler and Lopez made

their study[1] in 1947 they reported that average yields were
0.29 pounds of dry cacao per tree and that some of the better
cultivated haciendas were getting yields of about 1.00 pound
per tree. The 1954 Agricultural Census indicated that average
yields were 0.55 pounds per tree for those trees in production.
A later study by Retondi, the FAO expert, showed estimates of
average yields of 0.45 pounds per tree, but some of the better
farmers were getting in excess of 2.00 pounds per tree. Interviews with a small sample of growers and technical people indicated that production levels and yields have been increasing
since the 1930's, when the industry was at its lowest ebb. It
is not known whether yields are as high today as in the period
1910 to 1916, when Ecuador exported about 40,000 tons annually.
The old plantings of cacao have to a large extent been complete-
ly abandoned and have reverted to jungle or have been cut down
and the land planted to other crops. On the other hand, there
are many plantings that are not producing an optimum yield for
lack of weeding, pruning, spraying, and good cultural practices.
If these semi-abandoned plantings were given good attention,
Ecuador could increase production by 10 to 20 percent. There
are also a number of new plantings that have not come into production plus an even larger acreage of trees which are still
under the age for maximum production. If economic conditions
should make it profitable to export larger quantities of cacao,
Ecuador could increase its present production sharply without
waiting for new plantings to be made. According to the Junta
de Planificacion, cacao production should rise from 40,000
metric tons in 1963 to 90,000 metric tons in 1973, without an
increase in acreage.

Quality Standards and Trends

No official grade standards exist for cacao, but trading is
carried on under a system of commercial grades that are

---

1. Robert E. Fowler and Gustavo Lopez, The Cacao Industry
of Ecuador, U. S. Department of Agriculture Foreign Agriculture Report No. 34 (Washington: U. S. Government Printing
Office, July, 1949).

recognized and generally respected by importers and exporters.
The best quality cacao comes from Manabi Province and is
known by the trade as "arriba," meaning up or upland cacao.
It was from this area that the best cacao was produced before
the plantings became infested with "Witches'-broom" disease.
This cacao was in demand because of its stronger aroma and
flavor. With the introductions of new disease-resistant strains
and varieties, it is reported that the cacao produced in the
Manabi area is much milder in flavor and aroma. This has
resulted in a smaller and smaller volume being sold by the
cacao traders as "arriba." Exporters in Guayaquil report
that the introduction of the new disease-resistant varieties has
led to a pronounced decline in the quality of the cacao being
exported in recent years. Other factors which determine
quality are the amount of diseased or moldy beans and the
methods used for fermenting the cacao beans before they are
dried and sacked for shipment.

     The recommended method of handling and preparing the
cacao beans for market is to remove the beans from the pods
and place them in wooden boxes to ferment for three to five
days. During the fermentation process the beans should be
turned several times daily. The beans are then placed on a
platform or flat surface to dry. The drying can be done in the
sun or by mechanical dryers using heated and circulated air.
The beans must be thoroughly dried to prevent spoilage and
molding. Most producers do a fairly efficient job of drying
the beans before sending them to market because they know
that they will be heavily discounted if there should be moldy
beans in the shipment. But a large part of the crop is not
properly fermented before the beans are dried.

     The larger growers generally have special processing
houses in which they ferment the cacao and a large concrete
slab on which the beans are later dried in the sun. They also
have at least one or two experienced employees to supervise
and handle the fermenting and drying operations. These
growers normally send to market a relatively uniform and
high-quality product. Some of the smaller farmers sell the
cacao pods to local buyers who specialize in the fermenting

and drying operations. If these local buyers have adequate
facilities for processing the beans, they also produce a fairly
uniform and high-quality product. Many of the small growers
do not have adequate facilities for fermenting and drying the
beans, and this results in much cacao of poor quality arriving
at the ports.

Production Costs and Prices

No farm management surveys have been made in Ecuador
to determine what production costs would be under different
methods of growing, harvesting, and marketing. A number of
production cost estimates were found in the various reports
reviewed, but none of them was based upon farming operations
as carried out in practice. Most were budgetary type estimates in which costs were determined by totaling the costs of
various operations normally carried out in the production of
cacao on a supposedly typical farm. One of these reports
estimated that the cost of bringing cacao into production over
a five-year period by interplanting cacao with bananas would
give cost and income as follows:

COSTS AND INCOME FOR INTERPLANTING
CACAO AND BANANAS
(In Sucres)

Year	Costs per Hectare	Income per Hectare			Net Profit or Loss
		Cacao	Bananas	Total	
1st	3,619	0	0	0	-3,619
2nd	1,751	0	1,162	1,162	- 589
3rd	4,235	1,860	1,860	3,720	- 515
4th	4,472	4,220	1,740	5,960	1,488
5th	4,123	6,400	--	6,400	2,277

Estimates found in another report assumed costs and income of bringing a semi-abandoned planting of bananas and
cacao back into production over a five-year period as follows:

COSTS AND INCOME FOR SEMI-ABANDONED
PLANTINGS OF CACAO AND BANANAS
(In Sucres)

| Year | Costs per Hectare | Income per Hectare | | | Net Profit or Loss |
		Cacao	Bananas	Total	
1st	2,850	0	1,519	1,519	-1,331
2nd	1,652	0	1,519	1,519	- 133
3rd	2,013	700	1,500	2,200	187
4th	2,392	4,175	1,500	5,675	3,283
5th	1,975	5,030	1,500	6,530	4,555

If these estimates of costs and income are realistic, it takes a farmer putting in a new planting of cacao six years to recover his initial investment. The farmer bringing an old planting back into production could recover his investment and start to get a net return during the fourth year. Inquiries made as to costs of doing certain of the operations, such as clearing, weeding, and planting, and observations on field trips lead to the conclusion that the cost estimates listed above are some-what higher than actual costs in practice on most haciendas and are considerably above those of the small farmer who uses family labor that would be idle if not used for bringing the land into cacao production.

In a report on cacao published by FAO in 1955, it was shown that during the period from 1915 to 1935 when Ecuador's pro-duction and exports were declining production in Africa and Brazil was increasing at a rapid rate. [2] It was concluded that both Africa and Brazil could increase production during this period primarily because both use peasant methods of pro-duction in which labor costs would be less than those of the

2. United Nations, FAO Commodity Series, "Cacao," Bulletin No. 27 (November, 1955).

then existing large haciendas of Ecuador. When world prices
improved after 1946 the cost of production differential became of less importance, and Ecuador again began to regain
its position as an exporter. As long as the f.o.b. price to
growers remained above about 20 cents per pound the large
Ecuadorian haciendas could maintain their production. If
world prices should at some future date experience another
sharp decline this would no doubt have an adverse effect
upon Ecuador exports from commercial production. Direct
costs of producing cacao in Ecuador have been estimated at
about 10 cents a pound, but the f.o.b. price is roughly twice
as much. It should be pointed out that the f.o.b. price to
the grower is influenced by export taxes and levies. When
the export taxes and levies of various types are added they
total about 20 percent of the f.o.b. price to exporters.

COFFEE PRODUCTION

Coffee is produced in practically all the provinces of
Ecuador, but the greater part of the production comes from
the coastal province of Manabi, which produced 587,900
quintals out of 766,500 quintals total reported for the country
in the 1954 Census. All the other coastal provinces produced
less than 50,000 quintals each. The only Sierra provinces
producing more than a few hundred quintals each were Loja
and Bolivar with 38,600 quintals and 19,400 quintals, respectively. In Manabi Province, 61 percent of the farmers
covered by the census reported the production of coffee.
Most of the coffee produced in Ecuador comes from relatively
small farms.

Out of 106,910,000 trees reported in the 1954 Census,
only 83,400,000 were in production, which suggests that a
large number of young trees had been planted which had not
yet come into production. This is also indicated by some
unpublished coffee acreage estimates prepared by the Ministry
of Fomento, as shown in the table on the following page.

ESTIMATED COFFEE ACREAGE,
1953-62

Year	Hectares of Coffee Harvested
1953	60,665
1954	87,850
1955	101,643
1956	96,722
1957	93,215
1958	98,470
1959	101,371
1960	114,432
1961	113,873
1962	151,976[a]

a. The sharp increase from 1961 is questioned. Junta de Planificacion estimate for 1963 is 130,000 hectares and production of 42,900 metric tons.

Source: Direccion General de Agricultura, Ministerio de Fomento.

It appears that Ecuador has increased its plantings by about 50 percent since the agricultural census was taken in 1954. Hectares harvested do not necessarily indicate the extent of total plantings, as most farmers will have young trees which have not come into production. But hectares harvested over a period of years should give a trend of plantings as trees begin to bear after the third year. Exports plus internal consumption are also an indication of plantings. Export and internal consumption data are shown in the following table.

COFFEE EXPORTS AND INTERNAL CONSUMPTION,
1952-62

Year	Total Ecuadorian Coffee Exports in Bags[*]	Estimated Internal Consumption in Bags[**]
1952	340,000	67,800
1953	311,000	69,500
1954	351,000	75,000
1955	384,000	80,000
1956	426,000	85,600
1957	481,000	76,000
1958	500,000	103,500
1959	396,000	101,750
1960	524,000	111,500
1961	381,000	122,750
1962	551,000	125,000

Note: Bags weigh 60 kilograms or 132.276 pounds each.

Source: * U. S. Department of Agriculture, Foreign Agriculture Service to 1961; 1962, Banco Central del Ecuador.

** Banco Central del Ecuador, but the rounded data for 1954 and 1955 have been interpolated by the authors because of obvious typographical errors for those two years in the original source. The 1962 data are preliminary estimates as of June, 1963.

The data on exports plus internal consumption show considerable variation from year to year, which can be explained by differences in yields, stocks, and other factors. It appears, however, that plantings and production have been steadily increasing. On a trip through the Manabi Province, it was observed that new plantings of coffee were being made at a

somewhat greater rate than the retirement of old plantings.
If export markets are available there is a good probability
that Ecuador will continue to increase production at about
5 percent per year. A limiting factor is the export quota
under the International Coffee Agreement, which is set
currently at only slightly over the 1962 export level.

Production Methods

Most of the coffee plantings were made with bananas as a
shade crop or planted in the forest where the low-growing
brush and trees had been removed and a large part of the
larger trees left for shade. One also finds from time to time
both cacao and coffee interplanted with bananas as the shade
plant, but more frequently these cacao and coffee interplant-
ings are found in the forests. In drier sections of Manabi
Province there appears to be very little harvesting of the
bananas where coffee is interplanted. It is probable that the
bananas were used as a cash or food crop during the period
when the young coffee trees were coming into production.

The degree to which coffee plantings are given good attention
in Ecuador varies greatly from one farm to another and from
one area to another. To get good yields of high-quality coffee,
it is important that the plants be weeded and pruned regularly.
The berries should be harvested at proper stage of maturity
and then processed by the washing method. The literature
available in Ecuador and the observations made on field trips
indicate that most plantings are not given good cultivation.
Many plantings are not weeded more than once or twice annually. Harvesting of most plantings results in a large percentage
of immature berries. Once the berries have been harvested,
less than one-half are properly processed to obtain the top
quality and prices. The volumes of washed and natural coffee
exported from Ecuador and the corresponding prices from
1954 to 1961 are shown as follows.

WASHED AND NATURAL COFFEE EXPORTED, PRICES AND VOLUMES, 1954-61

	Washed Coffee		Natural Coffee		Percent of Total Exports
Year	Quintals Exported	Price per Quintal	Quintals Exported	Price per Quintal	Sold as Washed Coffee
1954	115,520	$69.9	341,803	$56.1	25.3
1955	112,705	56.2	379,680	42.7	22.9
1956	289,590	63.9	250,811	44.1	53.6
1957	319,319	52.2	308,194	41.1	50.9
1958	324,277	42.6	328,532	36.5	49.7
1959	271,288	37.8	244,654	29.3	52.6
1960	436,999	35.0	246,743	26.4	63.9
1961	220,828	33.4	290,021	25.3	43.2

Source: Banco Central del Ecuador: export permit data.

Although there has been some improvement in the quality of coffee exported since 1954, the percentage of washed coffee sold in 1961 dropped considerably below the level for the five preceding years.

Productivity Levels and Trends

Production of coffee has been expanding in Ecuador in recent years, but there appears to have been no increase in yields. The evidence, however, is very thin. The 1954 Census showed total plantings as 106,910,000 trees, of which 83,400,000 were in production.

Quality Standards and Trends

Ecuadorian coffee on the world markets sells at a discount in relation to that from Colombia and Central America. This is in large degree the result of lower quality of coffee from

Ecuador. The prices of washed coffee from Ecuador are considerably higher than the "natural" or unwashed, but even the washed coffee sells at considerable discount under Colombian coffee and in general below that of washed coffee from other Latin American countries. There has been, however, considerable improvement in the quality of Ecuadorian coffee exported over the past two to three decades.

Prior to 1929 all the coffee from Ecuador was natural or unwashed. During 1929 two growers in Manabi Province imported depulping machines and began washing coffee on a small scale. The new method of handling the berries following harvest demonstrated the advantages of washing as to both improvement in quality and economies in handling. However, most of the coffee growers were slow to adopt the new method. Ten years later there were so many complaints of exporters regarding the quality of Ecuadorian coffee that the government invited a mission of Colombian technicians to come to Ecuador to give demonstrations on how to harvest and wash coffee. The work of this mission is reported to have stimulated some interest among growers, but relatively little progress was made toward universal adoption of the washing method. In 1949 under the sponsorship of Messrs. Galo Plaza and Clemente Yerovi, the Ministry of Economy helped the farmers of Manabi Province to organize the Instituto Ecuatoriano del Cafe. In 1957 this Institute made another attempt to improve the quality of Ecuadorian coffee by establishing a modern washing plant at Lodana. This new plant is reported to have made some progress toward improvement in coffee quality, but as was shown previously, about one-half of the Ecuadorian export is still exported as natural coffee which sells at a discount of about 25 percent below washed coffee.

Part of the slowness of the Ecuadorian farmer to adopt better methods of coffee production, harvesting, and curing of the harvested berries can be attributed to the small size of the individual operator—also to the low cultural standards of the peasant farmer and his lack of financial resources to obtain better equipment. It should be pointed out, however, that coffee production in Colombia is conducted generally

by small peasant-type farmers, who have learned to produce
a coffee that sells at top prices on the world markets.   The
coffee industry in Colombia is well organized but the washing
process is generally done by small-scale equipment.

Production Costs and Prices

Without the benefit of a cost of production survey, it is
possible to provide only some crude estimates of how much it
costs the Ecuadorian farmer to produce a quintal of coffee.

A study made by FAO in Colombia and Guatemala recently
shows that labor was one of the major costs of coffee production
in areas of Colombia where production methods are similar to
those for Ecuador.   For the farmer whose labor is provided
by his family, especially women and children who have no alternative source of employment, he will continue to produce
coffee on a declining market much longer than the commercial
farmer who must pay cash for his labor.   In the previous table
showing exports of washed and natural coffee with the corresponding price for each, exports of washed coffee have increased from 1954 through 1960 in spite of a decrease of about
50 percent in prices.   This is an indication that coffee prices
on the world markets are still high enough to pay the cash
costs of harvesting and marketing.

The greater part of the washed coffee will be produced by
the larger and commercial-type farmer, whereas the peasant-
type producer will produce primarily natural or unwashed
coffee.   From 1954 to 1960 the price of washed coffee declined
from $69.90 per quintal to $35.00.   During this period exports
increased from 115,520 quintals to 436,999 quintals.   This
would indicate that at the price of $35.00 it was still profit-
able for the commercial farmer to produce coffee.

It should be pointed out that the $35.00 per quintal is the
f.o.b. price to importers at the port of export in Ecuador.
The price received by the farmer would be considerably less
as export taxes, marketing costs, and transport from the
farm to the market must be deducted.   When these costs are

deducted the grower will probably get about $25.00 per quintal
or about 25 cents per pound. The cost of bringing a hectare
of coffee into production is not greatly different for a commercial grower than that for bringing a hectare of cacao into
production. Yields of the two crops will also be somewhat
the same on a poundage basis, with coffee giving slightly more
pounds per hectare but less per tree. On the basis of discussions with producers and others familiar with the industry,
it is estimated that commercial production costs are about 20
cents a pound. The peasant producer's cash outlay would, of
course, be much less, probably about half of the cited estimate.

For the commercial farmer, declines in prices can quickly
cause them to abandon their coffee plantings, but the peasant-
type producer is very likely to continue producing even though
prices fall to levels that are ruinous for the commercial
grower. Since a very large part of the Ecuadorian production
is by small producers, it is probable that production will continue to experience a healthy growth regardless of world price
trends. The limiting factor for exports, however, will be the
quota assigned Ecuador under the new International Coffee
Agreement.

SUGAR PRODUCTION

Ecuador has produced sugar cane since colonial times, and
prior to World War I sugar was one of the country's major exports. Depressed conditions throughout the world in the late
1920's caused prices to decline and exports were discontinued
in 1932. From that date until 1957 local production was maintained generally at about the national needs; exports were in-
frequent and indeed in poor crop years it was necessary to
import.

Production Levels and Trends

Refined sugar production is confined primarily to the Costa,
in Guayas Province, where there are two large refineries

which have 16,000 hectares of cane in production in their own
haciendas, for which production of refined sugar in 1962 was
about 135,000 tons. These two refineries have recently
modernized their plants and produce sugar of good quality.
In Loja Province there is a new refinery of small size built
in 1961, which had a production of 3,000 tons of refined sugar
in 1962. Near Salinas in Imbabura Province there is another
small refinery that was completed in 1963.

The Ecuadorian sugar situation since 1950 is shown in the
following table.

SUGAR PRODUCTION, IMPORTS, EXPORTS, AND NATIONAL CONSUMPTION, 1950-62
(In Metric Tons)

Year	Production	Imports	Exports	Apparent National Consumption[a]
1950	52,000	--	3,900	48,100
1951	57,000	--	--	57,000
1952	59,000	--	--	59,000
1953	61,000	--	8,300	52,700
1954	58,000	5,300	--	63,300
1955	57,000	20,000	--	77,000
1956	73,000	--	--	73,000
1957	86,000	600	10,000	76,600
1958	83,000	--	14,700	68,300
1959	95,000	--	30,300	64,700
1960	115,000	--	13,000	102,000
1961	125,000	--	41,000	84,000
1962	138,000	--	62,000	76,000

a. Changes in stocks are not known and may account for
some of the indicated changes in consumption.

Source: Unpublished report of the FAO Mission in Ecuador.

The above data reflect the situation for refined sugar only and do not include production of panela, a locally made type of brown sugar, used by the Indian population throughout the Sierra. In 1956 there was estimated to be 21,794 hectares of cane planted for panela production and 9,109 hectares used for the production of aguardiente, rum, and other liquors. Recent revised estimates by the Junta de Planificacion show sugar production for 1963 of 150,000 metric tons and panela production of 56,000 metric tons. Acreage for 1963 was estimated at 20,000 hectares for sugar and 20,000 for panela.

Both of the refineries on the coast are in the process of further development and the two smaller refineries in the Sierras have not reached full development yet. If the present high prices for sugar in the world markets should continue all of the refineries can be expected to continue to expand production until the capacities of the refineries have been met. The aggregate rated capacity of the two large coastal refineries is 200,000 metric tons; and that of the two Sierra refineries is 40,000 metric tons.

If world prices should continue at something like present levels, the coastal refineries will probably make additional installation and be able to pass the present capacity by 1973. With a moderate decline in price they can still be expected to increase production to about the present refining capacity of 200,000 metric tons. Production costs at the Sierra refineries are high, and they can be expected to reach full capacity only if the internal demands of the Sierra increase and a government policy of protection is followed in case there should be a heavy decline in the present high world prices. Taking all factors into consideration it can be expected that Ecuador will be producing at least 220,000 metric tons of refined sugar by 1973. The production target is 270,000 metric tons.

There are several factors that will be of importance in determining how large a surplus will be available for export during the next ten years. National consumption of refined sugar will no doubt increase, but this rate of increase will probably be at a slower rate than took place from 1950 to 1960 when national consumption more than doubled. Shifts in demand from panela to refined sugar could be an important factor. Present consumption of panela is somewhat lower than refined sugar consumption, 53,400 metric tons compared with 88,800. Government policy with respect to either internal or export prices will be an important factor. The decrease in national consumption from 102,000 metric tons in 1960 to 76,000 metric tons in 1962 may have been caused by the increase in sugar prices, although in part it may reflect changes in stocks. If the future policy is to hold internal prices high to protect the newly established refineries at Loja and Imbabura Provinces, internal demands will remain modest. This will also encourage more panela consumption, which is not under controlled prices. The coastal refineries have relatively low production costs, but they are slightly higher than those of some of the important world producers. If the government should place high export taxes on exports, this would adversely influence the volumes they will produce for export. Considering all the factors involved and assuming the government follows a policy that encourages the continued development of the sugar industry, it is reasonable to expect sugar exports of about 90,000-100,000 metric tons by 1973.

Quality Standards and Trends

Prior to the improvements made in the two large coastal refineries about 1956, Ecuadorian sugar was of a dark-colored and coarse-grade quality. This was the type and quality most in demand by local consumers, because they were accustomed to using panela. Today the sugar produced by the modern refineries is highly refined white sugar that meets the standards of the world markets.

Marketing Methods in Use

The coastal refineries are vertically integrated corporations with marketing agencies that handle all marketing operations from the plants to the retail dealers. They also have offices, warehouses, and a sales organization at Guayaquil for handling export sales.

The panela production is primarily a home industry. It depends upon the local retail markets and local merchants as a sales outlet. Some of the panela is consumed on the haciendas where it is produced.

Production Costs, Price Levels, and Trends

The coastal refineries report their production costs at about 2.75 cents to 3 cents per pound. This is slightly higher than some of the more efficient exporting countries where production costs are as low as 2.5 cents per pound. It is slightly under the world market price for 1957-61 when the average monthly price at Caribbean ports was 3.53 cents (U.S.) per pound for shipment to destinations other than the United States. During 1962 and 1963 the shortage in Cuban supplies has resulted in prices rising to about 7 cents a pound at Caribbean ports. When two small Sierra refineries get into full production, their costs can be expected to decline somewhat but it is doubtful that they can be reduced below about 4.5 cents. If world market prices should continue to present levels there will be no problem for all refineries to meet competition. If world prices should return to the 1957-61 levels, the coastal refineries can still export at a profit but those in the Sierra will need to be protected by tariffs or through some type of subsidy measures.

The coastal refineries are large organizations that have low production costs, their own facilities for carrying on variety improvement programs, and are generally in a favorable position to bring about increased and efficient production for export. If given a continued favorable economic climate in which to develop and expand, they can be expected to provide at least 200,000 metric tons of production

by the year 1973.   The revised production target of the Junta
de Planificacion is 270,000 metric tons.

RICE PRODUCTION

Rice has been grown in Ecuador since colonial times but
it was a subsistence crop until the 1920's.   With the drastic
decline in cacao exports in the late 1920's, farmers began
producing more bananas and rice.   Rice exports during the
1930's followed in importance banana exports.   By 1940
exports of rice were second to bananas in volume but were
exceeded by cacao and coffee in value.   In 1946 exports
of rice reached 67,100 metric tons with a value of $15.2
million and were the first in value among all exports.   Since
1946 exports of rice have shown a declining trend, almost
vanishing in 1962.   Acreages harvested since 1954 have
shown a rather steady increase but commercial production
has varied considerably from year to year, output in 1962
being about the same as in 1946.   Data on acreages, production, exports, and consumption for milled rice are shown
in the table on the following page.

The data presented in the table include only the rice
that is produced and handled through commercial channels.
The government agencies preparing these statistics point
out that a rather large acreage is harvested and consumed
locally that never passes through the larger rice mills and
for this reason is not reported in the official statistical
records.

MILLED RICE ACREAGE, PRODUCTION, EXPORTS,
AND CONSUMPTION, 1946-62
(In Metric Tons)

Year	Hectares Harvested	Commercial Production of Milled Rice	Exports	Consumption
1946	--	102,100	67,100	--
1947	--	112,700	62,000	29,700
1948	--	87,500	63,100	37,100
1949	--	109,800	30,900	35,500
1950	--	62,300	61,600	48,400
1951	--	61,200	6,900	37,600
1952	--	69,600	56,500	44,100
1953	77,887	104,400	32,800	27,500
1954	37,938	46,000	19,500	41,200
1955	62,843	69,400	20,700	44,700
1956	50,209	60,200	11,700	50,100
1957	63,348	81,000	37,400	47,600
1958	84,245	62,100	37,100[a]	30,700
1959	87,539	78,300	22,200	41,300
1960	91,135	52,400	37,300	36,900
1961	94,646	84,400	23,900	46,700
1962	111,751	100,500	4,600	59,400

a.   From 1958 these export data cover paddy rice exports
only.

Source: Production, export, and consumption from Banco
Central del Ecuador.   Hectares harvested from unpublished
Report of Ministry of Fomento.

Note: Production data are total receipts at the rice mills,
and consumption data are movements out of mills less exports.   These data therefore represent commercial production
and consumption and do not include large volumes produced on
farms and consumed by the farmer's own family.

Revised Data on Milled Rice

Since this report was completed, the Junta de Planificacion
has prepared revised figures on milled rice (and other products)
for 1968 and 1973 and corresponding revised estimates for 1963
(as representing the actual situation). The 1963 estimates
follow (milled rice):

Acreage	110,000 hectares
Production	154,000 metric tons
Yield per hectare	1,400 kilograms
Exports	25,000 metric tons
Seed	7,700 metric tons
Waste	15,400 metric tons
Available for human consumption	105,900 metric tons
Refuse (3 percent)	3,200 metric tons
Human consumption	102,700 metric tons
Human consumption per capita	22.3 kilograms

These revised figures helpfully resolve conflicts among the
data cited here from other sources. It is believed, however,
that they do not affect the substance of the analysis on rice in
this section.

The Italconsult Mission made some studies in 1962-63 to
determine total paddy rice production and arrived at the
following estimates, based on both the 1954 Census and the
data of the Office of Agricultural Statistics, Ministry of
Fomento.

PADDY RICE PRODUCTION AND CONSUMPTION,
1954-61
(In Metric Tons)

Year	Hectares Harvested	Production[a]	Internal Consumption
1954	51,300	75,166	57,711
1955	78,500	102,056	81,307
1956	92,920	106,092	94,395
1957	104,200	127,794	90,410
1958	108,800	132,840	108,829
1959	115,800	143,542	128,059
1960	--	157,557	133,843
1961	--	152,233	132,998

a. Includes production available for sale and consumption after making deduction for seed and losses on farm.

Source: Unpublished reports of Italconsult Mission to Ecuador.

Analysis of the above table suggests that unless strong action is taken Ecuador will eventually arrive at a point where all of the national production will be used by the internal market. In the sections to follow, it will be pointed out that Ecuador has the land resources to increase greatly her production and exports of rice, provided these resources are efficiently and effectively used.

Rice Production Methods

Two types of rice cultivation are followed in Ecuador. One is locally known as winter rice because the crop is planted in December and January and harvested in May and June. This method might be called irrigated production because the rice is generally grown in water and is frequently irrigated by crudely constructed canals. The other method is known as summer rice as it is planted in May and June in the low-lying areas after the recession of the waters that flood these lands during the rainy season. This rice is harvested is September and October.

Most of the work of preparing the land, planting, cultivating, and harvesting of rice is done by hand. A large percentage of the rice growers are day laborers or sharecroppers who rent a small tract from the large land-holders. They normally pay for the use of the land at about three or four quintals for each hectare planted. They clear the land of trees and brush, then transfer the seedlings from a plant bed to the field where the seedlings are re-set in rows under several inches of water. During the growing season the weeds might be removed once or twice but frequently no attention is given the crop until time to harvest. Harvesting is done with a hand sickle and threshing is by tramping off the kernels on a packed earth spot in the field. The use of fertilizers and selected seed is the rare exception rather than the rule.

Production Levels and Trends

Production varies greatly from one area to another and for different plantings within the same area. Along the Daule River and in the Babahoyo and Milagro areas, average yields of paddy rice are estimated at 40 to 45 quintals per hectare, but individual plantings will vary from as little as 5 quintals to as much as 80 quintals per hectare. The extent to which average yields have increased or decreased over the past two decades is a debatable question. On a field trip in which visits were made to the Daule River and Milagro areas, a few plantings were seen where the yields of paddy rice would probably exceed 80 quintals per hectare, but these good plantings were rarely found. Most plantings were full of weeds, contained several varieties, and were generally poorly cultivated. It is doubtful if average yields have improved any since the industry emerged from a subsistence crop status in the 1920's. The bringing in and mixing of new varieties with the old ones could well have resulted in lower average

yields caused by uneven maturing and shattering of the over-
ripe stalks during harvest.

With the population increasing rapidly and the demand for
more rice for internal consumption increasing, Ecuador will
need to take steps to increase production if the country expects to maintain even its present level of exports. The
solution to this problem is a reduction in production costs and
increased yields and improvements in the quality of rice.
Unless the government initiates some very vigorous programs
for rice there is a strong probability that the export of this
product will become nil within a few more years.

There are ample, good quality rice-growing lands available
in Ecuador. The Daule River Basin has 233,200 hectares,
most of which is highly productive land and well adapted to the
production of rice, yet only 50,610 hectares were in cultivation
and improved pastures at the time the census was taken in 1954.
There were only 54,156 hectares which were not under farm
ownership. This would indicate that the landowners were not
making full use of 128,434 hectares of land, a large percentage
of which is well adapted to rice production. To bring all the
good rice production land into rice cultivation would require
capital outlays for irrigation, but there are still areas not
fully utilized in this river basin which can be placed under
rice with water control methods rather than irrigation. Water
control through the construction of dikes and the use of pumps
for both irrigation and drainage will be more practical and
economical than large irrigation and drainage systems.

East of and adjacent to the Daule River Basin there is an
area in the basin of the Guayas River which appears to be
equally well adapted to rice production. This area extends
from Vinces, Ventanas, and Puebloviejo in the north to several
miles south of the Duran-Cochancay Highway. This area consists of about one million hectares of land of which only about
25 percent was under cultivation and improved pastures when
the last census was taken. In the Milagro area some of the
best fields of rice were observed while on a field trip from
Guayaquil to Cuenca via Milagro and Cochancay.

Quality Standards and Trends

Ecuador produces a large number of varieties and strains of rice. Each variety has characteristics that determine its acceptance or non-acceptability for export. The principal varieties being grown in 1962 are listed with prices and esti-mated importance as follows:

PRINCIPAL RICE VARIETIES, GROUPING AND PRICE

Grouping	Varieties	Price per Quintal	Estimated Percent of Total Crop in Each Group
1	Chato	60 sucres	5
2	Chileno Magnolia Piedra	75 sucres	25
3	Canilla	80 sucres	45
4	Fortuna	85 sucres	20
5	Rexoro Nira Blue Bonnet Sun Bonnet Century Patna	90 sucres	5

Source: Interviews with various rice mills and technicians working in the rice trade.

The Chato variety is very popular among growers because of its short growing season and ease of threshing by hand methods, but it is not of good quality. Chileno, Magnolia, and Piedra are readily acceptable by local consumers but are not in demand for export. Fortuna is also highly regarded in the domestic market, but it is not well adapted for the export trade because of its thin hull, which results in fermentation during transport to the mills. The fifth group, which includes the Rexoro, Nira, Blue Bonnet, Sun Bonnet, and Century Patna varieties, is the type of rice most desired in the export markets. These are imported varieties that constitute a very small percentage of the total crop in Ecuador.

Nearly all of the rice is of poor quality as it arrives at the mills in Ecuador. It is common practice for the moisture content to be in excess of 20 percent. When the trip from the farm to the mill is a long one, there is fermentation that causes discoloration of the grains. The rice almost never arrives at the mill with a moisture content of under 14 percent, which limit is essential for its safe storage and transport. Another factor that is responsible for the poor quality of Ecuadorian rice is the practice of growers to use mixed varieties at time of seeding. This results in the rice maturing unevenly as well as the other objectionable features of mixing varieties. This failure to standardize on one or two types and grades is a problem in the development of an export market.

In spite of the general low quality of the Ecuadorian rice, there has probably been considerable improvement in over-all quality during the past ten years, and the country does not produce a quality that would be inferior to that found in a number of other Latin American countries where rice is grown primarily for local consumption. Countries producing for export have learned through long experience, however, that the export buyers can be very discriminating, especially when there is a general abundance on the market, and have improved their quality to meet this competition.

There are a few rice mills that have modern equipment and which do a creditable job of cleaning, drying, milling, and classifying the rice, but the small, poorly equipped, and inefficiently operated mills are in the majority. With the small volume of good varieties of rice these modern mills can produce a milled rice of top quality. But only a small percentage of the total arrivals are of good types, and an even smaller percentage is of good quality. The critical problem in Ecuador is not the lack of natural resources for producing a high quality exportable rice but the small percentage of mills equipped to mill rice properly and the inability of farmers and the local merchants to deliver a good type and quality of rice to the rice mills.

Prices and Costs of Production

High costs of production are another factor that makes it difficult for Ecuador to develop a larger export trade in rice. These high costs are attributable to the large amounts of hand labor used and the very low yields obtained in Ecuador. Again, it is not the lack of good soils, climate, and growing conditions but the failure or inability of the farmers to follow better rice-growing practices. Paddy rice yields for Ecuador and a selected group of rice-growing producing countries are shown as follows:

RICE YIELDS BY COUNTRY

Country	Average Production of Paddy Rice 1955-60 (million pounds)	Yield of Paddy Rice per Acre (pounds)
Spain	847.5	5,168
Italy	1,619.1	4,666
Egypt	3,082.3	4,539
Japan	32,651.2	4,053
Peru	597.0	3,575
United States	4,934.1	3,189
Argentina	407.9	2,956
Uruguay	124.0	2,884
Taiwan	5,325.2	2,765
Surinam	156.4	2,334
Mexico	528.3	1,854
Ecuador	278.2	1,686
Colombia	800.5	1,668
Brazil	8,944.7	1,370
Venezuela	125.0	1,136
Panama	228.1	1,018

Source: U. S. Department of Agriculture, Agricultural Statistics.

Of the countries listed in the above table, Spain, Italy, Egypt, United States, Argentina, Uruguay, Taiwan, Surinam, and Brazil are exporters, while Mexico is an important importer (Japan was an importer until recently); and Peru, Colombia, Venezuela, and Panama are occasional importers when local production does not meet national demand. Brazil is the only exporting country out of the group with lower average yields than Ecuador.

The United States, Italy, and Spain get yields two to three times those in Ecuador. In addition, they produce a rice for export that is of much better quality than that exported from Ecuador. The importers will give preference to exports of high quality and take Ecuador exports only at a discounted price. The low Ecuadorian wages help to some extent to counterbalance the higher yields and quality of the important exporters, but any advantages gained in this field are quickly lost because of the excessive amounts of hand labor used by Ecuadorian rice growers. Some comparative studies by the Economic Commission for Latin America of the amounts of labor used to produce rice are shown as follows:[3]

Country	Hours of Labor per Hectare
United States	36.0
Argentina	96.0
Chile	474.0
Colombia	649.0
Ecuador	1,051.0

When one considers the enormous quantities of hand labor involved in rice production and adds to this the low yields, it becomes evident why Ecuador finds it difficult to meet the competition of exports from other countries. It is clear that practices are such that labor is very inefficiently utilized.

---

3. United Nations, ECLA, "Productividad de la Agricultura Ecuatoriana," Boletin Economica de America Latina, Vol. VI, No. 2 (October, 1961).

The f.o.b. export prices of rice during 1961, when there were exports of both paddy and polished rice, were about $4.00 and $6.00 per quintal, respectively. This represents about 72 sucres per quintal at the port for paddy rice, but the price to the grower will be 10 to 50 percent less depending upon distance to market, amount of discount for moisture content, and middlemen's charges. For the grower who received only 40 sucres a quintal at the farm and who could get an average yield of 40 quintals per hectare, there would still be some net profit in growing rice at the high input of 1,051 hours of hand labor per hectare, provided that he could hire labor at 1 sucre per hour. This would leave the commercial farmer 549 sucres per hectare to cover his other costs and his profit. Unimproved riceland is reported to be leased out to tenant farmers and sharecroppers at 2 to 4 quintals of the rice harvest per hectare. The commercial grower's profits per hectare may be calculated as follows:

Income:	40 quintals at S/40		S/1,600
Less:	Hired labor	S/1,051	
	Seed	40	
	Value of land	120	
	Other miscellaneous expenses	100	1,311
	Net profit per hectare		S/ 289

It should be pointed out that the commercial farmer who can produce 40 quintals of rice per hectare is probably able to produce 500 exportable banana stems per hectare at a net profit of 2 sucres per stem for a net return of 1,000 sucres.

When farmers point out, as several of them did in the Milagro area, that they could not make a profit growing rice, they may have meant that rice growing was not profitable so long as they could find a market for bananas at the existing banana prices.

There were a few commercial producers who reported that they were making a profit from the growing of rice. Visits and interviews with a small sample of these growers showed that their success can be attributed to: 1) much higher than average yields; 2) the planting of better varieties and seed, which results in better quality and a higher price; 3) more efficient use of labor with a much smaller labor input per hectare; and 4) better leveling and water control during the growing season. The income and costs per hectare of these few high-grade commercial farmers are estimated as follows:

Income:	120 quintals at S/70		S/8,400
Less:	Labor 600 hours at S/2	S/1,200	
	Seed	150	
	Value of land	300	
	Use of machinery	500	
	Fertilizers	500	
	Other miscellaneous expenses	500	3,150
	Net profit per hectare		S/5,250

The commercial rice grower who can get yield of this magnitude and the better price for his rice is making much higher profits than he would receive from bananas. A banana yield of 500 stems for export is considered to be very good, and few producers can obtain a net profit of more than 5 sucres per stem, which would give a net profit of 2,500 sucres per hectare as compared to 5,250 sucres for the highly efficient producer of rice.

For the sharecropper, who is the primary producer of rice in Ecuador, the primary concern is to get as much return as possible from the labor of himself and his family, which might otherwise be unemployed. He normally arranges with a landowner to use some 2 or 3 hectares of land for which he will pay to the landowner about 3 quintals per hectare for each hectare harvested. Assuming that he gets a total crop of 50 quintals of rice from which he must use 10 quintals to pay the landlord and replace his seed, he will have a net of 40 quintals for sale. Assuming further that he will get only 30 sucres per quintal and has used 3,000 hours of labor to produce the crop, he will have a return of 1,200 sucres at the rate of only 40 centavos per hour for the labor of himself and family.

BALSA LUMBER PRODUCTION

The balsa tree produces the lightest commercial lumber in the world, the dried lumber weighing from six to eight pounds per cubic foot. The lighter types weigh about one-half as much as cork and have similar insulating properties against heat and cold. Ecuador is the only Latin American country which has exploited the balsa tree on a commercial scale, although the tree grows in moist tropical zones as far north as the southern border of Mexico and as far south as the tropical forests of eastern Bolivia. It is also grown on the island of Ceylon in Asia. It is a tropical tree that grows wild whenever the seedlings can get a fair amount of sunshine, and it reaches lumber size in about ten years.

During World War II there was a sharp increase in demand for balsa for the construction of rafts and certain types of aircraft. In 1945 Ecuadorian exports of balsa reached a value of $1,359,000 but declined to $532,000 in 1946 and $209,000 in 1947. By 1950 there had been considerable recovery in exports when the volume reached 3,487.9 metric tons with a value of $678,000. Since 1955 exports have remained at about the level obtained during the war.

The recovery in balsa exports following the postwar drastic decline was reported by the balsa exporters and sawmill owners to be due to its increased use in toys in the United States and to substitution of balsa for cork and other insulators in refrigerated truck bodies in Europe. Balsa is competitive with some of the new plastic materials as an insulator. It has the advantage of being cheaper and stronger from the construction point of view, but is more difficult to mold into odd forms and shapes and absorbs moisture unless specially treated to give its surface a complete waterproof seal. Very little research has been completed to determine what new uses might be found for this unusual type of lumber or how it might be more effectively used for the existing purposes.

BALSA EXPORTS, VOLUME, AND VALUE,
1950-61

Year	Volume of Balsa Exported in Metric Tons	Value of Balsa Exports	
		In Ecuadorian Sucres	In U. S. Dollars
1950	3,487.9	9,193,000	678,000
1951	5,566.1	17,520,700	1,168,000
1952	4,504.9	14,705,500	980,400
1953	4,258.5	14,778,100	985,200
1954	4,028.8	14,133,900	942,300
1955	3,999.2	15,752,900	1,050,200
1956	3,986.5	15,565,700	1,037,700
1957	6,597.8	29,247,800	1,949,900
1958	4,905.4	22,995,400	1,533,000
1959	4,489.3	23,218,600	1,547,900
1960	4,093.7	20,256,400	1,350,400
1961	3,762.5	20,593,200	1,255,100

Source: Banco Central del Ecuador.

Local lumber dealers and technicians generally report that it is of no value as a construction timber, but on closer questioning they admit that they have never given it a fair test. A few buildings were seen in Ecuador where balsa had been used as weight-bearing timbers and as sheathing protected from the rains. In each of these uses it was reported to have been standing up well and to be as good a material as some of the more expensive local lumbers. In one structure it was used as a sheathing in a roof that was covered with a waterproof roofing material. The owner of this structure pointed out that the thick balsa sheathing served a dual purpose of providing both strength and insulation from the sun. At Manta surfboards made from laminated balsa were being used and showed no signs of splitting or damage from the water and use. These surfboards had been given several coats of spar varnish in the same way as surfboards of other lumbers.

The balsa lumber would seem to have qualities that would make it an excellent material for construction as well as insulating purposes. It might be used for the inside layers of plywood with a more durable wood forming the outer layers. This would provide a lightweight plywood panel which would be easy to handle, would be sturdy, and would have high insulating properties. Unless someone of the industry or the government takes the initiative to carry out some very simple experiments with balsa, the potentialities of this very unusual timber will continue to be unknown. It is a product that can be grown very easily and economically, and one that will give a quick return because of its rapid rate of growth. Without the benefits of such experiments there is little basis for predicting whether exports will continue at present levels or expand at a very rapid rate. Furthermore, it will be impossible to develop an export expansion program without this essential knowledge regarding the characteristics and potential uses of this lumber.

Production Methods

To the question of how he produced balsa, one farmer replied that he merely let it grow like a weed, then cut it down some ten or fifteen years later as one would cut any other forest tree. This is probably as accurate a description as it is possible to give regarding the method of producing balsa in Ecuador. The tree reseeds naturally and the young seedlings sprout and grow on any land which has been cut over and left uncultivated in the humid areas at low elevations. It grows best if all other vegetation is cut out to give it ample volumes of sunlight, but being a fast growing tree there are few jungle plants which grow rapidly enough to smother it with shade. Some farmers in cleaning up the brush on a cut-over lot will thin out the undesirable shaped saplings, leaving the best shaped young trees ample space to grow. In general there is no production of balsa as a specialized crop. When it is grown in areas that have been cleared for some other crop the trees are permitted to grow on those lands that are not well suited to cultivated crops and on land along roadside and fence rows.

The trees are harvested from both the virgin forests and on the land where they have reseeded naturally following clearing of the land. There is generally no attempt to cut only a standard-size tree. As a consequence, logs arriving at the sawmill are of varying diameters and lengths. To get the logs out of the virgin forests, a notch is cut in the end of each log to take a chain hoop and the logs are then snaked by animal power from the forest to a central loading point on the highway or at a river landing. Most of the logs arrive at Guayaquil sawmills by river transport. The logs are lashed together to form rafts that are floated or towed down the rivers by small power barges and tugboats. Harvesting takes place throughout the year, but some farmers stop cutting during the periods of rice planting and harvesting. This results in great variations in the volume of logs arriving at the mills from one week to another. During the dry season the volume decreases greatly because the river flow is light and there is not enough water in the more distant regions to float the rafts. To assure that their mills will operate continuously, the two larger exporters have plantings of balsa which they exploit during the seasons of short supplies. The logs from these exploitations are generally hauled to Guayaquil in trucks.

There is a great variability in the quality of the lumber which different trees produce. Trees from the same lot will show variability in weight, color of lumber, and the tendency to develop "water core." They report that two trees grown together and apparently of the same age, variety, and type will produce different quality of finished lumber. But this is a contention which might not stand up if research were conducted to find out more about the varieties, strains, and growth habits of the balsa tree.

Costs of Production and Prices

Since cutting of balsa is a supplemental enterprise for most farmers, it was very difficult to get any precise information on production costs. The mills at Guayaquil pay from 30 sucres to 100 sucres per log delivered to the mill, depending upon the size and quality of the logs. The mill operators reported that

after paying transport and other costs, lumbermen exploiting
a balsa wood lot would net about 25 sucres per log. If balsa
were planted on a commercial basis, about 500 trees could be
harvested from a hectare of land every ten years providing
the producer a net return of about 1,250 sucres annually per
hectare. This would be a net return comparable to average
returns now obtained from other export crops such as coffee,
cacao, rice, and bananas. So long as there are natural
forests to exploit at no investment cost to the farmer, there
is little probability that he will make commercial plantings of
balsa. On the other hand, the returns appear to be large
enough that farmers will go into commercial production at
present rates of return if the demand for lumber should become large enough to exhaust the supply of logs in the natural
forest. If ways can be found through research to eliminate
the low quality trees, it will be possible to improve net returns to farmers without increasing the cost of the logs at the
mill. The present prices of logs delivered to the mills will
permit the mills to produce a lumber that will cost about 3
cents per board foot. Prices of this magnitude are close to
the marginal limits at which balsa might be substituted for
other insulating materials in making plywood and other types
of wallboards. However, the price of the raw material is
sufficiently low that it will justify economic and technical
studies to determine what are the potentialities of this lumber
for new types of uses.

CASTOR BEAN PRODUCTION

Ecuador has been a producer and exporter of castor beans
over the past decade. In the early 1950's there were no facilities for processing the castor bean in the country and all production was exported. Today, one or two of the national oil
processors are handling some castor beans but most of the
production is exported as beans. Exports since 1952 are
shown as follows:

Year	Export Metric Tons
1952	6,078
1953	8,771
1954	9,655
1955	6,487
1956	5,006
1957	7,638
1958	8,811
1959	9,403
1960	10,504
1961	18,496

Although exports have been increasing since 1956, in previous years they varied considerably from one year to another. Most producers of castor beans interplant the beans with corn. Since the bean will stand more drought than corn they are used as a "catch crop" to assure that some income will be available in case the corn crop is a failure due to long periods of dry weather. The recent increases are probably due in part to the expansion in cultivated lands in Manabi Province but it is also probable that most of the increase represents harvesting of the castor beans in those areas where drought has resulted in a loss of the corn crop.

The castor bean as it is grown in Ecuador requires much hand labor. If this labor can be more profitably used to harvest the corn, then the castor bean will go unharvested. The castor bean is an easy crop to produce and although yields normally are very low there is good assurance against a complete crop failure. For this reason it is a crop that farmers in the drier areas of Manabi Province will continue to cultivate, but farmers in general are not enthusiastic about it as a basic export crop. If world market prices should improve it would become much more popular among the farmers.

There is ample land area for the increase in castor bean production, but in those areas where this crop is well adapted to the soils and climate the potential income is normally much greater for cotton, corn, and extensive livestock production.

TAGUA NUT PRODUCTION

The tagua nut palm is indigenous to Ecuador, and it has been one of the traditional exports of minor importance for several decades. It is not a cultivated crop but is exploited in the wild state by primitive means. In Manta there is a button factory which operates exclusively upon tagua nuts or "vegetable ivory" as a source of raw materials. This factory provides work to about 100 people, mostly women. The export of buttons is of relatively small importance to the over-all economy of Ecuador, but the factory is of importance as a source of employment to the people of the city of Manta where there has been a surplus of unemployed labor.

The tagua nut, which resembles ivory when sliced open with a saw or carving knife, is also used for carving of trinkets, jewelry, and toys by artisans working in the home. The extent of this artisan industry is not known but is thought to be of minor importance. The amount of time required to make the carvings in relation to the value of the finished product would not appear to make it an industry which should be promoted.

In conversations with people who have had some experience with the tagua nut palm they were loud in their praises of this tree and reported many things about it that would warrant at least some preliminary research. The palm is reported to yield about three quintals of nuts annually which are valued at fifteen to eighteen sucres per quintal for making buttons. The nuts are also reported to have a very high oil and protein content. The button factory has been grinding the waste materials from button manufacture into a meal which is sold to one of the local dairy farmers. It was reported that the feeding of this material in small quantities resulted in large increases in milk production. This would indicate that it may contain some minerals or proteins that are normally lacking in the dairy ration. Another report was received that the tagua nuts were an excellent substitute for charcoal in forges in the blacksmith shops. Just how valid each of the reports were is unknown, but they appeared to have sufficient validity to warrant some chemical analysis of the nuts and some

investigation to determine the average productive capacity of
the plants. It is entirely possible that this palm, when planted
and cultivated under proper conditions, may be a very valuable
economic plant.

PYRETHRUM PRODUCTION

Pyrethrum is a relatively new plant in Ecuador. It was
first successfully introduced in 1941, when two brothers of
Finnish birth, Paul and Kaj Arends, imported two small
packages of seed from Kenya. In the beginning the Arends
brothers encountered a number of difficulties in getting the
seeds to germinate and to get flowers that would yield a high
percentage of pyrethrine. But after ten years of experience
they had developed a stock of plants and seeds which became
the base for the present industry. In 1943 the United States
Government shipped 100 pounds of seed from Kenya to Ecuador. The first shipment did not germinate, and the following
year another shipment of 135 pounds of seed was imported.
The total production of flowers in 1946 from the later shipment was only 600 kilograms. A number of the reports on
the United States program to develop the industry rapidly
referred to the program as a failure. But others point out
that this work had a great experimental value that made it
possible for private interests to develop the industry at a
later period. The failure of the United States Government to
continue work on experiments was due to the development of
D. D. T. , which filled the immediate needs of the emergency
program as they related to World War II demands for nontoxic
insecticide.

In 1950 the Arends brothers began negotiations with the
U. S. Industrial Chemicals Company to sell them pyrethrum
flowers if the industry should develop into a commercial
enterprise in Ecuador. By the end of 1953 there were 72
hectares of pyrethrum in production and 372 additional hectares planted that would come into production in 1954.

During the past ten years, commercial production of dry pyrethrum flowers has increased from 34,453 kilograms in 1953 to 1,050,000 kilograms in 1962. It is estimated that 2,250,000 kilograms will be produced in 1963, and that the area planted to pyrethrum will be about 8,000 hectares. If present plans of the four large exporting firms are fulfilled, Ecuador will have about 10,000 hectares planted to pyrethrum in 1965 and will be exporting as extract the equivalent of 4,500,000 kilograms of dry flowers. If the world market demands continue to increase for pyrethrum and prices stay at present levels, Ecuador could have as much as 20,000 hectares in production by the end of the year 1973, and exports of about 8,000,000 kilograms of dry flowers in the form of extract. It remains to be seen, of course, whether those levels can be reached.

A review of the development of the pyrethrum industry in Ecuador might well serve to illustrate some of the problems involved in introducing a new crop and the time required to bring such crops into full commercial production. It was ten years from the time the first seeds were introduced until experimentation had proven that the crop could be grown on a commercial scale. It was another ten years before production had become of sufficient importance to make an impact on foreign exchange earnings. It will probably be another ten years before production will reach optimum levels.

Production Methods

There are four large exporters of pyrethrum in Ecuador and all have farms where they produce flowers for their own account. In addition they contract with small farmers to produce flowers which they buy for drying and processing into the pyrethrum extract. At present 80 percent of the total production comes from the land which the exporters cultivate and about 20 percent is produced by small farmers. On all plantings the large exporters try to control the type of seed planted and some of them give varying amounts of technical supervision to the small grower on proper methods of cultivating and harvesting.

The pyrethrum is a perennial plant that starts producing about 300 days from the time the seeds are planted and continues to produce throughout the year for about four years. The seeds are first planted in beds, then later transplanted to the field when the seedlings are about three months old. The harvest during the first year will not yield more than 50 to 100 kilograms of dry flowers per hectare. The yields during the second year will reach 450 to 1,000 kilograms, then decline in the third and fourth years to about 500 and 200 kilograms, respectively. The best yields are obtained on lands at 8,000 to 10,000 feet altitude but it can be grown at sea level and as high as 12,000 feet. At low altitudes it is reported that the flowers yield less volume and give a lower percentage pyrethrine in the extract.

Harvesting is done by hand in Ecuador and is an operation that must be performed at the proper time to be sure the dry flowers will yield a good quality extract. Much of the harvesting is done by women and children, as it is not a heavy task. The large growers generally contract this work, paying ten centavos for each pound of fresh flowers picked.

The fresh flowers are then dried either in the sun or by mechanical dryers. Five pounds of fresh flowers will yield about a pound of dry flowers. In general, it is reported that a worker can pick 60 pounds of fresh flowers per day but some of the better laborers pick as much as 100 to 120 pounds.

Yields and Quality

The Ecuadorian dry pyrethrum flowers give an average yield of 1.3 percent of their weight in pyrethrine. But individual plantings may vary from 2.0 percent to 1.0 percent. The Arends brothers were reported to have yields of 1.6 to 1.8 percent at the time they began planting and contracting with other growers in 1953. An average yield of 1.3 percent, however, is comparable to that obtained in other important exporting countries.

The yield of dry flowers per hectare has no doubt declined somewhat as more and more small farmers have entered production. This is not considered as endangering the future of the industry. The small farmer can stay in production with low yields because he uses family labor which does not need to get a wage return equal to that paid by the large commercial grower.

Prices and Costs of Production

Prices and costs of production are factors which will determine the future for the Ecuadorian pyrethrum industry. Pyrethrum extract has certain nontoxic qualities which make it a superior product to D. D. T. and other chemical insecticides. However, the price of pyrethrum has remained high in comparison with other insecticides. The high price of pyrethrum is closely related to the amount of labor required for its cultivation and its percentage yield of pyrethrine in the dry flower. Since the insecticide qualities of the pyrethrum flowers were discovered in 1840 in Dalmatia, several countries have tried to develop an export market for the product. The only countries that have been successful are Japan, Kenya, Tanganyika, Uganda, Congo, and Ecuador. All are countries with low wage rates or large amounts of underemployed peasant labor.

In Ecuador, growers of pyrethrum report that 300 days annually of hand labor are required for each hectare cultivated and harvested. This means that one laborer can on the average handle one hectare if he devotes all of his efforts to this crop. Total returns per hectare vary widely from $75 to $350 depending upon age of the planting, yield of flowers, and yield of pyrethrine. Costs other than labor will also vary somewhat from about $50 to $100 per hectare. The lands used for pyrethrum in Ecuador are the paramos at 8,000 to 12,000 feet altitude where the only alternative use is for extensive livestock grazing. On the lowest yield lands where income is about $75 and cash costs $50, there will be $25 left to the laborer, and on high yield lands with an income of $350 and cash costs of $100 the laborer will get $250. A return of $25 is far below the wages a laborer may get if he can find continual employment at the going wages of about 10 sucres per day in the Sierras. On the other hand, an income of $25 per year for the work of women and children who are not employed at other tasks is a welcome source of income to the peasant Sierra family, where the total cash income is often as low as $25 to $50 per year for the entire family. The peasant farmer who is sufficiently skilled to get a gross return of $300 from a hectare of pyrethrum finds this a highly profitable enterprise. His cash outlay will average about $75 and give a net return for his labor of $225. This peasant, after tending his own plot of land, would probably be able to get at the best no more than 100 days annually of outside work which at 10 sucres per day will give a net of $55 annually. Assuming that this peasant, because of his greater skills, can command a daily wage of 20 sucres and get 100 days of outside work, he is still much further ahead by growing pyrethrum.

For the commercial grower who must hire laborers for the planting, cultivation, and harvesting of pyrethrum, the only way to be assured of a net profit is to get high yields per hectare. To do so means spending more for high yielding seeds and to lease the better quality lands. With a gross return of $350 and total costs of $100 for seeds and rental and land preparation, plus $150 cash labor costs, his net profits will be $100 per hectare. If wage rates should increase by 100 percent over the next ten years in the Sierras, the commercial farmer will find it unprofitable to continue growing pyrethrum unless yields of flowers or percentage yield in pyrethrine from flowers are increased. Most of the exporters producing pyrethrum recognize that labor costs will continue to increase and have taken steps to meet this problem. Most of them have programs of contracting with small peasant farmers for part of their needs. All of them are experimenting in an effort to increase per hectare yields of flowers and to increase the percentage of pyrethrine in the flowers. Experiments indicate that yields of flowers per hectare can be increased by some 50 to 100 percent above those now obtained on commercial plantings. Some of the exporters point out that the quality of the flowers can be improved considerably. Their goal is to raise the average

pyrethrine content from the present 1.3 percent level to
about 1.8 percent.

Relatively little work is being done to find ways to reduce
the high labor inputs required under present cultural and
harvesting methods. At the time the United States Government
desperately needed a nontoxic insecticide during World War
II, a number of harvesting devices were developed to save
labor in the harvesting operation. Several of these simple
devices seemed to offer a solution to this problem, but needed
further mechanical refinements. If harvesting costs could be
reduced to one-third of the present rate total costs of producing pyrethrum might be reduced sufficiently to permit pyrethrum to become more competitive with other insecticides.
If research on labor costs plus production research to improve yield and quality were successful in bringing the total
cost of pyrethrum extract down to levels comparable to that
of some of the more common insecticides, the potential market
for pyrethrum would expand several-fold.

FISHERIES PRODUCTION

Ecuador has had a fishing industry for many years, but
prior to 1950 it was a local industry that employed about
2,500 families who fished along the coast to supply the fresh
fish needs of themselves and those of the coastal towns and
cities. The 1954 Census showed that 4,167 families were engaged in fishing of which about 60 percent were engaged full
time in this occupation and the balance were occasional fishermen. The export of fish was begun about 1950 when total
exports were 501 metric tons. By 1954 exports had increased
to 2,518 tons, of which about 2,075 tons were tuna fish and the
balance other types, principally shrimp and other shellfish.
The export industry remained at about this level until 1958,
when foreign fishing companies became interested and began
fishing in Ecuadorian waters.

In 1959 the Van Camp interests bought out a local plant at
Manta and established an export canning industry. This

company is operated under the local name of INEPACA and
cans tuna for both local sale and export. At the time it was
organized there were seven boats operating out of this port.
In 1963 there were 30 boats operating. This canning company
has assisted the local owners of the fishing boats to increase
the fleet but the fishing proper is still a local enterprise that
is fully managed and operated by Ecuadorian nationals. In
1962 this company produced 300,000 cases of canned tuna,
about one-half of which was sold nationally and the other half
exported. The total catch of fresh fish for this volume of
canned production is about 14,000 tons.

In addition to the canning plant at Manta there are other
plants at Guayaquil which export primarily frozen shrimp.
The total catch of both shrimp and tuna for the country has
been reported as follows:

Year	Catch in Metric Tons	
	Tuna	Shrimp
1955	6,060	1,723
1956	6,789	2,342
1957	9,862	2,137
1958	11,806	2,721
1959	14,817	2,843
1960	19,103	2,842
1961	29,880	3,842

The above data do not include the volumes caught by the
smaller operators who sell their catches to the coastal towns
and cities as fresh fish. The total catch of all types of fish
and shellfish was almost 60,000 metric tons for 1961.

Until the establishment recently of the United Nations
Special Fund's Instituto Nacional de Pesca in Guayaquil, little
research had been conducted to determine what are the potentials of the Ecuadorian fishing grounds if they were exploited
to the optimum. It is known, however, that owing to the influence of the Humboldt Current, the Pacific Coast of South
America is one of the richest fishing grounds in the world. In

Peru the fishing industry is also of recent origin. Its annual catch has increased from about 1,000 tons in 1940 to over 2 million tons in 1960. Studies recently made by the Peruvian Marine Resources Institute indicate that Peru is still not exploiting its waters at more than one-half of their potential. A large percentage of the Peruvian exploitation is for anchovy which is processed into fish meal. The anchovy do not run near the shore in Ecuador, so it is probable that, with a shorter coast line, there will be less potential for increasing the Ecuadorian catch. It is the general consensus, however, that Ecuador can expand its fish catch by at least two to three times the present production.

Fishing methods have been improved considerably during the past five years. There has been an increase in number of fishing boats, and most of the recent increases have been motorized vessels. However, there are still many improvements which could be made in equipment that would permit the fleet to go further from shore and to improve greatly the fishing methods. At present most of the boats are not equipped to stay at sea overnight. This eliminates the possibilities of exploiting those fishing grounds that are more than fifteen to twenty miles from shore. There is also the probability that a number of the fishing grounds within this distance are still not fished.

At the Galapagos Islands it is known that fish are plentiful but as yet this ground has not been studied and is only exploited by the islanders in a very limited way. The Japanese have made some studies as to the potentials of these fishing grounds, but their studies have not been made public.

Costs of operating a fishing fleet are unknown because there have been no studies made of these operations. Canners report that they pay 1,500 sucres per ton for yellow-fin tuna and 1,200 sucres per ton for skipjack tuna. Prices in the retail markets along the coast indicate that fishermen receive prices two to three times these rates for the less exploited species. Shrimp, which are normally a relatively high-priced seafood in most countries, sell in the local markets at the equivalent of 8 to 12 cents per pound, a price that is only about one-fifth that of this species in some of the world's most important markets.

A 6-1/2 ounce can of tuna fish sells in the national markets for 12 to 16 cents, depending upon the location and types of retailing establishment. This price is above the capacity of the poorer classes to purchase tuna, but middle and high income groups are using larger and larger volumes. This is also a price that is well below that normally charged in the importing countries and indicates that Ecuador can export in competition with other exporting countries.

Labor costs are relatively low in Ecuador. Laborers get 18 sucres per day in Manta and somewhat higher rates in Guayaquil. Cans are costly as they are not made locally and must be imported from the United States. Cardboard cartons and labels are made locally but the prices of these items are somewhat higher than the imported ones of equal quality.

In summarizing Ecuador's capacity to produce more fish products for export, it appears there are possibilities to expand the present industry. The extent of this expansion is still an unknown factor. The first action that should be taken is to determine the size, location, and productive capacity of the fishing grounds. Under the United Nations Special Fund's Institute in Guayaquil, work has already been started. It will take two or three years of rather intensive research work to obtain a general idea of the potential of the fishing grounds; and several more years' work may be needed to determine the species which should be exploited most intensively, the fishing methods that should be followed, and other factors that should be investigated carefully before investing still larger sums of capital in the industry. If it should be discovered that there is an opportunity to enlarge the present industry several times its present production, it will be necessary to build an efficient fishing fleet and fishermen will need to be trained to use better fishing methods and more efficient types of fishing gear.

PANAMA HAT PRODUCTION

The Panama straw hat woven from toquilla straw was at one
time Ecuador's leading earner of foreign exchange. It is a
handicraft or home industry generally carried on as a sideline
to subsistence farming. The toquilla straw comes from a palm
type of plant that grows wild in the tropical forests of the coast.
The weaving of these hats probably predates the colonial period,
as it is the Indians who are most deft in the weaving process.
The industry is centered in the three provinces of Manabi,
Azuay, and Canar. The best quality hats are made at the towns
of Montecristi and Jipijapa of Manabi Province, but Cuenca,
capital of Azuay Province, is the most important weaving center.
About 80 percent of all hats exported are produced in Azuay and
Canar Provinces.

Up until 1946 the export of hats had been increasing steadily.
From 1944 to 1946 exports averaged slightly over $5 million
annually, and in 1946 reached the all-time high of $6,117,000.
Following World War II exports dropped rapidly as the United
States, the principal importer, began buying cheaper hats made
in the Philippines, Japan, and Italy. In 1955 exports were
valued at $992,400. In 1956 they recovered to $1,466,700. But
the number of hats exported annually has been decreasing since
1950, as shown in the table on the following page.

As a handicraft and home industry, the weaving of toquilla
straw hats will very probably continue for a number of years
for the national market, but exports are likely to continue to decline. These hats are worn by the local Indians and are a traditional item of their dress. If cleaned and blocked periodically,
a hat several years old looks like new and can normally be expected to last for a lifetime. For the national buyer, labor costs
are low and the costs of cleaning and blocking are small compared
to the costs of a new hat. The opposite is true for the buyer in
those countries where the hats are imported. The cost of cleaning and blocking will be more than that for the purchase of a new
hat of cheaper types. There is also the factor that most of the
buyers in these countries like to have a change of style frequently.
There are other people who look upon the wearing of a Panama hat
as a mark of prestige, and for these there is likely to be a small
export demand.

PANAMA HAT EXPORTS, VOLUME AND VALUE,
1950-62

Year	Number of Hats Exported	Value of Exports in U. S. Dollars
1950	4,245,600	3,751,100
1951	3,676,600	3,236,000
1952	3,024,900	2,767,800
1953	3,518,100	3,165,100
1954	1,982,700	1,607,800
1955	1,285,000	992,400
1956	1,910,200	1,466,700
1957	1,492,400	1,073,700
1958	1,248,200	864,200
1959	1,197,900	791,200
1960	1,800,900	1,104,100
1961	751,300	492,800
1962[a]	825,000	465,000

a. Preliminary estimate based on data for the first nine months of 1962.

Source: Direccion General de Aduanas del Ecuador.

The weaving of a toquilla straw hat is a very tedious and time-consuming process. Like any handicraft item, normally the more time consumed in its production the more valuable is the end product. This is especially true for the Panama hat. The best hats are woven by hand from a very fine quality small diameter straw. To weave a hat of this type may take a man or woman as much as a month if he should work at it continuously. The retail value of these best quality hats in foreign markets is often as much as $30 to $48, but the price received by the weaver will seldom be more than 250 sucres, or about $13 to $14. He will have paid about $1.00 for the raw materials used in the weaving, giving a net return for a month's labor of $12 to $13. Although this is a very small monetary return for the subsistence farmer who can weave no more than one or two hats of this type in a year, it is frequently a welcome source of supplemental income. The weaving of the coarse straw hats takes much less time, and a relatively inexperienced weaver or child can generally weave one in a week to ten days, working on it a couple of hours daily. These cheaper type hats seldom reach the export markets except through the occasional tourist who may visit the country and buy them as low-cost souvenirs. The price to the weaver for the caps is frequently no more than 4 to 5 sucres; and for the hats about 25 sucres or about $1.39 each.

In the provinces of Azuay and Canar, from which most of the previous exports have been made, the recent development of industries will cause surplus labor to be drawn from the hat-making work. In the towns of Montecristi and Jipijapa in Manabi Province, other types of handicraft industries have already caused many of the former hat weavers to shift their occupations. Within the next decade it is possible that exports could drop to no more than a few thousand hats annually, most of which will be bought by tourists while visiting the country.

COMPARATIVE ANALYSIS OF THE BASIS FOR CONTINUED INCREASES IN PRESENT EXPORT CROPS

In the previous discussions it has been shown that large acreages of fertile lands suitable for the production of nearly all of the present export products still exist. Much of this land is still in virgin forest located near the ports and can be developed if markets should be available for additional volumes. Factors other than land will be the ones that will limit the volume that will be produced for the export markets.

There is a general surplus of labor and much inefficient use of labor, but at certain times and places there is an acute shortage, especially during the planting and harvesting seasons for some crops. The shortage of skilled and highly skilled laborers is reported to be almost universal, and that for managerial and highly technical skills is even more acute. There is also a general shortage of capital for investing in the types of equipment and installations that will be needed to bring about a large increase in exports of high-quality products.

To increase exports and to diversify exports are the twin underlying purposes sought to be served by this study. The development of the Ecuadorian economy requires enhanced foreign exchange earnings; and diversification aimed at lessening present dependence on the big three of bananas, cacao, and coffee is desired as a means toward providing greater year-to-year stability in foreign exchange earnings. It must be recognized that the laudable aim of diversification is more difficult of attainment than that of enhancement of exports, and indeed the two aims may at times be in conflict. For example, the dramatic current and prospective increases in banana exports to Japan, under which Japan for the year 1963 ranked second only to the United States as a market for Ecuadorian banana exports, will further increase the dominance of the big three. That new Japanese market brings a welcome addition to Ecuador's foreign exchange earnings, but it makes more formidable the longer range goal of diversification.

Since the major export crops of bananas, coffee, cacao, rice, and sugar account for around 85 to 90 percent of the present export earnings, it is obvious that a small increase in the export of these crops will bring in larger sums of foreign exchange than the doubling or tripling of some of the minor exports such as castor beans, balsa, and pyrethrum. A program to bring about a small increase in the major crops exported will probably be less costly and easier to accomplish than one to increase greatly the export of some of the minor crops.

One of the serious problems in getting a larger production for export is the scarcity of skilled labor and technical employees. Most of the labor force has some experience in the production of bananas, coffee, cacao, sugar, and rice. It will be easier and less costly to improve the efficiency of this labor than to train laborers to handle new crops. It is also in the production of these major crops and sugar where there is already a large, established production base.

There are now 150,000 hectares planted to bananas. Production of 78 million stems resulted in export of only 33 million stems in 1961.[4] With production knowledge and present state of training laborers, it would be much easier to raise the quality of the bananas to exportable standards than to bring in an equivalent value of other and new crops for export.

With respect to coffee and cacao, where the land in production is 130,000 and 200,000 hectares, respectively, the improvement of yields and quality can accomplish more in shorter time than bringing new lands into production for new crops where it will be necessary to learn new production and marketing techniques.

For sugar there are now two large plantations in operation which have trained employees and the facilities for a large production increase. They also normally have unused refining capacity. Again it is easier to build upon this established production and marketing base than to develop a new industry requiring the opening up of new lands, training of labor, and the building of new marketing installations.

With 110,000 hectares planted to rice, the actual production level is about 154,000 metric tons, a yield of 1,400 kilograms of milled rice per hectare. Soil and climatic conditions are equally as good for rice production as in other rice-producing countries where yields are about two to three times as large as in Ecuador, and the rice produced is of a much higher quality than the Ecuadorian rice. With an acreage of this magnitude already devoted to rice, it would seem highly desirable to initiate a program for improving yields and quality. If rice exports could be returned to the levels of 1946 to 1948, in excess of 60,000 tons annually, the foreign exchange earnings from this crop would about equal those for all the exports of the minor crops in 1962.

---

4. Junta de Planificacion estimates for 1963 show production of 75 million stems of bananas (and 24 million stems of plantain).

What has been said is not to decry the aim of diversification, which is indeed highly desirable as a means both to the expansion of total exports and to the minimizing of risks. The important point is that diversification should be achieved by adding output and export of new products to the output and export of traditional exports rather than building new exports at the cost of neglecting opportunities for expansion of the country's traditional exports. Where choices must be made to devote land and scarce capital and entrepreneurial skills to one product rather than another, the risk-reducing advantages inherent in diversification must be weighed carefully against the advantages inherent in expanding exports of products for which production and distribution know-how already exist and for which the required increments of capital and other resources would probably bring more results and faster than the same resources devoted to a new industry.

Any programs to increase exports will require the expenditure of government funds, an assignment of government personnel, and the allocation of land, labor, and capital that could be used for other development. It is important in the formulation of this program that all these factors be used in a manner that will maximize the total export income rather than an increase in one product at the expense of a decrease in another of equal or greater promise.

From the standpoint of comparative production costs and availability of suitable land, Ecuador is in a favorable position with respect to many other countries which are producing bananas, cacao, coffee, rice, and sugar for export; but it will be a mistake to assume that the export levels for these products can be maintained and increased without giving further attention to lowering production and marketing costs, improving yields and quality, and to the efficient marketing of these products. Under the banana disease control program, the sigatoka disease is under generally efficient control, but that control must be continued on a more intensive basis. Panama disease is still a serious threat to the industry, and very little work is being done on variety tests and improvements, production

costs, marketing, and other factors that must be considered
if Ecuador is to continue as the world's largest exporter.

For cacao the pending International Agreement will generally limit the exports of each country to an annual quota. It
appears, however, that Ecuador will be exempted from the
quota because of its special classification as a flavor cacao
producer. That exemption will be a challenge to Ecuador to
maintain and build up the quality of its cacao and to increase
the share of "arriba" cacao. Ecuador producers will need to
recognize that improvement of quality and the lowering of
production costs are the principal factors that determine a
country's ability to maintain its position in the world markets.
There are already international quotas for coffee, yet Ecuador
is still selling about half of its coffee as unwashed, a type that
does not meet quality demands and commands a lower price.

The prospects for exporting more sugar and rice appear to
be very good, but it will be necessary to meet the production
cost levels of other exporters for both of these products. To
export more rice it will be essential to improve quality. Ways
will also have to be found to reduce the amounts of hand labor
used to produce rice, through more efficient utilization of
labor, and yields will have to be raised greatly.

In the planning of a production program for a group of export crops, there are no ready formulas for determining the
weights that each crop should receive or for determining what
proportions of the available governmental budget should be
spent on each type of research and promotion. What is required is a cost-benefit analysis, or more specifically: What
are the costs of the research and promotion in relation to the
estimated benefits in terms of possible export earnings?

There are indeed so many factors to consider that there is
the temptation to spread the resources available over too wide
a field with danger that none of the work will be effective in
bringing about real benefits. That temptation must certainly
be resisted. Another danger to be avoided is that of initiating
a program and then dropping it after a year or so of intensive

research, despite promising results. For example, at the
Pichilingue Experiment Station work was started several
years ago on bamboo, teak, African oil palms, and rubber
but has been abandoned even though each of these products
grows well and shows promise of being an important economic
crop. At the Latacunga School an investment has been made
in well-bred livestock for experimental purposes but no provision has been made to keep the needed type of records on
production, costs of production, and the economic advantages
of various management, handling, and feeding methods.

This chapter has been concerned only with present export
crops and products and hence priority recommendations for
an export program will be restricted at this point to these
present export crops and products. They may be classified
into three categories as follows:

Category I: Crops and products for which there
is a good opportunity for continued and increased
production at costs comparing favorably with
those in other exporting countries. This category
includes those crops which rank large in the
present exports and those that will not be unduly
restricted by limited world demands. This group
should get a high priority in any government program, and funds for the successful completion of
the relevant parts of the program should be assured
before crops in a lower category are considered.
In this category are: bananas, cacao, coffee, sugar,
rice, and fisheries products. Appropriate remedial measures will be required for cacao, coffee,
and rice, as noted elsewhere in this report.

Category II: Crops and products of lesser importance for which there are opportunities for
continued exports at present or larger volumes.
Included in this group are castor beans, balsa,
and pyrethrum. Products in this category merit
attention in government programs only if those
in Category I have been assured adequate financing
and attention.

<u>Category III</u>: Products which may continue to
be exported over the next ten years but in
smaller volumes than at present. Included in
this category are: tagua nut products and toquilla
straw hats. These products have ranked small
in total exports in recent years, their outlook
for the future does not look promising, and it
will be difficult to justify a government program
for the increase in their exports.

In the next chapter the prospects for new export crops will
be examined; and in Chapter 4 processing industry prospects
will be appraised.

CHAPTER **3** PRODUCTION
PROSPECTS

Most of the presently exported crops are grown in the tropical lowlands of the Costa. Coffee is the only major export which is produced in part in the Sierra uplands, and the only Sierra province which contributes an important volume to this export is Loja. In the search for additional products which may be exported, much more attention was given to the Sierra provinces than to the tropical lowlands. The population is roughly equally distributed between the Costa and the Sierra, and there is an urgent need to bring about a higher and more efficient use of labor in the Sierra. The Sierra also has a climate that differs greatly from that of the Costa, and for this reason it should offer opportunities for a diversification of the exportable products.

In searching for additional exportable crops, first and major attention was given to those products which are already being grown in the country. Some of these crops are not grown in sufficient volume to meet internal needs and additional quantities must be imported. Others are grown in large volumes but are not presently exported. For those crops which are grown in too small volume to meet the internal needs, an increase in production sufficient to eliminate present imports can have the same result upon the foreign exchange picture, as it would make more foreign exchange available for those products and items which must come from abroad.

CATTLE FOR BEEF PRODUCTION

Cattle were introduced to Ecuador by the first Spanish colonists; and cattle raising for both meat and milk is found in every province of the country. The breeds introduced by the Spaniards are known as criolla. In recent years there has been great improvement in the cattle breeds through the importation of Holstein-Friesian for milk production and Zebu for beef production. These imported breeding stocks have been crossed with the native criolla breeds, and most of the cattle grown strictly for beef production still show signs of the criolla cross. On farms where cattle are produced primarily for milk the criolla cross is much less pronounced, and there are many herds where no signs whatsoever remain of the original criolla crossbreeding. The total number of cattle as reported by the 1954 Census was 1,215,900 head of which 786,300 head were in the Sierra provinces and 429,600 head in the coastal provinces. It is estimated that the cattle population in 1962 exceeded 1.5 million head, and that the distribution between the Sierra and the Costa was proportionately about the same as in 1954. The increase in the Sierra, however, has been almost entirely in cattle for milk production. Milk production in the Costa has never been of any importance, and there the increase in cattle numbers has been almost entirely for beef production.

Adequate quantities of good quality feeds have always been a serious problem for the cattle industry in Ecuador. In the Sierra provinces competition for land for cultivated food crop production has limited the acreage available for pastures and the production of concentrates. The natural pastures of the coast have normally been of very poor quality. Most of them are of native grasses which have a low nutritive value, and many have been overgrown with thick underbrush. The coastal grazing areas are also subject to seasonal droughts, and almost no storage of feeds in silos and as hay has been practiced. The introduction of cultivated pastures by a very small number of the coastal livestock farmers in the last five years has shown that excellent pastures can be established on the coast if proper grasses are planted and the pastures handled in the proper manner. Guinea grass has given excellent results in both Guayas and Manabi Provinces. In those places where the droughts are not prolonged a hectare of guinea grass will support up to three head of cattle annually, provided the cattle are rotated on the pastures, giving each field or lot about a month to recover its growth after intensive pasturing for ten days to two weeks. In the sections of Manabi Province where the droughts are prolonged, with proper management a hectare of guinea grass should support at least one animal annually.

Assuming that there should be a continued expansion of acreage planted to bananas, rice, sugar, and cacao on the coast over the next ten years, there would still be at least 750,000 hectares that might be put into cultivated pastures for beef cattle feeding. If the present area of about 350,000 hectares of natural pastures is converted to improved pastures, there would be in total sufficient pasturelands on the coast to support more than one million head of cattle. This would represent increase in the coastal production of beef of about 100 percent. Another 150,000 hectares of cultivated pastures would bring the supportable herd to 1.5 million head.

It should be pointed out that an increase of 100 percent or more is not likely to take place without a rather extensive governmental program of experimentation, breeding, extension work among farmers, increases and improvement of the veterinarian services, and an increase in livestock production credit. If such a livestock production program should be initiated, it will probably take about ten years to bring the total cattle population up to the 1.5 million head potential. One of the farmers who is well trained in livestock and pasture production methods, and who now lives in the Santo Domingo area, reported that he had built up a 300-head herd of beef cattle over the past five years. He plans to build this herd to a total of 500 head, but estimated it would require another five years to reach this goal. Land will have to be cleared and planted to pastures, and the basic breeding stock will be grown from selections of the best female calves produced by the present herd. In the meantime he has been selling the steers to pay the costs of the operation and to provide the investment needed for further land clearing and pasture establishment.

Cattle production for milk production will no doubt continue to increase in the central and northern Sierra provinces, but there are only small possibilities of increasing cattle for beef production in these provinces. In the southern Sierra provinces of Azuay and Loja, and the upland regions of El Oro Province, there are still possibilities to expand beef cattle production. At the time of taking of the 1954 Census these three provinces had 300,000 head of cattle of which about one-fifth were dual purpose types and the balance were raised primarily for beef production.

Marketing installations and facilities are very poorly developed for the handling of livestock throughout the country. There are no organized shipping point markets where the farmers can sell their cattle, and they depend mostly upon itinerant buyers who go from farm to farm, buying cattle for sale and slaughter in the towns and cities. At these urban centers slaughtering facilities are antiquated. There are no cold-storage installations and meat must be consumed within a few hours after it is slaughtered. This type of marketing system results in large losses from shrinkage in transport and results in a lowering of meat quality. If increases should be forthcoming in cattle production the present marketing installations would handicap greatly the possibilities of developing an export market.

The development of new and more efficient marketing installations will require the investment of relatively large sums of capital, but this should be an economic investment over a period of years, as it would result in large savings and permit a more even flow of meats into the consuming markets. Although some of the countries along the western coast of Central and South America are still importing cattle alive for slaughtering upon arrival, this practice is rapidly being replaced by imports of frozen and chilled meats. If Ecuador should initiate a livestock production program for export, it is essential that it include the development of more efficient and better marketing installations.

Per capita consumption of both beef and total meats is still very low in Ecuador but has been increasing much faster than population growth during the past ten years. With the increase in consumer incomes in the cities, a considerable increase in national beef production will be required to meet the rising national demands. The production of meats from national slaughter of cattle, sheep, and hogs from 1955 to 1961 is shown in the following table.

MEAT PRODUCTION BY TYPE, 1955-61
(In Thousands of Pounds)

Year	Beef	Lamb	Pork	Total	Approximate Per Capita Consumption in Pounds[a]
1955	59,402	7,429	16,950	83,781	22.7
1956	64,327	12,962	24,489	101,678	26.8
1957	68,754	13,460	26,652	108,866	27.0
1958	75,534	14,317	27,300	117,151	28.2
1959	79,194	15,417	30,889	125,500	29.2
1960	80,784	15,842	32,649	129,275	29.5
1961	81,072	16,638	34,980	132,500	29.7[b]

a. Total per capita consumption will vary somewhat from this approximation as no adjustment has been made for small volumes of imports and exports.

b. Made up of 18.2 pounds for beef, 3.7 pounds for lamb, and 7.8 pounds for pork.

Source: Direccion General de Estadistica y Censos del Ecuador.

The development of the cattle industry is essential in any case to avoid the importation of meats that will become necessary if production should not be increased. To develop a surplus of beef production for export would require a major effort.

Interviews with a few farmers regarding the comparative returns from cattle and other crops indicated that they could get a higher net return from bananas if they could be assured of an export market for their entire production. Those who were producing both cattle and bananas in the Santo Domingo area, however, felt that cattle offered somewhat better prospects because of the long haul in getting bananas to market, seasonal labor problems for the harvesting of bananas, and the more stable market for cattle. In the eastern part of Manabi Province, several farmers reported that they were abandoning the production of bananas for cattle because cattle gave greater net returns.

Cattle experiments were initiated at the Pichilingue Experiment Station in 1962. No information is available yet from this source regarding the economics of cattle production. It is known from the present work that cattle can be successfully raised under the existing tropical conditions. Experiments on a number of new grasses indicate that cattle raising can be a highly profitable industry provided proper attention is given to pasture management, which is the basis of any successful livestock industry.

PORK PRODUCTION POSSIBILITIES

The production of pork has been increasing rapidly in Ecuador during the past ten years, as can be seen from the following data on hog population and slaughter.

PORK POPULATION AND PRODUCTION, 1950-61

Year	Hog Population (In Thousands)	Pork Production (In Thousands of Pounds)
1950	574	NA
1954	683	NA
1955	--	16,950
1956	994	24,489
1957	1,081	26,652
1958	1,150	27,300
1959	1,201	30,889
1960	1,270	32,649
1961	1,340	34,980

Source: Prior to 1955, U. S. Department of Commerce; 1955 to 1961, Ecuador, Ministry of Fomento. No figures available for the years 1951-53.

There are good hog feed possibilities in Ecuador. In the
Sierra provinces there is a large acreage devoted to the production of corn. At present corn yields are very low and most
of the production is needed for human food. If through the introduction of hybrid seed the corn yield can be increased, there
will be a surplus of this grain for hog feeding. In the coastal
provinces there are now large quantities of bananas that are
rejected at the port or remain on the farm because they do not
meet the quality standards for export. Some of the rejects are
now used as feed for hogs, and more could be so used. The
increase in pork production over the past ten years can probably
be attributed in part to the feeding of bananas.

A draft report of the Italconsult Mission reported pork production in 1961 at 16,000 metric tons and projected production
for 1967 at 32,500 metric tons and for 1973 at 54,300 metric
tons, or 119,460,000 pounds. With population at 4.5 million
in 1961 and projected to 5.4 million for 1967 and 6.5 million
for 1973, the cited production figures would represent per
capita consumption of pork of 3.6 kilos for 1961, 6.0 kilos for
1967, and 8.4 kilos for 1973 or about 18.5 pounds. Beef consumption per capita for 1973 was projected at 14.9 kilos, or
32.8 pounds from a level of 8.2 kilos in 1961; and lamb consumption per capita of 1.7 kilos or 3.7 pounds, unchanged
from 1961. Aggregate meat consumption per capita in 1973
would be 55 pounds.

In summary, the outlook for pork production is excellent in
Ecuador, but the Italconsult projections of per capita consumption and population would absorb the total projections of pork
production for 1973 of about 120 million pounds. And considerable export, then, would have to be based on more production
of pork than projected or on less consumption per capita than
projected. It is possible that both of these developments might
eventuate in some measure.

DAIRY PRODUCTS PRODUCTION

Although the early Spanish colonists brought cattle to Ecuador, the commercial dairy industry is of recent development. During the past twenty-five to thirty years there have been importations of Holstein-Friesian cattle that have increased the yield of milk per cow several-fold. The first importations were for the purpose of crossing the Holstein-Friesian with the local criolla breeds, but most of the importations in the past ten years have been to improve the production of pure-bred herds and the crossbreed herds that are predominantly Holstein. This improvement in the dairy industry has been limited primarily to the Sierra provinces of Carchi, Imbabura, Pichincha, and Cotopaxi. A trip through the Sierras from Latacunga to Ibarra will show what an enormous improvement has taken place since the first introductions of the Holstein-Friesian cattle. Although a few typically criolla cattle are still seen on the small Indian holdings and some criolla-Holstein crosses in the commercial herds, most herds of more than five animals are predominantly Holstein and a large percentage appears to be purebred.

No data were found to indicate the production per animal or the total production of milk prior to improvement in the breeding of dairy herds, but it can be generally assumed that prior to about 1940 a cow would not give more than 1 liter per day as an average for the entire year. Total milk production for the country at that time was probably less than 100,000 liters daily. The 1954 Census contained a question regarding the number of cows milked and the production on the day previous to the enumeration. For the entire country, the 220,200 cows milked averaged 3.26 liters each. In Loja Province, where most of the cattle are still of the criolla breeds, the average was 2.4 liters, whereas in Pichincha and Cotopaxi Provinces (where there were at that time mostly criolla-Holstein crosses), it was 5.2 and 4.4 liters, respectively. With the continued improvement in breeding the average today in the latter two provinces is probably between 8.0 and 10.0 liters daily. Several of the dairy farms visited in the commercial dairy area reported that minimum production would be about 8.0

liters per day per cow. Those who followed good feeding
practices average from 10.0 to 12.0 liters per day per cow.
Although there were reports of individual cows that were producing in excess of 18.0 liters daily, it is reasonable to expect under normal conditions of feeding and dairy management
practices that average production cannot be raised above 12.0
liters within the next ten years.

Official statistics on milk production from 1954 to 1961 are
shown as follows:

MILK PRODUCTION, 1954-61

Year	Milk Production (In Liters Daily)	Increase in Production Over Preceding Year	
		(In Liters Daily)	(In Percent)
1954	718,400	--	--
1955	820,000	101,600	14.1
1956	877,000	57,000	7.0
1957	957,000	80,000	9.1
1958	997,000	40,000	4.2
1959	1,027,000	30,000	3.0
1960	1,070,000	43,000	4.2
1961	1,110,000	40,000	3.7

Source: Direccion General de Estadistica y Censos del
Ecuador.

During this period of eight years, total production has increased by almost 400,000 liters daily or about 6.4 percent a
year. However, the increases in the last four years have
averaged slightly less than 4.0 percent per year. The extent
to which milk production will be further increased during the
next ten years can be estimated only in a very general way
and will leave much room for error. If the annual increase
in daily production averages 4 percent, then total daily production in 1973 would be 1.78 million liters; if the average is

6. 4 percent, then daily production in 1973 would reach 2. 34 million liters. If average production per cow can be raised from 8 to 10 liters at present to 10 to 12 liters per day, this would mean a further increase of 22 percent, or daily production of 2. 85 million liters by 1973.

One of the factors that has limited a more rapid increase in milk production has been the shortage of legume pastures and concentrates in the ration. The 1954 Census showed that Ecuador had 1, 775, 300 hectares in pastures of which 520, 800 were improved pastures. At that time the four principal dairy provinces had 537, 600 hectares in natural pastures and 76, 000 hectares in improved pastures. The Italconsult Mission estimated that the four dairy provinces had 1, 125, 000 hectares in natural pastures in 1962 and 521, 000 hectares in improved pastures. The improved pastures included only 15, 000 hectares of alfalfa. These pastures data make clear that it is possible to increase greatly the number of dairy cattle as well as the daily production per cow, through conversion of more natural pastures to improved pastures and through increase in alfalfa acreage. The larger and more productive herds brought about by improved pastures would bring within the realm of the attainable the daily production goal figure of 2. 85 million liters cited in the preceding paragraph.

The Agriculture Section of the Junta Nacional de Planificacion estimates that consumption of milk and dairy products has increased somewhat more rapidly than milk production during the past ten years. In 1961 about 6. 0 percent of the dairy products consumed were from imports. Assuming substantially no exports from the national production figure shown on page 84, this would indicate that production of milk in 1961 failed to meet the demands of the internal market by approximately 70, 000 liters daily, and that total domestic consumption of dairy products in that year amounted to the equivalent of about 1, 180, 000 liters of milk daily. If milk consumption in Ecuador should increase to 1973 at the rate of 6 percent a year (roughly twice the rate of population increase), a daily production of 2. 3 million liters would be required in that year, leaving a daily surplus of 480, 000 liters available for export.

The value of this amount of milk as a raw material for processing would run to upwards of $9 million a year.

COTTON PRODUCTION POSSIBILITIES

Cotton is indigenous to the tropical climates in all the South
American countries but its production has never been large in
Ecuador. The Agricultural Census of 1954 showed that 5,553
hectares of cotton were grown with a total production of 48,399
quintals. At that time nearly all the cotton was grown in Manabi Province. This province has climatic conditions which are
favorable for cotton production, but growers and technicians
report that there is a serious problem in controlling insect
pests. The quality of the cotton observed on field trips indicates that this crop can be grown for internal consumption in
considerably larger quantities, but it is very doubtful if yields
and quality can be increased sufficiently in the near future to
provide a surplus for export. The government has initiated a
cotton production program, but it will no doubt take several
years of experimental work to determine whether cotton can
be grown in sufficient quantities and at costs which will justify
a production program for meeting the total demands of the
national textile industry. Imports of semi-processed textile
materials, cloth, and ready-made clothing in 1961 amounted
to $8 million. It is possible that increases in national cotton
production during the next ten years will be sufficient only to
eliminate the necessity to import.

Several of the South American countries started cotton improvement programs several years ago. Most of them have
had some success in growing this product for national consumption, but Brazil and Peru are the only ones up to date
that have developed important export markets. The Brazilian
exports are of the short staple varieties and those from Peru
are long staple and pima type cottons. Both of these countries
have spent much time and experimental work in the development of export markets. It is very doubtful if Ecuador could
develop a cotton export industry without going through a similar long period of experimental and promotional work.

FRUIT PRODUCTION POSSIBILITIES

Ecuador produces all the tropical, subtropical, and temperate zone fruits normally found in each of these zones at other places in the world. The Italconsult Mission estimated the production of most of these fruits for 1961 and 1962 as shown in the following table:

FRUIT PRODUCTION, 1961-62

Fruit	Unit of Production	1961	1962
Apricots	Quintals	8,000	4,150
Apples	Units	9,450,000	12,000,000
Plums	Quintals	46,000	36,286
Peaches	Quintals	155,900	140,000
Figs	Quintals	44,000	31,150
Limes	Quintals	20,000	20,000
Lemons	Quintals	1,140,000	1,150,000
Mandarins	Quintals	98,040	100,000
Mangoes	(000 Units)	150,000	148,555
Mamey	(000 Units)	11,000	11,000
Oranges	(000 Units)	667,693	720,000
Naranjilla	(000 Units)	616,000	743,700
Papaya	(000 Units)	34,000	60,000
Pears	Quintals	337,739	316,000
Pineapple	(000 Units)	28,000	27,303
Grapefruit	(000 Units)	4,200	4,300
Grapes	Quintals	5,600	3,920
Melons	(000 Units)	438	650
Watermelons	(000 Units)	1,880	3,000

Note: Bananas have not been included as they have been covered in detail in the preceding chapter.

Visits to any of the local retail markets in the cities and towns of Ecuador will show that nearly all of these fruits can be found when they are in season, but the volume offered for sale is generally limited to the local demands. The quality will vary greatly from one town to another. For some products the quality of the different lots offered for sale on any particular day will also vary greatly. In the Ambato market, which is located in the apple-producing zone, a few of the apples were of good quality and size but most lots were of small-size apples which showed insect and disease damage. Interviews with the retailers revealed that no commercial orchards existed. Most farmers have a few trees or a small orchard of fruit trees for home consumption and they send to market any surplus production. This type of production will naturally result in fruit prices being very low at times when the growing conditions have been favorable and a relatively large volume by chance arrives on the market.

Several of the small operators who processed fruit in the Ambato area reported that they all depended on the short seasonal surplus of fruit from the home orchards of the local farmers. One reported that attempts to develop a commercial fruit-processing industry in the area failed for lack of a volume of fruit large enough to meet the demands of even a small-size canning plant.

In a field trip made through the Sierra from Cuenca to Ibarra and through representative areas on the coast, the only producers found that might be classified as commercial fruit farmers were several small farmers in the Milagro area who were growing less than five hectares each of pineapples. The typical pineapple grower was found to have less than one hectare in production. He was generally a subsistence farmer and part-time farm laborer who had planted a small lot of pineapples to give his family employment and to obtain some supplemental income. They had little technical knowledge about varieties, insect and disease control methods, cultural practices, and the use of fertilizers.

The field visits indicated that a commercial fruit industry might be developed for apples, pears, citrus fruits, and pineapples if the growers were trained to follow good cultural practices of variety selection, pruning, spraying, and fertilizing.

In spite of the lack of commercial fruit-growing industry in the country, exports have been made on a small scale for a few fruits. Data compiled from records of the Finance Ministry by the Italconsult Mission show the exports of fruit from 1958 to 1961 as follows:

FRUIT EXPORTS, 1958-61

| Product | Exports Annually in Units of Each Fruit | | | |
	1958	1959	1960	1961
Oranges	16,460,190	15,750,270	17,919,850	14,759,722
Mangoes	3,882,150	2,823,540	2,217,910	1,367,340
Pineapples	425,272	216,723	417,290	993,080
Melons	--	--	--	28,765
Avocados	--	--	--	7,000
Papaya	1,000	--	--	--

Only limited information was available showing to which countries these exports were made. It is known that oranges, mangoes, and pineapples move from Guayaquil to the ports along the northern Peruvian coast during the seasons when there is no production in the northern zone of Peru of these items. During some years oranges are shipped as far south as Lima during a short period when this product is not available from local harvestings. Fresh pineapples are imported into Chile in very small quantities, but the prices after the long sea voyage are very high in comparison with those of locally grown Chilean fruits.

No information is available as to production costs and production problems that may be encountered in the developing of a commercial fruit industry, as there are no commercial

plantings from which to make an analysis. The condition of
the deciduous fruit trees found in home orchards indicates
that climatic factors are favorable to the growing of apples,
pears, and peaches if the trees are pruned, sprayed, and
handled under normal commercial management and cultivation practices. Yields can be expected to be good but
probably somewhat below those of the temperate zones in
which the trees go through a dormant period due to winter
temperatures rather than the reduction in rainfall which
brings on the rest period in the Ambato area. The area in
which deciduous fruits can be grown is limited to the Sierra
from about the latitude of Ambato in the north to Loja in the
south. As one goes further south the dry season extends
over a longer period and supplemental irrigation will probably
be needed for planting south of Cuenca. The development of
an export market for fresh fruits from this area appears to
offer no possibilities because the costs of moving the fruits
to a port of export would be too great.

A very important factor to consider is whether farmers
will be willing to grow fruits for export at the income from
this enterprise in relation to that from other crops. The
Italconsult fruit specialist made some extensive inquiries
into the yield and price situation for most fruits and arrived
at the estimations shown in the table on the following page.

These estimations are based upon existing conditions and
prices as reported in interviews with a relatively small group
of growers. Under good commercial cultivation practices
the volume of production per hectare could be increased by
two to three times the volumes now obtained for all but bananas. Prices per unit for either processing or sale to exporters would have to be lower than those now obtained for
most of these products. Under good commercial practices
the gross income per hectare will be higher for citrus fruits
and pineapples than for bananas.

YIELD, PRICE, AND INCOME DERIVED
BY FRUIT FARMERS

	Yield per Hectare		Price per Unit	Income per Hectare
Product	Volume	Unit	In Sucres	In Sucres
Apricots	5,520	kgs.	2.80	15,400
Apples	12,700	apples	1.00	12,700
Peaches	5,854	kgs.	1.90	11,226
Figs	18,400	kgs.	1.20	22,080
Oranges	117,400	oranges	.10	11,745
Lemons	33,730	kgs.	1.20	40,476
Grapefruit	50,000	fruits	.40	20,000
Papaya	11,420	fruits	1.00	11,420
Mangoes	230,000	fruits	.15	34,500
Grapes	1,288	kgs.	16.00	20,208
Naranjilla	19,350	kgs.	1.80	34,830
Pineapple	12,174	fruits	1.50	18,261
Bananas	687	stems	13.00	8,931

Under normal commercial growing practices a farmer may expect to get 20,000 pineapples from a hectare and from a processor receive S/.50 each, for a gross return of 10,000 sucres. For the small grower who would depend almost entirely upon family labor for planting, cultivating, and harvesting the crop, pineapples would offer somewhat higher family income; but for the commercial producer who would need to hire labor the net income would probably be about the same as for bananas. Net returns from oranges or grapefruit sold for processing may give the commercial grower considerably higher net returns than bananas, but there would be a period of waiting for the citrus trees to come into production.

The Italconsult Mission has estimated that about 2,300 hectares were planted to pineapples in 1961-62, and that 75 percent of this acreage was located in Guayas Province near the town of Milagro. There should be no serious problems

in bringing the total hectares planted in the Milagro area up
to about 5,000 hectares within a period of four to five years,
if farmers should find that it was an enterprise that offered
them more net income than some of the competitive enterprises like bananas, rice, and livestock. With respect to
citrus fruits it is estimated that about 7,500 hectares were
planted to oranges, grapefruit, and lemons, but these were
scattered rather widely in the province of Manabi, Bolivar,
Guayas, Los Rios, and El Oro.

VEGETABLE PRODUCTION POSSIBILITIES

In addition to potatoes and other high altitude tuber crops
normally grown by the Sierra people of South America for
home consumption, in the Sierra of Ecuador there is also production of several other cool climate vegetables and tomatoes.
Information collected by the Italconsult Mission for some of
the more important of the vegetable crops which may have
some potential for export in fresh or processed form is shown
as follows:

POTENTIAL VEGETABLE EXPORTS

Product	Hectares Harvested	Yield (Kgs./hectare)	Farmers Market Price per Kilo (In Sucres)	Gross Return per Hectare (In Sucres)
Onions	3,250	29,393	2.00	58,788
Cabbage	3,000	23,000	.90	20,700
Cauliflower	900	15,916	.75	11,937
Tomatoes	1,350	25,555	2.10	53,666
Peas	1,350	1,617	2.00	3,234

Both tomatoes and onions give high returns per hectare, and
most growers would no doubt be interested in increasing the
acreage planted if markets could be found for the additional
production. At present prices received for the above listed

products it would be impossible to compete in the export
markets for the fresh commodity. It should be noted, however, that farmers' market prices vary widely and, moreover,
that production costs on a quantity scale for processing would
be markedly lower, as will be seen in Chapter 4.

HARD FIBERS PRODUCTION POSSIBILITIES

The production of cordage until recently has been primarily
an artisan or home industry for which the raw materials were
the fibers of the local cabuya or agave plant. This material
was also used to some extent for the weaving of burlap bags
but there were imports of jute for making high-quality rope
and sisal for bagging materials. The cabuya plant is found
throughout the Sierra provinces and the drier areas of the
coastal provinces. It is grown mostly along the fence rows
but is also grown in solid stands on some of the steeper slopes
in the southern Sierra provinces. Unpublished reports of the
Ministry of Fomento show that 22,727 hectares were planted
to cabuya in 1962, and the total production of fiber was estimated to be 23,000 metric tons.

A new cordage and burlap plant recently constructed at
Guayaquil has a capacity to use 120,000 pounds of cordage
material weekly and expects to be in full production by the end
of 1963. This plant will in the beginning depend primarily
upon the fiber of the cabuya plant for making both cordage and
bagging materials. They are experimenting with other fibers
such as kenaf, abaca, and banana stalk fibers. They are also
assisting local farmers in the Sierra area to purchase a simple
decorticating machine which is being manufactured locally.
The decorticating machine is reported to have a productive
capacity of 1,000 pounds of dry fiber per day. If each machine
were operated at capacity on a 5-day weekly basis, 24 machines
would be enough to supply the cordage plant with its needs.
With plantings being so widely scattered and the difficulties of
getting farmers to harvest continually, it is possible that it
will require as many as 100 to 150 decorticating machines well
placed in the cabuya-producing areas to meet the needs of the
cordage plant in Guayaquil.

The production of cabuya should present no problem since the new plant will not use more than about 3,000 tons out of the present production of 23,000 tons. A large percentage of the existing planting has not been harvested at the optimum for several years. This will permit a 10 to 20 percent increase in harvestings that can easily take care of both the new plant and the existing artisan industries. More efficient decorticating methods can also be expected to increase yields.

A Japanese firm has been experimenting with planting of abaca and ramie during the past three years at the Pichilingue Experiment Station and near Santo Domingo de los Colorados. They are now satisfied that both these crops can be successfully produced in Ecuador and are planning to plant 2,000 hectares for producing fibers to be sent to Japan for further processing.

If both the new cordage plant and the Japanese firm reach planned production goals within the next two to three years they will be able to produce about 8,000 tons of hard fibers and cordage materials for export. At present prices this tonnage will yield about $2 million in foreign exchange.

In the field trips through the country several plantings of kenaf were observed. The plantings appear to be growing vigorously and yields of raw fiber materials are reported to be high. The problem that is most likely to limit the production of this product will be the development of a retting or decorticating method that is efficient and economic. Reports from countries where kenaf has been grown over the past several years are that no one seems to have developed an economical method of getting a high yield of dry finish fiber from the raw fiber materials.

VEGETABLE OILS AND FATS
PRODUCTION POSSIBILITIES

Ecuador has faced much the same problems with respect to edible oils and fats during the last ten years as other South American countries. In spite of all the attempts made to increase production, increases in domestic consumption have made it necessary to import larger and larger quantities. Imports of vegetable oils and animal fats from 1955 to 1961 increased at the average rate of about 13.5 percent a year. The figures are listed below:

VEGETABLE OIL AND ANIMAL FAT IMPORTS, VOLUME AND VALUE, 1955-61

Year	Volume in M. T.	Value in Dollars
1955	7,224	1,615,892
1956	10,307	2,500,774
1957	11,711	2,924,678
1958	11,051	2,576,279
1959	13,588	3,879,224
1960	17,781	3,528,653
1961	15,592	3,466,718

Source: Boletin del Banco Central del Ecuador.

Unless steps can be taken to provide the vegetable oils and fats needs of the country from locally produced raw materials, the present rate of increase in imports indicates that by 1973 it would be necessary to spend almost $16 million of foreign exchange for importing these products, assuming prices as of 1961.

The first steps were initiated to develop a national edible oils industry in 1943 when the Industries Ales, C. A. was organized and built a plant at Manta for processing raw

materials. By 1957 there were seven oil processing plants
established in the cities of Guayaquil and Manta. The building
of these plants did not stimulate production of raw materials
and they found it necessary to obtain two-thirds of their supplies from imports. Since 1955 production of edible oils has
more than doubled, as indicated in the following table:

VEGETABLE OIL PRODUCTION, 1955-61

Year	In Thousand Liters
1955	727
1956	1,316
1957	1,574
1958	1,411
1959	1,481
1960	1,578
1961	1,714

Source: Direccion General de Estadistica y Censos del
Ecuador.

Although attempts have been made to obtain the needed raw
material from local sources, these oil processors are still
getting about half of their supplies from imports. There are
several locally grown products from which oil can be economically extracted, but production of these products has not developed as fast as the needs of the oil processors for raw
materials. Some of the most promising sources of raw materials are: African oil palms, coconut palms, cottonseed, and
peanuts.

The African oil palm seemed to offer excellent possibilities
as it is adapted to climatic conditions found in the tropical
areas of the northern Guayas Basin and those found in the
basins of the Esmeraldas and Mira Rivers. When in full production the African oil palm is reported to yield up to 1,800

kilograms of oil per hectare. Some of the difficulties in establishing an oil industry from these palms are the need for technicians who know the conditions under which the palm must be planted, the cultural techniques for getting optimum yields, and the waiting period of four years for the palm to begin yielding fruits after it is planted. Maximum yields cannot be obtained until the palms are about seven years old. Some palms were introduced into Ecuador in the late 1940's, and some experimental work was carried out, but farmers generally did not show interest in this plant. In 1952 one planting of 100 hectares was made, but no additional planting was made until 1959 when 52 more hectares were planted. Since 1959 new plantings are being made at a slow rate, and it is estimated that by the end of 1963 there will be about 785 hectares planted. If optimum production can be obtained from these plantings they will provide only about 1,400 metric tons of oil, or about 15 percent of the need of the oil processor for raw materials by 1973, assuming growth in domestic oil production at the 1955-61 rate.

The owners of the first planting of 100 hectares of oil palms encountered many difficulties during the first ten years. Through lack of technical advice the palms were planted 100 per hectare when the best yields and financial returns are obtained from 140 plants per hectare. Lack of credit for maintaining the new plantings in proper condition resulted in failure of the palms to start fruiting at the end of the fourth year. When the palms did start fruiting in 1958 difficulties of obtaining credit to purchase oil extracting equipment and government delays in issuing an import permit resulted in the loss of the first crop. After many difficulties the first production of 95 tons of oil was secured in 1960.

The first oil palms specialist with practical experience was employed by the FAO and assigned to Ecuador in 1961. If a specialist of this type had been available in 1952 when the first commercial plantings were made, production would have begun about five years earlier and there would probably have been much more interest shown by other farmers in this new crop.

It should also be pointed out that this experience of introducing a new crop in the country has required about ten years
of work and investment before it began to give a return of
commercial importance. With a well-designed program ade-
quately backed by credit and technical assistance to growers,
it can be expected that another ten years will have elapsed
before production will reach optimum levels. It was previously
pointed out that much the same conditions were experienced in
introducing and developing the pyrethrum industry. The FAO
oil palm specialist has estimated that with adequate governmental assistance to the industry, an annual production of
7,500 tons of palm oil may be reached by 1973. This will be
enough to eliminate about one-half of the present imports of
vegetable oils at current rates of consumption but only about
10 percent of the needs by 1973, assuming continuance of the
1955-61 rates of growth in oil consumption.

To reach even this modest goal, it is estimated that an investment of 192,696,000 sucres will be needed, of which
176,696,000 sucres will come from private sources and 16
million sucres from public sources. It is also estimated that
about 2,500 people will need to be employed in the industry of
which 25 will need to be specialists and three, highly trained
experts. Since there are no nationals trained to handle this
crop at present, it will be necessary that a large number of
the 25 specialists be trained abroad and the three experts will
need to be foreign technicians with many years of experience
in growing and extracting oil from the palm fruits.

In view of the fact that it will take about ten years to bring
a modest oil palm industry into production, it would seem advisable in the meantime that some source of vegetable oil be
found that can be developed more rapidly to meet the immediate
needs of the oil processors. Peanuts have been grown in the
country on a small scale for many years and appear to offer
some potential. The statistics on peanut acreage from different official sources show large discrepancies. The 1954
Census of Agriculture gives the following information:

Zone and Province	Hectares Harvested	Production in Quintals
Total for the Republic	2,532	24,476
Sierra total	1,946	17,649
Carchi Province	5	60
Imbabura "	1	10
Loja "	1,742	15,904
Pichincha "	198	1,675
Coastal total	586	6,827
El Oro Province	185	2,193
Guayas "	35	199
Manabi "	366	4,435

The Ministry of Fomento has estimated the acreage and production of peanuts from 1953 to 1962 as follows:

Year	Hectares Harvested	Production in Quintals	Average Yield Quintals per Hectare
1953	7,370	73,700	10.3
1954	8,355	108,200	13.0
1955	11,168	171,080	15.3
1956	9,473	153,560	16.2
1957	10,975	177,704	16.2
1958	9,225	144,063	15.6
1959	8,995	141,880	16.2
1960	8,430	135,000	16.0
1961	7,073	121,835	17.2
1962	6,586	115,664	16.8

With discrepancies of this magnitude existing in the official statistics, it is difficult to reach sound conclusions regarding the potential of this crop as a source of raw material for the oil-processing industry. It was observed on a field trip through Manabi Province that a large percentage of the farmers had a small patch of peanuts, which were probably grown for home consumption but with sale of any surplus above their home needs in the markets. There are approximately 33,000 farmers in Loja and Manabi Provinces where peanuts are grown and where climatic and soil conditions are favorable for the production of this crop. Most of the farms in these two provinces are very small units. If there were 20,000 farmers who sold an average of only 3 quintals each this would represent more than twice the production shown in the census and about one-half the production shown by the Ministry of Fomento estimates of total production. With a minor crop like peanuts, which represents only 1 percent of the total area covered by the census, there is always the possibility of under-reporting. The Ministry of Fomento figures are probably closer to the mark.

If a program should be initiated to produce peanuts for oil processing, it will be important to raise the hectare yields to twice the present levels. This is not an impossible goal to attain since most of the varieties and types presently grown are relatively low producers. It would mean that new varieties would need to be introduced and that farmers be given technical assistance in the planting, cultivating, and harvesting of the crop. For the production from Manabi Province the present oil processing plants can be expected to provide the installations and equipment for extraction of the oil from the peanuts, and marketing should not present a serious problem. It would be important that production be increased to levels that would justify the installation of some additional equipment. For production from Loja Province, it will be more logical to extract the oil locally and leave the protein cake in the area where there is a scarcity of protein concentrates for animal feeding.

Before embarking upon a program of peanut production for oil processing, some rather detailed feasibility studies should be made. These should pay particular attention to the production potentials of Manabi, Loja, and Azuay Provinces. The investment costs of bringing the industry into operation should be carefully studied to determine the number and type of additional marketing facilities that will be needed as well as the assistance that will need to be provided to the farmers who may be interested in producing peanuts on a commercial scale.

Cottonseed is already being used as a raw material for oil by the processors, and increases in cotton production will make additional volumes of seed available for oil processing. It appears doubtful, however, that cotton production will be increased beyond the national needs for textile fibers in the next ten years. These increases will be of relatively small importance in meeting the present and increasing requirement for oil.

FORESTRY PRODUCTS POSSIBILITIES

With the exception of balsa, lumber production in Ecuador is for the national market. There are still large forested areas of virgin timber, but most of the stands of good species are inaccessible. When a new road is extended into a forested area, it becomes profitable to carry out lumbering operations that exploit the better species while clearing the land for the planting of cultivated crops. All the forestry experts who have studied the Ecuadorian forestry potential have generally arrived at the conclusion that exploitation of the natural forest for export markets is an uneconomic operation. They point out that the numbers of trees of marketable species found in a forested tract are too small and the trees too widely separated to justify the costs involved in cutting and getting the logs to market. The same forestry experts point out that lumbering and sawmilling operations are very poorly organized and that this is a factor that is primarily responsible for the high costs of finished lumber.

In the cut-over areas of the Costa which are too steep for cultivated crops no attempts have been made at reforestation. If these areas were planted to the better species which have been found in the native forest it could eventually lead to a forestry industry that could supply lumber for export. However, this will be an investment that requires a long wait for a cash return, and private capital is too scarce and too much needed for more immediate developments to invest it in this manner. On the other hand it should be recognized that most developed countries have found that it was necessary to have a government reforestation program following the exploitation of the country's natural forest. The realization of this important fact has oftentimes come very late with the result that the program becomes much more costly than would have been necessary if action had been taken sooner. There is a need for feasibility studies designed to determine the country's forestry resource potentials and to develop the basis for a sound forestry program. Such studies and a program for reforestation will not bring an immediate increase in exports, but they can lead to the continuation of an industry that may be lost entirely unless early action is taken.

In contrast to the Costa, there has been an extensive forestation program in the Sierra using eucalyptus. These plantings of eucalyptus have been and will be of great value to this area as a source of forewood and in certain types of construction. It cannot, however, be looked upon as an export product.

Teak, which is a valuable timber, was introduced on an experimental basis to Ecuador about twenty years ago. The trees planted at the Pichilingue Experiment Station have made a rapid growth and appear to be free of diseases. In 1961, 694 pounds of seed from these trees were sold to farmers. In the field trips made in the coastal zone two additional plantings of teak were observed. Both were very small plantings but the trees appeared to be growing well. Replies to inquiries made at the Pichilingue Station as to what had been done toward following up on the original introduction of teak indicate that this experiment has been abandoned. It is desirable that introductions of new plants and experiments of this type be kept under continued study until such times as it has been definitely proven whether the newly introduced plants have potential economic value. Plant introduction experiments frequently require many years of testing before it can be determined whether a new plant will be of any economic importance. Such experiments, however, can generally be continued without the expenditure of large sums of public funds. Such simple things as taking measurements of the teak tree growth rates once a year and a few recorded notes on the condition of the health of the plants would not require more than a few hours' work. This type of experimental work will not cost more than a fraction of the cost of importing and planting of the original plants, but it can be important at a later period in determining whether a program of commercial development will be an economically sound venture.

Several improved varieties of rubber were also introduced into Ecuador about fifteen years ago. Unfortunately, this experiment has also been abandoned. At the time the Italconsult Mission rubber expert was in the country, it was necessary to identify the abandoned trees by personal inspection, a method which is far from infallible. The records on the origin and names of the original introductions had been lost and were not in the experiment station files. The Italconsult rubber expert concluded that rubber could be economically grown in Ecuador on a commercial scale for both national industries and export. The rubber development plan submitted to the government indicates it would take Ecuador twelve years to develop the rubber industry to the point where the national needs can be supplied. It was estimated that the government would need to spend about $1 million in experimental, seed introduction, and other types of promotional work, if the plan were to be a success. Private enterprise would need to spend an additional $5 million during the first eight years before the trees would begin producing and give an annual return of $1.8 million. If ample funds will be available for development programs, the rubber plan would doubtless be an economically sound venture. However, with the severe limitations on the amount of development funds that appear likely, there may be other products that can justify a higher priority.

If one of the large rubber-producing firms, which would have trained technical people to supervise the development operations, should show an interest in establishing a rubber-growing industry in Ecuador, the prospects for earlier successful development would be brighter. In any case, the experimental work already started should be reactivated and continued.

TOBACCO PRODUCTION POSSIBILITIES

Tobacco has been produced in Ecuador for internal consumption for more than thirty years. The varieties grown have been primarily of the black types that are common in Brazil and Cuba. Prior to 1956 there was a rather important cigarette and cigar manufacturing industry which was privately owned and operated. These plants were required to sell their total output to the state tobacco monopoly which controlled prices to both wholesalers and retailers. These price control policies, plus a failure to improve the quality of the tobacco plantings, resulted in the black-marketing of imported cigars and cigarettes. There is still a rather large production of tobacco for the production of locally made cigarettes, but the preference is general for the imported brands, which sell at much higher prices. Climate and soil conditions are favorable for the production of tobacco, and there is no doubt that all national demands could be met from local production if improvements were made in the quality of the locally grown tobaccos.

Following the break in diplomatic relations between the United States and Cuba, the Government of Ecuador contracted with Cuban tobacco specialists to experiment with tobacco production in Ecuador, and the American Tobacco Company sent an expert to Ecuador to try to develop an industry that would replace the imports formerly obtained from Cuba. This company has contracted with farmers in Guayas Province to produce about 50 hectares of tobacco in 1963. Using seed from imported sources of the Havana types, experimental plantings have shown that both regular and shade-grown types of tobacco can be successfully grown in Ecuador. The primary problem faced by the tobacco expert is that of training each grower in the proper planting, cultural, and harvesting techniques. Assignment of counterpart personnel to work with the foreign expert in learning these techniques would appear to be a wise investment.

The net returns from tobacco make it a highly profitable crop for the farmer who is favored with the soil and climatic

conditions and technical knowledge of production. It is also
a potential important earner of foreign exchange, especially
the shade-grown types. Farmers of the Connecticut River
Valley in the United States have averaged above $1. 85 per
pound for this type of tobacco during the past ten years, and
production has averaged in excess of 1, 000 pounds per acre.
Price to farmers of regular types of tobacco will be much
lower, averaging between 20 to 50 cents, depending upon type
and quality, but yields are normally somewhat higher. If
Ecuador can develop only 250 hectares of tobacco of the shade-
grown type for export it will bring in about $1 million in
foreign exchange. With the loss of the Cuban production to
U. S. tobacco manufacturers, it will be possible to export to
the United States several times this volume, if the exacting
demands with respect to quality and type can be met. The
question of whether Ecuador will be able to take advantage of
this golden opportunity will depend upon the ability of the local
farmers and technicians to learn and apply the techniques of
producing a quality product. In addition to training the technicians to grow the tobacco, it will be important to select the
farmers carefully and also to select with care the locations
for growing the tobacco at each farm. To get the quality that
will be essential to the success of the program, each farmer
will need to limit his acreage to the amount he can personally
supervise, probably not more than one or two hectares. The
initial development program should be designed to sacrifice
volume of production for quality. If Ecuador can establish a
reputation as a shade-grown tobacco area, then it will have
the basis for another important foreign exchange earner, perhaps in a decade or so to rival coffee or cacao.

COMPARATIVE ANALYSIS OF PRODUCTION
POSSIBILITIES TO DIVERSIFY EXPORTS

As has been shown previously, there is no question but that
Ecuador has the type of soils, climate, and other natural conditions for the production of a wide variety of both tropical and
temperate zone crops. For the tropical crops there is no
reason to conclude that yields cannot be got that are as high as

or higher than those in other tropical areas of the world. Yields and cost of production for some of the temperate zone crops may vary somewhat from those in the most favored temperate zone areas of other countries, but generally Ecuador's yields and costs are competitive among the products appraised. It can be concluded definitely that climate and soil conditions will in no way be factors which will limit production increases in the crops having export possibilities.

A large surplus of labor at attractive rates of pay is one of the major inducements for investment in Ecuador. With extensive underemployment as well as considerable unemployment and with population increasing at more than 3 percent a year, it is not likely that the availability of labor in general will be a factor limiting expansion of export crops for some years to come. Especially is this true of the Sierra, where the pressure of population on land resources has produced marked underemployment.

There is, however, a scarcity of skilled labor and technicians. Complaints are heard also of short-term shortages of labor in the planting and harvesting seasons for some crops in the Costa, and as production is expanded such complaints will be more frequent, leading perhaps to some shift of population from the Sierra to the Costa.

The availability of capital is the production factor which places limits on the rate of development of export crops and products.

Cattle producers need more loans to purchase breeding stock and fencing materials, and to develop pastures. Coffee and cacao producers generally recognize that present curing methods are responsible for low-quality products, but they lack capital to purchase the equipment that will permit better processing of these products. The processors of dried bananas are presently working with antiquated equipment because they lack capital to purchase more modern machinery. The present bottleneck to increased fish production is the lack of capital for additional and more modern fishing boats. In general it can be expected that lack of capital will be the factor that is the most serious problem in bringing about more rapid development.

It is evident that Ecuador will not be able to bring into production rapidly all the crops and products for which there is a suitable natural resource base.   This means that a system of priorities must be established in a governmental development program.   The several products discussed in this chapter may be classified into three general priority groups as follows:

Group I

Milk for Production of Cheese, Butter, Powdered Milk, and Canned Milk

The production base for this industry is more than adequate, and present production is already large enough to meet most of the domestic demands.   The potential is a large one.

Cattle for Beef Production

With the introduction of cultivated pastures and sound pasture management, there is a very large potential for beef cattle production in the Costa and in the southern Sierra provinces.   A major governmentally sponsored effort extending over about a decade will be required to achieve significant export earnings.

Pork Production

There is a good production base and production has risen sharply.   The problem is to restrain consumption moderately in order to divert some of this production into export markets.

Hard Fibers for Cordage and Bagging

There is now in production a large amount of cabuya that is not fully utilized, and the new cordage plant at Guayaquil has a capacity to meet national demands and still provide a surplus

for export.   The experimental work for production of abaca
(and the fine fiber, ramie) has largely been completed.

Vegetable Oils and Fats

These products will probably not be produced in sufficient
volume to permit exports over the next ten years but they
should be promoted to eliminate the need for imports now using
$3.5 million of foreign exchange annually, which may rise to
about $16 million by 1973.   Considerable experimental work
has been completed on the growing of the African oil palm.
With an oil palm expert already in the country to provide technical assistance, this enterprise is now at the stage where development can take place rather rapidly but it may take some
years to develop an export market, since it takes seven years
for the oil palm to come into full production and domestic consumption is rising rapidly.   Peanut production is already established in two provinces and could be increased.   Increases
in cotton for the national textile industry will provide some
additional cottonseed for processing.

Tobacco

This product can be placed in the first priority group because of the present international demand for a substitute for
Cuban tobaccos.   Foreign companies possessing the essential
technical knowledge and resources are already in the country
with a program to increase production for export.

Group II

This group includes those products which appear to have
definite export potentials but of lesser magnitude, and they require large amounts of new investment capital and highly quali-
fied technicians not presently available in the country.

Pineapples for Processing

A group of small farmers already have experience in growing the crop, but they will need much more technical assistance
to produce for a processing plant.

Citrus Fruits for Fresh Markets and Processing

Production volume is adequate or can be expanded readily but much must be done to assure quality standards for the export market.

Tomatoes for Processing

These are sections of the country where farmers know the techniques of growing tomatoes, and climatic and soil conditions are good, with potentially low production costs on a quantity basis. Both capital for processing plants and technicians will be required.

Group III

This group includes those products for which a great deal of experimental work will be required before it will be possible to initiate production. The possibilities of developing an export market within the next ten years are small unless well established foreign companies with both technical and capital resources should be induced to develop production and marketing.

The products included in this group are:

> Rubber
> Tea
> Black pepper and other spices

4

PROCESSING OF RAW MATERIALS

In the preceding chapter, Ecuador's production prospects for new export crop possibilities have been assayed. The present chapter will be concerned with the possibilities of establishing industries to process for export Ecuador's raw materials. The analysis will be concerned primarily with the same commodities treated in basic production terms in Chapters 2 and 3 but treated here in terms of processing or manufacturing possibilities.

EXTENT OF PRESENT PROCESSING FOR EXPORT

Ecuador's present exports consist almost exclusively of raw materials—chiefly farm crops—shipped in bulk or packaged, with processed materials amounting to no more than 3 or 4 percent of the total. The only sizable and rapidly growing processed items chiefly designed for export are fishery products, specifically canned and frozen tuna and frozen cleaned shrimp. Exports of pyrethrum extract and pharmaceutical products are growing but still small. Panama hats, tagua buttons, and other artisan products show a declining trend.

By all feasible means, Ecuador must seek to expand its traditional exports; but the new and beckoning opportunity for the Ecuadorian economy is that of developing industries to process the nation's resources and thereby multiply the values involved and to seek export markets for these products. In that way, Ecuador can export also the skills of its people in fashioning its materials and crops and significantly increase Ecuador's "take" from the sale of the products of its farms, fisheries, and forests.

Some processing of banana products has developed; in
recent years no less than thirteen separate processing firms
have made their appearance, with a number of these firms
beginning to export, primarily to Central European countries,
such items as dried whole bananas and dried slices. It might
be anticipated that something similar would in time develop
with semi-elaborated cacao or chocolate. Some soluble coffee
is also being exported on a small scale. In general, however,
the attitude appears to prevail that if processed products are
to be manufactured in Ecuador, production should be aimed
merely at satisfying the local market, thereby replacing the
imported product. This attitude is reflected in reports on
such products as glass, sulfuric acid, and tomato products, in
which the size of the operation is not determined on the basis
of optimum operating size or comparative cost of production
relative to other producing countries, but on the quantity of the
imported products.

Primarily with a view to satisfying local demand, a number
of "assembly" or "packaging" operations have been brought
into existence, which do very little to improve the Ecuadorian
economy or the balance of trade. If, for example, a food mix
is imported in bulk, together with the containers, and all that
is accomplished in Ecuador is to fill and seal the containers,
the added value is inconsequential. Clearly, the interests of
the Ecuadorian economy will be best served by seizing the
many excellent opportunities for manufacturing items from
local raw materials and wherever possible packaging them in
local containers.

GENERAL APPRAISAL
OF PROCESSING POSSIBILITIES

The opportunities for expanding present exports of processed materials and developing new products for export are many
and favorable. Ecuador enjoys numerous comparative advantages for the production of processed materials. So conspicuous are these advantages that one experienced observer has
remarked that Ecuador is "a sleeper"—meaning a land whose

potential is greatly in excess of its present development. Her
present significant position in the export of farm crops is
based fundamentally on an abundant supply of fertile lands, a
long growing and harvesting season, and competent labor at
rates among the lowest in the world. Rich fishing grounds
fed by the Pacific currents, year-round fishing, and low labor
costs similarly account for Ecuador's growing exports of
fisheries products.

It is of course true that labor rates will rise in Ecuador;
and true also that the greater the success in expanding production and exports the greater will be the rise. This is in
the nature of economic development, for it is increased output,
and especially increased output per man-hour or man-year,
that supplies the wherewithal from which increased wages can
be paid. In a developing economy, then, wage rates should
rise—and they will rise—as increasing productivity makes
that possible. Ecuador is such an economy, and there is no
safer prediction than to say that wage rates will rise markedly
over the next ten years from their present levels.

An equally safe prediction is to say that wage rates in the
rest of the world will also rise, in consequence of rising productivity. Insofar as the comparison is with wage rates in the
developed economies of North America, Western Europe, and
Japan, it remains to be seen whether the rate of economic development in Ecuador can be fast enough to begin to narrow
the present margin in wage rates; and even if the rate of increase in wages in Ecuador should be much higher than the
rate of increase in the developed economies, the present margin is so wide that the comparative costs advantage in Ecuador
would persist for many, many years.

To take a hypothetical example, let it be assumed that wage
rates will rise twice as fast in Ecuador as in the United States,
say at an annual rate of 6 percent in Ecuador and 3 percent in
the United States. The results of this hypothetical example
would be as follows, for the two specified sets of daily wage
rates:

Assumed Daily Wage Rates, 1963	Daily Wage Rate in 10 Years if Rates Increase Yearly at		Daily Wage Rate in 25 Years if Rates Increase Yearly at	
	3 percent	6 percent	3 percent	6 percent
Group A				
$ 0.50	--	$0.90	--	$2.15
1.00	--	1.79	--	4.29
1.50	--	2.69	--	6.43
2.00	--	3.59	--	8.58
Group B[a]				
$ 8.00	$10.75	--	$16.75	--
10.00	13.44	--	20.94	--
12.00	16.13	--	25.13	--
14.00	18.81	--	29.31	--

a.   These assumed rates may be compared with the following record of average gross hourly earnings of wage earners in the United States for 1962; contract construction, $3.82; durable goods manufacturing, $2.57; nondurable goods manufacturing, $2.17; retail trade, $1.75. An amendment to the Fair Labor Standards Act in 1961 provided for raising the minimum wage in steps from $1.00 an hour to $1.25.

Let it be repeated, then, that Ecuador's basic comparative cost advantages are both marked and durable.

These same favorable factors will be equally significant in the development of processing industries for the export trade. Only in the Sierra does population press on land resources. In the Costa her rich volcanic and alluvial soils will provide the basis for whatever expansion in present production may be needed to supply processing industries. The Oriente, forming half of the area of the country, is entirely underdeveloped. Even though there may be no immediate potential in those vast lands lying east of the Andes, they are there as a reservoir for

future development. The Sierra makes only a small contribution to present major exports—chiefly some upland coffee—
but it has a significant potential, especially for the development of processed products based on its advantages of a temperate climate, year-long green pastures, a skilled and energetic population, and highly favorable labor costs.

Many things must be done to exploit these potentials, but
the resource base is there and the world's markets are growing as standards of well-being are rising around the world.
The most severe limiting factor is the shortage of capital.
Large amounts of capital will be required to develop new processing industries with a really significant export potential;
and even the needed expansion of existing industries will require considerable increments of capital. Moreover, many
of these investment opportunities will require a relatively long
period of experimentation and development. These long "waiting periods" will pay dividends ultimately, but they do impose
a heavy burden of capital and interest costs during the years
when there is only outgo and no matching revenue. But there
is capital in Ecuador, and there are also possibilities of attracting foreign capital.

Perhaps the second most severe limitation is the lack of an
adequate supply of skilled technicians and managerial personnel. This problem is a long-term one and clearly will not
yield rapidly to remedial measures. It is, however, entirely
feasible to bring in a nucleus of needed foreign technicians
and managers with definite programs of training local personnel to take over their functions at the right time. Moreover,
where direct foreign investment is resorted to, one of the
great advantages is that the foreign concern can supply its own
nucleus of needed technicians for the initial period of organi-
zing operations and training local personnel.

There are of course other limitations to a more rapid development of processing industries, but they are factors that
are being corrected or that are correctable. For example,
there is an urgent need throughout Ecuador for more adequate
transportation and especially for more and better roads. As

one Ecuadorian put it: "El problema de esta economia es carreteras, carreteras, carreteras." Fortunately, something is being done about that need, though time will be required. There are strong complaints about the taxation of export industries or products. And there are strong complaints concerning the long, drawn-out, complicated, and time-consuming negotiations with government agencies that are involved in setting up new ventures or in expanding old ones. These limitations do constitute serious barriers, but clearly they are removable in time through legislative and administrative actions and through the pressure of public opinion as Ecuadorians become more conscious of the need for enhanced production and exports as a means toward the upbuilding of the economy and the improvement of standards of well-being.

In the succeeding section the opportunities for processing industries for export will be explored, product by product. These product appraisals will be presented, starting with "Banana Products" and extending through "Vegetables for Processing," followed by a "Miscellaneous" category.

SPECIFIC OPPORTUNITIES FOR PROCESSING FOR EXPORT

Banana Products

Because of the size of Ecuador's banana crop and the present marketing methods, there is a tremendous volume of material available for processing. With a total annual production of about 2,500,000 metric tons of which only about 38 percent is exported, 50 percent left on the farms, and 12 percent rejected at the port, vast quantities are available, both in the production areas and at the ports, which may be purchased at a price of 15 cents per stem or less, or about 0.2 to 0.3 cents per pound. Assuming a 10 percent yield of dried banana solids, raw material for one pound of banana solids would cost 2 to 3 cents, and would make the banana a cheaper source of food in terms of calories than a pound of sugar.

The present utilization and marketing of the banana crop is indeed so wasteful that not more than 1 percent of the materials that can be utilized for other than fresh fruit export is actually used. It is estimated that the value of such materials which are now waste products could approach the value of the exported bananas themselves.

There is little doubt that such utilization will increase gradually to an appreciable export volume of perhaps $5 million a year, if for no other reason than the extremely low cost of the raw material. In all the plants visited, operations were found to be primitive, unsanitary, and unskillful. The most rudimentary application of industrial engineering principles could result in a many-fold improvement in processing, cost reduction, quality improvement, and a consequent rapid increase in market acceptability.

Even with such improvements, however, the full potential of banana products for export cannot be approached without a reorganization of the present fresh banana marketing system.

The prevailing marketing system for fresh bananas for export places a heavy burden on the banana grower and thereby imposes conditions which lead to great waste of bananas. This condition arises primarily from the fact that grading and packaging of the products takes place at the port rather than in the area of production. The grower bears the burden of shipping the stems, almost invariably by truck, to the port where they are accepted or rejected by the buyer. Almost one in four stems is rejected, on the average; one reason for this high rate being that a single defective or undersized hand of bananas (out of the normal eight or more hands) means rejection of the entire stem. Similarly, a stem of perfect bananas will be rejected if the number of hands is less than an agreed minimum, usually eight; and in some cases the stem, however perfect otherwise, will be rejected if its apparent weight falls below a certain minimum. That minimum in some cases may be far above the Ecuadorian average of about 70 pounds per stem or the reported average of about 80 pounds for stems shipped to the United States.

The rejected stem is in many instances a complete loss to the grower, both as to its costs of production of 5 or 6 sucres and as to the cost of shipping the stem to the port of about the same number of sucres. If the reject can be sold at all, it will command generally only from 1 to 3 sucres.

Under these circumstances the grower does his utmost in harvesting to select only those stems that appear to meet specifications. On the average he will harvest only one stem in two. Many of the remaining one-half will be harvested later for the domestic market, some for animal feed, and some will go to waste.

Stated in aggregate terms, of about 78 million stems grown in 1962, 34 million stems were exported; 9 million stems were rejected at the port; and 35 million stems were left at the farm for the domestic market or for stock feed or allowed to go to waste. (It is not known how many stems are consumed by the Ecuadorian population. But even at 100 pounds per capita per year-- compared with 21 pounds in the U. S. market-- only 6.5 million stems would be required.)

It is evident that these marketing methods are in need of drastic change. In particular there is urgent need for inspection in the area of production and treatment and packaging designed to avoid spoilage and waste in transit. An obvious gain among many others in packaging hands of bananas would be to maximize the selection of export-grade fruit since the hand of bananas rather than the entire stem would be the unit required to meet export specifications.

From the standpoint of a major processing industry, the great advantage of such a marketing system would be to concentrate the rejects, together with the stalks and trunks, about packing plants in the area of production, where these materials could be utilized further in the manufacture of all kinds of by-products, such as edible processed banana products, chemicals, paper, and fiber. If containers for the fresh bananas could be manufactured from banana stalks and stems, then such a by-product could approach in value that of

the export bananas themselves. One stalk of bananas is
valued at the port at about $1.10 to $1.20 and, if packaged,
requires about one and one-half boxes valued at about $0.60
each.

Cane, Sugar

The production of sugar from cane is discussed in Chapter
2. With a total cane production estimated at about 3.5 million
metric tons, a sugar yield of about 11 percent, and only about
150,000 tons of sugar, it is clear that only a fraction of the
total cane production is devoted to sugar manufacture. Estimates for 1963 show the following distribution of cane acreage
for various end products:

Aguardiente	6,500 hectares
Panela	26,000 hectares
Sugar	20,000 hectares

With the sharp rise in sugar prices, it would be well to
consider the possibility of diverting more cane to sugar production for export or new plantings for the purpose. Cane is
normally hauled very cheaply by the use of rail cars. If it is
not feasible under the current extraordinarily high price of
sugar to employ temporarily makeshift assembly methods,
then thought might be given to the possibility of exporting the
flavorful panela for use in the manufacture of drinks and
sweets. At least one major processor is considering use of
panela.

Besides its use for sugar, cane is probably the least expensive raw material for alcohol. According to a competent
practitioner in the industry, a hectare of cane will produce
10,000 gallons of 95 percent alcohol from about 300 tons of
cane. Thus alcohol production is extremely cheap, and may
of itself be an export item. A much greater added value can
be obtained, however, by utilizing this distillate in the form
of alcoholic beverages such as rum, gin, and others. This
is already being done in a very profitable manner in at least
one plant. Certainly every assistance should be given to such

operations having the capability of developing a very substantial export of alcoholic beverages manufactured primarily from cane juice.

Coffee

Soluble instant coffee is now being produced in the Si Cafe plant in Guayaquil. The product is of good quality; and the surplus of total plant capacity over domestic sales has been sold in advance to London buyers. Present plant utilization is 1,200 kilos per 8-hour day. Production could be expanded easily by operating two or three shifts daily. It was reported, however, that further export is limited because the exporter's costs make it difficult to compete favorably on the world markets.

The coffee that goes into three pounds of roasted and ground coffee will produce about one pound of soluble coffee. The per pound price of the soluble coffee in retail markets is understandably about three times the per pound cost of the roasted and ground coffee, thus achieving approximate parity on the original poundage basis. The one pound of soluble coffee, however, will produce about twice as many cups of coffee as the three pounds of roasted and ground coffee. Hence, it is doubtful that a mass conversion of exports from the form of beans to the soluble extract will in the long run add to Ecuador's total export earnings.

Cacao

Export of cacao beans is a well-established operation, with the Ecuadorian flavor cacao commanding a premium price on the world market. There are good reasons for believing that this condition will continue, and export of the beans will expand, although many candy manufacturers are using less of the premium grades for blending.

The percent of the total cacao production which is exported has been varying from about 83 to 90 percent, with the lower percentages being exported in years of low total production,

and the higher percentages in years of relatively high total
production. This would indicate that cacao is exported only
after local requirements are satisfied, and that export could
be substantially increased if larger quantities were available.

Even with the favorable conditions for exporting cacao in
the form of beans, there is an excellent opportunity to multiply the "take" from a fraction of this cacao in the form of processed products. Small amounts of cacao butter are already
being exported, but the large opportunity is in processed and
packaged chocolate. There is in Ecuador a uniquely favorable
situation in which all the main ingredients are available locally at a fraction of the costs prevailing in the major chocolate
manufacturing countries. At this time a manufacturer of
chocolate in Guayaquil can purchase milk powder from the
Sierra for 33 cents a pound, skim milk powder for 22 cents a
pound, sugar for confectionery use at 6 cents a pound, and
top quality cacao at 24 cents a pound. With such prices for
the raw materials, good quality chocolates made in Ecuador
and packaged properly could compete successfully anywhere
in the world.

Castor Beans

With the withdrawal of Brazil from the export of castor
beans, Ecuador has become the major exporter from South
America, doubling its exports from 1960 to 1962, to more
than 20,000 tons, or about one-fifth of the world total, at an
average value of 5 cents a pound. With an oil yield of 48.6
percent, castor oil could be manufactured in Ecuador at a
cost of approximately 15 cents a pound. Although the use and
price of castor oil have gone down, prices have held rather
steady recently at somewhat under 20 cents a pound. It
appears therefore that Ecuador's crop of some 20,000 tons
of castor beans converted to castor oil would yield about
twice as much foreign exchange, as compared with the export
of the raw bean.

Cereals for Processing

The only cereal product that may have an export potential is barley malt, manufactured from a variety of barley specially developed for the purpose. The malt is of excellent quality, but at present costs it is doubtful whether it could be exported competitively with Canadian and other sources.

Dairy Products

Although Ecuador is currently importing about 6 percent of her dairy products and is attempting to expand production of milk for local consumption, the prospects for developing a substantial export of milk products are excellent, particularly in the Andean highlands of the Sierra blessed with year-round pastures. In these areas milk is now sold to dairies at a price of about 5.5 cents a liter, and the actual costs of production, even including such costs as land and equipment depreciation, are probably under 4 cents a liter, as compared with costs of 7.5 cents in Wisconsin, and 5 to 6 cents in Denmark, the most efficient producers in America and Europe, respectively.

In the Sierra area there are now dairy plants that are producing pasteurized milk, butter, cheese, and powdered milk. Several of the larger haciendas are also making butter and cheese. All the commercial plants are equipped to make butter and cheese; one is producing whole powdered pasteurized milk of excellent quality; and one plant is equipped for canned milk that will meet export standards. Most of the haciendas can produce butter of exportable quality, and a few are producing cheese acceptable to the export markets. It is not contemplated that any problem will be experienced in the processing of cheese and butter for export.

With very little change in milk production or processing facilities, the Cayambe area alone probably could develop a $5 million annual export, simply by the expansion of existing herds, pastures, and processing facilities. With the present low volume prices of 36.5 cents a pound for Swiss or Gruyere type cheese, 33 cents a pound for butter, 33 cents a pound for

whole milk powder, and 22 cents a pound for skim milk
powder, these products on a volume basis should be highly
competitive in neighboring Latin American markets and perhaps in some other markets as well. The competitive wholesale prices that would have to be met in the United States
market for Cheddar cheese are suggested by the following
averages reported for 1961 by the United States Department
of Agriculture: Wisconsin primary markets 37. 2 cents;
Chicago No. 1 fresh daisies 40. 9 cents, and New York No. 1
fresh daisies 42. 4 cents. Whether Ecuador would be able to
export cheese to the United States or Europe will depend on
the relative level of processing costs; but a market probably
exists in Peru, Colombia, and some of the other Latin American markets.

There will be problems in transporting the products from
the plants in the Sierra to the coast for shipment abroad and
for moving them across the borders into the neighboring
countries of Colombia and Peru. For all of these marketings
refrigerated transport and storage equipment will be needed.
Small quantities of butter and cheese are now moving across
the northern border into Colombia but the butter is of poor
quality by the time it reaches the town of Cali, Colombia.

Fibers

Silk

Experiments with production of mulberry leaves and manufacture of silk thread are being conducted in Cuenca. If expectations are fulfilled, one family could operate one hectare
of mulberries and realize an annual family income of 36, 000
sucres per year. This operation is expected to yield about
250 kilos of silk which can now be marketed in France at $14
a kilo. Thus gross return from one hectare would be $3, 500.

This prospect would be an excellent means of utilizing low-
cost labor and vastly improving returns in acres where land is
utilized to capacity. It should be pointed out, however, that

returns from crops such as tomatoes, pineapples, and avocados would be similar, and involve considerably less labor.

Cabuya

The cabuya or agave plant yields 2.5 to 3.5 percent coarse and very tough fiber which is sold at 12.5 cents a pound if cut, washed, cleaned, and combed; and at 10 cents a pound if not combed. As stated in Chapter 3, the new plant at Guayaquil, Cordeleria Nacional, now has a capacity of 120,000 tons a week of fiber products, including cabuya. A substantial part of this capacity is now intended for export.

Abaca

Abaca fiber is also very tough, but finer and much longer —up to 3 meters—than cabuya. Japanese experiments in Pichilingue and Santo Domingo de los Colorados have demonstrated the possibility of producing the plant in Ecuador. A planting will last for 10 to 30 years, and yields 2 to 3 tons of dried cleaned fiber per hectare per year. Plantings will soon be established in southern, less humid regions of Ecuador.

Ramie

Japanese experiments are most promising for production of this fine fiber which the Japanese textile industry mixes with synthetic fibers in the manufacture of such items as men's shirts. Anticipated yields are 3 to 4 tons of dry fiber per year per hectare, at a price of $500 per ton. Current plans are to expand production of ramie and abaca over the next five to ten years to 2,000 hectares. With a production of up to 4 tons a hectare at $500 a ton, an industry grossing $4 million a year would result.

Fisheries

Shrimp

Export of frozen shrimp, mainly to the United States, is already a multimillion dollar Ecuadorian export item, but it can be increased to several-fold. Although the close-to-shore beds up to a depth of 20 fathoms are already being fully exploited, so that additional fishing vessels would not increase the total catch, there is still the opportunity for increasing the shrimp catch substantially by fishing beyond the 20-fathom depth, and such catches are likely to be of the larger and more expensive species. A number of fishing grounds are not being exploited primarily because of absence of access roads and fresh water, as for example Porto Lopez, where a substantial fishery processing operation could be located.

The tremendous advantage Ecuador holds currently because of the availability of low-cost labor is illustrated by the fact that cost of cleaned, deveined frozen shrimp in Guayaquil is 25 to 33 cents a pound, as compared to 55 to 65 cents a pound in the United States. With New York prices ranging from 35 cents for the small shrimp to $1.24 for the large, a very large margin of value is added by performing in Ecuador the essentially manual operation of cleaning and deveining.

Tuna

One substantial operation now exists, and operates profitably, producing 150,000 cases of consumer size cans for the local market, 150,000 cases of institution size (4-pound cans) exported to the United States, and 3,500 tons a year of frozen tuna to Puerto Rico. Some opinion was expressed that quantities of tuna are limited, particularly in the winter season. According to the Instituto Nacional de Pesca, the United Nations Special Fund's organization in Guayaquil, it is only the yellow-fin tuna that is being fished perhaps more heavily than desirable, but the similar skipjack species can be exploited considerably more.

Advantages of processing tuna in Ecuador are that the fish can be brought to the processing plant fresh the very same day they are caught, thus yielding a better quality canned product. Also the processing can be accomplished with the aid of local low-cost labor. Prices paid to fishermen are about $67 a ton for skipjack, and $83 a ton for yellow fin.

Lobster (Langosta)

Fishing for lobster is not yet well organized, and the extent of the fishing resources is only partially known. It is believed, however, that enough exists to develop an annual export of significant volume.

Fish Meal

The Van Camp Company is planning a fish meal plant in Manta, to utilize tuna waste. The major raw material for fish meal, such as anchovies, is available in huge quantities off the north coast of Peru, but apparently not available to Ecuador because of the flow of the ocean currents, thereby seriously limiting the opportunities for a substantial Ecuadorian fish meal operation.

Forestry Products

Hardwood

Large-scale exploitation of Ecuadorian forests is not attractive because there is no care or cultivation of the forest resources. Species are thoroughly mixed with no solid stands of desirable species so that cost of extraction is high. Much of the lumber is crooked, wormy, and diseased. Nevertheless, logs of hardwood, particularly Cuangre O Virola, are available when needed, and are being exported in limited quantities to the United States for door frames, molding, and special plywoods. Another useful species, the Mangrove, grows exceptionally straight, and single poles can be obtained as long as 17 meters. The wood is very hard, and practically totally resistant to decay, so that it is very suitable for pilongs and in boat construction. Some 300 hectares of teak have been planted and are growing rapidly, showing promise as a possible export.

Balsa

The world's lightest known wood, rapidly growing, and of good insulating properties, balsa is already and long has been an export item. It is available in any quantity at an average price of about $3 a log 15 inches in diameter and 5 meters long. It is usually cut into standard 3 x 3 inch pieces, 3 or 6 feet long, and exported in this form. It may also be cut into thin strips for use in models, or in lamination with aluminum sheets or other woods. The current value of balsa exports of something over $1 million will probably be increased gradually as the demand increases with the development of new uses.

With the exception of balsa, and perhaps teak and mangrove, the greatest opportunity for the utilization of forestry products as export items is in the utilization of local labor in the fashioning of wood products such as toys, tool handles, gun stocks, parquet flooring, and specialty items.

Fruit for Processing

Pineapple

Pineapples of different varieties are grown successfully in Ecuador and are available during the April-June season for as little as 3 or 4 cents per 6-pound fruit. According to Italconsult, actual cost of production per unit is about one-fourth cent per fruit. At such low raw product costs, Ecuador could compete successfully in any market. Perhaps the simplest product to process and to sell would be a frozen concentrate. The value of the total current annual crop of about 30,000 tons at the current seasonal price of 55 cents a dozen (72 pounds) would be about $460,000. If it were converted to 3,000 tons of concentrate, which could readily be marketed at a price of $2.80 a gallon, its value would increase to $1,680,000.

The major pineapple commodity in world trade is canned pineapple, averaging over 10 million cases per year, and a value of well over $50 million. There is an opportunity, considering the low cost of the raw material and labor, for Ecuador to capture a share of this market. For such purposes, however, it would first be necessary to establish a specific variety of uniform size and quality. Above all, it must be emphasized that an operation of this sort would require both experienced technicians and managerial personnel.

The small current operation where sulfured pineapple slices and wedges are exported cannot be expected to develop into anything substantial because of the poor quality of the product.

Citrus

Quantities of citrus are available in some parts of the country also at attractive prices, which might make possible the establishment at this time of a juice concentrating operation. The tremendous differences in quality of the citrus could perhaps be coped with through blending in the concentrated fruit product, whereas this could not be done with citrus processed in other forms.

Papaya

This very flavorful and nutritious fruit is available in great abundance and at very low cost, averaging only about $24 a ton. Unfortunately, there is still no way of shipping this delicate fruit in the fresh state. Certainly work should be undertaken to attempt to find some methods by which papaya could be shipped abroad in the fresh form. At the same time, it is very likely that a concentrate and other products could be processed in the frozen form and exported as such.

Naranjilla

This fruit, endemic to Ecuador, having a delightful, exotic
flavor, is decidedly of potential value as an export product
provided a suitable means for its preservation is developed.
It is possible that it could be preserved and shipped as a
frozen concentrate. In order to provide a sufficient base for
a steady raw material supply, it would probably be necessary
to establish regular plantings rather than depend on the chance
seedlings that now provide the raw material.

Tropical Fruits

Avocado, mango, as well as many other species such as
the chirimoyo and the tree tomato, have a real potential, but
little is known regarding the conditions of their production in
Ecuador as compared with other countries. Investigations
should be carried out not only regarding the possibilities and
opportunities for exporting these products in the raw state as
fresh fruits, but as processed products as well.

Small Fruits (Strawberries, Raspberries, Blackberries)

Such fruits would be particularly suitable for the Ecuadorian
economy, since their production in other countries is meeting
with very serious problems of labor costs, particularly during
harvesting. There is an apparently highly successful area of
strawberry production in Tungurahua, with berries sold at 2
to 6 sucres per kilo. Gross income per hectare reaches
100,000 sucres. These small fruits lend themselves admira-
bly to freezing, and can also be utilized for the manufacture
of preserves.

Jams, Jellies, Preserves

Such products usually consist of about two-thirds sugar
solids and one-third fruit solids. There are areas in Ecuador
where cane and fruits are grown side by side. This provides
the unique opportunity of producing jams, jellies, or preserves
by evaporating down cane juice with fruit or fruit juice, without

the necessity of first refining the sugar. These products
could be manufactured in Ecuador at a fraction of the cost of
manufacturing in almost any other area in the world.

Meat Products

As with dairy products, present emphasis is on the increased production of meat for local consumption; however,
the same factors which dictate an expansion of meat production
for local consumption also indicate that the export of meat
products could develop into Ecuador's second most important
export.

The basis for this optimistic evaluation of meat export
possibilities is the availability of vast land areas, hitherto
unused, which will produce from 300 kilograms of meat per
hectare on natural pastures at a pasturage cost of about $2.80
per 100 kilos, to 1,800 kilograms of meat per hectare on
elephant or guinea grass or similar type pastures at a pasturage cost of about $0.85 per 100 kilos.

An example of one area where an extensive meat packing
and processing area could be developed is the Upano River
Valley east of Cuenca, which will be available for development
when a road into the valley is completed. Officials of the
Centro de Reconversion for the provinces of Azuay, Canar,
and Morona Santiago at Cuenca report that this one valley con-
tains an area of 265,000 hectares of lush pastures capable of
supporting four head of cattle per hectare. Such an operation
would make it possible to maintain over one million head in
this one location alone. Even at three head per hectare, the
potential would be impressive. If this valley could be developed as one integrated unit with one central meat packing, freezing, and processing operation, it could easily develop into a
$20-$25 million annual export of frozen, canned, smoked, and
cured beef products, plus a by-product industry of hides,
tallow, fertilizers, and pharmaceuticals.

Even without resorting to areas in the Oriente, such as the
Upano River Valley, there is more than adequate land in the

Costa region for the development of several such meat industry complexes. There it may be desirable to bring together a number of firms which are already raising cattle on fairly large tracts, to pool their lands and herds and establish one or more additional operations of such dimension.

Present plans for encouraging production of meat and erection of slaughtering plants in or near the major cities, primarily for local consumption, need not interfere with a project such as the above one which could be earmarked primarily for the export market.

Exports of the size indicated would place Ecuador as a beef exporting country in a size-class with such countries as Denmark or Uruguay. Such a goal would require a major effort over something like a 10-year period, as was made clear in Chapter 3. Much experimentation and technical assistance to producers would be necessary, and large investments would have to be made in pasture improvement, in increased herds, and in the development of processing complexes and marketing facilities. All phases of such a major effort would have to rest on the availability through whatever means of first-rate, technical know-how and managerial competence.

In the southern Sierra provinces of Azuay and Loja, where the production of pig meats is much better developed than in the other areas of the country, there are some small ham, bacon, and sausage plants that produce primarily for the local market. One of these plants is already exporting sausages and ham to the northern part of Peru where prices of these products are much higher than in Ecuador. In spite of the general scarcity of meat in Ecuador, it is probable that these exports will continue and increase slightly over the next ten years, and especially if the LAFTA agreements are effective in bringing about a general reduction in tariff rates.

Whether a significant surplus of pork for export in the form of cured hams, bacon, and sausages can be developed will depend on the course of production and per capita consumption. As was shown in Chapter 3, both production and consumption of pork increased markedly over the years 1955 to 1961. The Italconsult report cited the projected production of 120 million pounds of pork for 1973 and a level of per capita consumption which, with 6.5 million population in 1973, would absorb the same amount. Hence, an export surplus would have to rest on either more production or a smaller per capita consumption (the population increase being taken as one of the "certainties") or on some combination of both.

There is a possibility that some of the increased pork production could be diverted to the export market in the light of the sharp upward trend of pork production. For the six years 1955 to 1961 pork production increased at the average rate of 13 percent a year. If that average rate should continue to 1973, production for that year would amount to 151 million pounds, leaving a surplus over projected domestic consumption of 31 million pounds.

If that amount of pork could be converted into cured hams, bacon, and sausages for export to Latin American markets at an average price of 10 sucres per pound, foreign exchange earnings of almost $17 million would result.

One marked advantage of building an export industry around cured pork products is that the techniques are relatively simple and the necessary marketing installations are relatively easy to establish in comparison with those for slaughter and shipping of chilled and frozen beef.

Oils, Edible

Ecuador plants producing edible oils, margarine, and soap utilize whatever raw materials are available in the country, such as palm kernel oil, but they secure about half of their needs from imports.

Present plans for the expansion of the edible oil industry do not include provision for export, but merely for replacing present imports. Some African palm plantations are already in existence and may prove to be successful to the point that an export potential may ultimately develop. The same situation exists with peanuts. Other oil plants which may in time prove their value to the Ecuadorian economy are safflower, sunflower, sesame, tung, and cartomo.

Packaging Materials

It should be recognized that packaging materials used to contain the various export products constitute export items themselves. The added value to the Ecuadorian economy can be very substantial if these containers could be manufactured in Ecuador from local raw materials, in contrast to the use of imported containers which are filled and sealed locally only to be exported again. Even if nothing is gained in the cost of the container, it is obviously to the benefit of the Ecuadorian economy for the container to be manufactured locally. Moreover there is the expectation that many containers can be made at lower cost if they are made locally with local raw materials and labor.

Paper Containers

In a study made by Parsons & Whittemore, Inc. in 1957, banana stalks and sugar cane bagasse were found to be very satisfactory raw materials for paper manufacture. At the time it was suggested that one-third banana fiber and two-thirds bagasse be utilized because of the distribution of the two crops. Although detailed investigations are still required, it is likely that both of these materials can be used for the production of paper for use as wrapping paper, paper boxes, and paper bags. Certainly enough raw material is available from which to make enough paper not only for Ecuador's domestic use but for packaging for exports as well. Both these raw materials are very inexpensive, since banana trunks are available for little more than cost of transport to the paper mill and bagasse had only low value as a fuel. It was estimated that 1.25 hectares of banana trunks would yield one metric ton of paper.

Such paper could be utilized for the production of corrugated cardboard for cartons in which bananas and many other products could be shipped, or the containers could perhaps be fabricated more directly from banana and other fibrous materials by compression, molding, or other more direct methods.

With such a wealth of raw material, certainly a major research effort should be made to determine the best and most economical means of transforming these raw waste products into paper and cardboard containers of every kind.

Plastic Containers

Plastic non-rigid containers are being fabricated in Ecuador quite satisfactorily from imported polyethylene stock.

Glass Containers

Practically all the users of glass bottles interviewed seem to be satisfied with the present system of bottle return and multiple use. Some users claim that very few new bottles are required, with the original bottles lasting for years and perhaps hundreds of reuses. This very extensive reuse of bottles may be attributable in part to less critical inspection of bottle condition. In export trade, however, there is no opportunity for bottle returns. Thus as exports of bottled products increase, the proportion of one-use bottles required will increase. A full-scale glass operation need not be limited to the manufacture of glass containers. Furnace capacity can be sufficient for other glass products as well. The bottling lines could contain one or more fully automatic lines which would probably need to manufacture a minimum of several hundred thousand units before it would be economical to produce the molds and other specific items required. There could also be facilities for semi-automatic lines which would manufacture units required in smaller quantities.

Metal Containers

There now exist in Ecuador several small, semi-automatic operations for the manufacture of cans of many different shapes and sizes, for use in the paint, detergent, wax, and food industries. Production rate is small and costs are high, particularly because of inefficient use of the tin plate. For food, there is also a lack of assurance that every can made is hermetically sealed so that the food will not spoil after being processed.

A fully automated can manufacturing plant equipped with all the necessary control equipment should produce a minimum of about 40 million units annually to be economical. If the canning business in Ecuador should develop output approaching this volume, it would be worthwhile to set up such a plant and utilize present facilities for special job-lot manufacture.

Panama Hats and Other Artisan Products

Artisan products, including Panama hats, other fiber products, as well as objects made from gold, silver, semi-precious stones, wood carvings, etc., are presently being made by highly skilled workers who actually earn very little—sometimes as little as 2 to 3 sucres for a day's work. If this industry is to continue and develop, changes will have to be made so that a skilled worker can earn a reasonable income. The following are indicated:

> Instruction in the use of some simple machinery which may double or quadruple output per man, at very little cost in equipment.

> Instruction in design, to keep abreast of, if not to take a creative lead in, style changes. Panama hats, for example, might be designed to meet the requirements of the women's hat market; or the toquilla straw might be used for other products such as mats or screens.

More vigorous marketing, and a change in the
marketing system to yield a better price for these
hand-made products—perhaps for artisan products
other than Panama hats to seek outlets in major
resort or population centers in the United States
and Western Europe.

Pharmaceuticals

The present pharmaceutical industry is a long-established
enterprise which, in addition to supplying the local market,
exports substantially more finished items than the raw materials which it imports. Unfortunately, only about 10 percent of
the raw ingredients used are of local production (alcohol, oil,
sugar, cacao).

Every assistance should be given to this industry to encourage the development of additional proprietary items, the
utilization of raw materials for the extraction of enzymes
(e.g., papain from papaya), essential oils (e.g., eucalyptus),
flavors (orange oil, other fruit extracts), perfumes, insecticides (rotenone). Personnel and laboratory facilities of these
pharmaceutical firms are especially suited for such development work.

Pyrethrum

The present operation is developing very satisfactorily
with a current export value approaching $1 million and plans
to reach an export of $3 million within the next few years.
Practically all the crop is now extracted and exported as 20
percent active ingredient. A second extraction plant is being
erected, which together with the original plant will have adequate facilities to handle the anticipated increase in the
quantity of pyrethrum flowers harvested. With a production
cost of about 11 cents a pound, a price to the farmer of 16
cents, and the equivalent value of the finished product of 39
cents, this change from export of flowers to extract is very
profitable to the Ecuadorian economy. The major problem in
the orderly development of this export item is that of reducing
the high labor input.

Spices

The potential for the development of a spice industry in
Ecuador is now known. Some years ago some clones of
pepper were introduced to the Pichilingue Experiment Station,
which apparently grew successfully and in fact supposedly are
still thriving in their abandoned state. However, no records
of any kind on pepper production could be found at this time,
apart from the statement in the Development Plan for 1961
that gross receipts from a hectare of pepper should be about
$900. Black pepper is currently in considerable demand, and
processors are actively seeking new sources of supply of
pepper. Attempts to develop production in Puerto Rico are
reported as about to be abandoned because of high costs and
disease infestation. Since there is a vague, but apparently
promising history of successful pepper production in Ecuador,
further investigations, probably at the Pichilingue Station,
should be undertaken promptly. It is possible that cooperative
arrangements could be entered into with an experienced
foreign processor.

Other spice plants which should be investigated are cinnamon, anise, cardamon, oregano, and molle.

Tobacco

Production of cigarettes at about 50 million packs a year
has been maintained with little change for several decades
despite the population growth and the obvious increase in
cigarette consumption. This lack of growth may be due in
part to the 4 cents per package which is imposed on top of
the actual cost of 4 cents, for a total price per package of
about 8 cents; although a more important reason may be the
failure of the industry to develop a desired type. It is common
knowledge that large quantities of tax-free cigarettes from the
United States are smuggled into the country and sold through
black market channels.

Production of cigars, however, is even more disappoint-
ing, with total production dropping from 64 million in 1937 to

25 million in 1947, 1 million in 1957 and practically no production at all during recent years. The reasons given for this disappearance of cigar manufacture were that because of certain legislation, as well as mismanagement, it became unprofitable to produce tobacco in Esmeraldas Province, which traditionally produced the best quality tobacco. With the abolishing of the restrictive legislation, there is a revival of tobacco production in Esmeraldas as well as in El Oro. Prices for first quality cigar tobacco are 19 cents a pound, 13 cents for second quality, and 9 cents for third quality.

An examination of the quality of the cigars being manufactured indicated that perhaps a major reason for the disappearance of the locally manufactured cigar is its poor quality. Apparently what is required in addition to good quality tobacco leaf is a modern cigar manufacturing plant. During the past year the American Tobacco Company initiated the production of cigar tobacco in Ecuador in the hope of replacing their Cuban source. Their experiments are apparently successful, the major problem being the slowness of the educational process by which they would educate increasing numbers of Ecuadorian growers to produce the tobacco by approved techniques to maintain the proper quality. The company purchases the tobacco raw from the growers at a price of about $55 a cwt. for the regular, and $166 a cwt. for the shade-grown cut tobacco. Curing and stripping are done by the company, and the tobacco is then shipped to the United States for manufacture into Havana-type cigars. Yields were reported as 20 to 25 quintals per hectare of good quality aromatic tobacco.

In Pimampiro, a large hacienda owner reported that he had grown successfully 100 acres of burley type tobacco and is planning to process this crop into cigarettes. It is possible that such an operation could raise the quality of Ecuadorian cigarettes and thereby lay the basis for diverting consumers from the black market.

Vegetables for Processing

Tomatoes

Observation of the yields, quality, and costs of production of tomatoes in different regions leads to the conclusion that a tomato processing industry could be developed on a substantial scale, with products competing successfully on the world market. Even without a thorough search for the best varieties, tomato yields run to 50 tons per hectare and more. Red color, which is a critical quality factor, is excellent when tomatoes are grown at elevations where the temperature is primarily in the 60° to 80° F. range. Because of the extremely low labor costs, it might even be possible to continue with the pruning and staking methods now used, since tomatoes grown with such techniques are still produced at costs of about 0.6 cents a kilo as compared to 3 to 5 cents a kilo in such exporting areas as Italy or California.

Because of transportation cost barriers, the most obvious tomato product for export would be tomato paste. A special advantage for Ecuadorian grown tomatoes is their high solids content of about 8 percent compared with 5 to 6 percent in other countries. Thus to achieve a ton of 30 percent solids paste, only 3.75 tons of Ecuadorian tomatoes would be required compared with 5 to 6 tons of tomatoes grown elsewhere. Another advantage is the long growing and harvesting season leading to the need for only a fraction of the equipment needed for similar operations in four-seasons temperate zones. Because of the large labor requirements for the manufacture of whole canned tomatoes, this product too may become a major export item. With many fewer advantages, Italy now exports about $3.5 million worth of tomato products to the United States alone. A tomato processing export of similar size could be developed very quickly by the erection of the necessary facilities in one of several appropriate locations where tomatoes can be grown on a large scale. Qualified technicians and managerial personnel would be required.

Vegetables for Canning or Freezing

In addition to tomatoes, similar natural advantages exist for the production and processing of canning crops such as peas, green beans, broccoli, brussels sprouts, cauliflower, asparagus. With the very limited experience with these crops as canning crops, it would undoubtedly be desirable to experiment first with varieties, cultural practices, irrigation, fertilization, etc., before a full-scale processing operation is established. Because of the basic advantages enumerated above, however, such an operation of the proper size, properly managed, employing competent technicians and utilizing modern techniques, should be able to compete successfully, not only in the Latin American market but in other world markets as well.

Vegetables for Dehydration

Nutritional analyses performed by the Institute of Nutrition at Quito reveal that, in general, crops grown in Ecuador contain exceptionally high nutritive value, and are particularly high in total solids. This is of major importance in dehydration, since yields of dried products are higher and cost of drying is lower, with fewer pounds of water to be evaporated. Because of the very satisfactory yields of onions (average of 44 tons per hectare) and low price of the raw material (average price $42 a ton and low cost of production estimated by Italconsult at about $22 a ton), dehydration of onions appears to be particularly attractive. The world demand for dehydrated onions is developing rapidly, particularly because of recent increases in use of prepared foods such as dried soups, etc.

Another vegetable which could be dehydrated is garlic. Its possibilities should be investigated.

Watches and Other Assembly Operations

The Cuenca Reconversion Center has negotiated the establishment of a number of assembly operations, by Japanese interests, to take advantage of available skilled labor. In many cases, production cost is close to half in local contributions and somewhat more than half in imported parts. As production increases, local contribution is expected to increase. The products are expected to be exportable to other Latin American countries, particularly through LAFTA agreements. Local capital is participating with Japanese capital in these developments. Some examples are:

Watches

	Standard	Special
Local contribution in labor, etc.	$2.00	$ 5.00
Imported parts	3.00	20.00
Total price	$5.00	$25.00

First year's production - 60,000 units, to expand to 360,000 units a year, primarily for LAFTA market. Eventually 65 percent of production cost to be of local contribution.

Sewing Machines

Local contribution in labor, etc.	120 sucres
Imported parts	251 sucres
Total cost per unit	371 sucres (not sales price)

First year's production of 6,000 units to expand to 12,000 units a month.

Transistor Radios

	6-Transistor	8-Transistor
Local contribution in labor, etc.	38 sucres	
Imported parts	74 sucres	
Total cost per unit	112 sucres	162 sucres

First year's production - 2,000 units, to expand as rapidly as possible to 20,000 units, a good part of which is expected to be exported.

Miscellaneous Products

Cement

The two cement factories are not operating at full capacity and could therefore increase their output for the purpose of export. However, attempts to export to Costa Rica and to Florida were not successful because of high costs of transportation. It must be concluded that with the possible exception of some export by sea to nearby areas, cement is not likely to develop into a substantial export item.

Ceramics

In addition to artisan products, plans have been made for one commercial plant in Cuenca to produce good quality dishes and pottery, some of it for export.

Minerals

The only mineral resources of possible export potential of which reports were received in the course of this study are molybdenum and agate. Serious efforts should be made to determine the extent of the deposits and the feasibility of their extraction and utilization.

Plant Materials

Some naturally occurring plant materials could perhaps be exploited by being gathered from the wild, but in an organized manner. A few of these products are fig latex for ficin; rotenone root for insecticides; and eucalyptus, citronella, and geranium for essential oils. Investigations may show that it might be feasible to grow these plants and harvest them as cultivated crops in order to obtain the desired products.

Rubber

Little is known as yet concerning the possibilities for the production of cultivated rubber and the development of a rubber products industry in Ecuador. A good case for the development of rubber plantations on a large scale is made in an Ital-consult report, indicating that a plantation should begin to show a profit in the seventh year, and show a net profit of about $370 per hectare from the tenth year on. Rubber could become a major export item but at this time few conclusions can be reached regarding its possibilities. An official of the United States Department of Agriculture with experience in Ecuador has suggested the possibility of developing a rubber industry gradually and with very little investment by providing young nursery stock to small farmers who would plant a few trees each year together with other crops which they would produce for immediate returns.

Sorghum

This plant could possibly be grown in drier regions in the south and provide high quality starches and syrup for specific industrial and food purposes as well as animal feed.

Tagua Nuts

Tagua nuts are available only in Ecuador, but their export has fallen because of competition from plastic buttons and trinkets made of plastics. Also, labor inputs are very high and poorly paid. Prospects for expansion of the present exports of about $85,000 a year appear dim.

Tea

Tea is another crop with large export possibilities, but there is practically no knowledge of its present performance in Ecuador.

RECOMMENDATIONS

In attempting to put in effect a full-scale program for the rapid expansion and diversification of exports, the program should not be hampered by any consideration of expansion of production for local consumption. Certainly any product that can meet successfully competition in foreign markets will automatically capture the local market. At the same time it may be desirable in many cases to sacrifice the local manufacture of commodities which can be produced more economically elsewhere in return for greater concessions for the sale of Ecuadorian products abroad.

Raw materials frequently will require considerable study and research before full-scale manufacture can begin. Even with an active and energetic program, two or three years may be required to find suitable varieties and to select the best processing procedures and perhaps another year to do pilot plant studies; so that a minimum of three or four years may be required before a new industry can begin to produce at anything like a commercial scale. If the industry must wait on the improvement of pastures and the building up of herds, and the development of complex processing and marketing facilities, a decade may be required to attain planned full-scale operations.

In some instances raw materials and small-scale operations may already be in existence so that a full-scale operation can be erected rapidly.

Several approaches may be taken in initiating a new industry requiring extensive capital and technology. The operation may begin on a small scale with local capital and personnel, and develop gradually as capital, technical know-how, and markets grow. A second possibility is to purchase technology abroad, provide the capital locally, and develop the market. A third possibility, which can bring full-scale results almost overnight, is to invite from abroad a reputable company which is already established in the production of the commodity to bring in the capital, equipment, and technology, and produce and market with such local ownership participation as may be feasible, with maximum utilization of local labor, and with definite plans for training of nationals at all levels.

The following summarized discussion includes processed products only. The present and potential export of raw materials was discussed in Chapters 2 and 3.

MAJOR OPPORTUNITIES

Total Utilization of the Banana Plant

As a first priority in a program for expansion and diversification of exports, it is recommended that a major study be undertaken for two purposes: first, to find an optimal marketing method for maximizing the proportion of bananas suitable for export as fresh fruit; and second, to determine ways and means of making full use of the rejected bananas as well as the peels, stalks, and trunks.

Such a program of research and development should be made on a full scale, and by the most competent organizations available, and could easily require a budget of $500,000 and a period of three years for its successful conclusion. The program could be delegated to specialists in every category. Thus, for example, the study on grading, packing, and quality maintenance could be assigned to an organization with experience and competence in this area. Similarly, the problem of utilizing the banana rejects as processed food and the investigation of the presence and extractability of various chemical components in the banana could be assigned to a concern of standing in this field; and the problem of the manufacture of paper, cardboard, etc., from banana fiber could be assigned to such an organization specializing in that industry. These organizations would be required not merely to make feasibility studies pointing to possible uses for these waste products, but actually to develop procedures and execute them on a pilot-plant scale, to demonstrate the feasibility of such processes as they may develop. Following such a research program,

companies may be organized for the manufacture of these new
products; or companies operating similar plants in other
countries could be invited to invest in such plants in Ecuador.

An Integrated Meat Processing Industry

It is recommended that steps be taken leading to the development of one or more complete meat processing complexes,
devoted to the export of meat products, and with production of
a complete line of by-products.

For such a purpose it would be well to allocate large con-
tiguous tracts of land suitable for pasture, thus far largely
undeveloped, and to operate the entire area, preferably one of
100,000 hectares or more, as a single unit with all the livestock destined for processing in a single plant. Each such
complex would have the capacity of handling 200,000 or more
head of cattle per year.

Such a huge operation could not be developed overnight, but
could develop over a period of five to ten years, the time required being primarily the time needed to increase the herds,
to improve the pastures, and finally to erect the processing
plant and necessary marketing facilities. For the development of areas such as the Upano River Valley east of Cuenca,
the necessary roads would be needed also. Here it might be
most desirable, in order to obtain quick results, to invite
one of the large meat-packing companies to develop the entire
project. In the Costa, it may be possible to bring together a
number of producers who are already raising cattle on fairly
large tracts, to pool their lands and herds and establish one
or more additional operations of such dimensions. The major
factors needed in this type of operation are land, capital, and
technology and management, rather than labor.

An Expanded Dairy Industry

The dairy industry, particularly immediately to the north
and to the south of Quito in the Sierra, is already a well established, successful industry. All that is required is to

expand several-fold what is already being done quite satisfactorily. If rate of development is considered too slow, or
if capital is lacking, it might be desirable to invite a foreign
firm to establish new processing facilities, and perhaps add
to the dairy herds, in order to produce in a shorter period of
time large quantities of cheese, butter, powdered milk, and
perhaps canned milk.

An Expanded Fisheries Industry

The canning of tuna and the freezing of peeled and cleaned
shrimp is a substantial present industry based largely on exports. This export business can be expanded several-fold by
providing the opportunity for expansion of existing operations
through the provision of capital and technical assistance for
modernizing and enlarging the fishing fleet, building needed
processing and marketing facilities, and improving the efi-
ciency of fishing and processing methods.

New operations can be established in coastal areas such as
Porto Lopez between Manta and Salinas, and Bahia de Caracas
to the north of Manta, without interfering with present operations in Guayaquil and Manta. The new operations can be
branches of existing firms, or new local or foreign firms can
be invited to establish new plants. For example, processors
who are now canning forzen tuna and cleaning and deveining
frozen shrimp in the United States could possibly establish
operations in Ecuador to take advantage of the availability of
raw material and lower cost labor.

Fruits for Processing

The preparation of juice concentrates of pineapple, orange,
and perhaps other fruits, could begin quickly. There is
currently a large and rapidly expanding market for these concentrates to be used as a base for fruit drinks the world over.
As a preliminary measure, it will be necessary to organize
the raw material base. The processing facilities may be
erected by a local group of growers or other investors, who
could hire technical services from abroad. Growers of

these fruits would be approached and contracts made with them to provide given quantities of raw material at a given price for a given quality. The product can be disposed of in bulk by direct sale to drink manufacturers.

Another approach would be to invite an experienced foreign firm to erect a fruit concentrating plant and operate it in Ecuador, supplying all the necessary equipment and technology, and employing local labor.

Manufacture of jams, jellies, and preserves by combining cane juice with fruits directly, and packaging in locally constructed wooden containers, should be initiated immediately. This can be done in a locality where both the cane and the fruit are available, such as Uzhupud. A foreign firm could be invited to set up such an operation not only for Latin American markets but for other world markets as well.

Frozen berries should also be considered, and would be of interest to processing firms.

Vegetables for Processing

Although canned and bottled tomato products are low-cost commodities, the very low production costs in Ecuador give high promise of successful competition of the Ecuadorian product on world markets. Not enough is now known, however, about varieties, cultural methods, and disease control requirements for tomatoes as well as other vegetable crops, so that preliminary investigations are needed to establish the best practices for providing the raw materials.

The most direct procedure for establishing such an industry would be to have a local grower or group of growers, who would be in position to provide the raw material in the needed quantities and quality and at an acceptable cost, arrive at an agreement with a large vegetable processing firm. The foreign firm could establish the processing plant, manufacture the finished items, and export them to markets that they have previously developed.

The commodities that should be investigated promptly, in addition to tomato products, are peas, green beans, asparagus, cauliflower, broccoli, brussels sprouts, lima beans, dehydrated onions, and garlic.

Chocolates and Other Confections

Because of the availability at low cost of practically all the raw ingredients of good quality, and the low cost of labor, manufacture of chocolates and other confections in which cacao, sugar, and milk are used should be highly successful. The prospects are so good that firms manufacturing such products in the United States and Europe should be approached and urged to erect new plants in Ecuador, or transfer some of their present operations to Ecuador.

Containers

Paper containers and cartons should become a major export commodity. They should be made in Ecuador of local raw materials to be of maximum benefit to the country. An experienced foreign firm could be employed by the local investors to provide the technology for establishing paper and carton plants utilizing local materials such as bagasse or banana fiber. Another approach would be to invite foreign paper companies to set up such an enterprise in Ecuador.

Glass containers could also be produced by local enterprise with some foreign technical assistance; or some foreign firm could perhaps be interested in establishing a bottle-making plant in Ecuador.

Similarly, some foreign firm of standing could be invited to establish a full-scale can-making operation in Ecuador; or a local group could contract with such firms for technical service and licenses.

Sugar Cane Products

A recently completed report by CENDES, by Messrs. Esteve and Monnet, makes clear that the world sugar market is good not only currently and in the immediate future, but that it will continue to be profitable to export increasing quantities of sugar from Ecuador for many years. The cost of sugar production in Ecuador has been estimated to be as low as 2.75 cents a pound and certainly not more that 3-1/3 cents a pound. These low costs and the availability of the large global sugar quota from the United States strongly suggest that the expansion of sugar production in Ecuador for export should receive high priority. An ultimate goal of 100,000 tons of sugar exports might yield foreign exchange earnings of around $15 million.

One important producer in Ecuador has reported that 10,000 liters of alcohol can be produced from one hectare of cane at a cost of less than 1.1 sucres per liter. At this low cost, the production of alcohol from cane juice for export for all types of uses, including industrial, would be highly profitable. Whatever portion of this alcohol that can be exported as an alcoholic beverage should be exported in this form, because of the many-fold increase in value of the product processed in that form.

EXISTING INDUSTRIES THAT CAN BE EXPANDED FOR EXPORT

The following industries are already in existence, and many of them are already exporting their products abroad. They can be expanded substantially, although to lesser potentials than those of the nine product groups listed above.

Pharmaceuticals. If future development is based on additional proprietary items and locally produced ingredients, there is a possibility of an export market being further developed.

Pyrethrum. This industry is well organized and is currently converting all of the raw material to the more profitable 20
percent extract form for export. Demand for this natural
insecticide harmless to humans is expanding, the braking
factor being its higher cost compared with chemical insecticides. Research directed at improved yields and at reducing
the very high labor requirement would pay dividends.

Castor Beans. This growing output is still exported mostly
as beans, but plans for adequate extracting facilities are well
developed with a prospective doubling of foreign exchange
earnings from the same volume. Possible limiting factors
for future growth may be dropping world demand and falling
prices, which would reduce labor compensation to the extent
that labor would be attracted elsewhere.

Malt for Beer. This excellent local product requires a
further reduction in costs to be competitive now in adjoining
countries.

Cabuya and Abaca Fibers and Ramie. Work is well beyond
the experimental stage, and several well-equipped plants
should begin soon to export fiber products.

Wood Products. Excellent quality products are being manufactured now. What is needed is direct contact with large
foreign distributors of toys, tool handles, and flooring.

Tobacco. Every assistance should be provided to the
present attempt to produce cigar tobacco in Ecuador to replace
the former Cuban source.

Ceramics. The present modest beginnings should be encouraged to develop as rapidly as practical. Here, too,
foreign distributors such as department store chains could be
helpful in providing a market within a short time.

Assembly Operations. These, too, should be encouraged,
but only to the extent that they provide substantial added value,
and labor returns are such that will not discourage workers
from entering these enterprises.

NEW INDUSTRIES FOR WHICH ADDITIONAL
BASIC INFORMATION IS REQUIRED

For the following items, there are good reasons to expect
that an industry for export could be developed that might be
competitive; however, there is insufficient or no local experience with production of the raw material, not to mention manufacture of the processed products, to provide a basis for a
reasoned decision on their prospects of success.

Silk. Experimental work under Japanese direction is under
way and should provide the necessary information within the
next few years.

Papaya. This product is a raw material so abundant, so
cheap, and of such excellent quality that a serious effort
should be undertaken promptly to determine its possible uses
industrially as well as for processed food products. This research could perhaps be undertaken in a newly established
food technology laboratory in Ecuador, or it could be contracted for in some laboratory abroad. Similar studies could be
undertaken with other horticultural crops such as naranjilla,
avocado, and mango.

Spices. Many spice plants occur naturally and are known to
grow satisfactorily in certain regions of Ecuador, so that there
is reason to believe that pepper, cinnamon, anise, cardamon,
oregano, and molle could be grown in quantity and serve as a
basis for a substantial spice industry for export to a growing
world market. Research with locally occurring species and
imported varieties should be initiated to determine the economics of production of these plants as raw materials. Foreign
spice companies could be invited to participate in this research.

Yucca, Sweet Potatoes. These and perhaps other starchy
vegetables have the potential of serving as the raw material
for an array of industrial products generally manufactured
elsewhere, particularly in the United States, from corn. It
remains to be demonstrated to what extent starches, mucilages,
invert sugars, and similar products could be manufactured

economically in Ecuador from such raw material. The
necessary studies also could be carried out in food technology
laboratories to be established in Ecuador or elsewhere. Excellent work of this type has been done at the Southern Regional Laboratory of the U. S. Department of Agriculture at New
Orleans, which could be asked for advice on such investigation.

Oil Feed Crops for Livestock. Such crops as soybeans and
peanuts need to be investigated further before their potential can
be estimated.

Other crops that need study are rubber, tea, sorghum,
hops, and a number of plants that could yield essential oils,
such as eucalyptus, citronella, and geranium, or enzymes
from such fruits as the fig or the papaya.

CHAPTER **5** EXPORT
INCENTIVES

FRAMEWORK OF LAWS

The Industrial Development Law of 1962 was designed
specifically for encouraging the establishment or expansion
of those industries which manufacture articles for export,
those producing import substitutions, and assembly industries.
Four classifications are recognized:

Special - Industries listed by the Government during
the first quarter of each year as requiring
special stimulus by the State.

A   - Basic Industries: Export industries in
which imported materials are not more
than 50 percent of price; assembly industries in which imported parts are not
more than 90 percent of production costs;
import substitution industries in which
imported raw materials are not more than
50 percent of production costs and are at
least 0.2 percent of total imports.

B   - Consumer goods and construction materials
industries not included in (A); import substitution industries as in (A) but imports
aggregate less than 0.2 percent of imports
total; export industries in which imported
materials are more than 50 percent, but
less than 70 percent, of price; industries
producing raw materials.

C   - All other industrial activities not included
above.

The benefits granted under the law to each of these categories are summarized in a Development Center (CENDES or Centro de Desarrollo) report (September, 1962) as follows:

I. General and Permanent Benefits

    A. The government, private or public entities, and all those agencies enjoying governmental, provincial, or municipal benefits, or those participating in any way of public funds, will OBLIGATORILY make use of products from domestic industry.

    B. Exemption and deduction of actual taxes and those that may be created in the future:

        1. 100 percent of taxes on exported production (except income taxes).

        2. 100 percent deduction of taxes on gross profit from every reinvestment or new investment financed through credit or capital increase.

        3. 100 percent discount of taxes upon chartering a new corporation with industrial purposes or upon capital increase (stamp taxes, constitutive deeds and registration).

        4. To determine the taxable income the following items may be deducted:

            a. Investigations carried out toward betterment and innovation of production techniques;

            b. Training of technical and administrative personnel; and

            c. Donations made to institutions engaged in scientific research having juridical solicitorship, residing within the country, and related with the industrial activity.

   5. 100 percent exoneration of taxes on circulating
       capital.

II. Specific Benefits

   A. Exoneration of fiscal, municipal, provincial, and
       additional taxes and duties.

       1. Special Category: 100 percent during the first
           5 years.

   B. Exoneration of custom tariffs, consular tariffs, and
       additional duties on imports.

       1. Special Category: 6th to 10th year, 100 percent
           exoneration on all imports used in industrial
           processing. From the 11th year consular tar-
           iffs are exonerated in 50 percent; prior report
           of the National Planning Board.

       2. Category A: new and existing industries 100 per-
           cent permanent exoneration of custom tariffs
           and additional duties, and 50 percent exonera-
           tion of consular tariffs on all imports used in
           industrial processing.

       3. Category B: new and existing industries 100 per-
           cent permanent exoneration of custom tariffs
           and additional duties, and 50 per cent exonera-
           tion of consular tariffs on imports of new
           machinery, spare parts, and accessories.

       4. Category C: new and existing industries 70 per-
           cent permanent exoneration of custom tariffs
           and additional duties, and 30 percent of consular
           tariffs on imports of new machinery, accesso-
           ries, and spare parts.

C. Exoneration of taxes on sales from the date of effective production.

    1. Special Category: 100 percent exoneration of taxes on exported production (except income taxes).

    2. Category A: new industries 100 percent exoneration during the first 5 years.

    3. Category B: new industries 50 percent exoneration during the first 5 years.

    4. Category C: new industries 20 percent exoneration during the first 3 years.

D. Exoneration of income tax from the date of effective production.

    1. Special Category: 100 percent exoneration of taxes on exported production (except income taxes).

    2. Category A: new industries 75 percent exoneration during the first 5 years.

E. Accelerated method for depreciation of machinery and accessories.

    1. Special Category: 20 percent annual deduction during 5 years or exoneration of income tax payment (alternative).

    2. Category A: 20 percent deduction during 5 years or exoneration of income tax payment (alternative).

    3. Category B: 20 percent annual deduction during 5 years. (Optional)

4. Category C: 12.5 percent deduction during 8
    years. (Optional)

Certain liberalizing amendments were decreed August 28,
1963. The chief provisions of the decree are:

1. Assembling industries will receive exoneration on a
sliding scale during the first three years of operation if the
imported parts or materials do not exceed 75 percent of the
production cost. The following table illustrated the scale to
be used:

Percent of CIF Value of Imported Articles in Relation to Cost of Production	Percent of Exoneration From Import Duties
75 to 71	30
70 to 66	40
65 to 61	50
60 to 56	60
55 to 51	80
50 or less	100

2. In exceptional cases, the Junta de Planificacion may
recommend the increase of these stated percentages of exoneration.

3. New or existing industries will enjoy 100 percent exoneration from import duties and 50 percent exoneration from
consular fees on the importation of new machinery, accessories, replacement parts, or raw materials if these are not
produced in the country.

4. Assembly industries in all cases enjoy 50 percent exoneration from consular fees on the importation of parts and
materials.

5. Provisionally constituted businesses are granted a
grace period of 180 days in which to make application for
classification of the business under the Law of Industrial

Development. If at the end of that time they have not done so,
all taxes and fines will be due.

TAXES ON EXPORTS

Taxes on some items of export may be many and complex
and involve national as well as provincial and municipal imposts; they may be general revenue taxation as well as levies
for specific services, such as disease control, road maintenance, and port services. Particularly because of the regional assessments, it is difficult if not impossible to guarantee remission of taxes on exports, and more particularly so
if the export items are shipped from an inland location. For
all these reasons, it is difficult to generalize on taxation of
exports. Even the taxation of a particular commodity may
vary considerably, depending on the locality from which the
export shipment originates.

The following are some examples of taxes imposed on
some of the more important export items:

a. Canned Tuna:

Raw material   - 50 sucres per ton for Ecuadorian flag
                  vessels and 250 sucres per ton for
                  foreign vessels

Export stamps - 36 sucres per shipment

Income tax   - about 20 percent of gross profit
                  (waived for first 5 years)

Local tax   - about 3.5 percent of price (waived on
                  exports). This may apply to Manta,
                  Manabi Province only.

Taxes on im-
ported   - up to 30 percent of value
equipment

b. Bananas: Taxes at the national level:

National Defense (Law No. 227)   0. 25 sucres per stem

Treasury - Development Bank   1. 60 sucres per stem
(Laws No. 468, No. 573)

Port taxes (Laws No. 415,   0. 29 to
No. 264)   0. 72 sucres plus 5
                                   percent value
                                   f. o. b.

The following assessments are for designated
services rendered:

ANBE to finance activities to the
banana growers association
(Law No. 864)   0. 15 sucres per stem

Disease control (Law No. 999)   1. 20 to
                                   1. 60 sucres per stem

Port Labor (Law No. 964)   0. 093 to
                                   47   sucres per stem

In addition, the following regional and municipal
charges are made if the bananas originate, travel
through, or are shipped out of one or more of the
following provinces:

Esmeraldas	1. 05 to 1. 35	sucres per stem
Manabi	1. 17 to 1. 50	sucres per stem
Guayas	0. 37 to 0. 50	sucres per stem
Los Rios	1. 75 to 2. 30	sucres per stem
El Oro	3. 00	sucres per stem
Pichincha	1. 00	sucres per stem
Cotopaxi	1. 00	sucres per stem

c. Cacao: Taxes at the national level:

Treasury (Law No. 189) - 1.0 percent)
Treasury (Law No. 161) - 6.0 percent)
)
ALALC (Law No. 221)   - 1.0 percent) of the f.o.b.
) value
National Defense   - 5.0 percent)
(Laws No. 227, No. 264)   )

Law No. 505 provides for an additional assessment
of 5 percent of the f.o.b. value for the Department of
Agriculture, presumably for research and development
and quality control.

The Province of Los Rios imposes a provincial tax
of 1.0 sucre; and the Province of El Oro a 1 percent
tax.   There also exist cantonal impositions varying
from 0.2 sucres to 2.0 sucres per quintal.

d. Coffee: Taxes at the national level:

Treasury (Law No. 279)   - 1.0 percent of f.o.b. value

Treasury (Law No. 810)   - 0.90 sucres per quintal

National Defense (Laws   - 1/8 to 1.0 percent of f.o.b.
No. 202, No. 227)   value plus 3.0 sucres per
                                       quintal

ALALC (Law No. 221)   - 1.0 percent of f.o.b. value

For services rendered:

Coffee Educational Insti- - 4.5 sucres per quintal
tute (Law No. 570)
Panamerican Coffee   - 0.30 sucres per quintal
Bureau (Law No. 174)

Provincial and municipal:

El Oro	-	1.0 percent
Los Rios	-	5.6 to 7.2 sucres per quintal
Manabi	-	4.0 sucres per quintal or 1 percent of f.o.b. value
Guayas	-	1.4 sucres per quintal
Loja	-	4.0 sucres per quintal plus 1 percent of f.o.b. value

e. <u>Rice</u>:

National tax (Law No. 169) - 0.8 sucres per quintal

Provincial   - 1.0 sucres per quintal

Cantonal   - 0.2 to 2.0 sucres per quintal

Uniquely, rice exporters receive a subsidy of 3 sucres for each dollar of their foreign exchange proceeds.

New industries for export may enjoy liberal remission of most taxes, but the major problem is with the established export industries. From the foregoing tabulations it can be seen that these export products are taxed extensively. ANBE has reported that each banana stem which the grower exports is burdened with a tax of 27.78 percent of the price of that stem to the grower.

In a world in which the prevailing practice is to provide incentives for export and in which the exporters in each country must strive to meet the competition from other lands, the Ecuadorian practice of levying extensive taxes on exports merits careful and judicious review. At the same time it should be noted that the relatively modest taxes imposed to finance disease control, quality control, and research and development can be very effective in serving the interests of the producers.

The field of taxation is a complex one, and recommendations in that field must be approached with great care and
with a sense of responsibility, in full recognition of the
government's necessity to raise revenue appropriate to its
needs.   There must be practical recognition, likewise, that
any government will be exceedingly reluctant to give up one
source of revenue until it can see feasible alternative sources
of like amounts.   For all these reasons, the question of what
should be done with the many taxes on exports levied in Ecuador, in varying degrees by the national, provincial, and local
governments, is one that should engage the earnest attention
of the Ecuadorian Government.   Perhaps a special commission
set up for this specific purpose would be the most effective
procedure; or alternatively a special tax study commission to
review taxes generally, including export taxes.   Such a commission could undertake studies of the various taxation
measures and their impacts on the Ecuadorian economy; hear
witnesses, public and private; and formulate appropriate
measures.

EXPORT FINANCING

Export industries are usually in the special or "A" categories, and may obtain up to 80 percent of the necessary
financing of the fixed assets, excluding land, from the Comi-
sion de Valores at relatively favorable rates (about 8-9 percent).   Such loans, however, must be secured with equity of
sufficient value that the amount of the loan does not exceed
60 percent of the value of the equity put up as security.
Foreign and local investors are subject to the same conditions.
Apart from the equity requirement, the major problem involved in obtaining such loans is the length and difficulty of the
negotiations involved before such loans are approved by government authorities.

Exporters are required to deposit their foreign exchange
earnings with the Central Bank, and they receive from the
Central Bank the buying rate of 17. 82 sucres per dollar.   The
Central Bank assumes the obligation of selling foreign exchange

required for remittances abroad of dividends, profits, interest, and amortization at the official selling rate of 18.18 sucres to the dollar (within a maximum of 15 percent of such funds per year). In banana exports and shrimp exports, however, only about 70 percent of the declared value is exchanged at the official rate, and the balance at the free market rate. Understandably, exporters of these products look on their special treatment as merely softening the impact of the foreign exchange control which these and other exporters tend to regard as in effect merely another tax. That view is not justified, however, if the cost structure of the country is in the main adjusted to the official exchange rate through its application to imports and to exports generally. The free market rate applies to only a relatively small share of international transactions, primarily to certain invisibles such as tourist expenditures and certain capital transactions.

Exporters complain that heavy amounts of working capital are tied up in the delays incident to settlement of these accounts, capital which otherwise could be used in expanding their operations.

TRANSPORTATION

Although a major effort has gone into enlargement of transportation facilities, under which the Central Bank of Ecuador reports that facilities have been trebled since 1950, the lack of access roads is still the limiting factor in the development of many regions of Ecuador. The planned highway development program for 1964-68, however, will rapidly erase that lack; thereafter, feeder roads from farms to the many throughways will be the limiting factor. The railway system now has 1,116 kilometers of single-track lines, limited largely to the Sierra. Of the 10,800 kilometers of highways, according to the Central Bank report, 87 percent are all-weather roads, but most lack smooth surfacing, with consequent damage to the products transported over them. Air transportation between major population centers is well developed.

Modern port facilities are available at the new port of Guayaquil and dockside unloading will be available soon at Manta. In other ports ships are loaded from lighters.

Improvements in transportation facilities from inland points and in port facilities can reduce transportation costs and improve quality maintenance and thereby stimulate exports.

The relatively unfavorable geographic position of Ecuador relative to the markets of Europe, North America, and Japan makes ocean transportation rates a matter of extraordinary interest to the Ecuadorian economy. Vigorous pursuit of equitable rates to Europe, North America, and Japan in comparison with those from competing nations is an ever-present challenge.

POWER

The water power potential of Ecuador is considerable. Installed capacity increased from 111,000 kilowatts in 1960 to 132,000 in 1961, and is expected to approach 160,000 kilowatts in 1964. Reported costs of electric power vary from 0.12 sucres per kw-hr by a private industrial plant with its own hydro installation to 0.5 sucres from a municipally owned plant.

Because of some peculiarities of taxation, kerosene appears to be less expensive for generating steam than heavier oils. When oil must be utilized for electric power, however, the cost amounts to 1.0 sucre per kw-hr.

ANCILLARY SERVICES

Storage: Availability of storage facilities of proper type and size can be a very important part of the transport chain that links inland points of origin and dockside.

Storage of any kind in Ecuador, however, and particularly cold storage so necessary in the handling of many food and drug commodities, is almost totally lacking as a public service. Adequate facilities are found only on the oceangoing vessels which receive the products for export. Any industrial development requiring storage facilities must develop its own, rather than depend on public warehouses.

Sanitary inspection services: The presence of an organization having official government sanction and the respect and confidence of producers, exporters, and foreign buyers alike is essential for a food industry which hopes to capture an important share of the world market. No such organization exists in Ecuador. The Instituto Nacional de Higiene in Guayaquil and the Instituto Nacional de Nutricion in Quito, between them, could perhaps perform this function, but at present the Hygiene Institute visits processing plants only at their request. The Institute of Nutrition apparently has no contact with industry. From interviews with producers and exporters it was apparent that they lacked confidence in such official inspection agencies.

Quality control and grading inspection: Whatever quality control work is being done in Ecuador is being accomplished independently by industry associations, some well, some poorly, and some not at all. For example, the cacao industry has done a good job of quality control and grading on cacao and in maintaining the excellent quality standing of Ecuador cacao. In the coffee industry, on the other hand, Ecuador suffers from poor grading and poor quality control, its coffee in consequence being subject to a marked discount in price in international markets. In the banana industry the disease control program against sigatoka carried out by ANBE, with government participation, has been a notable success; but both marketing inefficiencies and the threat of the root fungus disease, mal de Panama, remain major challenges to that industry.

Many countries have adopted the policy of strict grading and inspection of all lots destined for export with the requirement that only high-quality goods meeting specific standards

can be exported. Where such a system has been adhered to
rigidly, it has rapidly gained the confidence of the world
buyers and thereby promoted the importing of such products.
The mere establishment of objective quality specifications is
an aid not only to the importer, who can buy with confidence,
but to the grower, manufacturer, or exporter in the country
of origin, who learns quickly what he can expect to export and
what he should not attempt to export because of the poor price
it will command or because it will be rejected.

Establishment and administration of such specifications of
quality, grading, and inspection may be in the hands of a
bureau in a government ministry or may be in more specialized agencies, such as a Standards Institution or a marketing
or customs service. In other instances such functions are
delegated to quasi-governmental organizations such as trade
associations or associations of producers or manufacturers.
With appropriate delegation of authority, these quasi-governmental organizations may be empowered not only to specify
the quality of the product to be exported but may also allocate
the entire output of a given product of a country by grade
specifications for various uses, such as for export as fresh
or processed, for local consumption as fresh or processed,
for industrial uses, for storage, or for waste disposal.

Such agencies may establish a grading and inspection
service themselves or they may retain the services of international firms who specialize in this area. By whatever
means this is accomplished, however, such a facilitating
function is urgently needed in Ecuador. A feasibility study
for determining an optimal procedure for grading and inspection of Ecuador's exports should be undertaken promptly.

Research and development: A considerable effort is expended for agricultural research, and considerable success is
already evident in this area, particularly in disease control
and cultural and varietal studies with some crops. Still more
needs to be done, including methods of work in the vitally
needed field of agricultural extension service to provide technical assistance to growers. There is apparently little or no

research effort supported by public or industry association funds on industrial development in the export industries.

Many of the new industrial attempts are poorly organized and inefficiently operated. Urgently needed are consulting services, ranging from the simplest kinds of management and industrial engineering to complex and elaborate research and development projects. As with grading and inspection, this function also can be performed by a government or quasi-governmental body, by trade associations, or by specialist firms. A number of countries have established productivity centers which study individual firms, in both developed and underdeveloped countries, with expert consultants and research facilities for providing assistance in plant layout, improvement in efficiency and in equipment utilization, quality control, and in developing new products or new processes.

It may be advisable to reduce the size and scope of such an operation, so that these services may be supplied not by one productivity center for all industry but by several centers, each covering either a given industry or a given geographic area. For example, the banana industry could well establish a research and development center to work on all problems of industrial uses of the banana. Such a center could operate its own facilities through its own technical staff or it could employ consulting firms to solve specific problems. At the same time the center could employ directly extension agents, who could undoubtedly bring about immediate and spectacular improvements in the quality and productivity of banana dehydration operations by working with existing plants.

Direct export promotion: Much can be done in this direction by providing an industry with up-to-date information on world markets, participation in trade fairs and exhibits, and making special market studies to determine how best to enter new markets. Such services can be performed by a government agency, such as an export promotion council, or these services also can be supplied by foreign consulting firms.

Encouragement of direct foreign investments: As stated in Chapter 4, the most rapid means of increasing exports of processed goods is to invite a major foreign processing concern that is producing a particular commodity to take advantage of special favorable opportunities existing in Ecuador to bring in both capital and technical know-how, to develop the industry and to export the product through their established marketing channels, with such local ownership participation or joint enterprise as may be feasible, with maximum feasible employment of nationals, and with a planned program of training nationals at all levels of the operation. Such encouragement can be accomplished by preparing for potential investors specific feasibility studies, such as those prepared by CENDES, and having them available at foreign consulates and embassies in Ecuador and at Ecuadorian consulates and embassies throughout the world.

CHAPTER 6 IMPORT MARKETS

The discussion presented in this chapter is based on visits to and interviews in import markets in the named countries, at different times over the period May 3-August 14, 1963, by the foreign trade specialist. Canada, Mexico, and Scandinavia are exceptions; because of time and schedule limitations, they were not visited in person, but discussions were held in other markets with nationals of those countries or other persons well informed on their trade. Wherever possible, advance notice of the visit to each city was sent by the Government of Ecuador to the appropriate Ecuadorian foreign service officer. The appointments and arrangements made by these officers were supplemented by others made through the specialist's own contacts in these markets. Discussions were held with importers, brokers, distributors, chamber of commerce officials, government officials, and representatives of international organizations as well as with Ecuadorian foreign service officials.

NORTH AMERICA

United States

The United States should continue to be Ecuador's chief customer as well as principal supplier for many years to come. Ecuador's exports of bananas, cacao, and coffee could increase at a moderate rate as the United States market expands with growing population. There are, however, particular problems that Ecuador must solve in her cacao and coffee exports to support their growth. In the cacao market the problem stems from the trend among chocolate manufacturers to discontinue the use of premium grades of cacao for flavoring. The problem in the market for Ecuador coffee arises out

169

of the poor grading and the mixing of highland coffees with
lowland coffees. Increases should occur in exports of such
items as canned tuna, frozen shrimp, pyrethrum, sugar, and
tropical woods. Tobacco is an excellent prospect, dependent
on the outcome of production developments in Ecuador.

Once rated on a par with Colombian highland coffee, Ecuadorian coffee has steadily declined in quality until at the
present time it is one of the lower grades of mild coffees and
is generally priced about 25 percent below the better grades.
In the Los Angeles area, for example, total imports of coffee
in 1962 amounted to about 32,000 tons, of which Ecuador
supplied only 527 tons, and brokers stated that no increase in
demand can be expected in the future unless quality and grading are drastically improved. Exporters in Guayaquil ad-
mitted that they mix highland and lowland coffees together in
order to ship as expeditiously as possible. The fact that the
coffee is shipped as soon as harvested or as promptly as possible is also a factor in keeping prices down, but exporters
point out that because of high interest costs they cannot afford
to hold the coffee for later shipment. The possibility of financing facilities for more efficient handling and storage might
well be examined. At the same time, better processing of the
beans and better grading should result in a considerable increase in the income from coffee exports. If financing facilities can be arranged to avoid present concentration of sales at
crop time, Ecuadorian exporters should have agents in the
principal markets to advise them as to the market needs and
to recommend time of shipment.

The indictment in July, 1963, of a leading fruit organization by a Federal Grand Jury in California for alleged
monopolistic practices in controlling most of the banana distribution in six western states (for which the courts have now
assessed penalties) has stimulated interest on the part of
local distributors in the possibility of dealing directly with
Ecuador suppliers. However, dealers are accustomed to
purchasing after inspection of the fruit and indicate their
reluctance to assume the risk of buying before seeing the
shipment.

A vegetable oil company in San Francisco is now working with growers in Colombia and Venezuela to produce safflower seed as a source of edible oil and is interested in the possibilities of production of that product in Ecuador. Safflower requires 120 days of dry weather for the growing period. This firm now buys some castor beans from an exporter in Guayaquil, but has been able to obtain only small quantities (about 500 tons per year).

A large broker in San Francisco who formerly handled Ecuador rice for resale overseas has discontinued buying from Ecuador because of unsatisfactory grading and very poor quality.

Canada

Because most of Canada's purchases of Ecuadorian products are made in the United States, Ecuadorian statistics do not indicate the actual amounts involved, and even Canadian reports do not identify all the commodities of Ecuadorian origin. Imports of bananas have held steady over the past three years at $25 to $26 million, and Ecuador bananas have constituted about one-third. However, as Ecuador statistics indicate, only a small fraction is sold directly to Canada; most banana purchases were made in the United States with about 60 percent being supplied by the United Fruit Company. Canadian per capita consumption of bananas has maintained a consistent level only slightly below the United States level, and it is not likely to increase. In view of the popular acceptance of Ecuadorian bananas, consideration should be given to the possibilities of obtaining a larger share of the market by promoting the direct sale of this commodity to Canada.

Imports of cacao beans in 1962 amounted to $8 million, 75 percent of which originated in Africa. Presumably a portion of the $1 million imports from the United States originated in Ecuador, but direct imports amounted to only $166,704. Cacao butter imports in 1962 amounted to $7 million, the principal suppliers being the United Kingdom, Ghana, and

Brazil, with Ecuador sales totaling only $5,407. Unless Canadian chocolate manufacturers can be convinced of the merit of a higher percentage of Ecuador flavor cacao for blending, there seems little likelihood of overcoming the Commonwealth preference and established buying habits.

The situation with regard to coffee is similar, although Commonwealth preference is not a serious problem with coffee. In 1962 Brazil provided $21 million of a total of $55.6 million of imports. Purchases from Ecuador jumped from $153,000 in 1961 to $415,000 in 1962, but unless there is improved grading and direct sales promotion this increased trade will not be maintained.

Ecuador exports of shrimp to Canada amounted to only $15,632 in 1962, but here again the statistics do not reveal whether the actual total may not be considerably higher through purchases in the United States. United States sales of shrimp to Canada were $2.4 million, out of total shrimp imports by Canada of $4.6 million. Practically all tuna imports are from Japan, indicating that little if any effort has been made to market the Ecuadorian product in Canada.

With regard to straw braid, there is no indication that any effort has been made by Ecuadorian exporters to sell to Canada. Canadian imports in 1962 amounted to $670,000, of which 80 percent came from Switzerland, 12 percent from the United States, and only $902 from Ecuador.

The fact that such a consistent pattern is evidenced in the trade in the above described commodities points to the lack of a serious effort on the part of Ecuador exporters to develop direct sales to Canada. Canada cannot be treated as part of the United States market, nor can Ecuador shippers hope to increase sales to this excellent buying area unless they do promote direct sales.

Mexico

In spite of the special concessions granted Ecuador under ALALC, of which Mexico is also a member, there would seem to be little opportunity in the foreseeable future for any appreciable volume of exports by Ecuador to Mexico. It would seem probable, however, that Mexico will seek to market various industrial products in Ecuador.

EUROPE

European Economic Community (EEC)

The Treaty of Rome which established the European Common Market provides for a common external tariff to be applied to imports from non-member nations. Associated overseas territories of the six member nations, many of whose products are in direct competition with Latin American exports, receive preferential import treatment. However, the common external tariff on minerals and other basic raw materials is very low, and in many cases these products are duty free. Latin American trade with the EEC has grown faster than with other major areas. From 1953 to 1961 exports to the EEC increased by 50 percent and accounted for more than half of the $1 billion total export gain by Latin American countries, five of which transact more than one-third of their trade with the European area.

Rates of duty under the common external tariff increase when commodities are purchased in semi-manufactured form, and the semi-manufactured goods of the nations have associated status with the EEC will be duty free. Thus the European Common Market will not encourage development of Latin American industries which manufacture products for export. Processed foodstuffs will face a tariff when exported from non-associated producers. Cacao butter, for example, will pay a duty of 20 percent, and the external tariff on soluble roasted and decaffeinated coffee will be 25 percent to 30 percent.

Producers of tropical foodstuffs in the associated territories of Africa will also enjoy the tremendous advantage of
no tariff. Other suppliers, including those in Latin America,
will be subject to duties of 20 percent on bananas, 16-21 percent on coffee, 5. 4 percent on cacao beans, and 80 percent on
sugar.

Both French officials and officials at the Office of the
European Economic Community asserted that Latin American
imports would not be precluded, although at the present time
France's price support of a number of products from her
former African colonies, particularly bananas, coffee, cacao,
and vegetable oils, does in fact practically eliminate the like-
lihood of Ecuador exports. The EEC, however, following the
lead of Germany, has voted to eliminate the price support
program. Within a few years, therefore, it is scheduled to
be discontinued and increased trade thereafter will be possible, provided an appropriate trade development program is
made effective. French experts expressed doubt that Africa
can supply the demand for vegetable oils, nor do they believe
African suppliers can compete on a price basis after the
support program is terminated. As regards bananas, French
buyers are accustomed to the African type and undoubtedly
will continue to purchase primarily from that source because
of tariff preference and long-established trade connections.
For the same reasons, Africa will continue as the main source
of coffee, although mild coffees, especially Colombian, will
still be in demand. Improved quality and grading of Ecuador
coffee will be needed to compete in this market, as is true for
other areas.

In order to keep informed as to developments and to present its economic problems, ALALC, rather than representatives from each member country, should maintain a commercial representative to the EEC in Brussels.

Belgium

In Antwerp, which is one of the three leading import distribution centers of Europe, there were many importers who

are well informed regarding Ecuador products, and in many cases had handled or do handle such products.

Belgium statistics show that for the years 1960 and 1961 Ecuador was the leading supplier of "fresh fruit," bananas of course being responsible, and the statistics on Ecuador's exports compiled by ANBE show Belgium second only to West Germany in Europe. The largest importer and distributor in Belgium is the United Fruit Company Agent, reportedly now owned by the United Fruit Company. Another leading importer now handles bananas from the Congo, which is increasing production and has the advantage of EEC tariff preference.

With respect to cacao, importers stated that Ecuador exporters do a good job of grading but, because contracts allow 2 percent loss of weight during shipment, have developed the practice of shipping less than 69 kilos per bag. African shipments are reported to arrive with weight loss rarely exceeding 0.5 percent. It was reported that Ecuadorian shipments consistently are at least 2 percent less than 69 kilos per bag, with fairly frequent claims of greater loss. Importers also commented on the higher freight rates from Ecuador than from competing areas, citing the rate on cacao of about $60 per ton from Ecuador compared with $30 from Brazil and $20 from Africa.

Because of the reduction in the manufacture of fine semi-sweet and bitter chocolates, which have been almost totally replaced in most countries except Holland, Germany, and Switzerland by cheaper sweet and milk chocolate bars, a steady decline in the demand for fine blending grades of cacao can be anticipated. This trend may lead to a reduction in the premium now being paid for the Ecuador cacao. This result may be retarded, however, according to Belgian importers, because Ecuador exporters have good distribution and good connections throughout the buying world.

The position of Ecuador coffee in world markets is almost the reverse of that of Ecuador cacao. Instead of obtaining the confidence of buyers by consistently good grading and thereby securing the cooperation of brokers and traders in the principal markets of the world, Ecuador coffee exports have declined from a premium position to a minor and insecure status. No importer in Belgium has confidence in the grading of Ecuador coffee, washed or unwashed. Most experts agree that Ecuador highland coffee is the equal of Colombian and in fact was long accepted, until recent years, as a premium coffee and should be restored to that position to assure a continuing market in the future.

Several importers in Antwerp indicated a definite interest in handling canned fish and fruit and frozen shrimp, for which there is a growing market throughout Europe.

Germany

Hamburg is the major port for distribution for Scandinavia, Austria, and Switzerland as well as West Germany, and virtually all sales of Ecuadorian products to those areas are handled through Hamburg importers. One of the largest of these is also a major shipper of Ecuador bananas to Japan. There is an increasing demand throughout Europe for bananas. There has been some sales resistance to bananas in boxes, primarily on the part of ripeners who still prefer stems which they are equipped and accustomed to handling. In Austria, on the contrary, buyers have shown a preference for boxed bananas. There has also been a growing market for dehydrated bananas, which are now being imported in increasing and substantial quantities.

Coffee importers had the same complaints with respect to grading of Ecuador coffees as reported in other countries.

There is a continuing demand for castor oil, and for the immediate future the market can absorb all Ecuador can supply. Eventually, however, exports from Africa and other areas associated with the EEC may replace imports from non-associated areas.

There is a steady demand in Europe for rice, but the unsatisfactory quality of Ecuadorian rice limits its use to animal
feed and breweries at very low prices. Importers stated that
the difficulty was due to improper handling and storage, resulting in fermentation due to dampness and inadequate drying
so that the rice is hard and discolored.

Cigar manufacturers would be interested in dependable
sources for shade-grown tobacco, but expressed doubt that
Ecuador will develop production of a satisfactory leaf for export in the near future. They also mentioned the difficulty of
finding responsible firms in Ecuador with which to work in
joint ventures.

Germany now imports tropical woods from all over the
world. Importers expressed interest if they could deal with
reputable suppliers who could furnish satisfactory quantities
and provided also freight rates do not preclude competitive
delivered prices, which seems to be the situation at present.

Importers here as elsewhere stressed the high freight
costs, inferior and inconsistent grading, and the consequently
lower prices commanded by Ecuador products, that is, with
the exception of cacao.

Netherlands

About half the bananas now imported into Holland are fur-
nished by the United Fruit Company, and trade statistics
show that about one-fifth of Holland's banana imports as originating in Ecuador. Total imports are about 60-70 thousand
tons a year. Surinam, a Dutch colony which will come under
EEC preference, is rapidly increasing production and expects
to reach 40,000 tons within two years. An estimated 10,000
tons now comes from Africa and that quantity might also be
increased, so that in the future imports from outside the EEC
area will be subject to increasing competition.

Cacao importers here reiterated the views expressed in
Belgium, London, and elsewhere, to the effect that Ecuador

cacao is well graded and commands a premium price, but
that there is a decreasing demand for premium cacao and
that excessive freight costs under the present Conference set-
up have an adverse effect on Ecuador's sales.

Commodity importers and brokers in Amsterdam generally
commented on the adverse position of Ecuador in selling to
Europe because of high freight rates. On rice, for example,
although reduced recently about 12 percent, the rate from
Ecuador is $24 compared to $18 a ton from Argentina.

Coffee agents and traders in Amsterdam likewise criticized
grading by Ecuador shippers and the necessity for stressing
high grade with proper processing of Ecuador's highland coffee.
There was general agreement that such action would in the
long run increase export earnings of Ecuador and ensure a
more stable market.

Rice dealers here reported that the grades shipped by Ecuador are usable only for chicken feed and by breweries, that is,
the lowest grades. Proper handling, particularly proper drying of the rice, from the time of harvesting until shipment
would result in higher prices and larger foreign exchange returns.

Rubber is another product for which proper handling would
increase the export earnings of Ecuador. Importers stated
that the apparent lack of know-how in smoking, cleaning, and
drying and the fact that the product is shipped in balls instead
of sheets, results in a loss of 25 percent and frequently more
in the price paid for Ecuadorian wild rubber.

Spain

The Trade Expansion Office of the Spanish Ministry of
Commerce is interested in increased trade between the two
countries and will enlist the assistance of their chambers of
commerce in promoting and publicizing trade opportunities.
They suggested also that the matter be discussed with the
Spanish Chamber of Commerce in Guayaquil, also with the

Spanish Commercial Attache in Lima. Spanish officials did
point out that the freight rate problem must be remedied before any successful trade development can be expected with
Spain.

The Ecuador Embassy in Madrid, which has apparently
done little if anything to stimulate trade, must play an active
role by keeping in contact with Spanish export and import
firms in Madrid and other commercial centers to develop an
interest in Ecuador products and to ascertain the possible interests of Spanish buyers. Ecuador exporters must be kept
informed, possibly through their chambers of commerce, of
such specific opportunities and on prices and other market and
competitive conditions. Chambers of commerce in Ecuador
should consider sending a trade mission with appropriate
publicity to the major cities in Spain, as well as to other parts
of Europe, to meet with chambers and trade associations.

Spain has an ample supply of bananas and coffee from the
Canary Islands and Spanish Guinea and a bilateral agreement
with Colombia for mild coffee (in exchange for trucks). However, there is a limited market for banana flour which might
be negotiated.

At the present time purchases of Ecuador cacao are apparently made through London brokers. The possibility of developing direct sales to Spain should be investigated.

There is a market in Spain for buttons and for hat braid,
and trade in both of these commodities would appear to offer
some immediate potential with suitable promotion.

The need for higher farm production is correspondingly increasing the demand for insecticides. This points to a potential for pyrethrum extract or a finished insecticide.

Although many United States and European pharmaceutical
manufacturers are producing in Spain, the increasing demand
would indicate a possible market for Ecuador products if they
can compete as to prices and are appropriately advertised.

Because of the decline in production of olive oil and the
desire to maintain exports of this high-priced product, substitutes are needed to supply domestic requirements which
cannot be fully met by supplies of soy, palm, and other vegetable oils from Spain and her colonies. At present, however,
freight rates probably preclude Ecuador from competing; any
increased trade with Spain is unlikely until the freight rate
situation has been improved.

Switzerland

Switzerland imports from 40 to 50 million kilos of bananas
per year, and it is a very popular fruit in this country. Every
fruit stand and store display bananas; the larger at 1.50 francs
per kilo, the smaller 1.20 (about 16 cents and 14 cents per
pound). The largest food chain, which has some 400 stores
and supermarkets, buys about half the total imports or 20
million kilos a year and reportedly uses bananas as a "loss
leader" selling at or below actual cost. This has resulted in
higher sales by the chain but has sharply curtailed sales by
independent stores as well as the sales of wholesalers serving
the independents.

However, the chain reported that they have recently discontinued purchases of Ecuador bananas, because they claim
they obtained more uniform fruit in better condition from
other countries, especially Colombia, Honduras, and the
Dominican Republic, which now are the prime suppliers to
this market, through the United Fruit Company. The fruit
buyer stated that Ecuador bananas in boxes are unsatisfactory
because too frequently half of the contents of the box were too
ripe, the other half too green, because of the varied size
bananas packed in the same boxes. They were bought from an
importer in Hamburg, who did confirm that the chain had discontinued purchases of Ecuador bananas. This situation
merits quick remedial action by Ecuadorian exporters or ANBE.

Imports of banana flour are not listed in the statistics, but
there is a limited market, possibly also for flakes or puree,
to the confectionary and bakery trades.

Cacao imports total about 12 to 15 million kilos per year, of which trade statistics show that Ecuador supplied about 1-1/3 million kilos. Most purchases are through Antwerp brokers, so that Swiss buyers have no direct contact with Ecuador suppliers.

Switzerland's imports of Ecuador coffee in 1962 were valued at $133,000, or some 268,000 kilos out of a total imports of 30 million kilos. Brazil and Colombia were the leading suppliers, in that order.

There is a substantial market in Switzerland for leaf tobacco imports totaling some 750,000 kilos, practically all of which is purchased at auctions in Amsterdam and Hamburg.

Swiss statistics show a heavy balance of trade in favor of Ecuador. As a result, the Government Trade Office is more concerned in increased sales to Ecuador and is not too much interested in further increasing their unfavorable position by larger purchases from Ecuador. However, if the large chain and other buyers continue to exclude Ecuador bananas, this factor in itself would swing the trade balance in the other direction. It would seem important, therefore, that some action be taken promptly to recover this substantial market for Ecuador bananas.

United Kingdom

In view of Great Britain's political and commercial ties with her Commonwealth countries and former colonies, there appears to be little opportunity for increased imports from Ecuador, with the possible exception of cacao.

European cacao trade is largely controlled by London brokers, and the London Cocoa Exchange continues as the most important in Europe, the other two, in Amsterdam and Hamburg, being comparatively unimportant. Ecuador cacao shippers would profit from a London agent to keep them informed as to the market and to obtain maximum sales to Europe. Chocolate manufacturers in Great Britain are using

a decreasing amount of Ecuador cacao. Cadbury's, for example, the largest chocolate manufacturer in Great Britain,
no longer uses the finer grades for blending, and reportedly
uses synthetic flavoring developed by their chemists. Other
United Kingdom manufacturers also are using less Ecuador
cacao, due in part to the declining production of high-grade
chocolates.

One well-known British broker expressed the opinion that
the increased production of the "Trinidad" variety in Ecuador,
which produces larger beans with less flavor, will in time
result in the reduction or even elimination of the premium
prices now paid for Ecuador beans. Brokers with whom the
subject was discussed agreed that Ecuador cacao shippers
do an excellent job of grading and do ship according to description. They also stated that Ecuador exporters ship light, so
that weights on arrival almost uniformly are close to the 2
percent allowable shrinkage specified in contracts. Importers
agree that losses in transit should not exceed 0.5 percent, as
is their experience with African and Brazilian beans.

Scandinavia (Denmark, Norway, and Sweden)

In aggregate, this area represents a rather substantial
market for various Ecuador products, particularly bananas
and coffee. However, as far as could be ascertained, there
is no direct trade connection between importers in any of
these countries and Ecuador, all the trade being done through
brokers and importers in Hamburg, Amsterdam, and Antwerp.
Business groups in these countries have expressed the view
that direct trade promotion by Ecuador should result in a substantial increase in the volume of trade.

ASIA

Japan

The international trade of Japan, both imports and exports,
is largely concentrated in the hands of the six largest Japanese

trading companies. Five of these firms were interviewed
during the course of the survey, all of whom indicated considerable interest in Ecuador, not only from the standpoint
of exports and imports but also from the standpoint of possible
industrial development and investment.

Until October, 1962, imports of bananas were restricted to
those from Taiwan, which became unable to supply sufficient
quantities to meet the growing demand in Japan. Since "liber-
alization, " imports have increased substantially. In 1962
banana imports totaled $12. 5 million, of which $4. 8 million
were from Ecuador. For 1963, the Japanese Ministry of International Trade and Industry anticipates total imports of $33
million with $15 million coming from Ecuador, which will
give Ecuador a large trade balance. The present duty of 70
percent of the f. o. b. value will be reduced within the next two
years to 30 percent, which is expected to reduce the retail
price and result in a further increase in sales. The better
grade of bananas now sells in the shops at the equivalent of
about 10 cents each.

For the next several years, Ecuador may expect an increasing market in Japan, which may even go as high as $20
million a year, particularly if the retail price is reduced
because of lower duty and increased volume of shipments.
Importers did point out that there is some objection to Ecuador
bananas as a result of the long haul because the fruit must be
cut when small and very green and therefore does not have the
desired flavor or size.

It was reported that a consortium of the six leading Japanese
trading companies and the United Fruit Company has organized
the Far Eastern Fruit Company for the express purpose of developing production of bananas in North Borneo or other areas
near Japan. The Japanese companies, according to this report, each have a 10 percent interest and the United Fruit
Company a 40 percent interest in the new organization, which
will grow Cavendish type, to which Japanese consumers are
more accustomed than to the Ecuador variety, the Gros
Michel. If plans progress as anticipated, the Far Eastern

Fruit Company expects to have sufficient production within seven to ten years to meet most of the demand in Japan, at which time they report that Ecuador fruit will no longer be imported.

It should be noted also that Japan has a positive ban on imports from any country where there is Mediterranean fruit fly; therefore, should there be any infestation of that fly in Ecuador, imports from Ecuador would immediately be prohibited.

Coffee consumption in Japan has been increasing at a very rapid rate. In 1962 imports amounted to about 250,000 bags, with Brazil and Colombia furnishing more than half of the total. Importers are not interested in Ecuador coffee because of poor grading and the unsatisfactory experience of one large importer a few years ago, which apparently is well known to the trade in Japan.

Because of increasing sales of chocolate, importers anticipate a slight but steady increase in cacao imports from Ecuador. Total annual imports amount to about 20,000 tons, and in 1962 purchases from Ecuador totaled $640,000. The largest consumer is the manufacturing company, Morinaga, and there are three other sizable manufacturers using Ecuadorian cacao. ASE grade is most popular, ASESC (SES) second in demand.

In 1961, imports of castor beans amounted to $48,000, and trading companies are interested and could handle larger quantities if available.

There is also a good demand for hides and deerskins, but quality and grading from Ecuador must be improved. One of the large trading companies specifically expressed an interest in getting in touch with suppliers.

Because of declining production in the Philippines, Japanese companies are particularly interested in cordage fibers. Two of the large trading companies are interested in the production of abaca in Ecuador. Last year they sent an expert with long experience in the Philippines to develop experimental plantings in Ecuador. These have been extremely successful, and they claim that they are producing a longer and stronger grade of fiber in Ecuador than that grown in the Philippines. Plans are under way to extend operations on a substantial scale. Although other companies expressed the opinion that the use of natural fibers would steadily decline because of synthetics, there is an interest in various fibers, most of which are now brought from the Philippines, North Borneo, Mexico, and East Africa. Abaca imports for 1962 totaled 23,800 tons, all from the Philippines and Borneo. This fiber is most in demand for cordage, because of its resistance to salt water, and for that reason is preferred over henequen or sisal. No one expressed interest in kenaf.

Some of the larger trading companies working in cooperation with Japanese fishing companies are looking into the possibilities in Latin America for production of fish. One of the largest and two fishing companies are now actively considering the possibilities of tuna operations in Colombia, the fish to be sold to the West Coast of the United States. A survey of the Galapagos was made by the Japanese in 1962, but apparently results were not considered too favorable, or at least that is the impression given.

There is a large demand in Japan for all kinds of lumber and particularly for tropical hard woods. In view of the reduced availability of Philippine mahogany, several of the major companies expressed interest in discussing this matter with responsible Ecuadorian interests, but the lack of an organized group in Ecuador to participate in joint ventures makes it difficult to interest Japanese firms. No interest was found in balsa. One of the trading companies sent the manager of their lumber department in Colombia to Ecuador in August, 1963, to look into the possibilities for hardwood lumber.

There is no market in Japan for Ecuador pineapple because of tariff protection given territory of residual Japanese sovereignty. Imports from Okinawa, the chief supplier, are duty free, whereas imports from other areas are taxed at about 55 percent ad valorem.

The brewing industry is largely supplied by local barley production so that there is no need for malt imports.

Because of the declining use of straw hats in Japan, as elsewhere throughout the world, there is no future market indicated for either straw hats or straw braid. In 1961, imports totaled only $12,000.

Use of plastics has practically eliminated the demand for tagua; 1961 imports totaled $11,000.

One Japanese importer indicated an interest in musk, which comes from a variety of deer indigenous to Ecuador. They would be interested in knowing whether any supplies are available in Ecuador, and prices.

Because of the long transportation and the cost involved, it would seem unlikely that any considerable amount of trade can be expected with Japan aside from bananas, cacao, and sugar (and also coffee provided Ecuador exporters will grade properly). The future market for cacao would seem reasonably assured, as long as Japanese chocolate manufacturers continue to produce high-grade candy. For the next five to seven years or so Ecuador may expect to sell $15 million to $20 million or more of bananas a year, but after that there is the possibility of a steady decline, depending on the degree of success achieved by the consortium described above in its efforts to develop production in North Borneo or other areas nearer Japan and depending on possible developments in transportation costs which would lower this major obstacle of long distance from Ecuador to Japan.

Some of the larger Japanese trading companies indicated specific interest in industrial development and a willingness to participate in financing such projects suitable for the ALALC market.

SOUTH AMERICA

Latin American Free Trade Association
(LAFTA, or ALALC in Spanish)

Ecuador faces a difficult problem in endeavoring to expand
its export sales to the other members of the Latin American
Common Market. This fact is recognized under the ALALC
convention by designating Ecuador as an underdeveloped
country. At the present time it has only two manufacturing
export industries: the oldest—straw hats—apparently has
virtually no future in Latin America or elsewhere because of
the declining use of straw hats by men throughout the world,
barring a revolutionary change in the industry in the direction
of better styling, lowered costs, and possibly a shift to
women's hats.

The second industry—pharmaceuticals—faces severe competition in other parts of Latin America where local, United
States, and European manufacturers are already established
and producing on a major scale.

Exports of raw materials and foodstuffs are faced with
parallel production in many other ALALC countries. Ecuador's
difficulties are further compounded by her geographical position and the cost of transportation to the larger population
centers, notably Buenos Aires, Montevideo, Rio de Janeiro,
and Mexico. It is evident, therefore, that the greatest potential is in the neighboring countries, particularly Colombia and
Peru, with opportunities also for some trade expansion with
Chile. In these markets as in other overseas markets, established Ecuador exporters are faced with handicaps in the
form of taxes, which encourage contraband trade and illegal
operations. In contrast, Colombia exempts from taxation the
first 40 percent of profits derived from exports.

In its current negotiations with ALALC, it would seem advisable to restrict the list of those commodities for which
special treatment is desired to the particular items which
Ecuador is now in a position to export to other parts of Latin

America or which will be available for export within a short
time. What has apparently been the practice up to this time,
of asking for concessions on any and all items which Ecuador
might at some time be in a position to export, defeats the basic
purpose of the common market development and tends to make
a farce of the tariff negotiations without serving any useful
purpose.

Colombia

This neighboring country offers the greatest potential for
expansion of Ecuador exports because of the concentration of
population and industry in such cities as Cali, Medellin, and
Bogota. Domestic production is inadequate to meet the needs,
particularly for some foodstuffs and certain industrial raw
materials. In view of the importance of the Cali-Medellin
market, Ecuador might find it advantageous to establish an
organized trade promotion program in that area, including an
office or offices to promote the sale of Ecuador products, to
cooperate with Colombian exporters to Ecuador, and to keep
in close contact with Colombian industry.

Chocolate manufacturers in the major cities of Colombia
have been increasing production, with a correspondingly greater demand for cacao, butter, and liquid. An estimated 20 percent of Ecuador production is going to Colombia. Until 1961
this trade was on a legitimate basis, but now as much as 80
percent may be contraband. It is reported that smugglers
can pay higher prices than legitimate exporters and still
undersell in Colombia, a situation which applies also to such
items as dairy products, rice, meat, and probably other items
as well. In view of this demand, as well as requirements for
the local market, serious study should be given to the possibility of establishing a cacao processing plant in Ecuador and in
requesting preferred tariff treatment under ALALC for cacao
butter.

The local dairy industry in the Cauca Valley has not kept
pace with the boom in population increase, and local products
are stated to be inferior and reportedly unsanitary. There is,

therefore, an excellent market for dairy products, particularly butter and cheese. Ecuador cheese is in demand, and considering present conditions, per capita consumption is already high and could be developed to a very substantial market.

The fishing industry has not been developed in Colombia, although there are now two small operations at Tumaco and Buenaventura. Colombians have not been fish-eaters, but the success of the two present operators indicates that a market can be developed. Ecuador tuna is well regarded, and in view of local buying power in Medellin and Cali, a substantial market for frozen shrimp is also indicated.

Mention was made of a possible market in Colombia for Ecuador brandy, but no information on the potential was secured.

The volume of Ecuador handicrafts, rugs, and wood carvings now sold in Cali would support the idea of an organized promotion of such items. At the present time, most, if not all, of the trade is contraband. Reportedly many of the items now sold marked "Product of Colombia" are actually produced in Ecuador. If not actually made in Ecuador, rugs sold in this area of Colombia are made of Ecuador wool.

Although Ecuador malt is now being exported to Colombia, serious efforts should be made promptly to expand this market before it is lost to local suppliers. Because of the demand there is a substantial increase in barley production in Colombia, and a new maltster is now operating near the Ecuador border.

Colombia is primarily a meat-eating country, at least in the Cauca Valley, where meat is relatively high priced, and, judging from that served in the better restaurants in Cali, of inferior quality.

There is considerable demand for fresh oranges as well as orange juice and other tropical fruits, including pineapple. The small local production of pineapples, although on the increase, does not and probably will not meet domestic needs, nor is the local pineapple as good as the Ecuadorian.

Improved agricultural methods in Colombia are increasing the demand for insecticides. While a market can be developed for pyrethrum extract, Ecuador should give serious study to the potential for manufactured insecticides in Latin America. The extract makes possible a saving in transport costs, but there is a demand also for the finished product.

Rice production costs in Colombia are high and production is usually inadequate to meet local demands, but the quality of Ecuador rice must be improved to obtain a permanent place in this market and create a greater consumer demand. A substantial amount reportedly is now being smuggled over the border.

Tea production has been started in Colombia on a reportedly substantial basis and local consumption has been steadily on the increase.

As is generally true throughout Latin America, production does not meet needs for various types of vegetable oils. The Cali area offers an opportunity to market a substantial quantity when available on a constant supply basis. This is particularly true of peanuts and peanut oil. Establishment of peanut production on a substantial basis could be followed by the manufacture of peanut butter, for which there is every reason to expect that a volume market could be developed throughout the ALALC countries.

The wool and textile industry in Medellin is now producing excellent woolen fabrics for suitings as well as rugs and will require an increasing quantity of wool, most of which must be imported.

Peru

The Lima area, with two million population, offers a major market for Ecuadorian products, especially meat and dairy

products, bananas, pineapples, and possibly lumber. A
serious trade promotion program by the government in cooperation with the chambers of commerce in Ecuador could result in a substantial increase in Ecuador exports. Such a
program should be initiated possibly through a trade mission
by the chambers of commerce of Quito and Guayaquil and by
having a commercial attache at Ecuador's embassy.

Lima importers and retailers indicated an interest in
Ecuador products which can compete on a price and quality
basis with, for example, cattle from Argentina, cheese from
Europe, and bananas and pineapples from other parts of Peru.
Peruvian officials likewise indicated that such trade would be
welcomed.

According to various estimates, the Lima area alone offers
an annual market for 100,000 head of cattle, $500,000 worth
of bananas, and more cheese, butter, and other dairy products
than Ecuador would be in a position to offer for many years.
Prices and uniform quality are the governing factors.

Retailers stated that past difficulties would have little if
any real effect on sales of Ecuador products of the desired
quality at competitive prices.

Chile

The Chilean Government, as well as local industry, has
indicated a special interest in developing trade with Ecuador.
A Chilean mission visited Quito in April, 1963, and entered into
an agreement with the Planning Board and the Central Bank to
study several proposals for joint cooperation and participation
to develop commerce between the two countries. These proposals included sugar, steel, canned fruit, bottling of Chilean
wines in Ecuador, assembly plants, fibers, fisheries, and
others.

Under the sugar program, Ecuador would agree to increase
production and guarantee a minimum annual quota to be shipped
to Chile for refining. The Chileans believe that Ecuador can

produce at competitive prices and much below reported costs
of present producers in Chile.

The steel plan contemplates processing of Chilean billets
in Ecuador into bars and other merchant shapes but not including sheets or rolled products. On the basis of present
Ecuadorian consumption, the Chileans believe this plan would
save Ecuador about $1 million annually in foreign exchange
and at the same time, of course, assure a market for Chilean
steel.

The Chileans are especially interested in coordinating the
fishing industries of Chile and Ecuador, and would like also
to include Peru in such a program. They recognize, however,
that the inclusion of Peru in such a program might be extremely difficult; in any event they see the possibility of Chilean investment in Ecuador, provided a law is enacted similar to the
one in Chile under which 50 to 75 percent of profits for a
specified number of years must be used for expansion. Under
their proposal Chile would build the vessels needed and presumably manufacture most of the equipment.

They foresee also the possibilities of joint Chilean-Ecuado-
rian companies which could market Ecuador products such as
bananas and cacao in Chile and sell Chilean products in Ecuador. Such companies might also set up assembly plants using
material and parts made in Chile. They are much more interested in such joint ventures than in an exchange of trade.

Argentina

Argentina annually imports about $4 million worth of ban-
nanas, $4 million worth of cacao, and $20 million of coffee,
with Brazil supplying about 90 percent of the total. With increased prosperity and buying power it is estimated that total
imports of bananas may exceed $6 million, with correspond-
ing increases in the other items.

Ecuador's problem in reaching this market is transportation. Whereas it takes four weeks by vessel from Guayaquil to Buenos Aires, it takes only seventy-two hours from Brazilian ports to Buenos Aires. Furthermore, under an agreement between the Argentinian State Line and the Gran Colombiana Line, the latter picks up the merchandise in Guayaquil for transshipment in Peru to Argentine vessels, so that the voyage is lengthy and freight rates are high.

The ultimate solution, for products of high value in relation to weight or bulk, would appear to be air freight.

Ecuador export potentials include pineapples, coffee, cacao (in limited amounts), and, despite the fact that there are many United States and European manufacturers producing in Argentina and Uruguay, pharmaceuticals and veterinary supplies. Fibers and insecticides are further possibilities. Argentina would expect to sell various industrial materials, machinery, and parts.

Uruguay

Opportunities for trade between Ecuador and Uruguay appear very limited and from a practical standpoint nonexistent.

There is a substantial market for bananas and pineapple, both of which now come from neighboring Brazil, but they are far inferior in quality to the Ecuador products. In view of the long voyage by sea, however, the future of any such trade is problematical. Uruguay is also a large market for veterinary and pharmaceutical supplies; here as in Buenos Aires the major United States and European manufacturers are well represented.

OBSERVATIONS ON PROBLEM AREAS
FOR ECUADOR'S EXPORTS

Ocean Freight Rates

As indicated throughout this report, transportation is one of Ecuador's primary problems and since geographic position makes this a continuing condition, priority should be given to a careful study of the possibility for reduction of transportation costs from Ecuadorian ports to major overseas markets. The scope of such a study might include the following:

> Comparison of northbound rates from Ecuador, Colombia, and Peru.

> Comparison of rates on cacao from Brazil to Europe with those from Ecuador to Europe.

> Comparison of rates on coffee with those on other commodities for both Ecuador and Colombia.

> Appraisal of the surcharge on shipments from Guayaquil in the light of the new port facilities at that port.

> Analysis of the effect on Ecuador's export trade of the unanimous vote in the West Coast Steamship Owners Association.

> Appraisal of the effect on Ecuador's export trade of her 20 percent partnership in the Gran Colombiana Steamship Line.

Promotion of Ecuador Exports Abroad

Any promotion of the sale of Ecuador products in overseas markets, either by the government or by exporters, is conspicuous by its absence. Sales promotion has been left entirely in the hands of the fruit companies and foreign importers and distributors. In effect this means that the future of an important phase of the economy of the country has been almost entirely neglected by those most directly concerned. As pointed out previously, there is now no direct connection between the buyers in Northern Europe and other areas, including Switzerland, and the exporters in Ecuador, all trade being through middlemen in other countries.

As a first step, the government should eliminate most of the nonproductive services now required of its consular officials and require them to devote a considerable portion of their time to trade promotion. During the course of this survey, discussions were held with a number of Ecuadorian foreign service officers, and the investigator was strongly impressed by the high caliber of these officers and equally by their dedication to the task of promoting the interests of Ecuador abroad. These observations, it may be added, proceed from a background of thirty years of experience involving close and frequent contact with foreign service personnel of many countries. The Ecuadorian foreign service personnel generally evidenced an intimate knowledge of commercial and trade developments and the need for greater promotion of Ecuadorian products in those markets, in spite of the fact that their time and that of their staff, where they have any, is taken up with handling requirements for certification of shipping documents, a nonproductive and virtually useless operation.

The government might well study the possibility of abolishing the requirement for consular invoices and consular certification of shipping documents. No European country requires consular certification, and the United States recently discontinued such procedure, as have Mexico, Costa Rica, and a number of other countries. This can be done without loss of revenue, because the relevant fees can be applied to the commercial invoice or bill of lading and collected through the steamship lines, together with freight charges, or at the port of entry.

With the elimination of the certification of shipping documents by the Foreign Service, consular officials could devote
most of their time to trade promotion, and the career service
could be made up in large part of men who specialize in commercial work. They could promote Ecuadorian products in
areas abroad, advise Ecuadorian exporters as to business
opportunities, and report regularly on market conditions and
prices in their respective areas, as well as interesting potential private investors in investment opportunities in Ecuador,
an activity which consular officials of other countries have
carried on effectively. With the elimination of consular invoices the consular staffs in large ports could be materially
reduced with resulting savings to the government.

Standardization of Grading and Packing

There is a definite and strong need for improved grading
and packing of Ecuadorian export products in order to improve the reputation and standing of those products in overseas
markets and also to increase foreign exchange earnings, both
by obtaining higher prices and by expanding markets. Such a
development is essential at the present time in view of the
competition in overseas markets and particularly in the
ALALC countries. Furthermore, effective trade promotion
is only possible when assurance can be given to buyers that
the commodities will meet satisfactory quality standards.

If trade groups prove unable or unwilling to develop and
maintain satisfactory grading and packing, the government
might consider the possibility of setting up a nonpolitical independent agency or a quasi-governmental authority to carry
out such a program.

Tourism

Proper use of a modest budget for tourism can attract a
substantial amount of foreign exchange quickly and stimulate
local investment in facilities. Ecuador has numerous advantages for the tourist trade, yet little is known of these advantages outside of Ecuador; and Ecuadorians take them for

granted as parts of the familiar environment. Merely to list
a few of Ecuador's attractions is to suggest their appeal: the
perpetual spring of its Sierra; the grandeur of its mountains
and "avenue" of snowclad volcanoes; the verdant beauty of its
intermontane valleys; its steep cultivated slopes; the strange,
other worldly fascination of its bleak Andean passes and
paramos; the majestic beauty of its high altitude rain forests;
the pastoral charm of many of its landscapes and year-round
pastures; the Old World charm of its ancient cities, living
museums of sixteenth and seventeenth century Spanish colonial
architecture and decoration; its quaint Indian life. To the west
are the Pacific beaches of the Costa and the rich fishing
grounds; and not far away to the east are the tributaries of
the Amazon and the fascination of the Oriente jungle.

Much will have to be done to realize this tourism potential
and time will be required—more and better roads, better air
transport schedules, more and better hotels and other tourist
facilities, and effective promotion—but the resource base is
there to build upon.

If consular certification of shipping documents can be eliminated, the foreign service officers also could do a great deal
to promote tourism, particularly in such centers as New York,
Los Angeles, and Chicago.

Promotion of Industrial Investment

During the course of the survey a number of companies in
the United States, Europe, and Japan appeared to be favorably
inclined toward possible investment in Ecuador. They all
stated, however, that they had received no practical encouragement or cooperation from either government officials or business in Ecuador. In some of these cases, they are looking in
other areas where they have been approached with specific investment opportunities and with cooperation from local busi-
nessmen. But some, and potentially important ones, are still
looking toward Ecuador.

In spite of its natural wealth and the undoubted opportunities for development projects, Ecuador will be unable to compete in attracting private investment capital unless specific investment opportunities are outlined in detail and brought to the attention of potential investors.

CHAPTER ***7*** OUTLOOK--
1968-73

ECUADOR'S OVER-ALL ECONOMIC TARGETS:
1968-73

The Perspective in Synthesis

Ecuador's economic growth in the decade of the 1950's was
appreciable and paralleled an even greater expansion in exports—the dynamic factor in the economy. In the period
1950-60, the gross domestic product had increased at an
annual rate of 5 percent, making possible a per capita growth
rate of 2 percent. (See table on page 200.) Exports, however,
increased at an annual rate of 9 percent.

No fundamental structural changes had occurred in the
economy in this period, in line with the limitations of the
scope and level of investment, whose rate in relation to the
gross domestic product had risen only from 11 to 15 percent.

In the most recent years, the growth in exports has been
declining, and the rate of expansion of the economy has consequently been affected.

For the future, Ecuador's "big three" export products—
bananas, cacao, and coffee—cannot be counted on alone to
supply the same basis for future growth in the economy as
they did in the decade of the 1950's. The outlook for these
"big three" traditional exports is for an annual growth rate
of less than 5 percent in the period to 1973, and the expected
rate of increase of the population is about 3 percent.

199

GROSS DOMESTIC PRODUCT BY TYPE OF EXPENDITURES, 1950 AND 1960-62,
PROJECTIONS FOR 1968 AND 1973
(Millions of Sucres, at 1960 Prices)

	Population (000)	Gross Domestic Product (at market prices)				Gross Domestic Product per Capita	Consumption per Capita
		Total	Consumption	Investment	Exports[a] less Imports		
1950	3,203	8,694	7,216	939	539	2,714	2,253
1960	4,208	14,060	11,814	2,200	46	3,257	2,806
1961	4,326	14,461[b]	12,478	2,210	-227	3,246	2,884
1962	4,480	15,006[b]	12,861	2,250	-105	3,350	2,870
Projections							
1968	5,359	20,690	16,797	3,724	168	3,860	3,134
1973	6,282	27,000	21,082	5,400	518	4,305	3,356
Percent Avg. Annual Increase							
1950-60	2.8	4.9	5.0	8.9	--	1.8	2.2
1962-68	3.1	5.5	4.5	8.8	--	2.4	1.5
1968-73	3.2	5.5	4.7	7.7	--	2.2	1.5
1962-73	3.1	5.5	4.6	8.3	--	2.3	1.4
Percent Distribution							
1950		100.0	83.0	10.8	6.2		
1960		100.0	84.0	15.6	0.4		
1968		100.0	81.2	18.0	0.8		
1973		100.0	78.1	20.0	2.0		

a. Goods and Services.

b. Composition estimated on the basis of partial data.

Sources: Junta Nacional de Planificación; Banco Central; World Bank (Ecuador Transportation Study); SRC Staff.

In this stage of Ecuador's economic development, growth
in per capita output and income at the rate of 2 percent or
more per year requires industrial and export diversification
and a greater investment effort. The economic development
programming effort initiated towards the end of the decade of
the 1950's and the evolution of the Latin American economic
integration movement should help to make possible the
achievement of the desired growth targets. This potential
is based on the possibility of combining the present effort
of the Government of Ecuador to expand investment and diversify industry with new industrial exports as well as new
primary products exports.

Present government efforts center on (1) supplementing
traditional exports with other tropical crops and fisheries
products; (2) expanding and diversifying industrial production,
including the output of products to supplement or supplant imports; (3) increasing public investment in such areas as transport, electric power, and housing; and (4) reorganizing ar-
chaic aspects of the administrative, budgeting, and revenue
structure. These major objectives, however, even if they
were to be realized, would not by themselves assure success
in the attainment of the desired over-all growth targets. Substantial new industrial exports will have to be developed if an
expanding Ecuadorian economy is to be able to obtain those
minimum essential imports, especially of capital goods and
raw materials, necessary for economic growth.

The possibility for achieving substantial new industrial exports rests in part on the prospects for the Latin American
integration movement. It is the aim of LAFTA to promote
the development in the larger countries of "integration" industries—machinery and equipment, transport equipment,
steel, aluminum and other metals, and chemicals—for export to all LAFTA countries, and to encourage in the smaller
Latin American countries, such as Ecuador, the development
of exports of consumer goods, nondurable and durable, some
industrial materials, and some capital goods components.

Ecuador's minimum essential imports over the next ten years will require a doubling of capital goods imports, which would account for one-half of all imports by 1973; raw materials and industrial supply imports would rise by 50 percent and account for one-fourth of all imports by that year. A large share of the increment in Ecuador's imports under LAFTA plans would be supplied by the Latin American integration industries, in return for which Ecuador would supply primary products, consumer goods, industrial materials, and capital goods components. These proposed arrangements were reviewed at the November, 1963, meeting of the Latin American Social and Economic Council in Sao Paulo, Brazil.

Ecuador's official growth targets call for the production of goods and services in 1973 80 percent above the 1962 levels; or an average annual rate of growth of 5.5 percent.[1] This rate would make possible a per capita growth rate of 2.3 percent[1] a year, in line with the Alliance for Progress growth targets for the Latin American region as a whole. Population is expected to grow at a rate of 3 percent[1] a year, to reach 6.3 million by 1973, compared with 4.5 million in 1962. Investment would have to double the 1962 level and account for 20 percent of gross domestic product by 1973. The programmed expansion of public investment expenditures is expected to call forth a similar rate of growth in private investment.

---

1. The indicated growth target percentages have recently been revised by the Junta de Planificacion. The following annual rates of growth are now contemplated in the General Plan of Development:

Gross National Product	6.25 percent
Gross National Product per capita	3.15 percent
Population	3.10 percent

These revisions are noted here, but it has not been possible to incorporate them in revisions of any of the tables of this chapter since other corresponding changes in the Plan were not available to the authors in Washington during the period of revision of Chapter 7.

Agricultural and Manufacturing Production Goals

According to plans, Ecuador's economic structure would
change, with manufacturing production rising to make up one-
fifth of total production of goods and services, while agriculture would continue to be the dominant base of the economy,
accounting for one-third of the total. (See table on page 204.)
Agricultural production targets calling for a 5 percent annual
rate of growth in output reflect ambitious programs for expanding the area under cultivation as well as increasing agricultural
productivity. More ambitious industrial production targets call
for a 140 percent increase (from 1961) in output by 1973, with a
7. 6 percent annual rate of growth and the development of 22
high priority industrial projects, consumer durable and nondurable goods, and industrial materials—paper, paperboard,
chemicals, fertilizer, cement, steel wire, tools, textiles, and
food products—to supply the needs of an expanding population,
to substitute for imports of consumer goods and industrial materials, and to provide an export margin in some cases. These
targets would require an expanded share of imports of capital
goods and other industrial materials.

Import Substitution Needs

In the decade of the 1950's, imports expanded much more
rapidly than domestic output, at an annual rate of 8 percent,
compared with 5 percent. For the next ten years, imports
which could ordinarily be expected to grow at 8 to 9 percent a
year, given a 5. 5 percent[2] growth of the economy as a whole,
must be held to a growth rate of no more than 5 percent a year,
even with a considerable growth of exports if equilibrium in the
balance of payments is to be maintained. Such restraint of imports would require that net new industrial output substituting
for imports would account for 30 percent of total industrial
production by 1973. This estimate is based on an import elasticity of demand of 1. 5, which was the rate in the 1950's.

---

2. Now revised to read 6. 25 percent; see footnote on page
202.

GROSS DOMESTIC PRODUCT BY ECONOMIC SECTOR -- 1950, 1960, AND 1961,
PROJECTIONS FOR 1968 AND 1973
(Millions of Sucres, at 1960 Prices)

| | Gross Domestic Product (at factor cost) | | | | | |
	Total	Agriculture	Mining	Manufacturing	Construction	Electricity, Transport, Trade, and Services
1950	7,532	2,922	171	1,202	205	3,032
1960	12,128	4,367	296	1,908	500	5,057
1961	12,540	4,645	310	1,927	501	5,157
Projections						
1968	18,242	6,536	430	3,156	780	7,340
1973	23,841	8,342	540	4,616	1,040	9,303
Percent Avg. Annual Increase						
1950-60	4.9	4.1	5.6	4.7	9.3	5.3
1961-68	5.5	5.0	4.8	7.3	6.5	5.2
1968-73	5.5	5.0	4.7	7.9	5.9	4.8
1961-73	5.5	5.0	4.7	7.6	6.2	5.0
Percent Distribution						
1950	100.0	38.8	2.3	16.0	2.7	40.3
1960	100.0	36.0	2.4	15.7	4.1	41.7
1968	100.0	35.8	2.4	17.3	4.3	40.2
1973	100.0	35.0	2.3	19.4	4.4	39.0

Sources: Banco Central del Ecuador; (World Bank) Ecuador Transportation Study; SRC Staff.

In these circumstances, the composition of imports may be expected to change, with a rising share going to capital goods and fuel imports, and a smaller share going to imports of consumer goods and production materials and supplies. A doubling of capital goods imports, for example, would require that there be no appreciable increase in the volume of consumer goods imports.

Export Goals

As indicated, the "big three" traditional exports of bananas, cacao, and coffee alone, which have been accounting for about 85 percent of total exports, cannot be counted on alone to supply the basis for future growth in the Ecuadorian economy owing to their limited growth prospects less than 5 percent a year. Some expansion of other existing exports and the development of new exports of primary products are possible. Ecuador also has the possibility, however, of developing new industrial exports within the framework of the Latin American economic integration movement. These exports would be in the fields of primary products, consumer goods (nondurable and durable), industrial materials, and capital goods components. A modest though essential target for new industrial exports would be a level equivalent to one-eighth of total exports by 1968, and one-sixth by 1973, amounting to $24 million and $43 million respectively.

With these targets for industrial exports, which are geared to the integration of the Latin American economy, and with expansion of exports of fisheries products, pharmaceuticals, pyrethrum extract, sugar, and other agricultural products, and a limited growth of exports of the "big three," Ecuador's exports could be expected to rise from the 1962 level of $143 million to a 1973 level of $297 million, reflecting an annual growth rate of 6.9 percent.

This export growth target would still require a major national effort as regards the "big three" as well as with respect to other primary products, and especially the new industrial

integration industry counterpart products. Such an export
effort will be essential if Ecuador's over-all economic growth
targets are to be achieved.

THE PERSPECTIVE FOR ECUADOR'S TRADITIONAL EXPORTS: 1968-73

In assessing the outlook for future earnings from Ecuador's
traditional exports, each product was examined as fully as the
data available permitted.

In view of the great importance of bananas, cacao, and
coffee to Ecuador's trade, the market possibilities for these
products were explored in depth, as detailed hereafter. The
findings indicate that substantial over-all growth in earnings
from these products can be anticipated. Aggregate earnings
from the "big three" are projected at $174 million in 1968 and
at $201 million in 1973. But the relative importance of these
products will diminish somewhat from their present levels.
Their combined projected value represents 82. 3 percent of the
total projected value of traditional exports for 1968, and 79. 2
percent for 1973.

For sugar, which has only recently emerged as a significant export product, export earnings are projected at $11. 2
million in 1968 and at $10. 4 million in 1973. For rice, the
projections are $2 million for 1968 and $3 million for 1973.

Total earnings from all traditional export products are projected at $211 million for 1968 and at $254 million for 1973.
It should be noted that these totals do not include projected
earnings from LAFTA trade, which are treated separately.

Following are detailed analyses of prospects for exports
of bananas, cacao, coffee, sugar, and rice. Other products
are considered separately, but in less detail. A tabular summary of prospective export earnings for 1968 and 1973 is
shown on page 249.

Bananas

World Imports and Consumption Trends

World imports of bananas have risen sharply over prewar levels. In 1961 they totaled 182. 6 million stems (50-lb. equivalent), an increase of over 60 percent above the prewar average of 111. 1 million stems.

Western Europe accounted for the larger part of this gain; its 1961 imports were well over twice as great as its prewar average—76. 2 million stems as against 33 million—and its share of world imports was 40 percent compared to the prewar average of 30 percent. France, West Germany, and the United Kingdom were the big buyers; their combined imports represented about 70 percent of total 1961 Western European imports.

United States imports, on the other hand, while still topping all areas and continuing to show annual increases in the aggregate, have declined in their relative share of global imports. In 1961, U. S. imports totaled close to 80 million stems (43. 6 percent of the world total), against a prewar average of 61 million stems (55 percent of the world total).

In per capita consumption of bananas, the United States and Canada continue to lead the world, but both appear to have reached a saturation point—the United States at a level of around 21. 5 pounds and Canada at about 20 pounds. In the long term, U. S. per capita consumption has declined, and that in the face of falling prices. (Averaged on a 10-year base, 1952-61, per capita consumption was only 20. 9 pounds, whereas the prewar, 1930-1939 average was 22. 6 pounds.)

Switzerland and Germany are edging close to these levels; each showed a per capita consumption rate in 1961 of 19. 2 pounds, up from 6. 6 and 4. 6 pounds, respectively, in 1952. And a number of other Western European countries have reached relatively high consumption levels: France, Belgium, Norway, and the United Kingdom all registered per capita consumption rates of over 15 pounds in 1961.

Prices

Unlike other commodities that move in international trade, no true world price exists for bananas; each major importing area has its own price base, largely related to source of supply. (See Table 4 in Statistical Appendix.)

In the United States, prices are based on Central American bananas and quoted in terms of "wholesale price, f.o.b. port of entry." (Actually, it is not possible to calculate true export values or f.o.b. unit prices, since the necessary data are not available. In Central America, the central banks calculate f.o.b. values by deducting from the U. S. wholesale value the costs incurred after loading and prior to sale in the United States, but this information is not published.)

In West Germany prices are quoted separately for bananas from Ecuador and Colombia, in terms of "import price, Hamburg."

United Kingdom prices are quoted as "wholesale price London" for imports from Jamaica.

For France, three prices "f.o.b. French ports" are quoted—for Guadeloupe, Cameroon, and Guinea.

Prices in all these markets have declined from their 1957 levels. In the United States the price dropped from $8.04 per 100 pounds in 1957 to $6.26 in 1962; in West Germany the comparable drop was from $7.71 to $6.35; in the United Kingdom from $13.92 to $12.47; and in France, from $12.24 to $8.95.

Ecuador's Banana Trade

The readiest index to the spectacular rise of Ecuador's banana trade is its growth relative to world exports. In the period 1957-61, Ecuador exports averaged 25 percent of total world exports, compared to 16 percent in 1951-55, and 4 percent 1945-49.

Today, bananas are the mainstay of the Ecuadorian economy. As noted in Chapter 1, aggregate export earnings from bananas in the years 1958-63 averaged 60 percent of all export earnings.

The United States is by far Ecuador's primary market for bananas; during the years 1958-63 it bought over 60 percent of Ecuador's yearly shipments.

In Western Europe, Germany and Belgium are the chief outlets for Ecuadorian bananas. During the years 1958-63 exports to these countries averaged 29 percent of exports to all destinations. But the trend in these two important markets is downward; exports to Germany have declined steadily—from 7.6 million stems in 1958 to 5.3 million in 1962; to Belgium—from 3.8 million to 2.5 million stems. And partial 1963 figures reflect still further declines in these markets.

Preliminary data for the first seven months of 1963 indicate that global shipments were roughly 19 percent higher than in the same period in 1962—23 million stems, as against 19.4 million stems in 1962. This increase, however, was accounted for largely by the greatly accelerated exports to Japan— 3,891,000 stems, as against 308,000 stems in 1962. Exports to two other destinations showed increases: the United States, up by roughly 475,000 stems and Holland, up by 150,000 stems. Shipments to other destinations registered decreases or remained unchanged from 1962 levels.

The Banana Outlook

The foregoing facts about world trends and consumption clearly indicate shrinking markets for Ecuador in some areas and lower rates of growth in others.

In the United States the market potential for bananas can be expected to be limited to population growth, in view of the apparent saturation point in per capita consumption, alluded to above.

In Western Europe, the competitive position of Ecuador
(as well as of other Latin American exporters) will be seriously affected by EEC policies. The preferential tariff treatment
accorded by the Common Market countries to their associated
territories has far-reaching implications for Latin American
banana exports. The Rome Treaty provides for a common external tariff of 20 percent ad valorem, applicable at the end of
a transitional period (1970) to imports from third countries,
while the tariff to be applied to associated countries is to decrease to zero.

Currently, the following ad valorem duties apply:

	General Rates (percent)	Rates Applicable to Associated Countries (percent)
Benelux	15.0	12.0
France	20.0	15.0
Germany	Free	Free
Italy	32.4	28.8

As noted, German imports are duty free. A special proto-
col of the Rome Treaty provides for a duty-free quota for West
Germany based on 1956 imports. However, the quota is subject to annual adjustments according to an established formula,
and imports above the established quota are to be subject to the
general 20 percent EEC duty. The effect of this provision has
already been felt; in 1962 imports above the duty-free quota
were subject to a 6 percent tariff. It may be anticipated that
pressure will be exerted on Germany to allocate increasingly
larger shares of its imports to associated territories.

Furthermore, national policies in certain EEC countries
still further prejudice imports from Latin America. In France,
a system of import licenses, implementing restrictive agreements, assures the banana market for imports from Martinique
and Guadeloupe and the French associated territories of Africa.
Imports from these areas enjoy a 5 percent advantage over
other imports.

Italy's tariff wall is even more restrictive. Imports from
Somali are duty free, while imports from EEC countries are
subject to a 25.2 percent ad valorem rate, and those from
third countries, 31.2 percent. But still other factors affect
imports from outside the national orbit: (a) under a recently
concluded agreement with Somali, Italy guarantees to absorb
the latter's entire banana production for a period of five years
(presumably, regardless of prices); and (b) imports and distribution of bananas are controlled through a state monopoly.
These various controls not only effectively bar imports from
other areas, but also inhibit growth in consumption.

Belgium, which has thus far proved a favorable market for
Ecuador may also be expected to deteriorate as a customer
because of Common Market policies. Until now, because of
the low quality and high production cost of Congolese bananas,
the latter have offered little competition to imports from third
countries. Ecuador and other Latin American exporters have
been able to market their bananas, despite the 15 percent
tariff to which they are subject. But improvement in the
Congo's production and the higher tariff contemplated by the
Rome Treaty will undoubtedly have adverse effects on future
imports.

Finally, as regards the United Kingdom while not a member
of the EEC, it never has been a favorable outlet for Latin American bananas. Preferential treatment of the Commonwealth
countries and a 15 percent tariff have made the United Kingdom
market noncompetitive for Latin American imports.

Ecuador Banana Exports -- 1968 and 1973

A quantified forecast of Ecuador's banana exports for the
two 5-year periods ending in 1968 and 1973 is detailed in the
table on page 213, which was developed on the basis of the
following assumptions, deriving from the considerations discussed above:

1. The common denominator for all exports is price per
    stem. A constant price of $2.50 per stem is assumed.

This represents the average price per stem 1958-62
as reflected in Ecuador's export earnings in that period.

2. Exports to the United States are predicated on the as-
    sumptions that:

    a. Ecuador will continue to maintain its present share
        of the market (40 percent).

    b. U. S. imports will increase in line with population
        increases projected at an over-all rate of growth
        of 7. 3 percent and 7. 9 percent, respectively, in the
        two 5-year periods, or average annual rates of in-
        crease of 1. 44 and 1. 60 percent.

3. Exports to Western Europe are projected on the as-
    sumption that they will decline at the rate of 10 percent
    in the first 5-year period and 15 percent in the following
    five years. (The higher rate of decline in 1969-73 takes
    into account the end of the transition period provided for
    in the Treaty of Rome and the subsequent higher tariffs
    that will apply.)

4. Exports to Japan cannot be projected on a historical
    basis, since a real momentum in Ecuador's exports
    to this country has only just begun to manifest itself.
    However, in the light of recent sharp increases in ship-
    ments, it is assumed that exports will total 15 million
    stems by 1968 and 20 million stems by 1973.

5. For exports to other areas, including Chile, Canada,
    and markets not yet represented in Ecuador's banana
    trade, the following allowances have been made for the
    two periods:

    1968 - 10 percent of actual 1962 global exports.

    1973 - 10 percent increase to these areas over
           the estimated 1968 level.

PROJECTED EXPORTS OF BANANAS FROM ECUADOR,
BY VOLUME AND VALUE: 1968 AND 1973

Destination	1968		
	Volume (1000 stems)	Unit Value (dollars)	Total Value (millions)
United States	22,270	2.50	$55.7
Western Europe	8,500	2.50	21.3
Japan	15,000	2.50	37.5
Other	3,400	2.50	8.5
Total	49,170		$123.0
	1973		
United States	24,030	2.50	$60.0
Western Europe	7,250	2.50	18.1
Japan	20,000	2.50	50.0
Other	3,750	2.50	9.4
Total	55,030		$137.5

The above projected levels of banana exports would represent the following aggregates and percentages of increase in
volume and value:

	Volume (1000 stems)	Value (million dollars)
Average 1958-62		
1958	33,307	83.1
1973	49,170	123.0
	55,030	137.5
Aggregate Percent Increase		
1958-62 to 1968	47.6	48.0
1968 to 1973	11.9	11.8
1958-62 to 1973	65.2	65.5
Avg. Annual Percent Increase		
1960[a] to 1968	5.0	5.0
1968 to 1973	2.3	2.3
1960 to 1973	3.9	4.0

a. Using 1958-62 average as 1960.

Cacao

World Imports and Consumption Trends

World imports of cacao in 1961 and 1962 rose sharply—to 1,014,000 and 1,020,000 metric tons, respectively—bringing the 1958-62 average to 877,300 tons, or 23.6 percent above the 1952-56 average of 710,000 tons.

Europe accounted for the major part of this increase. Virtually all of the Western European countries showed substantial annual increases in their cacao imports during this period; their aggregate imports in the past five years averaged 25 percent higher than in 1952-56. Eastern Europe more than doubled its imports in the period.

United States imports, while registering sharp fluctuations from year to year, averaged 6 percent higher in the past five years than in the 1952-56 period.

Per capita consumption followed the trend set by imports, with most Western European countries exceeding the consumption levels of other importing countries. As might be expected, per capita consumption has been increasing and is highest in those countries which are leading exporters of cacao products —Switzerland, the Netherlands, Austria, Belgium, and the United Kingdom. In 1961, all of these countries showed per capita consumption rates of over 2 kilos, with Switzerland topping the list with 3.2 kilos.

In the producing countries consumption is negligible; in fact, it appears to be on the decline. In 1958 and 1959, consumption in these countries represented 8 percent of total world consumption; in 1960, 7.5 percent; and in 1961, 6.7 percent. The notable exception is Colombia, where per capita consumption in recent years has been averaging 1.44 kilograms.

Prices

Few agricultural products have been subject to as wide
price fluctuations as cacao. Between 1952 and 1962, spot New
York prices for Bahia and Ghana ranged between the 1954 high
of 55. 7 cents and 57. 8 cents per pound, respectively, and 21. 3
cents and 21 cents per pound in 1962. Prices in other markets
were similarly erratic. In Belgium the average price range,
c. i. f. Antwerp, for Congo 1-A was 55. 7 cents per pound in
1954 and 20. 2 cents per pound in 1962; in Italy the importers'
selling price f. o. b. Milan for Sao Tome was 81. 5 cents in 1954
and 45. 7 cents in 1962; and in France the average prices ranged
between 70. 1 cents in 1954 and 24. 3 cents per pound in 1962.
The 1962 price index in all markets was between 20 and 30 percent below 1957 levels.

Ecuador's Cacao Exports

Ecuador's exports of cacao (all flavor grade) have moved in
line with fluctuations in world exports. Ecuador's exports in
1950-54 averaged 55, 976, 000 pounds and in the period 1957-61,
64, 771, 000 pounds, an increase of close to 16 percent, compared to the 17. 8 percent increase in world exports.

What is significant about Ecuador's exports is not only that
they have more or less paralleled the trend in total world
cacao exports, but that they have been capturing an increasing
share of the world flavor-cacao market. In the period 1952-56,
Ecuador's share of the flavor market averaged 38. 8 percent;
in the years since then its share has averaged slightly above 43
percent. This performance is particularly noteworthy in the
light of declining relative world demand for flavor cacao.
Whereas in the period 1952-56, flavor-cacao exports averaged
9. 5 percent of over-all world exports, for 1960-62 they averaged only 7. 5 percent.

(It is to be noted that no world trade figures are available
on "flavor" cacao. The foregoing assessment of global trade
and Ecuador's share of the market was made possible by the
identification (by the Cocoa Study Group) of the countries whose

production is wholely or largely of the flavor variety and which
were therefore to be exempted from quota restrictions. This,
in turn, permitted compilation of Table 32, FLAVOR COCOA
EXPORTS by Principal Producing Countries, as given in the
Statistical Appendix to this study.)

As with bananas and coffee, the United States is Ecuador's
principal market for its cacao production. During the past
decade exports to the United States have averaged around 50
percent of Ecuador's total cacao shipments.

Western Europe has been taking an increasing share of
Ecuador's cacao, averaging close to 38 percent of total shipments during the years 1957-62, as against 23 percent in the
period 1952-56. West Germany continues to be Ecuador's
principal European market, the Netherlands the second largest.

In South America, Colombia has been an important buyer of
Ecuador's cacao, although legal or recorded shipments to this
market show a decline. During 1953-56, exports to Colombia
averaged 13,350,000 pounds and represented close to 23 percent of Ecuador's total cacao exports; in the years 1957-62
recorded shipments averaged only 8,800,000 pounds, about
14.5 percent of total exports. These are official export
figures which do not take account of contraband shipments. It
is commonly believed in the area that a large part of Ecuador's
exports to Colombia are contraband shipments; and it may be
that total exports have actually increased. The Central Bank
of Ecuador has estimated that there has been no diminution in
those exports but that a large share has been diverted into
clandestine channels. Colombian import data show estimated
contraband shipments of 3,400 metric tons in both 1960 and
1961 and 2,000 tons in 1962, indicated as coming largely from
Ecuador.

In recent years the most spectacular gain has been recorded
by exports to Japan. These have risen from initial shipments
of 163,000 pounds in 1959 to 4,483,000 pounds in 1962.

The Cacao Outlook

World demand in 1970 for grindings (excepting the Soviet bloc) was projected by the FAO Cocoa Study Group on the basis of population and income growth, taking into account the expected values of price and income elasticities under three alternative assumptions as to the price level and two alternative assumptions as to rate of income growth.

Thus calculated, the results indicated that: (1) the choice of alternative rates of income growth had very little influence on the total demand for grindings, and (2) aggregate demand in 1970 could amount to slightly below 1,100 thousand metric tons at a price of 30 cents per pound, to around 1,160 thousand tons at a price of 24 cents per pound, and to slightly over 1,250 thousand pounds at a price of 18 cents per pound. The study noted, however, that "a few years of comparatively stable prices favorable to consumers and educational efforts to promote consumption of various cacao products could result in a structural change which would shift the demand schedule upwards."

A major unknown factor in projecting future world demand for grindings lies in the lack of a basis for forecasting probable level of imports into the USSR and Eastern Europe, since imports into those areas are likely to be influenced not by the factors which determine imports into free societies but rather by policy considerations of the central governments. With these uncertainties in mind, it was nevertheless assumed by the Cocoa Study Group that imports into that area of 200,000 to 250,000 metric tons may be reached by 1970.

Calculated against actual world grindings (exclusive of the USSR and Eastern Europe) in 1957-59, which averaged 808,300 metric tons, the foregoing projected levels of demand would represent aggregate 10-year rates of growth of 35 percent, at an assumed price of 30 cents per pound; 45 percent at 24 cents per pound; and 55 percent at 18 cents per pound. The corresponding average annual rates of increase would be 3.1 percent, 3.8 percent, and 4.5 percent.

The projected level of 250,000 metric tons for the USSR and
Eastern Europe would mean a 375 percent increment over the
1957-59 average grindings of 52,500, or an average annual rate
of increase of 16.8 percent.

Tested against actual grindings during the period of 1960-62
these projections appear to be on the low side. In the case
of world grindings (exclusive of the USSR and Eastern Europe),
the 1960-62 grindings were 15.2 percent higher, representing
an average annual increase of 4.8 percent. In the case of the
USSR and Eastern Europe, the average annual increase came
to 14.3 percent.

For purposes of establishing a base against which to project
Ecuador exports in 1968 and 1973, this study assumes the
following levels of demand, which have been calculated (without
reference to price) at the actual average annual rates of increase registered during the years 1960-62 over the 1957-59
level, as set forth in the paragraph above:

	Average 1960-62	Estimated 1968	Estimated 1973
	(in 1,000 metric tons)		
World grindings (excluding USSR and Eastern Europe)	931.5	1,293	1,635
USSR and Eastern Europe	78.5	200	390
Total World	1,010.0	1,493	2,025

Ecuador Cacao Exports -- 1968 and 1973

Forecasting future levels of export for Ecuador presents
special difficulties, since no information is available that would
provide a basis for estimating future global demand for flavor
cacao. In the light of the declining share of flavor cacao in
over-all cacao exports in the years 1957-62, alluded to earlier,
projecting global flavor-cacao exports even at their present

ratio to over-all cacao exports would probably be over optimistic. On the other hand, Ecuador's increasing share of
global flavor-cacao exports warrants a more favorable outlook
for Ecuador than for other countries involved in the trade.

The levels of cacao exports projected for Ecuador in 1968
and 1973, as developed below, were predicated on the following
assumptions:

1. That all flavor cacao will be exempt from quota re-
    strictions, as specified in the revised Draft Internation-
    al Cocoa Agreement.

2. That the Agreement will serve to stabilize prices as
    envisaged.

3. That flavor cacao will command a price of 24 cents per
    pound. (Ecuador's exports in 1961 averaged 21.8 cents
    a pound; in 1962, 22.7 cents a pound.)

4. That global flavor-cacao exports will continue to decline
    in their relative share of over-all cacao exports, but at
    a somewhat lesser rate—to 6 percent in 1968 and 5.5
    percent in 1973, compared with 7.5 percent in 1960-62
    and 9.5 percent in 1952-56.

5. That Ecuador will increase its present share of global
    flavor-cacao exports to 47 percent in 1968 and to 50 per-
    cent in 1973, compared with the average of 43.8 percent
    for 1958-62 and 38.8 percent in 1952-56.

The projections are as follows:

	1968	1973
	(metric tons)	
Global cacao exports (all grades)	1,493,000	2,025,000
Global Flavor cacao exports	89,000	111,400
Ecuador Exports	42,100	55,700
Ecuador Export Earnings	$22.3 million	$29.5 million

The above projected levels of cacao exports would represent the following aggregates and percentages of increase in volume and value:

	Volume (metric tons)	Value (million dollars)
1958-62 Average	30,181	19.1
1968	42,100	22.3
1973	55,700	29.5
Aggregate Percent Increase		
1958-62 to 1968	39.5	16.8
1968 to 1973	32.3	32.3
1958-62 to 1973	84.6	54.5
Avg. Annual Percent Increase		
1960* to 1968	4.2	2.0
1968 to 1973	5.7	5.7
1960 to 1973	4.8	3.4

* Using 1958-62 average as 1960.

Coffee

World Imports and Consumption Trends

World imports of coffee beans during the years 1958-62 showed steady annual increases; they rose by approximately 10 million bags[3] from 37 million in 1958 to 47 million in 1962.

The United States is the world's number one market for coffee. Although its relative share of over-all imports has been decreasing somewhat, it continues to absorb over half of the world total. Its imports during 1958-62 averaged 22.5 million bags.

3. Bags, as used in this context, refers to the standard coffee bag of 60 kilos, or 132.276 pounds.

Europe's imports during this period increased from 13. 8 million bags in 1958 to 18. 5 million in 1962, paralleling rising standards of living in Western Europe and reflecting the sharp upswing in imports by Eastern European countries, which rose from about a half million bags in 1958 to over a million bags in 1962. But within Western Europe, itself, there are wide disparities in import levels. The European Economic Community, the second largest market in the world, consumes almost twice as much coffee as the rest of Western Europe and over ten times as much as all of the Eastern European countries combined.

Two countries, the USSR and Japan, showed the largest relative increases in coffee imports in 1962. The USSR's imports totaled over 400,000 bags, compared to 68,000 in 1958. Japan's increase, although not so spectacular, was nevertheless significant; imports rose from 106,000 bags in 1952 to 256,000 in 1962.

In per capita consumption of coffee, four Western European countries lead the world. Sweden heads the list with 24. 3 pounds in 1962; Denmark next with 21. 4 pounds, followed by Finland and Norway with around 19 pounds each. In the United States, per capita consumption has remained remarkably steady for some years, during the years 1958-63 amounting to either 15. 8 or 15. 9 pounds.

With respect to world imports of soluble coffee, only scattered data are available. In any event, import figures would not provide an index to world consumption, since to a very large extent the consuming countries produce their own soluble coffee requirements.

The available data indicate that world consumption of soluble coffee has been increasing steadily. In terms of green-coffee equivalent, [4] consumption rose from 4,745,000 bags in 1958 to 6,367,000 bags in 1962, averaging 13 percent of the world's total coffee imports during this period.

---

4. Most of the statistics on soluble coffee are stated in terms of green coffee equivalent.

The United States is by far the largest producer and consumer of soluble coffee. Production during the years 1958-63 averaged 3,865,000 bags, of which 3,775,000 bags were absorbed by the domestic market, the balance going to exports. This consumption level represented close to 17 percent of over-all United States coffee consumption (which during this period averaged 22,513,000 bags). The United States is both an importer and exporter of soluble coffee. Its exports, however, have consistently exceeded imports and are on the increase; in 1958 they represented 3.1 percent of soluble production; in 1962, 7.2 percent. Imports ranged between a high of 2.9 percent of soluble consumption in 1959 and a low of 2.0 percent in 1961.

There are no firm figures on European consumption of soluble coffee; however, according to a report[5] in 1962 about 9.0 percent of the total volume of coffee (18.5 million bags) consumed by Western European countries was in the form of soluble coffee. The same source estimates that in 1962 Eastern European countries consumed the equivalent of 25,000 bags of soluble coffee, or about 2.4 percent of their over-all coffee consumption.

Prices

Historically, coffee prices have been subject to wide cyclical fluctuations and have varied with respect to not only quality but markets as well. In all markets current prices are sharply below the 1954 peaks, but the fall in robusta prices has been more pronounced than the price decline for the mild, quality grades of coffee.

The New York spot price for Santos 4 averaged 79.7 cents a pound in 1954; the average in 1962 was 34 cents a pound. In West Germany the price of Santos "extra" dropped from 82.1 cents to 37.65 cents over the same period. And in France, the

---

5. Coffee Report No. 260, January-February, 1963, issued by Jacques Louis-Delamare et Cie., Le Havre, France.

drop in price for Ivory Coast robusta, ex-warehouse Le
Havre, was from 55.34 cents in 1954 to 30.84 cents in 1962.
For Manizales, the 1962 New York spot price was 40.82 cents
as against 80.09 cents in 1954, and in West Germany the price
of Kenya "A" dropped from 80.29 cents to 63.96 cents a pound.

Even more than import prices, retail prices differ markedly from country to country, depending on the rates of duty and
internal taxes that apply and on processing and distribution
costs, which also vary from country to country. A recent
comprehensive review of the world coffee economy[6] noted the
differentials between the 1958 United States retail price and
prices in other major markets as shown in the table on page
224.

Ecuadorian Coffee Trade

Coffee has long been a major support of the Ecuadorian
economy. Shipments in 1962 reached an all time peak of
551,100 bags. Averaged over two 5-year periods, exports
in 1958-62 were over 20 percent higher than in 1953-57.
But, increased shipments have not meant increased export
earnings. The sharp fall in coffee prices since the peaks of
1954 has resulted in diminishing returns from this important
product. Average export earnings in the years 1958-63,
$20.9 million, were 18.7 percent below the 1953-57 average
of $25.7 million.

The United States continues to be Ecuador's chief market
for coffee, although its proportionate share of aggregate Ecuador shipments has been declining; its imports have dropped
from 66.5 percent of Ecuador's total coffee exports in 1953-57
to 62.9 in 1958-62.

---

6. The World Coffee Economy, Commodity Bulletin Series
No. 33, Food and Agricultural Organization of the United
Nations.

STRUCTURE OF RETAIL COFFEE PRICE IN SELECTED COUNTRIES IN RELATION TO THAT IN THE UNITED STATES, 1958

Country	Difference Between National and U.S. Retail Price (U.S. Dollars per Kilogram)				Index of National Retail Price (U.S. Retail Price = 100)
	Import Unit Value Difference	Duty and Tax Difference	Gross Margin Difference	Total	
Netherlands	+0.04	--	-0.07	-0.03	98
Canada	+0.10	+0.11	-0.14	+0.07	104
Norway	+0.21	--	+0.12	+0.33	118
Switzerland	+0.13	+0.13	+0.14	+0.40	122
Sweden	+0.17	+0.16	+0.09	+0.42	123
United Kingdom	-0.04	+0.04	+0.57	+0.57	131
Belgium	-0.04	--	--	+0.64	132
France	-0.04	+0.61	+0.08	+0.65	135
Spain	+0.33	+0.82	-0.26	+0.89	148
Denmark	+0.04	+0.25	+0.68	+0.97	152
Greece	-0.03	+0.37	+0.91	+1.25	167
Austria	+0.18	--	--	+1.60	186
Yugoslavia	+0.01	--	--	+1.65	189
Finland	-0.02	+1.47	+0.25	+1.71	192
Italy	+0.05	+1.20	+0.54	+1.79	197
Germany, Western	+0.33	+1.20	+1.24	+2.77	250

Western Europe, on the other hand, has been taking increasingly larger shares of Ecuador's coffee. In 1958-63 its purchases have averaged 33.7 percent (159,100 bags) of total coffee exports, as against 18.4 percent (109,300 bags) in 1953-57. In both periods, France, Western Germany, Italy, and the Netherlands have been the chief buyers.

The Global Outlook for Coffee

Global coffee consumption can be expected to rise substantially given: (1) relatively stable prices (as envisaged by the International Coffee Agreement); (2) the currently indicated rates of growth in population and income in the traditional coffee-consuming countries; (3) increased demand in line with anticipated rise in standards of living in low-income countries; and (4) the newly emerging demand in previously non-coffee-drinking countries, such as the United Kingdom and Japan. But demand will be influenced, as well, by less predictable factors —vagaries in consumer preference, technological developments affecting coffee and coffee substitutes, and government policies with respect to foreign exchange, tariffs, and taxes as they relate to coffee imports.

Because of the overriding importance of coffee to many Latin American economies, and, more recently, to some of the African nations, coffee and the coffee market have been subjected to continuing study by national and international bodies, as well as by the trade.

A number of recent studies,[7] involving projections of global coffee consumption, were examined as a means of establishing

7. Agricultural Commodities Projections for 1970, published by the Food and Agriculture Organization, 1962. The World Coffee Economy, Commodity Series No. 33, published by FAO in 1961. Analysis of Trends in the International Coffee Market, prepared by Joao Oliveira Santos, for the Course on the Coffee Economy, given at the Brazilian Coffee Institute, 1963. Coffee Consumption in the United States: 1920-1965. U. S. Department of Commerce, 1960.

a base against which to project Ecuador's exports in 1968 and
1973. Since the FAO coffee projections are based on the same
methodology and premises with respect to population and income growths as those for cacao, these were selected as the
base for calculating Ecuador's future coffee exports.

The FAO projections for coffee are part of an over-all assessment of future prospects for principal agricultural commodities, evaluated according to three main areas: high-
income countries, low-income countries, and the Sino-Soviet
area. Estimates are expressed in terms of 3-year averages
and cover a 12-year period in order to even out cyclical dis-
turbances, to minimize unforeseen developments, and to allow
time for changes in policy to take effect.

Thus calculated, world consumption (excluding the Sino-
Soviet countries) in 1970-72 is estimated at about 51.8 million
and 54.9 million bags, representing an increase of 33 to 40
percent over the 1958-60 level, or the equivalent of 2.4 to 2.9
percent a year. If the consumption level estimated for Eastern Europe and the USSR is included in the higher of the two
projected levels for other importing countries (54.9 million
bags), the over-all average annual increase would come to
3.6 percent.

The table on the following page shows a breakdown of these
estimates according to major importing areas.

These projected consumption levels did not consider the
effects of possible price declines or of increases or decreases
in soluble coffee consumption, for these reasons:

1. Price declines would have to be relatively sharp to
    influence consumption substantially, since in the
    principal importing countries, with the major ex-
    ception of Italy, the price elasticity of demand is
    low. The FAO study estimates that a drop in retail
    price of 10 to 30 percent in the period under con-
    sideration might result in a rise in world con-
    sumption of only 3 to 6 percent. It also noted that

ESTIMATED COFFEE CONSUMPTION BY IMPORTING COUNTRIES
(In Thousands of Bags[a])

	Average 1958-60	1970-72 Low	1970-72 High	1970-72 as Percent of 1958-60 (Index 1959 = 100)	
North America	22,480	28,920	30,210	129	134
Oceania	180	250	617	142	157
Western Europe	14,350	19,150	20,016	138	143
EEC	(9,400)	(12,950)	(13,483)	158	178
Mediterranean Countries	(660)	(1,050)	(1,150)	121	126
Other European "	(4,280)	(5,150)	(5,383)	134	140
Others	2,030	3,520	4,016	173	198
Total	39,040	51,840	54,859	133	140
USSR and Eastern Europe	684[b]	3,330[c]			487

a. Weighing 132.276 pounds; converted from FAO metric-ton base.

b. Actual imports, 1958-60.

c. According to the FAO, "Only the roughest estimates can be made of future coffee consumption in Eastern Europe and the USSR. It is to be expected that imports will depend on policy considerations rather than consumer taste. In Eastern Europe consumption has recently averaged about 0.4 kilograms per person against 0.9 kilograms in prewar years. In the USSR, a tea-drinking country, coffee consumption is insignificant. However, if it is assumed that Soviet trade with coffee producing countries will continue to expand, the region may take larger imports of coffee in the future. But, even if East European and USSR imports increased fivefold, to about 250,000 tons by about 1970, per capita consumption in Eastern Europe would still be considerably below that of Western Europe, while in the USSR it would be less than that of any other area of the world except Asia."

227

declines in import prices are not followed by proportionate declines in retail prices; that a 10 percent decline in import prices might bring about a
drop of only 6 to 7 percent in retail prices.

2. Currently envisaged increases in soluble coffee
    consumption would not materially affect over-all
    coffee consumption.

Ecuador's Coffee Exports -- 1968- 73

Ecuador's prospective coffee exports will be influenced not
only by global demand but by the quota limitations of the International Coffee Agreement. Ecuador's basic quota, as fixed
by the Agreement, is 552,000 bags per year. As specified in
the Agreement, annual export quotas will be reviewed at the
beginning of each coffee year by the International Coffee Council,
and in the light of estimated world imports the Council will fix
annual export quotas "which shall be the same percentage for all
exporting Members of the basic export quotas as specified in
Annex A (of the Agreement). "

Ecuador's basic quota represents 1.2 percent of total basic
quotas. (Actual shipments in 1962 closely approximated the
basic quota; they totaled 551,000 bags.)

Ecuador exports of coffee, as projected below, were based
on the following assumptions:

1. That consumption in the importing countries,
    including Eastern Europe and the USSR, will
    increase at a slightly higher rate than the 3.6
    percent projected by the FAO—i. e. , at 3.8
    percent per annum, in line with the actual in-
    crease in 1959-62 imports.

2. That Ecuador will maintain a constant 1.2
    percent share in world imports.

3. That prices will be stabilized at the 1958-62
    level. For Ecuador this would imply an average
    of 32.2 cents per pound, the average price re-
    flected by Ecuador's export earnings of this
    period.

The projections follow:

	1968	1973
	(Thousands of Bags)	
Consumption in importing countries	55,570	66,960
Ecuador's Exports	667	804
Ecuador's Export Earnings	$28.4 million	$34.2 million

These projected levels of coffee exports and export earnings
would represent the following aggregates and percentages of
increases:

	Volume (1,000 bags)	Value (million dollars)
1958-62 Average	472.6	20.1
1968	666.8	28.4
1973	803.5	34.2
Aggregate Percent Increase		
1958-62 to 1968	41.1	41.3
1968 to 1973	20.5	20.4
1958-62 to 1973	70.0	70.1
Avg. Annual Percent Increase		
1960* to 1968	4.5	4.4
1968 to 1973	3.8	3.8
1960* to 1973	4.2	4.2

* Using 1958-62 average as 1960.

Sugar

World Production, Consumption, and Trade

During the past eighteen years sugar production in all countries was greatly expanded, as a result of protectionist policies and technological improvements, both in agriculture and processing. World production of centrifugal sugar increased by 130 percent between 1947-49 and 1960-61, with the greatest increase taking place in Asia (excluding China) and South America, where production rose by 100 and 115 percent, respectively. Very substantial increases also took place in the North and Central American countries, other than the United States.

World consumption, over the past decade, rose by 5.2 percent a year, as against less than 2 percent for population. Per capita consumption levels vary widely from region to region. In North America and Oceania consumption remained stable at high levels (between 45 and 47 kilos); in North Western Europe it increased in the first part of the decade, but since then has shown little change (the average for the region in 1956 was 43.3 kilos).

World trade in sugar has not kept pace with world production, largely because of the drive towards self-sufficiency in importing countries. World exports, which in 1953 amounted to 41 percent of production, declined to only a little over 30 percent of production by 1961. Exports by countries outside the Communist bloc have continued to expand slightly, from an average of 8.7 million metric tons in the period 1955-59, to 10.4 million in 1960, when Cuban shipments to the United States market were first supplanted by imports from other sources, principally Latin American.

World imports increased from an average of 14.6 million metric tons in the period 1955-59 to a peak of 19.7 million in 1961; however, most of this expansion can be accounted for by the emergence of the Sino-Soviet area, formerly a marginal net exporter, as the major outlet for Cuban sugar. Imports by

countries other than those within the Sino-Soviet area have
varied little in recent years, from an average of 13.8 million
metric tons in 1955-59 to 14.3 million in 1960, 14.0 million in
1961, and 14.5 million tons in 1962.

The Outlook for Sugar

According to the United Nations Food and Agriculture Organization's analysis of current trends in the world sugar
economy, indications are that by 1970 consumption outside the
Sino-Soviet area will increase by 36 to 44 percent, at a rate
of 2.7 to 3.2 percent a year, compared with 3.8 percent
during the 1950-60 decade. This projection, however, is
based on an assumption of constant prices; and if retail prices
were to drop substantially, demand would react sharply in
countries with low consumption levels. For example, consumption could increase by about 10 percent in the Far East,
if retail sugar prices were to decline by 10 percent.

Taking into account the change in Cuban trade (that is, assuming that countries outside the Sino-Soviet area will continue to import about 2 million tons of Cuban sugar a year and
that the balance of Cuba's supplies will go to the Sino-Soviet
area) world trade is expected to expand by 9 to 14 percent by
1970. Production during the decade of the sixties is likely to
rise by 45 to 53 percent. (This large increase is projected in
the light of the substantial increase in production which has
occurred since the disruption in the Cuban sugar trade.)

During the 1960's, net import requirements of the industrial-
ized countries, North America, Western Europe, and Japan,
are expected to rise by somewhat less than 10 percent. As
illustrated in the table, most of the projected increase will
result from estimated expansion of Japanese imports from the
1957-59 level of slightly over 1 million tons per year to close.
to 2 million tons a year in the period 1969-71. These estimates are believed to be reasonable in view of the present low
sugar consumption in Japan, the high rate of economic growth
assumed, and the limited possibilities for expanding domestic
sugar production.

PROJECTION OF NET IMPORTS OF SUGAR
FOR THE MAIN IMPORTING REGIONS
(EXCLUDING THE SINO-SOVIET AREA)

Region	1957-59		1969-71		
	(thousand metric tons, raw value)			(Index, 1957-59=100)	
		L	H	L	H
North America[a]	4,931	5,450	5,450	110	110
Western Europe	3,179	2,700	2,700	85	85
Japan	1,191	1,850	1,950	155	164
Total industrialized countries	9,301	10,000	10,100	108	108
Near East	811	1,000	1,200	123	148
North Africa[b]	679	600	700	90	103
Rest of Africa[c]	329	500	660	152	200
Total Near East and Africa[c]	1,819	2,100	2,560	115	141
Grand Total	11,120	12,100	12,660	109	114

a. Including Puerto Rico and Hawaii.

b. Algeria, Egypt, Libya, Morocco, Tunisia.

c. Excluding South Africa, Mauritius and Reunion.

Source: Agricultural Commodities: Projections for 1970,
Food and Agriculture Organization, of the United Nations.

It should be recognized that price will have an important
bearing on future levels of consumption. World price, which
declined from the 1957 level of 5.16 cents per pound to a low
of 2.91 cents per pound in 1961. recovered substantially
during the middle and latter part of 1962 and by the end of the
year had risen to over 4.5 cents per pound. In view of the anticipated increase in world consumption and the substantial

reduction in world stocks, plus sharply reduced Cuban output, prices are expected to strengthen further in the 1963-64 crop year.

Over the long term, price movements will be strongly influenced by the trade and selling policies of Cuba and the Sino-Soviet countries. The latter could continue to absorb 4 to 5 million tons of sugar a year for some time to come, despite the increased domestic production projected for the USSR. Mainland China, for example, has a very low per capita consumption level (3 kilos in 1958) and, with outside financial assistance, could become a very large market. However, if for political or other reasons, the Sino-Soviet area ceased to be a large net importer, a substantial surplus would result and prices would be severely depressed. Lower prices would, of course, reduce the rate of production expansion, but such an eventuality would, nevertheless, create great difficulties.

The Outlook for Ecuador

Ecuador's sugar production increased from an average of 60,000 tons during 1950-54, to 165,000 tons in 1962, but until 1957 its domestic output was absorbed almost entirely by the local market. Since 1957, however, it has become a net exporter of sugar, with Japan as its chief outlet until 1961, when exports showed a sharp upswing, following inclusion of Ecuador in the United States global sugar quota.

In view of the production and consumption trends projected for the various regions of the world, the United States and Japan will in all probability remain Ecuador's chief outlets for its exportable sugar surpluses.

Under the United States Sugar Act, Ecuador has a basic quota of 27,049 short tons (raw value) plus an allowance of 308 tons for each 100,000 tons in excess of a total of 9.7 million tons imported into the United States, in a given year. In 1961, Ecuador exports to the United States totaled 31,285 short tons and in 1962, they were more than twice that level—65,148 tons.

Ecuador's future exports to the United States will depend, first of all, on future United States levels of consumption. Since per capita consumption is considered to be at the saturation level, aggregate increases in United States sugar consumption are expected to follow population increases. This would mean average annual rates of increase of 1.41 percent in the period 1963-68 and 1.53 percent in 1968-73. But, additional factors will have a bearing on Ecuador's prospects in the United States market: (1) United States import requirements and the overages above the 9.7 million tons which serve as a benchmark for additions to basic quotas (which, in turn, will depend on domestic availabilities); and (2) Ecuador's own future consumption requirements and exportable surpluses.

So far as long-term prospects for United States production are concerned, no forecasts are feasible at this time, in view of the manifold uncertainties as to world supply and price and their effect on United States subsidies for domestic sugar production. Ecuador's exportable surpluses will depend not only on domestic requirements, but on its future production. Finally, an added uncertainty in projecting Ecuador's prospective exports to the United States is presented by possible shortfalls in deliveries by other countries against their quotas, which could affect imports from Ecuador (upwards).

Since it is not feasible to reduce these imponderables to mathematical form, Ecuador's sugar exports to the United States are projected to increase solely in line with United States population growth, as noted above, calculated against its actual exports in 1962 of 65,481 short tons. This would result in potential exports of 69,900 tons in 1968 and 75,400 tons in 1973.

For Japan, in the absence of any alternative yardstick, exports are projected on the basis of Ecuador's share in Japan's over-all sugar imports during 1958-61 (the only years for which data were ascertainable), which averaged 1.23 percent. For these projections, Ecuador's future participation in Japan's imports is projected at that average, figured against the higher of the two import levels projected for Japan by the

FAO for 1969-71, which represents an average annual increase in imports of 4. 2 percent. [8] Thus calculated, Ecuador's sugar exports to Japan would approximate 23,500 short tons in 1968 and about 29,000 short tons in 1973.

In South America, Chile and Uruguay are the only net importers of sugar. Ecuador may be successful in establishing a market in Chile, but at present there is no basis for a quantified assessment of this possibility.

The selection of a price level at which to project future sugar exports presents even greater difficulties than the projection of quantities. The uncertainties with respect to production engendered by the break in the traditional movement of Cuban sugar in world trade have had wide repercussions in the price area. At the beginning of 1962, world prices for sugar were nearly one-third lower than early in 1961, and continued to drop further. The international export quota system had ceased to operate and, although reductions in European and Cuban production had already been indicated, large world supplies and sales by Eastern European countries continued to depress the market. By the end of January, prices had dropped to below 2 cents a pound (the lowest level in a quarter of a century). They rose sharply, however, in the following months, partly under the influence of the Cuban crisis, reaching a little over 4. 5 cents a pound by the end of 1962. By May, 1963, the world price had peaked at 12. 6 cents, but has since dropped to an average for January-October, of 8 cents a pound. In the light of current estimates of world production and costs of production, informed sources estimate that world sugar prices might average 6 cents a pound in the 5-year period to 1968 and 5 cents a pound to 1973.

---

8. At this rate of increase, Japan's imports in 1968 would total 1,740,000 metric tons; in 1973, 2,120,000 metric tons— or converted to a short ton-base, to 1,920,000 and 2,335,000 tons, respectively.

Ecuador's sugar exports in 1968 and 1973, projected at the volumes and values detailed above, would represent the following export earnings in 1968 and 1973:

PROJECTED EXPORT EARNINGS IN SUGAR
FOR 1968 AND 1973

Exports to:	1968		1973	
	Volume (1,000 s.t.)	Value (million dollars)	Volume (1,000 s.t.)	Value (million dollars)
United States	69.9	$ 8.4	75.4	$ 7.5
Japan	23.5	2.8	29.0	2.9
Total	93.4	$11.2	104.4	$10.4

Rice

World Production, Trade, and Consumption

World rice production, excluding Communist Asia and the USSR, amounted to 150.4 million metric tons in the 1961-62 crop year, an increase of only 5,000 tons over the preceding season. Prior to this, output had increased at a rate of about 3 percent a year for the past decade. The prospects for 1962-63 were for larger crops in all producing regions as a result of greater acreage allotments, 2 million more than in 1961-62, and anticipated higher yields. Total production for the year was estimated at 153.2 million metric tons.

The leveling off of rice production in 1961-62 caused a shortage of supplies in the major exporting countries, and world trade declined in 1962 for the second successive year. Though output in the exporting countries was expected to be up an average of 5 percent in 1962-63, generally, production over the last decade has not kept pace with the increases in trade and consumption.

Excluding the Sino-Soviet area, rice exports rose from an average of 3.8 million metric tons of milled rice in calendar years 1951-55 to 5.5 million metric tons in 1961, an increase of 45 percent. In 1958, world production of rice exceeded consumption by 3.8 million metric tons. By 1962, this surplus had already been erased; in fact, several importing countries did not receive their full requirements and three leading exporters, Vietnam, Cambodia and the United Arab Republic limited export sales in order to conserve supplies for domestic consumption.

In 1961, the Asian countries accounted for 62 percent of world imports of rice. Among them, by far the largest importers are Indonesia, Malaya and Ceylon whose combined imports in 1961 represented 37 percent of the world total. In recent years, demand has been particularly strong in Indonesia—now accounting for one-sixth of world trade—owing to lagging production, internal distribution problems, and inflationary pressures which have impeded government procurement.

On the export side, three countries—Burma, Thailand, and the United States—supplied over two-thirds of all the rice entering world trade in 1961. Mainland China's exports in 1961 were about one-third of what they had been in the preceding five years, 850 million pounds as against an average of 2.5 billion for 1956-60. After three seasons of unfavorable growing conditions, the outlook for China is now more optimistic and expectations were that Chinese exports would recover somewhat in 1962, though not to the 1956-60 level of shipments.

Prices

Reduced supplies caused free market prices to rise sharply in the first half of 1962, while contract prices remained at their 1961 levels; on the whole, the general price level was expected to be about 10 percent higher than in 1961. As illustrated in the

following table, prices for rice entering private trade have
fluctuated widely and in 1962 were at their highest levels
since 1954. Contract prices, on the other hand, have remained relatively stable and, because of the volume of rice traded
under contracts, have prevented the world rice market from
showing more marked disequilibrium.

FAO EXPORT PRICE INDEX (1957-59 = 100)

	1957-58 Average	1959	1960	1961	Prelim. 1962
Private trade	104	92	83	95	110
Contract trade	101	99	95	97	97
Total trade	103	95	88	94	104

The contract system developed in its present form during
the postwar period of acute scarcity, when the assurance of
supplies was of vital concern to importing countries. While
the proportion of rice traded under contract has diminished as
world production has recovered, for various economic and
political reasons, a number of exporting and importing countries still regard the contract system as the most satisfactory
method of trading. In 1961-62 the volume of rice trade under
bilateral contracts amounted to 2.3 million metric tons, about
45 percent of world trade.

The Outlook for Rice

In general, the long term outlook for the world rice economy is clouded by the conflicting national policies of the rice
exporting and importing countries. If the trends of the past
decade were to continue throughout the 1960's, demand would
exceed production and, if at the same time prices remained
relatively unchanged, rice exporting countries would have
little difficulty finding markets. If, on the other hand, plans

in the traditional importing countries for achieving self-sufficiency in rice were realized, supplies would increase at a higher rate than consumption, tending toward a global surplus.

Export prospects for rice are further clouded by two facts: (1) the share of rice in total agricultural trade has diminished, from 3 percent to 2 percent during 1953-63 and (2) export earnings from rice did not improve during those ten years, despite increases in aggregate shipments. There has been a shift in the pattern of demand and most of the gain in the volume of exports in recent years was accounted for by the cheaper grades of milled and broken rice. Consequently, while there may be opportunities for further expansion of rice exports, the profitability of the grades involved does not appear favorable. The terms of trade for rice in relation to manufactured products has been declining since 1953; thus the exporting countries have suffered a "real" loss in terms of their purchasing power against the goods which they need to import.

The outlook with respect to various regions, as summarized in the January, 1963, issue of the FAO Monthly Bulletin of Agricultural Economics and Statistics, indicates that the opportunities for expanding exports to traditional Asian markets are limited by self-sufficiency policies, which have been enacted wherever growing conditions are suitable, and strict government controls on trading. Import markets in other areas are therefore becoming increasingly important. These are broken down into six regions (including 80 importing countries) as follows: Latin America, West Africa, the Near East, Western Europe, USSR, and Eastern Europe.

The combined imports of these areas, amounting to over 2 million metric tons a year, valued at $250 million and representing one-third of total world rice imports, have more than doubled in the past decade; for, although production has risen by 25 percent, consumption has increased by over 50 percent. Current consumption of rice in these 80 countries represents only about 3 percent of global consumption, but they are nevertheless important, because of the rate of growth in their

consumption, which has averaged 5 percent a year since
1950-52, and because they import such a high proportion of
their consumption requirements.

By 1970, the total population in these 80 countries is expected to increase by 13 percent over 1960. With improved
living standards, assuming prices remain relatively constant,
by 1970 consumption in these areas could increase by 1.5 to
2 million metric tons a year. The over-all outlook points to
increased import demand in West Africa, the Near East, and
Western Europe, while imports into Latin America and Eastern Europe are expected to fluctuate and may actually decline
if domestic production plans are realized.

The Outlook for Ecuador

In the period 1952-62 Ecuador's exports of rice have
fluctuated widely from a high of 57,183 tons in 1952 to a low
of 4,650 in 1962. Excluding 1962, which was unusually low,
the 5-year averages for the preceding decade compare as
follows: 1952-56, 28,591 metric tons; 1957-61, 25,683 metric
tons. In addition to year to year fluctuations in export
volumes, there have not really been any consistent markets
for Ecuadorian rice, appearing to indicate that importing
countries purchase rice from Ecuador only in years when
there is a shortage of supplies elsewhere or when domestic
production fails to meet demand.

Since 1954, almost all of Ecuador's export of rice have
been to Western Hemisphere countries. In the past few years,
Venezuela, which has been an erratic producer because of
plant disease, has been the major market, but recently,
through the introduction of disease-resistant varieties, high-
support prices and irrigation, production in that country has
risen sharply and now amply covers domestic needs. In
Colombia, Panama, and Costa Rica, which have been sporadic
but nevertheless important purchasers of Ecuadorian rice,
there have been substantial increases in domestic output as a
result of government support. Colombia, in fact, has already
achieved self-sufficiency. Thus, with so many of the Latin

American countries aiming at self-sufficiency, the outlook for
Ecuador expanding exports to this area does not look promising.
As regards prospects in the growing markets of the Neat East
and Africa, Ecuador's ability to compete in or even gain access
to these markets will depend on whether it succeeds in improving the quality standards of its exportable rice. Since measures
toward this end will require time to take effect no improvement
in the situation can be expected in the short run. Even maintenance of present volume and value levels will require active
measures.

For purposes of these projections it is assumed therefore
that rice exports will amount to $2 million in 1968 and $3
million in 1973.

Pyrethrum

World production of pyrethrum has traditionally been limited
to five or six countries and of these only three—Kenya, Tanganyika, and Ecuador—are currently producing sufficient quantities to make them important factors in the world market.

Kenya has for many years been the world's largest producer
and today provides over 80 percent of world supplies of pyrethrum. Its production in 1961-62 totaled 10,580 long tons of
flowers and its exports amounted to 8,694 long tons. In recent
years exports of extract have risen sharply; they rose from
172 long tons (valued at 1.3 million pounds sterling) in 1958,
to 737 long tons in 1962 (valued at 2.7 million pounds sterling).
Export of flowers, on the other hand, declined over the same
period—from 1,806 long tons (valued at 525,000 pounds sterling) to 1,521 long tons (valued at 440,000 pounds sterling).

Tanganyika, the second largest producer of pyrethrum, increased its production of flowers from 726 long tons in 1959-60
to 1,452 long tons in 1961-62, and it is estimated that its production by the end of 1962-63 will come close to 2,300 long
tons. In 1962 Tanganyika exported 33 long tons of extract,
valued at 253,715 pounds sterling—all to the United States.

Ecuador is the world's third major producer of pyrethrum.
Total area in production at the end of 1961 was estimated at
1,230 hectares, yielding a harvest for the year of 544 metric
tons. United States import data for 1961 show purchases of
294,000 pounds of flowers and 55,000 pounds of extract,
valued at $480,000 and for 1962, 238,000 pounds of flowers
and 53,000 pounds of extract, valued at $465,000. The drop
in Ecuador shipments in 1962 is accounted for by the fact
that a substantial part of current production was used for new
plantings, as a result of which 1963 production is expected to
double the 1962 level.

All the major producers continue to rely heavily on the
United States as a market for their output, although efforts
are being made, largely by the African producers, to extend
their sales areas. In 1962, United States imports of pyrethrum
(in all forms) were valued at $4.8 million, substantially below
the 1961 level of $6.4 million. But the trade estimates that
the United States market alone could expand by as much as 20
percent a year, with sales in 1965 approaching $15 million.

Since the United States has been Ecuador's principal outlet
for its exports of pyrethrum, the following assessment of its
prospective export earnings in 1968 and 1973 is limited to a
consideration of the potential of the United States market.

Ecuador's prospects for increasing its earnings from pyrethrum are most encouraging, partly as a result of the increasing demand for natural insecticides and partly because
of the uncertaintities with respect to production in Kenya,
since their independence. While it is not anticipated that
the political situation will deteriorate to the same extent
as in the Congo, there is, nevertheless, some doubt about
Kenya's economic stability. This prospect may explain why
Mitchell Cotts, Ltd. expanded their interests in Ecuador.

With this expansion in acreage planned by Mitchell Cotts, it
is estimated (by the U. S. Department of Agriculture) that
Ecuador's production in 1964 should reach 2,500 metric tons

of flowers. More recent estimates, obtained in Ecuador by the SRC team, indicate the possibility of reaching production levels of 4,500 metric tons in 1968 and 8,000 metric tons in 1973.

A major difficulty presents itself in attempting to assess the potential export volumes and values of these prospective production levels, for these reasons:

1. Ecuador's share of the United States market will depend on world supply, which cannot be predicted at this time in view of the uncertainties with respect to world production, arising from the unsettled political conditions in Africa.

2. In turn, because of the unpredictability of world supply, long-range price trends are conjectural at best.

3. Finally, no basis is available for estimation of the probable expansion of extraction facilities in the coming decade which, in turn, precludes estimates of separate export values for flowers and extract.

In the absence of a basis for projecting price trends of pyrethrum, the present price of about 40 cents a pound (flower basis) has been used in computing projected export values for Ecuador for 1968 and 1973, taking 4,500 metric tons for 1968 and 8,000 metric tons for 1973 as tonnage goals. Thus figured, export earnings would amount to roughly $4 million in 1968 and to $7 million in 1973.

Castor Beans and Castor Oil

Exports of castor beans have risen appreciably during the past decade. Shipments during 1957-61 averaged 10,870 metric tons, representing an average annual increase of 8.8 percent over the preceding five years. Export earnings in 1961 amounted to $2.2 million. Assuming the same rate of increase in tonnages shipped and constant prices, export earnings would reach $3. 6 million in 1968 and $5. 6 million in 1973. But even more significant increases may be expected. In view of the processing facilities which are planned for producing castor oil, combined exports of castor beans and oil could reach $4. 0 million in 1968 and $6. 5 million in 1973.

Abaca and Ramie

These two fibers give promise of developing into substantial export earners, under the guidance of a Japanese firm. The development of commercial plantations, however, is still in the initial stage and therefore there is no adequate basis at this time for prediction of production levels. The following export earnings may be considered as reasonable expectations: earnings from abaca—$500, 000 in 1968 and $1. 0 million in 1973; earnings from ramie—$1. 0 million in 1968 and $2. 0 million in 1973.

Fisheries Products

Ecuador's export earnings from its fisheries products have shown significant gains since their sharp upswing in 1955, when they first topped the $1 million level. In 1962, exports of fresh and frozen tuna and other fish, canned tuna, and frozen shrimp were valued at $4. 8 million, with shrimp accounting for roughly two-thirds of the total.

In the absence of data showing Ecuador's exports by country of destination, [9] an attempt was made to establish the relative

---

9. According to the available official sources, data on Ecuador's trade for major species by country of destination are available only for the first two quarters of 1962. These data, however, are subject to question because they represent export permits rather than records of actual exports. Moreover, it is believed that there is considerable contraband trade in shrimp and lobster, which of course is not reflected in the data.

importance of the U. S. market by relating U. S. import valuations to Ecuador's total export valuations of fisheries products
in the 5-year period, 1958-62, as detailed in the table on the
following page. These figures confirm the general view that
shipments to destinations other than the United States are relatively small, but they also disclose serious discrepancies. As
will be noted, U. S. import valuations exceed total Ecuador
export valuations for 1959, 1960, and 1962, with the disparity
particularly sharp in 1962—a difference of roughly $1.4 million
or about 28 percent. For the 5-year period, Ecuador import
valuations average $4.2 million, as compared with the U. S.
import valuation average of $4.5 million.

The available data indicate a very sharp upward trend in
exports of frozen and canned tuna (and other fish classified
with tuna) and a relative decrease in the proportionate share
of shrimp in export earnings from fisheries products. Export
earnings, therefore, are projected separately for the two
species. The following assumptions underlie the projections:

1. That the export value of frozen and canned tuna
    (and other fish classified with tuna) will increase
    at an average annual rate of 20 percent above
    their 1958-62 average of $1,228,000.

2. That the export value of shrimp and lobster will
    increase at an average annual rate of 5 percent over
    their 1958-62 average of $3,000,000.

Thus calculated, export earnings would reach the following
levels in 1968 and 1973.

	1968	1973
	(millions of dollars)	
Tuna and other fish	$3.1	$7.6
Shrimp and lobster	3.8	4.9
Total fisheries products	$6.9	$12.5

COMPARISON OF TOTAL ECUADOR EXPORTS AND U. S.
IMPORTS OF FISHERIES PRODUCTS, BY VALUE, 1958-62
(In Thousands of Dollars)

	Tuna Frozen[a]	Tuna Canned[b]	Other Fish Products[c]	Total Fish	Shrimp[d]	Tot:
1958						
Ecuador exports	141	340	3	484	3,667	4,1!
U. S. imports	160	205	-	365	3,122	3,4!
1959						
Ecuador exports	470	491	5	966	2,970	3,9:
U. S. imports	814	312	-	1,126	2,943	4,0(
1960						
Ecuador exports	346	507	5	858	2,737	3,5!
U. S. imports	878	445	-	1,323	2,793	4,1!
1961						
Eucador exports	510	1,673	4	2,187	2,541	4,7:
U. S. imports	649	882	-	1,531	2,986	4,5!
1962						
Ecuador exports	685	995	4	1,684	3,100	4,7!
U. S. imports	1,156	903	-	2,059	4,081	6,1.
1958-62 Avgs.						
Ecuador exports				1,228	3,000	4,2:
U. S. imports				1,280	3,169	4,4(

a. U. S. imports include tuna, yellow fin, skipjack, swordfis shite bass, and albacore.

b. U. S. imports include tuna, bonito, and types of fish NES (not elsewhere specified).

c. Ecuador exports include secondary fish products (mouths, intestines, etc.).

d. Ecuador exports include other crustaceans (crayfish, etc.)

Sources: U. S. export figures from official import statistics, Bureau of the Census, U. S. Department of Commerce; Ecuador export figures from 1962 Memoria del Gerente General del Banco Central.

An examination of possibilities with respect to whale oil does not indicate favorable prospects for Ecuador's entry into this market. Among the facts leading to this conclusion are:

1. The whaling catch is subject to quota control, under the International Whaling Convention. The five participating countries (Japan, Norway, the USSR, the United Kingdom, and the Netherlands) reached agreement in late 1962 on an over-all annual quota of 15,000 blue whale units, to be effective until the end of the 1965-66 season.

2. Participating countries also pledged themselves not to add to the total number of whaling factory ships operating in the Antarctic. This limitation was agreed to because the ever-increasing fleets were inflating costs and rendering the activity increasingly unprofitable.

3. As a result of over exploitation, prices have declined sharply. In 1962, the average price of whale oil fell to 45 pounds sterling per ton, the lowest level since 1945. At the peak of the market (in 1951) whale oil sold for 170 pounds sterling per ton.

Forestry Products

Traditionally, Ecuador's export earnings from its forest resources have derived from one product—balsa. Shipments reached their peak in 1957, when exports were valued at close to $2 million. Since then, however, there has been a steady erosion of earnings from this product; in 1962, exports were valued at $1.2 million.

In the light of the increasing use of plastics, which are displacing the use of balsa, the commercial value of this product is seriously threatened. As stated in Chapter 2, there are possibilities for new and increased uses of balsa, but a research program to that end would be required. In the absence of plans

for such a research program, there is no basis for projecting
these potential increases in balsa export earnings. On the
other hand, the unique qualities of this light wood will undoubtedly continue to be in demand. For projection purposes it appears reasonable to assume stabilization of balsa export earnings at $1 million for both 1968 and 1973—with full recognition
that an energetic search for new uses could materially increase
those levels.

In view of the beginning that has been made in exporting hardwoods, aggregate earnings from forest products may be expected to increase. Exports of hardwoods, which until 1962 had
been negligible, took a sharp upturn in 1962, when shipments
reached a value of 9.9 million sucres (a little over $0.5 million.)
Available information provides no basis for assessment of
future earnings. The composition of the 1962 hardwood exports,
for example, is not known; nor is it known to what extent those
exports might have represented an accumulation of exportable
supplies, in contrast to an expected flow. There appear, however, to be good prospects of developing export markets for
Ecuador's Cuangre O Virola and mangrove resources and from
the teakwood plantings, which are reported to be growing rapidly. Tropical hardwoods are in demand in both the United States
and Japan. There are many uncertainties, but $500,000 for
1968 and $1 million for 1973 appear to be reasonable expecta-
tions. This would mean aggregate export earnings from forestry products of $1.5 million in 1968 and $2 million in 1973.

Pharmaceutical Products

In the absence of full-scale information on production plans
for the various pharmaceutical products now being produced
for export and the prospective markets for which they are
intended, future export earnings from these products are projected at the levels indicated in the projections developed by
the Junta de Planificacion—i. e., $1.2 million in 1968 and
$1.4 million in 1973.

Miscellaneous Products

For other traditional products—Panama hats and other hand woven products made of toquilla straw, fresh fruits and conserves, tagua nuts, and numerous others of relatively minor importance—these over-all export earnings are assumed:

1968 — $5 million

1973 — $7 million

The prospective export earnings from the products reviewed above are tabulated in the following table.

PROSPECTIVE EXPORT EARNINGS:
TRADITIONAL PRODUCTS, 1968 AND 1973
(In Millions of Dollars)

	1968	1973
Bananas	$123.0	$137.5
Cacao	22.3	29.5
Coffee	28.4	34.2
Subtotal, "Big 3"	$173.7	$201.2
Sugar	11.2	10.4
Rice	2.0	3.0
Pyrethrum	4.0	7.0
Castor Beans and Castor Oil	4.0	6.5
Fibers (Abaca and Ramie	1.5	3.0
Fisheries Products	6.9	12.5
Forestry Products	1.5	2.0
Pharmaceutical Products	1.2	1.4
Miscellaneous Products	5.0	7.0
Subtotal, Other Traditional	$ 37.3	$ 52.8
Total Traditional	$211.0	$254.0

OTHER POTENTIAL EXPORT OPPORTUNITIES

The foregoing assessment of prospective export earnings has been limited to products and industries which are already established as export earners and, consequently, for which informational bases for quantified projections were available. But as was made clear in Chapters 3 and 4, there are numerous other potential export opportunities in the form of existing products which can be further developed for export or processed in Ecuador for export. It was also made clear in Chapter 4 that further export opportunities exist through the establishment of assembly industries to turn out finished products for the LAFTA markets, comparable to those already planned in Cuenca. There is, however, no basis for quantifying those prospects at this stage since their realization will be dependent on research, experimentation, and development programs not yet planned.

Finally, in Chapter 7 there was presented an analysis of the opportunity facing Ecuador under the programs envisaged by the Latin American Free Trade Association for the development of exports to the LAFTA countries of consumer goods, industrial materials, and capital goods components. These export opportunities would proceed from "complementarity agreements" to be drawn up under the aegis of LAFTA to lay the basis for exports from Ecuador (and other small LAFTA countries) in exchange for her imports of "integration industry" products— iron and steel, aluminum, ferro alloys, chemicals, machinery and equipment, and transport equipment—from the larger LAFTA countries. There is no basis for identifying these industries at this stage pending the further development of the Latin American integration movement, clarification of the role of Ecuador in LAFTA, multi-national negotiation under LAFTA of "complementarity agreements," and the consequent programming in Ecuador. In the light of present knowledge of plans for the Latin American integration movement, LAFTA export goals for Ecuador consistent with those plans are estimated at $24 million for 1968 and $43 million for 1973.

NEED FOR EXPORT DIVERSIFICATION

The Crux of the Problem

The prospect that Ecuador's traditional "big three" export products, which currently account for 85 percent of all exports, can be expected to increase by less than 5 percent a year in the period 1962-73 highlights the urgent need for export diversification if Ecuador is to achieve minimum acceptable targets for over-all economic growth.

During the decade of the 1950's export volume had increased at a rate of 9 percent a year and export value had grown at the somewhat lesser rate of 5 percent a year, sustaining an over-all rate of growth for the economy as a whole of 5 percent a year. The Ecuadorian national plan recognizes that the "big three" export products alone cannot be counted on to supply the basis for the future growth of the economy and places first priority on industrial development and diversification. Yet industrial development and diversification alone, especially of the order of magnitude proposed in the national plan, would not be sufficient to support an adequate rate of economic growth. In a growing small country economy, import demand usually rises at a faster rate than the over-all production of goods and services. If imports were to be confined to the limits permitted by an export growth rate of 4 percent, the share of industrial production that would have to be dedicated to new import substitution, alone, would be so great (equivalent to virtually half of all industrial output), that only a very small margin would remain to supply the needs of a growing population for industrial products. In fact, economic development and the expansion of industrial capacity would be hampered by severe restrictions on imports of capital goods. If it is to reach an over-all growth target of 5.5 percent[10] per year in the production of goods and services, Ecuador has no ready alternatives to the expansion of exports by diversification (that is, the addition of new export products, not the substitution of new for old).

---

10.   Now revised to 6.25 percent; see the footnote on p. 202.

Minimum Import Needs

A 5 percent annual rate of growth for imports would make possible the accommodation of a growing Ecuadorian economy in the process of industrial development and diversification to a declining role of imports in the over-all economy. (See tables on pages 253 and 254.)

Industrial development and diversification would complement import demand, which ordinarily tends to rise even more rapidly than exports. In these circumstances, the composition of imports can be expected to change, with a rising share going to capital goods and fuel imports and a smaller share going to imports of consumer goods and raw materials and industrial supplies. (See table on page 254.) In order to permit a doubling of capital goods imports, for example, no appreciable increase in the total volume of consumer goods imports could be expected. The share of capital goods imports, in relation to total imports, would rise from 44 percent in 1960 to 50 percent in 1973, whereas the share of nondurable consumer goods imports would fall from 16 percent in 1960 to 11 percent in 1973. (Nevertheless, the potential expansion of Ecuador's imports, which would increase by roughly two-thirds between 1962 and 1973, would provide an attractive new, though small, market for Latin American and other countries, as will be shown in the following section of this chapter.)

The incidence of a 5 percent growth rate for imports and its compatibility with an expanding Ecuadorian economy are best seen in a comparison of the changing coefficient of imports in relation to the production of goods and services in the economy as a whole, as well as in relation to investment, consumption, and industrial production. As indicated in the table on page 256, imports rose in relation to the gross product from 10 percent in 1950 to 12 percent in 1962, providing a firm base for the appreciable growth in output experienced in the decade of the 1950's. In the long term, to 1973, a growing Ecuadorian economy could accommodate itself to a decline in the import coefficient to 11 percent, although this would require an impressive industrial development effort, import substitution, and change in the composition of imports.

COMPOSITION OF ECUADOR'S IMPORTS: 1950, 1960, AND 1962;
PROJECTIONS FOR 1968 AND 1973
(In Millions of Dollars at 1960 Prices)

	Total	Consumer Goods (nondurable)	Consumer Goods (durable)	Fuels	Raw Materials and Supplies	Capital Goods
Imports (f.o.b.)						
1950	47.8	8.8	3.2	0.8	14.4	20.6
1960	102.2	16.6	5.9	4.3	30.7	44.7
1962	96.2	16.0	6.0	5.0	29.0	40.2
Projections						
1968	128.9	17.4	6.4	7.1	37.4	60.6
1973	164.5	18.6	7.4	11.5	44.8	82.2
Percent Avg. Annual Increase						
1950-60	7.9	6.6	6.3	18.3	7.9	8.1
1962-68	5.0	1.4	1.1	6.0	4.3	7.1
1968-73	5.0	1.3	3.0	10.1	3.7	6.3
1962-73	5.0	1.4	1.9	7.9	4.0	6.7
Percent Distribution						
1950	100.0	18.4	6.6	1.6	30.2	43.1
1960	100.0	16.2	5.8	4.2	30.0	43.8
1968	100.0	13.5	5.0	5.5	29.0	47.0
1973	100.0	11.3	4.5	7.0	27.2	50.0

Sources: Banco Central del Ecuador; SRC staff.

IMPACT OF A 5-PERCENT GROWTH RATE FOR IMPORTS ON THE ECUADORIAN ECONOMY,
1968-73
(Import Coefficients[a] in Percent)

Year	Total Imports in Relation to Gross Product	Imports of Capital Goods in Relation to Investment	Imports of Consumer Goods in Relation to Consumption	Imports of Fuel, Raw Materials and Supplies in Relation to Industrial Production
1950	10.3	41.2	3.1	17.6
1960	13.7	38.2	3.6	25.5
1962	12.1	33.6	3.2	24.6
Projections				
1968	11.7	30.6	2.7	19.2
1973	11.5	28.6	2.3	16.9

a. The coefficient of imports in relation to gross product, investment, consumption, and industrial production.

Capital goods imports, which accounted for 41 percent of total investment in 1950 and 34 percent in 1962, would be reduced to 29 percent in 1973, as a doubling of the volume of investment would be achieved with a marginally greater share of machinery and equipment requirements to be produced in Ecuador. Imports of fuel, raw materials, and industrial supplies had increased notably, in relation to industrial production, from 18 percent in 1950 to 25 percent in 1962, reflecting the significant process of industrial development experienced in the decade of the 1950's. For the future, to 1973, the proportion of fuel and industrial materials imports, in relation to industrial production, would have to be reduced to 17 percent if an over-all 5 percent annual growth rate in imports is to be compatible with over-all economic growth. This is possible, but will require a major industrial development and import substitution effort.

In essence, it may be concluded that a 5 percent growth rate for imports is compatible with over-all economic growth goals. A 3 percent import growth rate, on the other hand, would limit capital goods imports, as well as fuel and industrial materials imports, to such an extent as to be incompatible with economic growth targets for a 5.5 percent[11] annual rate of growth in the production of goods and services.

Industrial Production for Exports, Import
Substitution, and Growth

Industrial development in Ecuador, in the period of 1973, has the formidable but attainable task of achieving a rapid rate of expansion to provide a broadly diverse range of products to satisfy growth in population and per capita income, substitution of imports, and substantial new exports within the framework of the evolution of Latin American economic integration. (See table on page 256.) Industrial production targets, as a whole, call for a 67 percent increase by 1968 and a 140 percent increase by 1973, representing an annual growth rate of 7.6 percent.

11. Now revised to 6.25 percent; see footnote on page 202.

ECUADOR'S REQUIREMENTS FOR INDUSTRIAL DEVELOPMENT: 1961-73

(Value in Millions of Sucres at 1961 Prices)

		Industrial Production		
	Total	Domestic Consumption	Import Substitution (new)[a]	Export Demand for Integration Products
1961	2,603	2,553	--	50
1968	4,347	2,956	891	500
1973	6,269	3,563	1,846	860
Percent Avg. Annual Increase				
1961-68	7.6	2.1	--	39.0
1968-73	7.6	3.8	15.7	11.5
1961-72	7.6	2.8	--	27.0
Percent Composition				
1961	100.0	98.1	--	1.9
1968	100.0	68.0	20.5	11.5
1973	100.0	56.8	29.4	13.7

a. Assumes gross product growth rate of 5.5 percent* per year; import demand growth rate of 8.3 percent (with an elasticity coefficient of 1.5), and import capacity of 5.0 percent a year, requiring import substitution equivalent to an import growth rate of 3.3 percent per year. If import capacity were to rise at only 3.0 percent a year, the requirements for import substitution would be equivalent to an import growth of 5.3 percent a year.

* See footnote on page 202.

Sources: Junta Nacional de Planificacion; SRC staff.

256

The Junta de Planificacion and the Centro de Desarrollo
have been carrying out an intensive program of industrial
project preparation and development in the fields of consumer
goods and industrial materials, covering the broad range of
products required for an expanding Ecuadorian economy and
the substitution of imports. The preparation and promotion of
projects for new industrial products for export remains to be
developed, however. Some of the implications of these industrial development targets in relation to a minimum growth
rate of 5 percent would be that by 1973, for example, approximately 30 percent of industrial production would be dedicated
to net new import substitution; and new industrial exports, in
the framework of Latin American economic integration, would
account for 14 percent of industrial production. In combination,
industrial production for substitution of imports and for new
exports would make up 43 percent of all industrial output. Both
of these targets would have to be achieved if an expanding
Ecuadorian economy is to accommodate to a 5 percent growth
rate for imports. If production for import substitution or exports were to expand with a lesser growth, the Ecuadorian
economy would be faced with an inadequate supply of imports
of industrial materials and capital goods.

Export Targets

The minimum requirements of an expanding Ecuadorian
economy for imports highlight the urgent need for development
of substantial new exports. In comparison with the perspective
for less than 5 percent annual rate of growth for traditional
"big three" exports, it may be estimated that Ecuador needs
an over-all export growth of at least 5 percent a year, to 1973,
to support minimum import needs within the framework of a
growing economy and equilibrium in the balance of payments.
(See table on page 258.)

PROJECTIONS

COMPOSITION OF ECUADOR'S EXPORTS: 1950, 1960, AND 1962:
OF TRADITIONAL EXPORTS AND TARGETS FOR LAFTA EXPORTS, 1968 AND 1973
(In Millions of Dollars)

	Total	Bananas	Cacao	Coffee	Other Traditional Export Products	LAFTA Integration Products
1959a	59.7	16.7	16.1	14.2	12.7	
1960	146.2	88.9	21.4	21.9	13.9	
1962	142.9	82.9	15.7	20.9	23.4	
Projections						
1968	234.9	123.0	22.3	28.4	37.3	23.9
1973	297.1	137.5	29.5	34.2	52.8	43.1
Avg. Annual Rate of Growth Percent						
1950 to 1960	9.3	9.3	2.9	4.4	0.9	
1962 to 1968	8.6b	6.8	6.0	5.2	8.1	
1968 to 1973	4.8c	2.3	5.8	3.8	7.2	12.5
1962 to 1973	6.9d	4.7	5.9	4.6	7.7	
Percent Distribution						
1950	100.0	28.0	27.0	23.8	21.2	
1960	100.0	60.8	14.6	15.0	9.5	
1962	100.0	58.0	11.0	14.6	16.4	
1968	100.0	52.3	9.5	12.1	15.9	10.2
1973	100.0	46.3	9.9	11.5	17.8	14.5

a. At 1960 prices.

b. The annual rate of growth for traditional export products ($211.0 million) would be 6.7 percent.

c. The annual rate of growth for traditional export products ($254.0 million) would be 3.8 percent.

d. The annual rate of growth for traditional exports would be 5.4 percent.

258

EXPORT POSSIBILITIES IN THE LATIN AMERICAN
INTEGRATION MOVEMENT

The Integration Perspective

The Latin American economic integration movement may
make significant progress in the next ten years. The Latin
American Free Trade Association, which is only six years old,
already is credited with some accomplishments, and there is a
widespread hope that it may become a major force in shaping
the development of the economies of Latin America. Leading
authorities engaged in the effort to accelerate the economic
development of Latin America believe that free trade is not
enough—that a special drive must be undertaken to program the
development of the new Latin American "integration industries."
These integration industries are those new industries whose
optimum development requires an investment and production
focus geared to a multi-national market—iron and steel, aluminum, ferro alloys, chemicals, machinery and equipment,
and transport equipment.

A key to the programming of Latin American integration industries lies in the development of "complementarity agreements," on the style of the European Iron and Steel Community
and the European Coal Community. For the smaller countries,
it is envisaged that the "complementarity agreements" would
provide a counterpart market to match their incremental market
for integration industry products. The smaller countries, such
as Ecuador, which can be expected to provide a small but significant market for integration industry products, would be
assisted in developing export programs for specialized types of
consumer durable goods, industrial materials, and capital goods
components, which have a high income elasticity of demand in
comparison with the perspective for its traditional export
products. A goal for Ecuador would be to achieve new industrial exports of $40 million to $50 million over the next ten
years. Within the context of a potential expansion of intraregional trade from the present level of approximately $1
billion to a 1975 level of more than $6 billion, this should be
possible, although a major programming effort would be
required.

Integration Industry Programming

Intraregional trade has already been raised from an estimated $700 million in 1959 to $1,000 million in 1962, from approximately 7 percent to roughly 10 percent of the total trade of the region. LAFTA has been effective in providing a forum for the study of common problems and opportunities. A beginning has been made in the lowering of tariff barriers between countries and a number of small shifts have occured in trading patterns. Despite the many difficulties that lie ahead, there is the general hope that the Association will hold together and will exert a growing influence on the economic development of Latin America.

The perspective for Latin American economic growth within the framework of economic integration is impressive. With an expected growth in population of almost 50 percent over the present level of more than 200 million to a level of approximately 300 million in 1975, the production of goods and services would rise from the 1960 level to $78,000 million to a 1975 level of $172 billion, an increase of 120 percent, if the Alliance for Progress growth targets are achieved. (See table on page 261.) Investment in the region would expand from $13,000 million to $40,000 million over the period.

Such magnitudes of growth would signify a much greater rate of expansion in integration industry production, as a consequence of high demand elasticities, as well as the substitution of a margin of extraregional imports. Production of machinery and equipment may be expected to rise from the 1960 level of approximately $1,000 million to $7,000 million in 1975. Steel output would increase from 5 million to 24 million metric tons over this period. Motor vehicle production would expand from a 1961 level of 356,000 units to 1,300,000 units in 1975. Paper and paperboard output would grow from the 1961 level of 1,874 thousand metric tons to 8,000 thousand metric tons. Even the production of cotton yarn and textiles, not considered as an integration industry product, would experience a growth from

PERSPECTIVES FOR LATIN AMERICAN ECONOMIC GROWTH
CONSONANT WITH INDUSTRIAL DIVERSIFICATION AND INTEGRATION, 1960-75
(Values at 1960 Prices)

	1960	1975	Increment		Percent Annual Average Increase
			Amount	Percent	
Population (in millions)	199.0	292.0	93.0	46.7	2.6
Gross domestic product (billion dollars)	78.4	172.5	94.1	120.0	5.4
Gross domestic investment (billion dollars)	12.8	40.3	27.5	214.8	8.0
Production:					
Machinery & equipment (billion dollars)	1	7	6	600	13.9
Steel (m.t. finished product equiv.)	5	24	19	380	11.0
Motor vehicles (thousand units)	356[a]	1,300	944	265	9.0
Paper & paperboard (thousand m.t.)	1,874[a]	8,000	6,126	327	10.2
Cotton yarn & textiles (thousand m.t.)	537	1,655	1,118	208	7.8

a. 1961.

Source: United Nations Economic Commission for Latin America, The Latin American Common Market: 1959, and later studies.

537 thousand metric tons in 1960 to 1,655 thousand metric tons in 1975. [12]

Above all, Latin American intraregional trade would expand from the 1962 level of $1,050 million to $6,650 million in 1975 if economic integration targets are achieved. (See table below.) Finally, intraregional trade would account for one-third of all Latin American trade in 1975 compared with its present share of 10 percent.

LATIN AMERICA AND ECUADOR:
PERSPECTIVES FOR TRADE DEVELOPMENT
(In Millions of Dollars)

| | Exports | | Imports |
	Total	Intraregional	Extraregional
Latin America			
1962	10,550	1,050	9,570
1975	20,120	6,650	11,800
Ecuador			
1962	143	10	88
1973	297	60	104

The Latin American Economic and Social Council, it is reported, will promote the study of the evolution of a free trade area to a common market, the need for regionwide planning, the requirements for regional infrastructure projects, and cooperative arrangements towards integration, and the development and use of natural resources on a regional basis.

12. See The Latin American Common Market, United Nations Economic Commission for Latin America (Santiago, Chile, 1959).

Special studies will be made of the integration industries from the viewpoint of requirements for a planned complementary expansion within an enlarged regional market. Investigation of concrete industrial opportunities for the smaller countries will be promoted with a view to overcoming or reducing the inevitable inequality which, in the short run, would arise from a reciprocity that tends to favor the larger, better endowed countries. Specific feasibility studies, within this framework, would be undertaken. Such a regionwide planning framework would help individual countries to program their own development, in keeping with the requirements of an evolving regional economic integration.

Ecuador's Opportunity

Ecuador's requirements for machinery and equipment would total an estimated $76 million in 1973, compared with the 1962 level of $32 million. (See table on page 264.) Requirements for transport equipment would amount to $46 million, in comparison with the 1962 level of $19 million. The need for motor vehicles would rise to more than 4,000 units per year. Steel utilization would reach 260,000 metric tons per year (as estimated by ECLA, in The Latin American Common Market, in 1959).

These integration industry products, many of which could be imported from other Latin American countries, provide the basis for the programming of complementarity agreements. Ecuador must now seriously program the production and export of new industrial products within the framework of Latin American integration.

At the present time, Ecuador's intraregional trade accounts for only 7 percent of Ecuador's exports. A goal would be to achieve $40 to $50 million of new industrial exports, and a total level of intraregional trade of about $60 million with a view to raising the intraregional trade share to one-fifth of total trade. (See table on page 261.) The programming for these goals warrants high priority.

ECUADOR'S PROJECTED REQUIREMENTS FOR
SELECTED PRODUCTS: 1962-73
(Values at 1960 Prices)

Product	1962	1973
Transportation equipment (million dollars)	19	46
Machinery and other equipment (million dollars)	32	76
Automotive vehicles (thousand units):		
Stock	24	46
Annual demand	n. a.	4
Steel (thousand metric tons)	n. a.	260

Source: United Nations Economic Commission for Latin
America.

CONCLUSION

A telescopic view of the findings of this study with respect to
the outlook for Ecuador's exports for 1968 and 1973 is presented
in the table on the following page, which highlights the following
significant prospects:

1. The "big three" are expected to show substantial gains
   in the aggregate (4.9 percent from 1962 to 1973) but are
   expected to decrease somewhat in relative importance.
   Bananas, cacao, and coffee combined, it is estimated,
   will have dropped to 73.9 percent of prospective total
   earnings in 1968 (as against 83.6 percent in 1962) and to
   67.7 percent in 1973.

2. Other exports, including products projected to move in
   the LAFTA trade, are expected to assume increasing
   importance. Their share of export earnings is projected
   at 26.1 percent in 1968 and 32.3 percent in 1973.

3. Traditional exports in total are expected to grow at an
   average annual rate of 5.4 percent in the period 1962-73;
   and aggregate exports, at a rate of 6.9 percent per annum.

PROSPECTIVE EXPORT EARNINGS FROM TRADITIONAL AND OTHER PRODUCTS,
1968 AND 1973 COMPARED WITH 1962
(In Millions of Dollars)

	1962		1968		1973	
	Value	Percent of Total	Value	Percent of Total	Value	Percent of Total
Traditional Exports						
Bananas	$ 82.9	58.0	$123.0	52.3	$137.5	46.3
Cacao	15.7	11.0	22.3	9.5	29.5	9.9
Coffee	20.9	14.6	28.4	12.1	34.2	11.5
Combined "Big Three"	(119.5)	(83.6)	(173.7)	(73.9)	(201.2)	(67.7)
Other	23.4	16.4	37.3	15.9	52.8	17.8
Total Traditional Exports	$142.9	100.0	$211.0	89.8	$254.0	85.5
LAFTA Trade	--	--	23.9	10.2	43.1	14.5
GRAND TOTAL	$142.9	100.0	$234.9	100.0	$297.1	100.0

Percent Annual Rate of Growth	Traditional Exports	Aggregate Exports
1962 to 1968	6.7	8.6
1968 to 1973	3.8	4.8
1962 to 1973	5.4	6.9

265

FINDINGS

Export Pattern

Agricultural products account for about 94 percent of Ecuador's exports of about $140 million; fisheries products about 4 percent; manufactures and minerals about 2 percent; and forest products under 1 percent. Bananas, cacao, and coffee have aggregated from 84 to 90 percent.

The United States has taken about 59 percent of Ecuador's exports, Europe 30 percent, and Latin America 9 percent. In the last several years Japan has developed into a growing market for Ecuador's bananas and cacao.

Dollar value of Ecuador's exports has risen since 1953 but bananas have been responsible, cacao and coffee export values falling because of lower prices and rice exports falling sharply in tonnage. Marginal exports have doubled their share in five years but remain at about $23 million. By contrast, banana exports, in which Ecuador leads the world, aggregate $83 million.

Production Base for Present Exports

Ecuador has ample lands of good quality accessible to the sea and low-cost labor to support output of bananas, cacao, coffee, sugar, and rice several times larger than the present export volumes of each of these crops.

Rich fishing grounds and low-cost labor are likewise the factors behind the growing fisheries products industry; growing

production and exports of pyrethrum are based on the highly
suitable soils of the high Andean paramos and low-cost labor.

From the standpoint of comparative production costs and
availability of a suitable natural resource base, Ecuador is in
a highly favorable position for expanding the output and exports
of bananas, cacao, coffee, sugar, rice, pyrethrum, and fisheries products. It now appears that only coffee exports will be
limited by quota, but their proceeds can be improved markedly
by better handling and grading, thereby raising quality and
prices.

Diversification is highly desirable as a means to both expansion of total exports and the minimizing of risks. It is also
essential in view of the outlook for limited growth in the markets
for Ecuador's existing principal exports. However, it should be
achieved by adding output and export of new products to the existing base of traditional exports rather than by developing new
exports at the cost of neglecting opportunities for expansion of
traditional exports. Where choices must be made to devote
land and scarce capital and technical and managerial skills to
one product rather than another, the risk-reducing advantages
of diversification must be weighed carefully against the advantages inherent in expanding exports of products for which production and distribution know-how already exist in the country,
and for which the required increments of capital and other resources would probably bring more results and faster than the
same resources devoted to a new industry.

Production Prospects for New Exports

Cattle for Beef Production

The coastal zone of Ecuador has ample lands suitable for
beef production, even assuming a marked expansion of acreage
devoted to bananas, cacao, sugar, and rice. Conversion of the
present area of about 350,000 hectares of natural pastures to
improved pastures growing such grasses as guinea grass or
elephant grass—proven both at the Pichilingue Experiment
Station and on coastal farms—would provide sufficient pasture-

lands to support more than one million head of beef cattle, or
a twofold expansion in beef production in the Costa. With development of another 150, 000 hectares of cultivated pastures,
the herd could be raised to 1.5 million head. Still further and
significant possibilities for beef production exist in the southern
Sierra provinces of Azuay and Loja and in the upland sections of
El Oro Province. In all of these areas Ecuador has the advantage
of an open climate and soils and rainfall sufficient to yield excellent pastures at low cost. These advantages point to a potential for a new export industry of major proportions.

Pork Production

Both pork production and pork consumption have been rising
very rapidly but projections indicate the possibility of achieving
a significant margin to support an export industry in cured hams,
bacon, and sausages.

Dairy Production

This industry is already well established in the lush year-
round pasturelands of the cool and temperate Sierra, and enormous progress has been made over the past two or three decades
in importation of Holstein-Friesian cattle, thereby increasing
the yield of milk per cow several-fold. Despite the growing
domestic consumption of dairy products and the present imports
of about 6 percent, there is a good base for expansion of milk
production to permit the export of butter, cheese, and powdered milk. All of these products are now successfully produced at
relatively low cost.

Fiber Production

Production of cordage from the widely distributed cabuya, or
agave, plant has long been a home industry. The recent establishment of a large cordage and burlap plant at Guayaquil and the
highly successful experiments at Pichilingue and Santo Domingo
with abaca and ramie by a widely experienced Japanese company
now point toward production for export of about 8, 000 tons of
fibers to yield around $2 million.

Tobacco Production

Experimental plantings under the technical guidance of the
American Tobacco Company have shown that regular and shade-
grown types of tobacco can be grown successfully in Ecuador;
and that company is now trying to develop an industry to replace
the imports formerly obtained from Cuba. If these efforts are
successful, a new foreign exchange earner rivaling cacao or
coffee can develop in a decade or so.

Vegetable Oils

Despite the good prospects for expanding production of
African oil palm, peanuts, and cottonseed, rising domestic
consumption now requiring imports annually of around $3-4
million may leave no margin for export. It will be of foreign
exchange significance, however, if production can supply
domestic needs or even a material part thereof. A continuation of the rate of increase of imports of edible oils over the
past seven years would require about $16 million of foreign
exchange to cover such imports by 1973.

Forestry Products

Ecuador has enormous areas of virgin forests but they are
largely inaccessible under current conditions, and of uncertain
commercial value. There can be development for export ultimately, especially of tropical hardwoods, but apart from balsa,
lumber production has been mainly for the national market.
Small amounts of wild rubber are occasionally exported, and
the Italconsult Mission rubber expert has concluded that rubber
can be grown economically in Ecuador on a commercial scale
for both domestic needs and export. Something like twelve
years of development would be required, however, to obtain
any significant output. Prospects for earlier development
would be brighter if an existing major rubber producing firm
with trained technicians could be interested.

Other Products

Ecuador, with its wide range of climates, produces practically all the tropical, subtropical, and temperate zone fruits and likewise the usual temperate zone vegetables as well as the tuber crops such as white potatoes, yams, and yucca. Both ample lands of good quality and low-cost labor are available for marked expansion if needed.

Cotton is grown in Ecuador, and large areas with suitable soil and climatic conditions are available for expansion. It is unlikely, however, that expansion over the next ten years will do more than meet the needs of the domestic textile industry, given the higher returns available from alternative products.

Processing for Export

Ecuador's present exports consist almost exclusively of raw materials and chiefly farm crops, with processed materials amounting to no more than 3 or 4 percent of the total. The only sizable and rapidly growing processed items chiefly designed for export are fisheries products, canned and frozen tuna, and frozen cleaned shrimp.

By all feasible means Ecuador must seek to expand its traditional exports, but the new and beckoning opportunity is that of developing industries to process the nation's resources and thereby multiply the values involved. To export also the skills of its people in fashioning its materials and crops is to increase significantly Ecuador's "take" from the sale of the products of its farms, fisheries, and forests.

The opportunities in Ecuador for expanding present exports of processed materials and developing new processed products for export are many and favorable, for Ecuador enjoys many comparative advantages. Her present significant position in the export of farm crops is based fundamentally on an abundant supply of fertile lands, a long growing and harvesting season, and competent labor at rates among the lowest in the world. Rich fishing grounds fed by the Pacific currents, year-round fishing, and low labor rates similarly account for Ecuador's growing exports of fisheries products.

These same factors will be equally, if not more, significant in the development of processing industries for the export trade. Moreover, these comparative advantages are lasting ones—the inherent advantages of soil and climate and the durable advantages of low labor rates. Wage rates in Ecuador will rise from their present low levels as economic development and productivity progress, but so will wage rates in competing countries. It remains to be seen to what extent the present gap, compared with the developed countries, can be narrowed; and—to cite a hypothetical example—even if wage rates should rise twice as fast in Ecuador as in the United States, the cost advantage in Ecuador would still be spectacular twenty-five years hence.

It must be recognized that world markets have their limits and that access to those markets is generally based on the achievement of costs as low as or lower than those of competing exporters. In consequence, the development of processing industries for export should be confined to those products for which there is a clear case of comparative international advantage. In seeking to enter world markets for new processed products, Ecuador must exploit the same prime advantage of low costs which has underlain the success of her traditional exports. If her costs are significantly lower for a given quality than those of her competitors, Ecuador can find a place even in crowded markets; and here one of Ecuador's advantages lies in her relatively small size.

Many things must be done to exploit Ecuador's potentials. There must be efficient organization and management, clear command of technical know-how for both production and marketing, and adequate capital. All these resources are in short supply in Ecuador. Perhaps the most severe limiting factor is the shortage of capital, but of almost equal significance is the shortage of skilled technicians and managerial personnel for new ventures. These limiting factors will yield only slowly, but there are possibilities of overcoming both for more rapid development by attracting foreign capital for joint investment or otherwise and attracting foreign technicians and managers for the necessary period of training nationals.

Several approaches may be taken in initiating a new industry requiring extensive capital and technology. The operation may begin on a small scale, with local capital and personnel, and develop gradually as capital, technical know-how, and markets grow. A second possibility is to purchase technology abroad, provide the capital locally, and develop the market. A third possibility, which can bring full-scale results almost overnight, is to invite from abroad a reputable company which is already established in the production of the commodity, to bring in the capital, equipment, and technology to produce and market the product and train nationals, with such local ownership participation as may be feasible.

Major Opportunities for Processing for Export

Banana Products

Only about 38 percent of Ecuador's banana crop of about 75 million stems is exported; 50 percent is left on the farms; and 12 percent is rejected at the ports. The stems not exported are generally sold at from 1 to 3 sucres a stem for domestic consumption, for present limited processing, or for animal feed, although many stems are wasted or never harvested. Vast quantities are available for processing at a cost of about 0. 2 to 0. 3 cents a pound. The present utilization and marketing are indeed so wasteful that not more than 1 percent of the materials that can be utilized for other than fresh fruit export is actually used.

It is estimated that the value of present unutilized or waste products could approach the value of the exported banana themselves. Full utilization of the rejected bananas, as well as the peels, stalks, and trunks, would involve processing of puree and dehydrated bananas and chips; manufacture of animal feed; extraction of chemical components; and the manufacture of paper and cardboard.

Meat Products

The export of meat products could develop into Ecuador's second most important export. Availability of vast land areas

which will produce meat on improved pastures at a feeding
cost of about $0.85 per 100 kilograms is the primary basis for
this estimate. An integrated meat-processing operation in
such a location as the Upano River Valley east of Cuenca, with
facilities for packing, freezing, and processing could develop
a $20-$25 million export of frozen, canned, smoked, and cured
beef products plus a by-product industry of hides, tallow,
fertilizers, and pharmaceuticals. Even greater potentialities
exist in the Costa zone for the development of several such meat
industry complexes, possibly through bringing together a number of firms already raising cattle on fairly large tracts. These
potentialities would place Ecuador as a beef exporter in a size-
class with such countries as Denmark and Uruguay. A major
effort would be required in experimentation; in technical
assistance to producers; in investment in improved pastures,
increased and improved herds, and development of processing
and marketing facilities. All phases of this effort would have to
rest on technical know-how and experienced managerial competence.

Export of pork products is more problematical because of
the sharp rise in pork consumption. If the rate of increase in
pork production since 1955 should continue to 1973, however,
there is the possibility of a surplus over projected domestic
consumption of around 30 million pounds. Converted into
cured hams, bacon, and sausages for the Latin American
market at about 10 sucres per pound, this would realize foreign
exchange earnings of about $17 million.

Dairy Products

Although Ecuador is currently importing about 6 percent of
her consumption of dairy products, the prospects for developing a substantial export industry are excellent. In the lush
year-round pastures of the Andean highlands, milk is now sold
to dairies at about 5.5 cents a liter and can be produced at
under 4 cents a liter, compared with 7.5 cents in Wisconsin
and 5 to 6 cents in Denmark, the most efficient producers in
the United States and Europe, respectively. The processing
industry already exists and is producing excellent butter,

cheese, and powdered milk at attractive prices that would be highly competitive not only in neighboring Latin America but in many other markets as well.

Fisheries Products

Canning of tuna and freezing of peeled and cleaned shrimp are already a substantial industry based largely on exports of around $5 million. This export business can be expanded several-fold by the provision of capital and technical assistance for modernizing and enlarging the fishing fleet, building needed processing and marketing facilities, and improving the efficiency of fishing and processing methods. Although the close-to-shore shrimp beds up to a depth of 20 fathoms are already being fully exploited, there is the opportunity of increasing the catch substantially by fishing beyond the 20-fathom depth, and such catches are likely to be of the larger and more expensive species. And some close-to-shore fishing grounds, such as Porto Lopez, are not being exploited primarily because of the absence of access roads and fresh water. The yellow-fin tuna is thought to be fished currently more heavily, perhaps, than is desirable, but the smaller skipjack tuna can be exploited considerably more.

Sugar Cane

The present high price for sugar, the low cost of production in Ecuador of around 2. 75 cents a pound, and the availability of larger sugar quotas from the United States strongly suggest the possibility of diverting more cane to sugar production for export or increased plantings. Of the approximately 52, 000 hectares in cane production, it appears that 20, 000 are devoted to sugar, some 26, 000 hectares being used for production of panela and 6, 500 for aguardiente and other liquors. Of 1962 sugar production of 150, 000, exports were 62, 000 tons. Capacity of existing refineries is about 240, 000 tons.

Alcohol from cane juice and various alcoholic beverages offer further export possibilities, based on the very low cost of production of alcohol in Ecuador.

Fruits for Processing

Ecuador's tropical, subtropical, and temperate zone fruits offer significant opportunities for processing industries for the export trade, based primarily on the very low costs of production. Examples are pineapple for frozen concentrates now, to be used as a base for fruit drinks, ultimately also as a canned product after establishment of a specific variety of uniform size, color, and other quality specifications; oranges for frozen concentrates; naranjilla, an Ecuadorian fruit having a delicious and exotic flavor, perhaps for a frozen concentrate. Others, such as papaya, mango, chirimoya, tree tomato, are delicious fruits but not enough is known of their possibilities for processing.

These tropical and subtropical fruits, as well as the usual temperate zone fruits that are grown in the Sierra, would also lend themselves to processing in the form of jams, jellies, and preserves. In some areas of Ecuador, fruit and cane grow almost side by side, thereby offering the possibility of evaporating down cane juice with fruit or fruit juices without the necessity of first refining the sugar. Such jams, jellies, and preserves could be manufactured in Ecuador at only a fraction of the costs in almost any other area of the world.

Temperate Zone Vegetables

Temperate zone vegetables grown in the Sierra give high promise for freezing or canning at extremely low costs. Examples are tomatoes, peas, green beans, asparagus, cauliflower, broccoli, brussels sprouts, and lima beans. Onions and garlic for dehydration are other good prospects. One marked advantage, apart from the salient advantage of good farm labor at very low rates, is the long harvesting season, leading to the need for only a fraction of the equipment required for similar operations in four-seasons temperate zones with a harvesting season of only a few weeks.

Chocolate and Other Confections

Ecuador has a uniquely favorable situation in which all the main ingredients are available locally at only a fraction of the costs prevailing in the major chocolate manufacturing countries. A manufacturer of chocolate in Guayaquil can purchase whole milk powder from the Sierra at 33 cents a pound, skim milk poweder at 22 cents, sugar for confectionery use at 6 cents, and good quality flavor cacao at 24 cents. With such low raw material prices and low labor cost, good quality chocolates made in Ecuador and attractively packaged could compete successfully anywhere in the world.

Containers

Packaging materials used to contain the various export products constitute export items themselves, and the added value can be very substantial if these containers can be made in Ecuador from Ecuadorian raw materials. Moreover, many containers can probably be made from banana fiber and sugar cane bagasse, both available in Ecuador in great volumes at little or no cost. Corrugated cardboard boxes could be made from such paper for shipping bananas and other products; and perhaps such containers could be fabricated even more cheaply by molding or compression.

Glass bottles will need to be manufactured in Ecuador as exports of bottled products increase since these bottles cannot be returned for reuse as in the practice in the domestic trade. Metal cans are made now in several small plants for use in the food, detergent, paint, and wax industries. Production rate is low, costs are high, and quality control is precarious. A fully automated can-manufacturing plant will be needed as the domestic and export canning industry grows. No Ecuadorian metal would be used, but there would be obvious savings in transport costs as well as labor cost savings.

Other Products

Existing industries which have the possibility of expanding their exports are pharmaceuticals, castor oil, pyrethrum, tobacco, fibers from abaca and ramie, malt for beer, fabricated wood products for such items as parquet flooring and tool handles and toys, ceramics, and assembly transistor radios and watches and sewing machines for export to the LAFTA countries.

Exports of such artisan products industries as Panama hats from toquilla straw and buttons and trinkets and costume jewelry from tagua palm nuts, or "vegetable ivory," are on the downgrade. To revive the Panama hat industry exports would require revolutionary changes in production and marketing practices in the direction of lowered labor inputs (to assure better earning rates) and improved styling with a possible shift to women's hats and table mats and other decorative household items.

Export Incentives

Legal Framework

The Industrial Development Law of 1962 was designed specifically to encourage the establishment or expansion of industries which manufacture articles for export, those producing import substitutions, and assembly industries. The law was well designed, and the benefits are substantial. It was further liberalized by amendments decreed in August, 1963.

Taxes on Exports

Taxes on some exports, including bananas, cacao, coffee, and canned tuna, are many and complex and include national, provincial, and municipal imposts. Generally these imposts are for general revenue but some of them are levies for specific services, such as disease control, road maintenance, and port services. In the aggregate the imposts may amount to around one-fourth of the f.o.b. price to the grower; 27.78 percent for bananas, according to the banana growers association (ANBE).

Uniquely, rice exporters receive a subsidy of 3 sucres for each dollar of foreign exchange proceeds.

Export Financing

Export industries may obtain up to 80 percent of their necessary financing of fixed assets, excluding land, from the Commission de Valores at the relatively favorable rate of about 8 to 9 percent. Such loans, however, must be secured with equity of sufficient value that the loan does not exceed 60 percent of the value of the equity. Foreign and local borrowers are subject to the same conditions. Complaints are heard about the length and difficulty of the negotiations; and likewise about the equity requirement.

If an exporter must resort to the commercial loan market, the interest rate will be high, probably 12 percent or more.

Exporters are required to turn over their foreign exchange proceeds to the Central Bank which gives them sucres at the official rate of 18 to the dollar (actually 17.82, the buying rate), in contrast to the free market rate, currently strengthening at under 19 sucres to the dollar but for the year ended June 30, 19 having ranged from 23.27 in July, 1962, to 21.23 in June. On banana and shrimp exports, however, only about 70 percent of the declared value has to be turned over to the Central Bank at the official rate, the remaining share being exchangeable at the free market rate. On the other hand, the Central Bank sells foreign exchange required for remittances abroad of dividends, profits, interest, and amortization at the official selling rate of 18.18 sucres to the dollar (within a maximum of 15 percent of the funds for such purposes per year.)

Understandably, exporters would prefer to obtain the higher free market rate for their foreign exchange earnings and tend to regard the application of the official rate as in effect merely another tax. That view is not justified, however, if the cost structure of the country is in the main adjusted to the official exchange rate through its application to imports and to exports generally. The free market rate applies to only a relatively small share of international transactions, primarily to certain invisibles such as tourist expenditures and certain capital transactions.

Storage

Storage facilities as a public service are almost totally lacking. Any industrial development requiring storage facilities must be provided with its own.

Sanitary Inspection

An organization having official government sanction and the respect and confidence of producers, exporters, and foreign buyers alike is essential for an export food industry. Ecuador has no such organization, although the Instituto Nacional de Higiene in Guayaquil and the Instituto Nacional de Nutricion in Quito, between them, could perhaps perform this function; but at present they do not. From interviews with producers and exporters, lack of confidence in official inspection agencies was apparent.

Quality Control and Grading Inspection

Whatever quality control work is being done in Ecuador is being done by industry associations—some well, some poorly, and some not at all. The cacao industry has done a good job. In the coffee industry, on the other hand, Ecuador suffers from poor grading and poor quality control, its coffee exports being subject to a marked discount despite the potentially premium quality of Ecuador's upland coffee. The banana growers association (ANBE), with some governmental participation, has carried out a disease control program against sigatoka with notable success; but marketing inefficiencies and the threat of the root fungus, "mal de Panama," remain major challenges.

Grading and inspection services are urgently needed in
Ecuador for its growing exports.

Research and Development

A considerable effort is expended in Ecuador for agricultural
research and considerable success is already evident, particularly in disease control and cultural and varietal studies with
some crops. Still more needs to be done, including work in the
vitally needed field of agricultural extension service to provide
the badly needed technical assistance to growers.

There is apparently little or no research supported by public
or industry association funds on industrial development in the
export industries.

Direct Foreign Investment

The most rapid means of increasing exports of processed goo
is to invite a major foreign processing concern to take advantage
of special favorable opportunities in Ecuador to establish a processing plant, bring in the necessary technicians to get the oper
ation started and to train nationals, and to export the product
through the firm's established marketing channels, with such
local ownership participation as may be feasible.

OBSERVATIONS ON IMPORT MARKETS
FOR ECUADOR'S EXPORTS

North America

United States

The prospect is that the United States will continue for many
years to be Ecuador's chief customer as well as principal
supplier. Bananas, cacao, and coffee imports from Ecuador
could increase at a moderate rate with the growth of the United
States market as population increases. Problems must be met,
however, in cacao and coffee. There is a trend away from use
of premium-grade cacao in chocolate manufacture, which

constitutes a threat to Ecuador.   A more immediate threat is in
the coffee trade because of the strong complaints about poor
grading of Ecuador coffees, which were once rated on a par with
Colombian highland coffee.

Other products from Ecuador for which the United States could
be a growing market are canned tuna, frozen shrimp, sugar,
pyrethrum, and tropical woods.   Tobacco has excellent prospects
if present production developments in Ecuador are successful.

Canada

Most of Canada's considerable purchases of Ecuadorian
products are made in the United States.   To cultivate the Canadian market better,   there is a need for direct promotion by
Ecuador exporters.   Bananas, tuna, shrimp, coffee, and straw
braid offer opportunities.

Mexico

No significant opportunities are seen for Ecuador's exports
in this market, although Mexico's growing industries will seek
markets in Ecuador.

Europe

European Economic Community (EEC)

There is an urgent need for the establishment of an ALALC
office in Brussels with a representative to EEC to serve the
interests of the Latin American countries.   EEC is a serious
threat to Latin American exports to Europe, both through the
preferential treatment of imports from Associated Territories
and through the common external tariff on imports from non-
member countries, particularly on semi-finished or finished
goods because of the higher rates.

Belgium

Grading of Ecuador cacao receives a fine rating in Belgium,
but there is complaint that the allowable shrinkage of 2 percent

is abused, with nearly all shipments at least 2 percent under 69 kilos per bag, whereas African shipments rarely exceed 0.5 percent loss.

Belgium importers displayed no confidence in grading of Ecuador coffee, which has declined from a once premium status to a present discount. To assure a continuing market, drastic improvements in grading will be required.

Germany

Hamburg importers handle virtually all sales of Ecuadorian products to Scandinavia, Austria, and Switzerland as well as to West Germany. There is an increasing demand throughout Europe for bananas, and especially in Germany where per capita consumption is only a pound or two below that of the United States. Some resistance to boxed bananas was expressed, probably due to poor grading. Austrian buyers have expressed a preference for the boxed fruit.

Importers complained of poor grading of Ecuador coffee, and rice importers complained of improper handling and storage of Ecuador rice, resulting in fermentation, hardness, and discoloration, restricting its use to animal feed and breweries at very low prices.

Netherlands

As in all other markets in Europe, cacao importers reported that the Ecuador product is well graded and commands a high premium price but that high freight rates and the decreasing demand for premium cacao are having an adverse effect on Ecuador's sales. Ecuador will face increasing competition from the EEC Associated Territories of Surinam and the African countries. A stable market for coffee from Ecuador will necessitate improved processing and grading, especially of the highland coffee. Ecuador rice is usable only for chicken feed and by breweries, at very low prices, because of poor handling and storage.

Spain

Spanish officials, although expressing hope for increased
trade and suggesting promotion by Ecuador groups, reported
that the ocean freight problem would have to be remedied before
much increased trade can be expected. There is a market for
banana flour, buttons, hat braid, insecticides, and pharmaceutical products.

Switzerland

Bananas are a very popular fruit in Switzerland, per capita
consumption being on a par with that of West Germany and only
a pound or two below that of the United States. Because, however, of unsatisfactory experience with boxed bananas from
Ecuador, the largest food chain reported that it had recently
discontinued the purchase of Ecuador bananas. Quick remedial
action is suggested. Bananas are bought through Hamburg
importers. The confectionary and bakery trades are potential
markets for banana flour, flakes, and puree.

Ecuador flavor cacao still commands a considerable market
in Switzerland, mostly through Antwerp brokers. Ecuador
coffee has only a minor place.

The Government Trade Office is more concerned with increasing sales to Ecuador, because of the present heavy
balance in favor of Ecuador.

United Kingdom

The European cacao trade is largely controlled by London
brokers, the London Cocoa Exchange continuing as the most
important in Europe. They agreed that Ecuador cacao shippers
do an excellent job of grading and shipping according to description, but complain of light shipments, uniformly close to the
2 percent allowable shrinkage in contrast to about 0.5 percent
on shipments from Africa and Brazil. Chocolate manufacturers in Great Britain are using a decreasing amount of Ecuador
flavor cacao, and the opinion was expressed that Ecuador's

increased production of the "Trinidad" variety will in time bring about the reduction or even elimination of the premium now paid for Ecuador beans.

The importance of the London cacao trade suggests that Ecuador's cacao producers or shippers would find it advantageous to have an agent in London to keep them informed as to the market and to promote maximum sales to Europe. A promotional campaign to present the merits of Ecuador's flavor cacao for blending might counteract and reverse the present trend in many countries toward elimination of the more expensive flavor cacao in blending.

Apart from cacao, there appears to be little opportunity for increasing Ecuador's exports to the United Kingdom, because of her ties to the Commonwealth countries and to her former colonies.

Scandinavia (Denmark, Norway, and Sweden)

There are opportunities through direct promotion of a substantial increase in Ecuador's exports to the Scandinavian countries, particularly bananas and coffee. All or almost all the trade is now handled by importers and brokers in Hamburg, Amsterdam, and Antwerp.

Asia

Japan

The major Japanese trading companies, who dominate international trade in Japan, expressed considerable interest in Ecuador, in terms of both trade and industrial development and investment.

A sharp increase of banana imports from Ecuador has developed, and this trend will continue for some time. Since October, 1962, Japan has no longer restricted her banana imports to those from Taiwan, which was unable to meet Japan's growing needs; and the ad valorem duty is to be reduced within the next two years from 70 percent to 30 percent, as a further stimulus. Imports of $20 million from Ecuador are expected.

This trade may be threatened some years hence, depending on the degree of success achieved by the consortium formed by the leading Japanese trading companies and the United Fruit Company to seek to develop banana production in North Borneo or other areas in the Far East. The consortium hopes to be able to meet most of Japan's needs within seven to ten years.

Coffee consumption is increasing rapidly in Japan, but importers indicated lack of interest in Ecuador coffee because of poor grading and the unsatisfactory experience of one importer a few years ago, which apparently is well known in the trade.

A small but steady increase in cacao imports from Ecuador is expected. Demand is increasing also for castor beans, cordage fibers, tropical hardwoods, hides and deer skins, and deer musk.

Because the growing imports of bananas and cacao from Ecuador will give Ecuador a large trade balance, the major Japanese trading companies are seeking opportunities for industrial development investments in Ecuador, not only to meet their own needs but also to export to the LAFTA markets and others. Examples are the experimental work in Ecuador on abaca and ramie fibers, the arrangements for assembly operations in Cuenca for the LAFTA market, the search for tropical hardwood supplies to replace the declining Philippine sources, and the interest in tuna operations.

South America

Latin American Free Trade Association (LAFTA)

Ecuador's difficult problem of expanding its exports to LAFTA markets is recognized in the LAFTA Convention by its designation as an underdeveloped country. With few export manufacturing industries, Ecuador is faced with parallel raw

materials and foodstuffs production in many LAFTA markets;
and her geographical position practically excludes her from the
major population centers of Mexico, Buenos Aires, Rio de
Janeiro, and Montevideo.

The greatest potential is in the neighboring west coast
countries of Colombia and Peru and, to a lesser extent, Chile.
The extensive contraband trade, encouraged by Ecuador's
taxation of exports, is a handicap to legitimate exporters.

Colombia

Concentration of population in such cities as Cali, Medellin
and Bogota offers Ecuador its best opportunities for export
expansion.   Domestic production of some foodstuffs and certain
industrial raw materials is inadequate.   An Ecuadorian trade
promotion office, particularly in the Cali-Medellin area, might
be advantageous.

There is a growing demand for cacao and cacao butter, but
much of this market has become contraband over the past three
years.   A growing demand exists also for dairy products,
especially butter and cheese.   Other products in demand are
wool, canned tuna, frozen shrimp, handicrafts, malt for beer,
and insecticides.

Peru

The Lima area, with two million population, and northern
Peru offer a major market for meat products, dairy products
such as cheese, butter and powdered milk, bananas, pineapple,
and possibly lumber.   Organized trade promotion would be
helpful.

Chile

Joint participation and cooperation to develop commerce
between Chile and Ecuador have engaged the attention of officials of both governments recently.   Products under review
include sugar, steel, canned fruit, wines, fisheries, fibers,

and assembly plants.   Potential Ecuador exports would be
bananas, cacao, sugar, fruits, and fisheries products.   Chile
in turn would seek outlets for her manufactures.   Joint Chilean-
Ecuadorian companies are proposed to conduct the two-way
trade.

Argentina

Brazil supplies about 90 percent of Argentina's imports of
bananas, cacao, and coffee.   Because of the distance and high
cost of transport, trade opportunities in Argentina for Ecuador
are severly limited.   There are opportunities, however, for
pineapples, limited amounts of premium cacao, pharmaceuticals, veterinary supplies, fibers, and insecticides.

Uruguay

The market in Uruguay for Ecuadorian products is sharply
limited for the same reasons of distance and transport cost
which have been stated for Argentina.   The bananas and pineapples sold in Montevideo are far inferior to the Ecuadorian
products, but the long voyage by sea practically closes the
market for Ecuador shippers.   Pharmaceuticals, veterinary
supplies, fibers, and insecticides might offer possibilities.

OBSERVATIONS ON PROBLEM AREAS IN EXPANSION
OF ECUADOR'S EXPORTS

Ocean Freight Rates

High freight costs relative to those from competing countries
are a major problem for Ecuador.   Serious efforts should be
made to overcome this handicap through careful study of the
facts and through representations to the carriers, associations,
and conferences.

Promotion of Ecuador Exports Abroad

Promotion of Ecuador's exports in foreign markets, either
by government agencies or by producers or exporters, is conspicuous by its absence, promotion being left entirely in the
hands of fruit companies, foreign importers, and distributors.

Little or no promotion work is done by the Ecuadorian consular officials, their time being given over to the highly unpro-
ductive task of certifying shipping documents. Most countries
have eliminated that task, shifting it to the steamship lines or to
port agencies.

Standardization of Grading and Packing

There is a strong need for improved grading and packing of
Ecuadorian products—notably coffee—in order to improve the
standing of these products in foreign markets and also to increase foreign exchange earnings through higher prices and
expanded markets.

Tourism

Ecuador has salient attractions for tourism, and an organized promotion would pay dividends in foreign exchange earnings
and in the stimulation of local investment in facilities.

Promotion of Industrial Investment

The attraction of direct investment capital requires not only
the enactment of favorable laws, as has been well done in Ecuador, and the conduct of surveys, which again has been well
started in Ecuador, but a determined and systematic program
of bringing specific investment opportunities to the attention of
potential investors. Ecuador has a solid base of comparative
advantages on which to build such a program.

OUTLOOK FOR ECUADOR'S EXPORTS, 1968-73

Detailed projections for 1968 and 1973 are presented in
Chapter 7 along with stated assumptions and analyses. The

specific projections there outline aggregate $211 million for
1968 and $254 million for 1973, including projected exports of
the big three—bananas, cacao, and coffee—of $174 million for
1968 and $201 million for 1973. Still further and major export
possibilities in processing and manufacturing will be dependent
on the planning and carrying out of development programs.

RECOMMENDATIONS

The terms of reference for this study included a review and
assessment of Ecuador's present export base and recommendations directed at expanding existing exports through improvements in production and marketing techniques, as well as developing new products for export. Recommendations and
suggestions in this regard which are covered in the main text
may be summarized, as follows:

General Recommendations

1. Organization of a systematic development and promotion
program for expansion and diversification of Ecuador's exports,
with provision for the active participation of industry and trade
groups, directed at:

a. Enhancement of earnings from Ecuador's traditional
exports of bananas, cacao, coffee, sugar, and rice, through
both volume expansion wherever possible and quality upgrading,
to take maximum advantage of the existing base of production
and distribution know-how, developed lands, capital, and
facilities.

b. Diversification of exports to minimize the risks
inherent in the present dependence, to the extent of 85 to 90
percent, on export earnings from bananas, cacao, and coffee,
both by expansion of other present exports and by the development of industries to process a growing share of the products
of Ecuador's farms, fisheries, and forests for export and
thereby increase Ecuador's foreign exchange "take. "

2. Provision in the program for extending technical assistance to producers, managerial assistance to both old and new enterprises, and assistance in product and market research for both old and new industries—with the aim of achieving efficient organization and management and clear command of technical know-how for both production and marketing for the export trade.

3. Emphasis in the program on improvements in quality and lowering of costs, in recognition of the principle that access to limited world markets must be based on costs for a given grade or quality as low as or lower than those of competing exporters.

4. A selective program of technical and economic feasibility studies be initiated in those areas in which existing knowledge is insufficient to provide the basis for specific development action, including those listed below in the Summary of Feasibility Study and Research Proposals.

5. Development of new industries for the export trade be limited to those for which there is a strong possibility of comparative international advantage, based on the combination of favorable physical conditions, low labor rates and ready access to ports which has underlain Ecuador's success in her traditional exports.

6. For those industries for which Ecuador lacks capital and technical know-how, the speed of development be accelerated through negotiating arrangements under which reputable and experienced foreign concerns could be induced to establish such industries in Ecuador, bringing in capital, equipment, and managerial and technical personnel for production of the product and its marketing through their established channels, with such local ownership participation as may be feasible and with a systematic program for the training of Ecuadorian nationals at all levels of the enterprise.

Recommendations for Principal Processing Industries
for the Export Trade

1. A program be initiated, through the feasibility and research study proposals summarized below, looking toward the
total utilization of the banana fingers, peels, stalks, and
trunks—and involving the processing of puree and dehydrated
bananas and chips, manufacture of animal feed, extraction of
chemical components, and the manufacture of paper and cardboard, including that needed to package bananas and other
Ecuadorian exports.

2. Steps be taken to initiate a major national effort in the
direction of establishment of a meat products export industry,
including the necessary experimental work; technical assistance to producers; investment in improved pastures and increased herds; and development of integrated processing and
marketing facilities for production for export of frozen, canned,
smoked and cured beef products, and such by-products as
hides, tallow, fertilizers, and pharmaceuticals.

3. An organized program be initiated for expansion of the
existing dairy products industry to produce for export on a
major scale such products as cheese, butter, powdered milk,
and canned milk, involving improvement of pastures, increase
of herds, and increased processing capacity.

4. A major program of expansion of production of fisheries
products, be initiated with provision for additional capital
and technical assistance for modernizing and enlarging the
fishing fleet, building needed additional processing and marketing facilities, and improving the efficiency of fishing and processing methods, including capacity and techniques for fishing
beyond the 20-fathom depths and needed facilities for close-
to-shore fishing in grounds not now exploited.

5. Strenuous efforts be made to increase the production of
sugar for export, to take advantage of the present and prospective favorable market, through diversion of a larger share of
the output of cane to sugar production, through increased
plantings for sugar production, through increased utilization

of existing refining capacity, and through expansion of refining
capacity.

6. Arrangements be made with a concern experienced in the
production of fruit concentrates to establish and operate facilities in Ecuador for the manufacture of frozen fruit juice concentrates from pineapples and oranges, and their marketing
through the concern's established channels; and to establish
laboratory facilities for appraising the possibilities of processing such other Ecuadorian fruits as naranjilla, chirimoya,
tree tomato, papaya, and mango.

7. Steps be taken to establish chocolate manufacturing for
export to take advantage of the relatively low cost of all the
required ingredients in Ecuador.

Recommendations on Export Incentives and Facilitating Functions

1. An ad hoc commission be established by the Government
to investigate the impact of taxes on certain exports, to hold
public hearings, and to submit its conclusions and proposals.

2. Consideration be given to the modification of the present
subsidy on rice exports, of 3 sucres for each dollar of foreign
exchange earnings, to apply only to those exports meeting minimum standards of quality and thereby to upgrade rice exports
and enhance earnings.

3. Consideration be given to the establishment of a similar
incentive to improve Ecuador's coffee exports, including a
special differential for the separate grading of Ecuador's highland coffee.

4. Steps be taken to provide professionally competent and
impartial sanitary inspection for Ecuador's growing processed
food industries, with particular reference to exports; and that
consideration be given to accomplishment of this objective
through a mandate to the existing Instituto Nacional de Higiene
in Guayaquil and Instituto Nacional de Nutricion in Quito with

provision for technical advice and assistance to those Institutes
by outstanding foreign experts in sanitary inspection.

5. Provision be made through appropriate legislative and
administrative action for mandatory minimum standards of
quality control and grading for the export trade; and that both
the establishment of standards and grades and inspection be
delegated to industry organizations or institutes under appropriate governmental supervision or participation with provision
for technical assistance and advice by specialists in this field.

6. A pervasive and competent agricultural extension service
be established to provide badly needed technical advice and
assistance to growers to upgrade production and marketing
methods and improve crop quality; and that this service seek
and utilize such foreign technical assistance as may be needed
and feasible, with particular reference to rice production and
coffee handling and grading.

7. Steps be taken to encourage the establishment by private
interests, or if necessary under mixed private and public aus-
pices, of a technical services organization to render, for a
fee, technical assistance to both old and new enterprises
manufacturing for export, including advice and assistance on
production, marketing, and financial problems and with appropriate laboratory facilities for testing.

8. A careful study be made of ocean freight rates from
Ecuador's ports and competing ports to North America, Western Europe, and Japan as a basis for such representations to
the carriers, associations, and conferences as the facts may
warrant.

9. Promotion of Ecuador's exports be made a prime function
of Ecuador's consulates and to permit their concentration on
these tasks, that the requirement of consular certification of
shipping documents be abolished, shifting the function to the
carriers or to port agencies.

Recommendations Based on Import Market Visits

1. Ecuador urge LAFTA to establish an office in Brussels with a representative to EEC to serve the joint interests of the Latin American countries in an effort to minimize the threat to their exports, stemming from the preferential treatment of imports from the Associated Territories.

2. Ecuador take advantage of the economic integration program of ALALC through seeking to accelerate the development of "complementary agreement" industries to process its products for export to other ALALC countries in exchange for the products of the integration industries in the larger Latin American countrie

3. The Government of Ecuador and the Association of Cacao Exporters develop and carry out a promotional program to encourage the use of Ecuador's flavor cacao in blending and to counteract the trend in both Europe and the United States away from its use in favor of synthetic flavoring or lower grade cacao.

4. The Government of Ecuador and the Association of Cacao Exporters take prompt action with respect to the criticism that cacao shipments from Ecuador are consistently underweight by the allowable 2 percent shrinkage in contrast to only 0.5 percent shrinkage in shipments from Africa and Brazil.

5. Strenuous and urgent measures be taken to improve the grading of Ecuador coffee and, in particular, to grade and market separately Ecuador's highland coffee, both to prevent loss of markets and to upgrade the product and thereby enhance earnings.

6. Similar strenuous and urgent measures be taken to improve the handling and processing of Ecuador's rice to prevent further loss of markets and to upgrade the product, removing it from the low-price animal feed and brewery markets.

7. The Government of Ecuador urge ANBE (National Association of Banana Exporters) to tighten its inspection procedures for boxed bananas in response to the criticisms made in Hamburg

and Switzerland; and to take steps aimed at correcting the situation which led the large Swiss retail food chain to discontinue the sale of Ecuador bananas.

8. The Government of Ecuador and ANBE keep informed on the progress of the Japanese trading companies-United Fruit Company consortium in their efforts to develop banana production in North Borneo or elsewhere in the Far East for the Japanese market.

9. That the Government of Ecuador consider sending a mission to Japan to take advantage of the expressed desire of the major Japanese trading companies to seek industrial development investments in Ecuador for ALALC markets and others.

Feasibility Study and Research Proposals

Crop Research Programs

Rice Research Program, including: Variety tests to determine which of the known varieties give the best yields and quality under Ecuadorian conditions.

Cultivation and fertilizer tests to determine the most effective land leveling, water control, and cultivation practices.

Rice drying tests to determine the most effective methods of reducing the moisture content to safe storage limits on the farm prior to shipment to the mill.

Farm management studies of costs of production and studies of marketing methods.

Coffee Research Program, including: Harvesting and handling tests to determine, under Ecuadorian conditions, the most effective methods of harvesting, depulping, and washing coffee.

Grading tests to determine the most effective methods of grading Ecuadorian coffee.

Farm management studies of production costs and studies of marketing methods and storage financing.

Cacao Research Program, including: Harvesting and handling tests to determine the most effective methods, under Ecuadorian conditions, of fermenting and drying.

Shipping tests to determine the most effective methods of minimizing shrinkage in transport.

Nutrition and flavor tests to determine the characteristics and advantages of Ecuador's flavor cacao in blending in chocolate manufacture and in other principal uses.

Variety tests to determine the effect of the increasing trend toward the "Trinidad" variety on the grading of Ecuador's cacao and to reassess the present varietal composition in the light of current market trends and the present knowledge of disease control.

Farm management studies of production costs and studies of marketing methods.

Pyrethrum Research Program, including: Variety and cultivation tests to determine the most effective methods of increasing (a) the yield of flowers per hectare, and (b) the yield of pyrethrum per ton of flowers.

Harvesting and mechanical tests to seek to develop a simple and inexpensive mechanical device to reduce the present high labor input.

Farm management studies of production costs and studies of marketing methods.

Balsa Research Program, including: Technical studies of the feasibility of new uses for balsa including its use in association with other materials in the manufacture of plywood, doors, door frames, wallboards, ship interiors, soundproofing, and insulation.

Studies of potential costs of production and marketing on the assumption that balsa was grown under commercial conditions.

Banana Research Program, including (see also below, under Processing Industry Research Programs): Intensive disease control tests to seek possible ways and means of eradicating or controlling "mal de Panama."

Farm management studies of costs of production and studies of marketing methods and costs.

Processing Industry Research Programs

Banana Processing Research Program, including: Study of grading, packing and quality control to determine the most efficient means of performing these functions and the most effective locus.

Technical investigation to determine the presence and extractability of various chemical components in the banana and the peel, including pilot plant feasibility tests.

Technical investigation to determine the most efficient methods of producing animal feed from waste products with corresponding feeding tests; and with pilot plant feasibility tests.

Technical investigation to determine the feasibility of producing paper and cardboard from banana stalks and trunks, both with and without admixture of cane bagasse, and with pilot plant demonstration.

Detailed study of marketing methods and processes currently used in the banana industry with particular reference to the implications of those methods and processes in an effort to develop a processing industry to utilize all products of the industry; and with a view to formulating the changed marketing methods and procedures that would be required for the establishment of such a processing industry.

Meat Processing Industry Research Program, including: Experimentation to determine the most suitable grasses for both the Costa and the Southern Sierra, with animal nutrition tests.

Experimentation to determine the most effective methods of pasture management.

Farm management studies of costs of production in the present livestock industry in the Costa.

Technical and economic study of meat-processing methods to determine the most efficient methods for Ecuador, optimum size of processing plants, and estimated costs.

Marketing methods and potentials study to determine most effective method for an Ecuador industry and to estimate export market potentials for each major product.

Research Programs for Potential Processing Industries, including: Tomatoes and other vegetables: varietal, cultural methods, and disease control studies to establish the best practices for providing raw materials.

Jams, jellies, and preserves: study of the feasibility of direct production from cane juice and fruits.

Canned pineapple: varietal studies to establish a specific variety of uniform size, color, and other quality specifications.

Pepper and other spices: varietal and cultural studies to determine the economics of production of spices and their processing in Ecuador.

Sorghum: varietal and cultural tests to determine the suitability of this product for the drier areas in southern Ecuador as the basis for the processing of high-quality starches, syrups, and animal feed.

Tea: varietal and cultural tests to determine whether a marketable product can be produced in Ecuador.

Molybdenum and agate: Exploratory studies to determine the approximate extent of the deposits and the feasibility of their extraction.

STATISTICAL APPENDIX

STATISTICAL APPENDIX

Included in this Appendix are 107 tables, covering trade statistics on 16 commodities.

These data were assembled to serve a dual purpose:

1. To provide the field specialists working on this project with basic information on various aspects of the world market for those Ecuadorian products which move in international trade and which constitute the present base of Ecuador's export earnings, as well as products which were being examined for their potentials as possible new export commodities.

2. To provide the statistical base for assessing and projecting Ecuador's exports for 1968 and 1973.

Every effort was made to assemble series through 1962 and to present the data according to a consistent pattern. In some instances, however, 1962 figures were not available, and some inconsistencies were unavoidable because of differences in statistical terminology employed by the various sources used.

Table   Page

CASTOR OIL

CASTOR BEANS & CASTOR OIL

COCOA

305

307

308

309

Table 1

A B A C A

UNITED STATES IMPORTS BY COUNTRY OF ORIGIN,
Average 1955-59, Annual 1960-62

Country of Origin	Quantity [1] (in long tons)				Value (in dollars)			
	Average 1955-59	1960	1961	1962[2]	Average 1955-59	1960	1961	1962[2]
Mexico[3]	1,639	189	267	201	207,472	53,766	89,561	69,632
Costa Rica	1,669	16	3	2	815,578	2,266	1,620	675
Other Central America	4,017	-	-	-	1,763,237	-	-	-
Other America	1,159	-	-	16	180,619	-	-	13,598
Indonesia	241	60	21	89	96,037	31,946	11,452	29,993
Philippines	30,267	19,392	25,444	29,791	11,376,957	9,867,513	10,069,322	8,205,647
Singapore	205	1,117	2,319	878	94,392	568,551	1,005,614	301,071
Other Asia	68	5	-	38	22,005	1,127	-	14,618
Other Countries	237	25	1	78	43,769	6,453	369	26,794
TOTAL	39,502	20,804	28,055	31,093	14,600,066	10,531,622	11,177,938	8,662,028

[1] 2,240 lbs. [2] Preliminary. [3] A large percentage of these figures is believed to be ratine fibers rather than true abaca.

Source: U. S. Department of Agriculture, Foreign Agricultural Service.

312

Table 2

BANANAS

WORLD EXPORTS BY PRINCIPAL PRODUCING AREAS,
5-Year Averages for 1935-39, 1945-49, and 1951-55, and Annual 1957-61
(In Thousands of 50-lb. Stems)

Producing Area	5-Year Averages			1957	1958	1959	1960	1961	1962 4/
	1935-39	1945-49	1951-55						
ECUADOR	1,920	3,054	19,190	33,500	38,052	44,838	50,674	44,451	
Brazil and Colombia 1/	16,841	8,484	16,242	18,239	20,474	19,682	19,812	20,982	
Central America 1/	36,458	42,413	45,716	52,903	54,311	50,414	53,122	57,251	
Caribbean 2/ and Mexico	29,883	11,022	15,453	20,518	21,667	26,896	28,576	29,229	
Africa 3/	12,463	10,701	22,161	24,012	22,463	22,495	24,513	26,206	
Other 3/	6,122	772	2,306	2,597	3,959	3,980	4,213	5,170	
World Total	103,687	76,446	121,068	151,769	160,926	168,305	180,910	183,289	
				Percent Distribution					
World Total	100.0	100.0	100.0	100.0	100.0	100.0	100.0	100.0	
ECUADOR	1.9	4.0	15.9	22.1	23.6	26.5	28.0	24.3	
Brazil and Colombia	16.2	11.1	13.2	12.0	12.7	11.7	11.0	11.4	
Central America	35.2	55.5	37.8	34.9	33.7	30.0	29.4	31.2	
Caribbean and Mexico	28.8	14.4	12.8	13.5	13.5	16.0	15.8	16.0	
Africa	12.0	14.0	18.3	15.8	14.0	13.4	13.5	14.3	
Other	5.9	1.0	1.9	1.7	2.5	2.4	2.3	2.8	

1/Includes Costa Rica, Guatemala, Honduras, Nicaragua, and Panama. 2/Includes Dominican Republic, Guadelupe, Jamaica, Martinique, Trinidad, and Windward Islands. 3/Includes Asia and Oceania. 4/Not available, pending conversion of export data to new reporting on pound basis, which became effective January, 1962.

Source: U. S. Department of Agriculture.

313

Table 3

B A N A N A S

WORLD IMPORTS BY PRINCIPAL IMPORTING COUNTRIES,
5-Year Averages for 1935-39, 1945-49, and 1951-55, and Annual 1957-61
(In Thousands of 50-lb. Stems)

| | 5-year Averages | | | 1957 | 1958 | 1959 | 1960 | 1961 | 1962 [1] |
	1935-39	1945-49	1951-55						
North America									
Canada	2,250	3,809	5,748	6,362	6,469	6,774	7,569	7,238	
United States	61,192	53,506	62,247	68,687	71,265	77,218	82,824	79,600	
Total	63,442	57,315	67,995	75,049	77,734	83,992	90,393	86,838	
Europe									
Belgium-Luxembourg	914	1,029	1,896	2,507	2,684	2,694	2,784	2,870	
France	7,416	3,838	11,339	13,524	15,390	14,889	15,369	15,976	
Germany, West	5,512	313	6,112	14,916	18,608	18,882	19,801	20,733	
Italy	954	87	1,579	1,919	2,747	2,695	3,832	4,531	
Netherlands	1,273	67	1,120	2,050	2,273	2,506	2,621	2,998	
Spain	2,084	3,962	2,560	4,278	3,389	4,305	4,450	4,500	
Switzerland	282	347	746	1,261	1,489	1,545	1,975	2,096	
United Kingdom	13,186	4,562	10,639	14,057	13,813	14,963	15,416	16,465	
Other 2/	1,422	643	3,521	5,585	5,385	5,538	5,816	6,102	
Total	33,043	14,848	39,512	60,097	65,778	68,017	72,064	76,271	
South America 3/	7,960	5,876	9,018	9,757	12,262	12,420	12,788	12,800	
Africa	564	811	1,236	1,326	1,344	1,513	1,784	1,561	
Asia 4/	5,570	341	1,479	1,491	2,050	1,985	2,226	3,565	
Oceania 5/	524	463	725	1,015	1,440	1,423	1,504	1,570	
WORLD TOTAL	111,103	79,654	119,965	148,735	160,608	169,350	180,759	182,605	

1/Not available, pending conversion of export data to new reporting on pound basis, which became effective
January, 1962. 2/Includes imports by Austria, Denmark, Finland, Ireland, Norway, and Sweden. 3/Primarily
Argentina. 4/Virtually all Japan. 5/New Zealand.

Source: U. S. Department of Agriculture.

Table 4

B A N A N A S

WORLD IMPORTS, DISTRIBUTION BY MAJOR IMPORTING AREAS,
5-Year Averages for 1935-39, 1951-55, 1957-61, and Annual 1957-61
(In Thousands of 50-1b. Stems)

	Total	United States	Canada	Western[1] Europe	South America	Africa	Asia	Oceania
5-Year Averages								
1935-39	111,103	61,192	2,250	33,043	7,960	564	5,570	524
1951-55	119,965	62,247	5,748	39,512	9,018	1,236	1,479	725
1957-61	168,411	75,919	6,882	68,445	12,005	1,506	2,263	1,390
Annual								
1957	148,735	68,687	6,362	60,097	9,757	1,326	1,491	1,015
1958	160,608	71,265	6,469	65,778	12,262	1,344	2,050	1,440
1959	169,350	77,218	6,774	68,017	12,420	1,513	1,985	1,423
1960	180,759	82,824	7,569	72,064	12,788	1,784	2,226	1,504
1961	182,605	79,600	7,238	76,271	12,800	1,561	3,565	1,570

Percent Distribution of World Imports

	Total	United States	Canada	Western[1] Europe	South America	Africa	Asia	Oceania
5-Year Averages								
1935-39	100.0	55.1	2.0	29.7	7.2	0.5	5.0	0.5
1951-55	100.0	51.9	4.8	32.9	7.5	1.0	1.2	0.6
1957-61	100.0	45.1	4.1	40.6	7.1	0.9	1.3	0.8
Annual								
1957	100.0	46.2	4.3	40.4	6.6	0.9	1.0	0.7
1958	100.0	44.4	4.0	41.0	7.6	0.8	1.3	0.9
1959	100.0	45.5	4.0	40.1	7.3	0.9	1.2	0.8
1960	100.0	45.8	4.2	39.9	7.1	1.0	1.2	0.8
1961	100.0	43.6	4.0	41.7	7.0	0.9	1.9	0.9

[1] Includes total banana imports of prewar Germany.

Source: U. S. Department of Agriculture.

Table 5

B A N A N A S

ECUADOR EXPORTS TO MAJOR IMPORTING COUNTRIES BY VOLUME AND PERCENTAGE DISTRIBUTION: 1958-62

(Volume in Thousands of Stems 1/)

Importing Country	1958 Volume	1958 % of Total	1959 Volume	1959 % of Total	1960 Volume	1960 % of Total	1961 Volume	1961 % of Total	1962 Volume	1962 % of Total
United States	15,223	52.6	21,850	62.9	24,218	67.5	20,991	64.2	21,499	62.8
Canada	-	-	326	0.9	351	1.0	131	0.4	472	1.4
Chile	1,164	4.0	1,474	4.2	1,660	4.6	1,534	4.7	1,504	4.4
Germany, West	7,606	26.3	7,105	20.4	5,924	16.5	6,114	18.6	5,350	15.5
Austria	-	-	122	0.4	165	0.5	156	0.5	194	0.6
Belgium	3,796	13.1	3,300	9.5	3,144	8.8	2,838	8.7	2,465	7.2
Netherlands	-	-	72	0.2	-	-	69	0.2	433	1.3
Norway	15	0.1	-	-	-	-	20	0.1	104	0.3
Sweden	938	3.2	-	-	-	-	40	0.1	219	0.6
Switzerland	192	0.7	512	1.5	402	1.1	595	1.8	580	1.7
Japan	-	-	-	-	-	-	229	0.7	1,437	4.2
Other	-	-	-	-	1	-	-	-	1	-
TOTAL	28,935	100.0	34,761	100.0	35,865	100.0	32,717	100.0	34,258	100.0

1/ Actual stems, as distinguished from conversion to 50-lb. stems, as given in U. S. statistics.

Source: Associación Nacional de Bananeros del Ecuador.

316

Table 6

B A N A N A S

U. S. IMPORTS FROM PRINCIPAL SOURCES: 1957-61
(In Thousands of 50-lb. Stems)

	1957 Volume	1957 % of Total	1958 Volume	1958 % of Total	1959 Volume	1959 % of Total	1960 Volume	1960 % of Total	1961 Volume	1961 % of Total
TOTAL U. S. IMPORTS	68,687	100.0	71,262	100.0	77,218	100.0	82,824	100.0	81,468	100.0
ECUADOR	20,871	30.4	22,308	31.3	31,649	41.0	35,093	42.0	29,318	36.0
Central America	42,498	61.9	45,749	64.2	41,997	54.4	45,515	55.0	49,508	60.8
Costa Rica		13.0		12.9		9.2		10.4		14.2
Guatemala		6.7		7.8		7.7		10.6		8.1
Honduras		23.0		24.6		20.0		17.3		26.0
Nicaragua		0.2		0.2		0.2		0.3		0.1
Panama		19.0		18.7		17.3		16.4		12.3
Other	5,318	7.7	3,205	4.5	3,572	4.6	2,216	2.7	2,642	3.3

Source: U. S. Department of Agriculture

317

Table 7

B A N A N A S

ARGENTINA IMPORTS BY COUNTRY OF ORIGIN: 1957-62
(In Thousands of 50-1b. Bunches)

Country of Origin	1957[1]	1958[1]	1959[1]	1960[1]	1961[1]	1962[2]
Brazil	9,213	12,135	10,326	9,880	10,851	
Paraguay	200	180	165	265	254	
Bolivia	-	-	-	-	1	
ECUADOR	-	-	-	-	1	
TOTAL	9,413	12,315	10,491	10,145	11,108	

[1] Actual bunches.   [2] Not available.

Source: U. S. Department of Agriculture.

318

Table 8

B A N A N A S

BELGIUM-LUXEMBOURG IMPORTS BY COUNTRY OF ORIGIN: 1957-62
(In Thousands of 50-1b. Bunches)

Country of Origin	1957	1958	1959	1960	1961	1962
Belgium Congo	498	399	562	747	489	
ECUADOR	866	1,191	1,072	1,010	1,168	
Colombia	871	715	627	532	582	
Netherlands	-	1	2	2	7	
Honduras	-	-	-	265	-	
Dominican Republic	-	-	-	-	400	
Others	283	390	436	363	236	
TOTAL	2,517	2,696	2,760	2,918	2,982	2,794[1/]

[1/]Total for 11 months (January-November).

Source: U. S. Department of Agriculture.

319

Table 9

B A N A Ñ A S

WEST GERMANY IMPORTS BY COUNTRY OF ORIGIN: 1957-62
(In Thousands of 50-1b. Stems)

Country of Origin	1957	1958	1959	1960	1961	1962
Belgian Congo	168	94	62	33	-	-
Canary Islands	452	256	224	390	413	847
Guatemala	2,100	585	695	713	831	1,474
ECUADOR	6,712	10,667	9,538	8,987	9,189	8,828
Colombia	4,650	4,871	5,996	6,592	7,252	5,841
French Cameroon	101	228	68	-	-	-
Honduras	518	877	1,475	679	582	357
French W. Africa	2	-	-	-	-	-
Brazil	-	5	145	5	-	-
French W. Indies	35	177	2	2	-	-
Dominican Republic	289	631	713	2,529	2,428	2,883
Panama	-	127	-	-	93	122
Portugal	21	39	19	-	-	-
Costa Rica	-	14	-	-	24	-
Guinea, Spanish	16	35	33	-	-	-
Ethiopia	-	6	-	-	-	-
Congo Republic	-	-	-	-	-	61
Others	27	22	-	14	40	241
TOTAL	15,090	18,634	18,969	19,943	20,853	20,593

Source: U. S. Department of Agriculture.

Table 10

B A N A N A S

JAPAN IMPORTS BY COUNTRY OF ORIGIN: 1957-61
(In Thousands of 50-1b. Bunches)

Country of Origin	1957	1958	1959	1960	1961
Formosa	1,070	1,589	1,648	1,808	2,864
ECUADOR	-	-	-	1	215
Panama	-	-	-	8	150
Direct from China Port	103	16	-	-	-
Other	50	25	5	52	34
TOTAL	1,224	1,630	1,653	1,869	3,264

Source: U. S. Department of Agriculture.

321

Table 11

B A N A N A S

NETHERLANDS IMPORTS BY COUNTRY OF ORIGIN: 1957-62
(In Thousands of 50-1b. Stems)

Country of Origin	1957	1958	1959	1960	1961	1962
Belgium	300	350	391	416	396	440
Colombia	980	935	800	697	896	518
ECUADOR	394	556	615	558	579	574
Honduras	30	151	243	280	161	206
Dominican Republic	184	223	337	355	626	728
Guatemala	-	15	97	288	163	456
Panama	152	12	-	-	34	75
Germany	15	11	22	17	79	44
Surinam	-	-	-	11	35	63
Other	-	27	7	6	37[1]/	4
TOTAL	2,055	2,280	2,512	2,627	3,008	3,109

[1]/Includes 34,127 stems from Costa Rica.

Source: U. S. Department of Agriculture

322

Table 12

B A N A N A S

PER CAPITA CONSUMPTION IN SELECTED COUNTRIES: 1952-61
(Pounds)

	1952	1953	1954	1955	1956	1957	1958	1959	1960	1961[1]
United States[2]	18.9	21.7	20.2	19.5	20.3	20.2	20.6	22.0	23.3	21.9
Canada	19.4	20.3	19.4	18.8	19.2	19.2	19.0	19.4	21.2	19.8
Switzerland	6.6	7.7	8.2	8.8	10.1	12.3	14.3	14.8	18.5	19.2
Germany, West	4.6	5.1	7.5	9.1	12.1	13.9	17.2	17.2	17.7	19.2
France				13.5					15.5	17.4
Belg-Luxembourg	9.9	10.8	11.5	12.3	12.8	13.7	14.3	14.3	15.2	15.1
Norway	3.1	3.3	4.6	5.0	7.9	18.1	17.9	14.6	15.0	16.7
United Kingdom				13.4					14.7	15.6
Denmark				13.5					12.4	11.9
Netherlands	4.4	5.1	5.7	6.8	8.2	9.3	10.1	11.0	11.3	12.9
Sweden	12.1	13.0	13.0	14.5	13.0	12.8	11.7	11.5	11.3	11.3
Austria		0.7	2.0	3.3	3.5	4.6	5.5	7.9	8.8	8.8
Spain				5.3					7.6	n.a.
Italy				2.0					3.9	4.6
Finland				3.9					3.7	4.0
Japan				0.6					1.0	1.7
Chile	8.8	6.0	8.2	5.7	3.7	3.7	4.0			

[1]Preliminary. [2]The average for the ten-year period, 1952-61, was 20.8 pounds, compared to the average for the prewar decade (1930-39) of 22.6 pounds.

Source: U. S. Department of Agriculture and Analisis y Proyeccion de las Exportaciones del Ecuador, by Hans Linnemann.

Table 13

B A N A N A S

PRICES AND PRICE INDICES IN SELECTED COUNTRIES: 1957-62
(Price in Dollars per 100 Pounds; Indices 1957 = 100)

Year	United States wholesale price f.o.b. port of entry[1]		West Germany import price Hamburg[2]		United Kingdom wholesale price London[3]		France f.o.b. French ports[4]	
1957	8.04	100.0	7.71	100.0	13.92	100.0	12.24	100.0
1958	7.40	92.0	6.62	85.9	13.61	97.8	10.70	87.4
1959	6.58	81.8	6.12	79.4	12.56	90.2	8.25	67.4
1960	6.48	80.6	6.03	78.2	12.74	91.5	9.12	74.5
1961	6.29	78.2	6.26	81.2	13.42	96.4	8.98	73.4
1962	6.26	77.9	6.35	82.4	12.47	89.6	8.95	73.1

[1] For Central American bananas. [2] Imports from Ecuador. NOTE: Imports from Colombia somewhat higher. [3] Imports from Jamaica. [4] Imports from Guadalupe. NOTE: Imports from Cameroun somewhat lower; imports from Guinea somewhat higher.

Source: FAO, Production Yearbook, 1961 and Commodity Review, 1963.
   U. S. Department of Labor, Bureau of Labor Statistics.

Table 14

C A S T O R   B E A N S

EXPORTS BY PRINCIPAL EXPORTING COUNTRIES,
Average 1950-54, Annual 1957-62
(In Short Tons[1])

Country of Origin	Average 1950-54	1957	1958	1959	1960	1961[2]	1962[2]
North America							
Haiti[3]	3,999	2,509	657	1,376	1,734	2,583	551[4]
South America							
Brazil	55,282	35,031	27,498	10,870	-	276	-
ECUADOR	7,182	8,597	9,712	10,365	11,579	20,282	2,535[5]
Peru	105	1,819	6,381	1,051	1,545	1,359	736[5]
Total	62,569	45,447	43,591	22,286	13,124	21,917	3,271
Africa							
Angola	6,515	25	14	6	-	-	-
Cape Verde Islands	-	141	130	131	-	-	-
Congo, Republic of the	2,192	1,720[6]	697[6]	531	203	-	-
Ethiopia	4,127	2,986[6]	2,735[6]	3,638	5,789	4,440	1,323[4]
Former French W. Africa[7]	911	580	589	712	1,089	1,102	-
Kenya	4,016	4,845	7,765	4,420	3,708	3,049	852[4]
Libya	243	1,344	5,536	5,021	2,119	2,425	1,212[4]
Malagasy (Madagascar)	1,828	1,367	1,152	997	591	1,326	696[8]
Mozambique	2,774	2,049	1,621	2,541	2,527	1,027	1,047[5]
Tanganyika	9,985	15,562	20,000	15,898	20,560	12,039	3,197[5]
South Africa, Republic of	-	-	8,500	1,040	1,834	1,723	1,543[5]
Sudan	7	4	20	45	4,130	3,745	3,891[9]
Uganda	9,078	1,968	2,928	2,663	1,886	1,926	1,522[4]
Total	41,676	32,591	51,687	37,643	44,436	32,802	15,283
Asia							
China, Mainland[10]	16,535	9,590	8,708	12,125	8,818	5,071	3,086[5]
Hong Kong	662	1,901	185	1,177	5,388	2,620	453[9]
India	19,608	-	-	-	-	-	-
Indonesia	1,634	22	134	-	493	248	-
Iran[11]	2,538	2,660	5,657	4,292	797	-	-
Pakistan	-	5,042	11	2,885	3,696	3,920	2,240
Thailand	16,104	28,651	17,351	34,646	26,429	35,947	55,160[12]
Total	57,081	47,866	32,046	55,125	45,621	47,806	60,939
GRAND TOTAL	165,325	128,413	127,981	116,430	104,915	105,108	80,044

[1] 2,000 lbs.   [2] Preliminary.   [3] Year ending September 30.   [4] January-May.   [5] January-June.
[6] Year ending September 10.   [7] Now the independent countries of Senegal, Republic of Mali,
Mauritania, Ivory Coast, Upper Volta, Niger, Dahomey, and Guinea.   [8] January-October.
[9] January-September.   [10] Unofficial estimates.   [11] Year beginning March 21.   [12] January-
November.

Source: U. S. Department of Agriculture, Foreign Agricultural Service.

325

Table 15

C A S T O R   B E A N S

IMPORTS INTO PRINCIPAL IMPORTING COUNTRIES,
Average 1950-54, Annual 1957-62
(In Short Tons[1]/)

Country	Average 1950-54	1957	1958	1959	1960	1961[2]/	1962[2]/
North America							
United States	77,811	17,179	9,432	10,166	1,516	2,038	10,087
Europe							
Belgium-Luxembourg	9,404	4,860	5,027	3,207	6,796	3,317	3,187[3]/
France	14,193	19,000	23,410	17,544	27,552	11,430	28,771
West Germany	14,334[4]/	20,918	22,875	23,982	31,206	24,779	29,407
Italy	7,136	8,416	8,568	4,541	10,744	10,401	10,101[5]/
Netherlands	3,111	3,124	3,506	4,610	4,317	3,139	2,644[5]/
Portugal	1,031	662	784	430	-	-	-
Spain	482	2,251	882	1,871	1,003	531	6/
United Kingdom	21,857	6,512	15,530	13,815	10,269	12,822	23,152
Total	71,548	65,743	80,582	70,000	91,887	66,419	97,263
U. S. S. R.	-	10,141	10,582	8,488	9,149	2,094	2,205[7]/
Africa							
South Africa, Republic of	827	1,379	442	59	-	-	-
Asia							
Japan	18,410	24,547	23,805	29,983	30,224	35,800	19,180[8]/
GRAND TOTAL	168,596	118,989	124,843	118,696	132,776	106,351	128,735

1/2,000 lbs.   2/Preliminary.   3/January-July.   4/Average 1951-54.   5/January-October.
6/January-March.   7/January-May. Includes Eastern Europe.   8/January-June.

Source: U. S. Department of Agriculture, Foreign Agricultural Service.

326

Table 16

C A S T O R   B E A N S

ECUADOR EXPORTS BY COUNTRY OF DESTINATION: 1952-61
(In Metric Tons)

Country of Destination	1952	1953	1954	1955	1956	1957	1958	1959	1960	1961
North America										
United States	6,058	8,260	7,976	4,770	1,383	-	617	2,014	594	3,619
Canada	-	-	-	-	-	-	409	205	-	-
Total	6,058	8,260	7,976	4,770	1,383	-	1,026	2,219	594	3,619
South America										
Colombia	-	-	-	74	141	-	-	-	-	50
Venezuela	-	-	-	5	-	-	50	51	25	251
Chile	20	-	7	5	-	-	141	112	111	-
Total	20	-	7	84	141	-	191	163	136	301
Europe										
Belgium-Luxembourg	-	-	205	256	203	634	952	1,433	1,999	2,238
France	-	-	-	154	-	-	-	-	-	-
West Germany	-	511	-	-	51	5,237	2,460	2,350	201	711
Netherlands	-	-	1,468	1,224	3,227	1,767	2,331	3,136	6,969	10,637
Italy	-	-	-	-	-	-	739	-	305	102
Spain	-	-	-	-	-	-	102	-	-	-
United Kingdom	-	-	-	-	-	-	-	102	-	889
Total	-	511	1,673	1,634	3,481	7,638	6,584	7,021	9,474	14,577
Asia										
Japan	-	-	-	-	-	-	1,007	-	300	-
TOTAL	6,078	8,771	9,655	6,487	5,006	7,638	8,811	9,403	10,504	18,496

Source: U. S. Department of Agriculture, Foreign Agricultural Service.

327

Table 17

CASTOR BEANS

UNITED STATES IMPORTS BY COUNTRY OF ORIGIN: 1957-62
(In 1,000 Pounds)

Country of Origin	1957	1958	1959	1960	1961	1962
Mexico	121.0	-	-	-	0.3	-
El Salvador	56.0	-	-	-	-	-
Haiti	1,696.4	1,665.1	2,508.1	1,463.2	124.8	3,779.2
LW WW I	72.6	-	-	-	-	56.2
ECUADOR	-	1,116.5	3,949.1	1,343.7	3,949.9	15,669.4
Paraguay	2,179.1	388.5	162.1	224.9	-	669.3
Brazil	30,233.7	15,694.3	13,713.4	-	-	-
Italy	-	0.4	-	1.0	-	-
Netherlands	-	-	-	-	-	0.8
TOTAL	34,358.8	18,864.7	20,332.7	3,032.8	4,075.0	20,175.0

Source: U.S. Department of Commerce.

328

Table 18

C A S T O R   B E A N S

UNITED STATES IMPORTS BY COUNTRY OF ORIGIN: 1957-62
(In Metric Tons[1/])

Country of Origin	1957	1958	1959	1960	1961	1962
Mexico	54.9	-	-	-	0.2	-
El Salvador	25.4	-	-	-	-	-
Haiti	769.5	755.3	1,137.7	663.7	56.6	1,714.2
LW WW I	32.9	-	-	-	-	25.5
ECUADOR	-	506.4	1,791.3	609.5	1,791.6	7,107.6
Paraguay	988.4	176.2	73.5	102.0	-	303.6
Brazil	13,713.9	7,118.9	6,220.4	-	-	-
Italy	-	0.2	-	0.5	-	-
Netherlands	-	-	-	-	-	0.4
TOTAL	15,585.1	8,557.0	9.222.8	1,375.7	1,848.4	9,151.3

[1/]Computed from U. S. import data. One metric ton equals 2,204.6 pounds.

Source: U. S. Department of Commerce.

Table 19

C A S T O R   B E A N S

BELGIUM-LUXEMBOURG IMPORTS BY COUNTRY OF ORIGIN: 1957-61
(In Metric Tons)

Country of Origin	1957	1958	1959	1960	1961
Western Hemisphere					
Brazil	708	1,000	-	-	-
ECUADOR	1,677	1,046	811	2,404	1,986
Paraguay	-	988	520	-	-
Peru	531	1,110	100	-	526
Other	102	-	-	698	-
Total	3,018	4,144	1,431	3,102	2,512
Europe	-	71	-	1/	-
Africa					
Congo, Republic of the	18	129	-	-	-
South Africa, Republic of	91	216	-	-	-
Tanganyika	79	-	509	-	-
Kenya and Uganda	340	-	306	-	-
Other	139	-	166	-	-
Total	667	345	981	-	-
Asia					
China, Mainland	-	-	-	2,047	-
Thailand	510	-	204	-	-
West Pakistan	100	-	-	-	-
Iran	114	-	-	-	-
Total	724	-	204	2,047	-
Other Countries	1	1/	293	1,017	498
TOTAL	4,409	4,561	2,909	6,166	3,010

1/ Less than 500 kg.

Source: U. S. Department of Agriculture, Foreign Agricultural Service.

330

Table 20

C A S T O R   B E A N S

FRANCE IMPORTS BY COUNTRY OF ORIGIN: 1957-61
(In Metric Tons)

Country of Origin	1957	1958	1959	1960	1961
Western Hemisphere					
Argentina	-	-	-	650	394
Brazil	1,830	3,213	-	-	-
Paraguay	-	-	-	2,087	1,192
Total	1,830	3,213	-	2,737	1,586
Africa					
South Africa, Republic of	1,384	2,784	1,372	917	-
Former French West Africa[1]	554	535	770	2,049	2,376
Malagasy	830	1,528	662	784	344
Congo, Republic of the	729	588	582	292	77
Ethiopia	-	-	330	607	-
Morocco	-	-	705	923	448
Sudan	-	-	-	-	940
British Africa	10,189	11,388	7,025	7,773	2,981
Portuguese Africa	-	-	-	119	100
Total	13,686	16,823	11,446	13,464	7,266
Asia					
China	-	-	2,032	2,032	-
Thailand	-	-	-	546	464
Pakistan	-	-	-	846	-
Iran	479	-	-	-	-
Lebanon	-	-	1,051	1,247	995
Total	479	-	3,083	4,671	1,459
Other Countries	1,242	1,201	1,387	4,123[2]	59
TOTAL	17,236	21,237	15,916	24,996	10,370

[1] Now the independent countries of Togo, Senegal, Republic of Mali, Mauritania, Ivory Coast, Upper Volta, Niger, Dahomey, and Guinea. [2] All from Yugoslavia.

Source: U. S. Department of Commerce, Foreign Agricultural Service.

Table 21

C A S T O R   B E A N S

WEST GERMANY IMPORTS BY COUNTRY OF ORIGIN: 1957-62
(In Metric Tons)

Country of Origin	1957[1]	1958	1959	1960	1961	1962
Western Hemisphere						
Haiti		513	55	1,273	2,207	50
Brazil		12,234	3,772	-	-	-
ECUADOR		4,517	3,465	4,897	6,812	4,963
Paraguay		1,057	3,004	2,360	6,540	6,940
Peru		2,218	220	152	194	-
Argentina		-	-	989	2,053	810
Other		-	291	39	-	29
Total		20,539	10,807	9,710	17,806	12,792
Africa						
Ethiopia		-	230	-	98	-
Kenya and Uganda		-	1,850	223	-	-
Portuguese W. Africa		-	1,145	1,633	-	-
Sudan		-	53	3,592	78	-
South Africa, Republic of		-	306	408	128	443
Tanganyika		-	894	886	251	-
Mozambique		-	-	-	1,283	817
Other		-	-	42	49	-
Total		-	4,478	6,784	1,887	1,260
Asia						
China, Mainland		-	1,309	4,642	314	781
Indonesia		-	-	101	199	-
Pakistan		-	1,416	1,109	-	539
Vietnam, North		-	99	149	200	-
Thailand		200	3,648	2,626	2,065	11,290
Other		-	-	1,130	-	-
Total		200	6,472	9,757	2,778	12,610
Other Countries		12	-	2,058[2]	9	17
TOTAL	18,977	20,752	21,756	28,310	22,480	26,678

[1] Detail by country of origin not available. [2] Includes 2,044 metric tons imported from Yugoslavia.

Source: U. S. Department of Agriculture, Foreign Agricultural Service.

332

Table 22

C A S T O R   B E A N S

ITALY IMPORTS BY COUNTRY OF ORIGIN: 1957-62
(In Metric Tons)

Country of Origin	1957	1958	1959	1960	1961	1962
Western Hemisphere						
Brazil	-	274	24	-	-	-
ECUADOR	-	778	-	303	-	-
Other	1/	-	22	-	-	-
Total	1/	1,052	46	303	-	-
Africa						
Congo, Republic of the	210	101	-	-	-	-
Ethiopia	1,368	1,565	2,137	2,907	4,482	3,955
Libya	3,316	3,138	550	1,917	2,155	2,618
Kenya	490	408	74	190	-	-
Uganda	-	127	-	61	-	-
South Africa, Republic of	178	50	26	-	-	-
Tanganyika	999	942	339	1,992	1,612	1,034
British Equatorial W. Africa	-	-	164	191	-	-
Other	16	3	4	4	-	-
Total	6,577	6,334	3,294	7,262	8,249	7,607
Asia						
China, Mainland	-	251	699	1,424	-	-
Thailand	-	-	35	303	-	-
Pakistan	583	-	46	456	-	-
Iran	541	37	-	-	-	-
Iraq	-	99	-	-	-	-
Total	1,124	387	780	2,183	-	-
Other Countries	64	-	-	-	1,188	1,857
TOTAL	7,765	7,772	4,120	9,747	9,436	9,464

1/ Less than 500 kg.

Source: U. S. Department of Agriculture, Foreign Agricultural Service.

333

Table 23

C A S T O R   B E A N S

JAPAN IMPORTS BY COUNTRY OF ORIGIN: 1957-61
(In Metric Tons)

Country of Origin	1957	1958	1959	1960	1961
Western Hemisphere					
El Salvador	-	45	59	-	-
ECUADOR	-	700	300	-	299
Total	-	745	359	-	299
Africa					
Tanganyika	769	3,323	915	962	1,087
Kenya	-	3,115	427	-	153
Mozambique	-	-	-	300	255
Total	769	6,438	1,342	1,262	1,495
Asia					
China	-	-	-	-	538
Indonesia	-	-	-	147	25
Thailand	21,351	14,196	24,470	20,883	27,286
Cambodia	-	167	976	4,196	2,142
Philippines	-	-	1	582	602
Indirect from Chinese Port	61	50	52	319	-
Other	88	-	-	30	91
Total	21,500	14,413	25,499	26,157	30,684
TOTAL	22,269	21,596	27,200	27,419	32,478

Source: U. S. Department of Agriculture, Foreign Agricultural Service.

334

Table 24

C A S T O R B E A N S

NETHERLANDS IMPORTS BY COUNTRY OF ORIGIN: 1957-62
(In Metric Tons)

Country of Origin	1957	1958	1959	1960	1961	1962
Western Hemisphere						
Haiti	235	269	-	101	76	-
Brazil	-	-	102	-	-	-
ECUADOR	1,467	1,320	2,242	2,084	1,623	1,608
Peru	152	1,096	-	49	249	51
Paraguay	-	189	241	236	549	108
Argentina	-	-	-	438	249	735
Total	1,854	2,874	2,585	2,908	2,746	2,502
Africa						
Kenya and Uganda	100	-	52	78	-	-
Tanganyika	100	53	298	284	-	-
Portuguese E. Africa	100	-	55	-	-	-
South Africa, Republic of	110	-	336	-	-	-
Libya	-	202	411	-	-	-
Other	60	-	100	-	-	-
Total	470	255	1,252	362	-	-
Asia						
Iran	48	-	-	-	-	-
West Pakistan	156	-	199	142	101	102
Thailand	304	-	102	-	-	229
China, Mainland	-	53	46	504	-	-
Total	508	53	347	646	101	331
Other Countries	2	-	-	-	-	-
TOTAL	2,834	3,181	4,182	3,916	2,848	2,833

Source: U. S. Department of Agriculture, Foreign Agricultural Service.

335

Table 25

C A S T O R B E A N S

UNITED KINGDOM IMPORTS BY COUNTRY OF ORIGIN: 1957-62
(In Long Tons)

Country of Origin	1957	1958	1959	1960	1961	1962[1]
Western Hemisphere						
ECUADOR	-	798	300	-	500	
Peru	-	1,393	629	849	233	
Brazil	-	1,678	-	-	-	
Total	-	3,869	929	849	733	
Africa						
Nigeria	501	307	460	717	794	
South Africa, Republic of	402	3,830	1,187	300	1,134	
Rhodesia and Nyasaland	59	879	288	-	-	
Tanganyika	2,547	2,950	6,600	3,868	5,458	
Kenya	1,034	1,875	1,605	1,499	2,553	
Uganda	104	139	794	-	-	
Total	4,647	9,980	10,934	6,384	9,939	
Asia						
Pakistan	1,167	10	469	-	-	
Thailand	-	-	-	-	145	
Total	1,167	10	469	-	145	
Other Countries	-	7[2]	4[2]	1,936[3]	631[3]	
TOTAL	5,814	13,866	12,336	9,169	11,448	20,671

[1]Detail by country of origin not available. [2]Foreign countries. [3]Commonwealth countries and the Irish Republic.

Source: U. S. Department of Agriculture, Foreign Agricultural Service.

Table 26

C A S T O R   O I L[1]/

EXPORTS FROM SPECIFIED COUNTRIES,
Average 1950-54, Annual 1957-62
(In Short Tons[2]/)

Country of Origin	Average 1950-54	1957	1958	1959	1960	1961[3]/	1962[3]/
North America [4]/							
United States	344	168	201	247	235	405	296
South America							
Brazil	25,694	53,036	60,977	52,601[6]/	46,138	100,128	40,420[5]/
Paraguay	1,110	280	46	1	-	-	8[7]/
Total	26,804	53,316	61,023	52,602	46,138	100,128	40,428
Europe							
Belgium-Luxembourg	4,503	1,229	2,014	1,192	2,191	775	25[8]/
West Germany	1,873	2,548	2,267	3,924	4,449	1,114	3,724[9]/
Rumania	-	1,151	2,210	3,382	2,168	4,188	4,740[6]/
United Kingdom	994	882	895	905	1,022	965	1,041[10]/
Other	873	798	831	849	460	1,750	549
Total	8,243	6,608	8,217	10,252	10,290	8,792	10,079
Africa							
Angola	285	1,123	1,930	1,516	973	814	612[8]/
Other	1,103	90	141	109	86	27	-
Total	1,388	1,213	2,071	1,625	1,059	841	612
Asia							
Hong Kong	49	13	20	11	4	-	-
India	29,346	47,539	22,662	39,511	64,456	25,968	25,420[9]/
Total	29,395	47,552	22,682	39,522	64,460	25,968	25,420
Oceania							
Australia[11]/	91	91	89	77	54	39	-
TOTAL	66,265	108,948	94,283	104,325	122,236	136,173	76,835

[1]/ Crude and refined oil combined as such. [2]/ 2,000 lbs. [3]/ Preliminary. [4]/ Commercial castor oil only. [5]/ January-August. [6]/ January-June. [7]/ January-March. [8]/ January-July. [9]/ January-October. [10]/ January-November. [11]/ Year ending June 30.

Source: U. S. Department of Agriculture, Foreign Agricultural Service.

Table 27

C A S T O R   O I L

IMPORTS INTO PRINCIPAL IMPORTING COUNTRIES,
Average 1950-54, Annual 1957-62
(In Short Tons[1]/)

Country	Average 1950-54	1957	1958	1959	1960	1961 [2]/	1962 [2]/
North America							
United States	43,220	60,715	41,816	58,164	53,726	59,278	52,807 [3]/
Canada	2,370	2,837	2,412	2,960	2,324	2,529	689 [3]/
Total	45,590	63,552	44,228	61,124	56,050	61,807	53,496
South America	200	198	256	319	269	241	-
Europe							
Austria	479	743	656	751	992	955	508 [3]/
Belgium-Luxembourg	598	277	452	405	377	709	487 [4]/
Denmark	503	444	493	553	578	424	-
France	1,580	11,650	18,026	7,571	19,535	28,647	23,799 [5]/
West Germany	1,520	2,210	2,941	2,114	2,373	2,680	2,685 [5]/
Netherlands	473	992	801	693	891	1,039	780 [5]/
Sweden	906	985	1,033	1,009	1,476	879	813 [6]/
Switzerland	1,007	1,383	929	911	-	1,543	882 [7]/
United Kingdom	9,918	19,483	16,313	14,806	24,789	18,441	14,204
Other	667	1,304	336	189	235	809	58
Total	17,651	39,471	41,980	29,002	51,246	56,126	44,216
Africa	618	398	627	365	65	-	-
Asia	213	250	275	185	218	219	151
Oceania							
Australia [8]/	1,922	1,611	1,387	1,272	2,264	1,687	-
New Zealand	158	208	294	312	274	262	-
Total	2,080	1,819	1,681	1,584	2,538	1,949	-
GRAND TOTAL	66,352	105,688	89,047	92,579	110,386	120,342	97,863

[1]/2,000 pounds. [2]/Preliminary. [3]/January-July. [4]/January-June. [5]/January-October.
[6]/January-September. [7]/January-August. [8]/Year ending June 30.

Source: U. S. Department of Agriculture, Foreign Agricultural Service.

338

Table 28

C A S T O R   O I L

UNITED STATES IMPORTS BY COUNTRY OF ORIGIN: 1957-62
(In Short Tons)

Country of Origin	1957	1958	1959	1960	1961	1962
Western Hemisphere						
Brazil	30,851	37,438	40,797	20,977	55,407	44,497
Other	752	452	42	198	345	121
Total	31,603	37,890	40,839	21,175	55,752	44,618
Europe						
West Germany	1,892	1,553	1,994	2,998	335	3,060
Yugoslavia	-	-	-	2,645	1,375	1,277
Other	-	336	327	760	-	-
Total	1,892	1,889	2,321	6,403	1,710	4,337
Africa						
Angola	467	2,038	624	675	930	165
Congo, Republic of the	-	-	268	352	308	161
Portuguese West Africa, n.e.c.	206	-	-	-	-	-
Total	673	2,038	892	1,027	1,238	326
Asia						
India	26,547	-	13,787	24,960	-	218
Japan	-	-	325	160	578	3,308
Total	26,547	-	14,112	25,120	578	3,526
TOTAL	60,715	41,816	58,164	53,726	59,278	52,807

Source: U. S. Department of Commerce, Bureau of the Census.

339

Table 29

C A S T O R   B E A N S & C A S T O R   O I L

UNITED STATES IMPORTS AND PRODUCTION,
Average 1950-54, Annual 1956-62
(In Short Tons[1])

	Average 1950-54	1956	1957	1958	1959	1960	1961	1962
Total U.S. Imports of Castor Beans	77,811	21,206	17,179	9,432	10,166	1,516	2,038	10,087
Imports of Castor Beans from Ecuador	6,559	1,960	-	558	1,974	672	1,975	7,835
Total Ecuadorian Production of Castor Beans	7,182[3]	18,025	11,825	20,610	19,500	21,800	22,815[3]	24,250[3]
Total U.S. Imports of Castor Oil	43,220	44,392	60,715	41,816	58,164	53,726	59,278	52,807
U.S. Production of Castor Beans	13,449[4]	1,880	10,160	20,560	12,165	15,635	19,000[3]	22,000[3]

1/2,000 lbs. 2/Exports of castor beans. 3/Preliminary. 4/Less than 5 years.

Source: U. S. Department of Agriculture, Foreign Agricultural Service.

Table 30

C O C O A

FLAVOR COCOA EXPORTS BY PRINCIPAL PRODUCING COUNTRIES,
Average 1952-56 and Annual 1957-62
(Metric Tons)

Producing Countries*	Average 1952-56	1957	1958	1959	1960	1961	1962
Ceylon	2,834	2,679	2,643	2,678	2,224	2,668	2,398
Comoro Islands	40	52	35	33	36	42	11
Costa Rica 1/	2,030	2,660	1,920	2,880	2,955	2,550	3,000
Dominica	170	86	151	143	155	99	n.a.
ECUADOR	25,846	26,856	22,150	28,540	36,452	32,426 2/	31,335 2/
Grenada	2,290	1,184	1,832	1,931	1,832	2,453 3/	2,272 2/
Indonesia	454	470	486	302	330	443 3/	28
Jamaica	1,282	256	344	1,115	1,624	1,116	2,231
Madagascar	297	368	322	228	344	435	338
New Guinea 4/	690	5,489	2,575	3,735	4,780	6,500	9,860
Nicaragua	121	119	102	184	309	895	n.a.
Panama	2,042	1,553	1,270	1,680	1,449	1,194	1,104
Sta. Lucia	272	291	186	267	236	284	n.a.
St. Vincent	n.a.	n.a.	n.a.	n.a.	n.a.	n.a.	n.a.
Surinam	35	168	112	223	269	138	317
Trinidad and Tobago	8,396	7,176	8,246	7,232 5/	7,237	5,686	5,916
Venezuela	16,645	14,978	13,509	10,416	11,973 5/	9,793 1/	10,776
Western Samoa	3,017	3,118	4,099	3,914	3,634	3,350 1/	4,696
Total	66,461	67,503	59,582	65,501	75,839	69,673	74,282

*As identified in Appendix B of the Draft International Cocoa Agreement, as revised by the FAO Cocoa Study Group at its Sixth Session, Port-of-Spain, March 25-30, 1963.

1/ Exports of flavor cocoa for Costa Rica have been calculated at 25 percent of total exports. (The Draft International Cocoa Agreement, Appendix B, specifies this percentage of Costa Rica's production as consisting of flavor cocoa.) 2/ Unofficial estimate. 3/ Eleven months. 4/ New Guinea exports of flavor cocoa calculated at 75 percent of total exports. (See footnote (1) above.) 5/ May include some semi-manufactured cocoa.

Source: Revised Draft International Cocoa Agreement, March 1963, and Cocoa Statistics, FAO, Rome.

Table 31

C O C O A

WORLD EXPORTS BY COUNTRY OF ORIGIN,
Average 1952-56 and 1958-62; Annual 1958-62
(Metric Tons)

Continent and Country	Average 1952-56	Average 1958-62	1958	1959	1960	1961	1962
North & Central America							
Costa Rica	8,113	10,648	7,685	11,522	11,822	10,213	11,996
Cuba	396	738 1/	554	1,048	611	na	na
Dominican Republic	21,564	18,768	24,096	21,722	26,970	11,696	9,355
Granada	2,290	1,984	1,432	1,931	1,832	2,453*	2,272*
Haiti	1,853	na	1,889	na	na	na	512
Jamaica	1,282	1,286	344	1,115	1,624	1,116	2,231
Mexico	2,512	6,211	5,033	5,393	3,089	5,475	12,066
Panama	2,042	1,339	1,270	1,680	1,449	1,194	1,104
Trinidad and Tobago	8,396	6,863	8,246	7,232	7,237	5,686	5,916
Other	1,190	1,423 1/	1,232	1,501	1,462	1,498	216 2/
Total	49,640	52,356	51,780	54,000	58,000	41,000	57,000
South America							
Brazil	107,132	93,596	103,435	79,577	125,457	104,170	55,340
ECUADOR	25,846	30,181	22,150	28,540	36,452	32,426	31,335
Venezuela	16,645	11,293	13,509	10,416 3/	11,973 3/	9,793	10,776
Other	80	310	442	281	371	138	317
Total	149,700	135,420	139,540	118,810	174,250	146,700	97,800
Asia & Oceania							
Ceylon	2,834	2,522	2,643	2,678	2,224	2,668	2,398
Indonesia	454	238	486	302	330	44 4/	28
New Guinea	919	7,319	3,434	4,979	6,373	8,666	13,144
New Hebrides and Papua	826	803	921	857	955	617	663
Western Samoa	3,017	3,939	4,099	3,914	3,634	3,350*	4,696
Total	8,050	14,804	11,580	12,730	13,510	15,200	21,000

Table 31 (Continued)

COCOA: WORLD EXPORTS BY COUNTRY OF ORIGIN

Continent and Country	Average 1952-56	Average 1958-62	1958	1959	1960	1961	1962
Africa							
Angola	318	271	328	244	245	370	168
Cameroon	52,634	56,982	54,414	53,357	58,898	58,302	59,938
Congo (Brazaville)	42	531	289	391	521	824	629
Congo (Leopoldville)	2,981	4,893	4,753	3,795	5,211	4,700*	6,007
Comoro Islands	40	31	35	33	36	42	11
Gabon	2,650	2,957	2,366	2,513	3,326	3,191	3,391
Ghana	224,154	320,441	200,494	254,216	307,661	411,855	427,977
Ivory Coast	65,115	72,407	46,333	63,269	62,896	88,467	101,069
Liberia	455	769	606	793	994	671	782
Malagasy Republic	297	333	322	228	344	435	338
Nigeria	106,343	155,046	89,050	145,096	156,395	186,864	197,824
Sao Tome and Principe	8,259	8,899	7,933	6,944	10,169	10,347	9,100
Sierra Leone	2,131	3,149	2,873	2,659	3,301	2,334	4,579
Spanish Equatorial Region	17,345	24,378	23,786	19,206	33,339*	20,753*	24,806*
Togo	8,725	9,461	6,917	8,362	9,414	11,534	11,079
Total	491,490	660,570	440,500	561,110	652,750	800,690	847,800
GRAND TOTAL	698,900	863,180	643,400	746,600	898,500	1,003,800	1,023,600

*Unofficial or estimate. 1/Average 1958-1960. 2/Information unavailable for many countries. 3/May include some semi-manufactured cocoa. 4/Eleven months.

Source: Cocoa Statistics, FAO, Rome.

343

Table 32

C O C O A

WORLD IMPORTS BY COUNTRY OF DESTINATION,
Average 1952-56 and 1958-62; Annual 1958-62
(Metric Tons)

Continent and Country	Average 1952-56	Average 1958-62	1958	1959	1960	1961	1962
Europe, Western							
Austria	7,270	10,330	8,421	10,228	10,580	12,096	10,323
Belgium	8,934	12,218	6,838	10,144	14,458	14,748	14,900
Denmark	3,021	3,983	3,035	3,464	4,225	3,973	5,220
France	47,589	59,458	55,993	56,228	56,667	59,178	69,225
Germany, West	76,200	114,035	90,272	103,919	113,529	125,475	136,980
Italy	17,766	29,905	22,065	26,625	28,026	36,008	36,803
Netherlands	58,114	86,736	62,102	75,696	83,564	109,140	103,180
Norway	3,927	4,311	3,932	4,018	4,171	4,844	4,592
Spain	14,270	22,337	22,396	21,163	23,996	22,795	21,333
Sweden	6,893	7,381	6,387	6,844	7,092	8,017	8,566
Switzerland	10,314	13,453	7,860	12,168	15,518	18,139	13,581
United Kingdom	116,703	97,176	92,574	86,918	98,445	92,993	114,949
Other	8,633	13,718	8,580	12,768	13,773	15,809	17,659
Total	379,630	475,042	390,460	430,180	474,040	523,220	557,310
Europe, Eastern	31,720	70,955 1/	40,000	77,410	101,410	65,000	n. a. 2/
North and Central America							
Canada	13,361	14,276	11,031	12,658	15,375	15,958	16,357
United States	246,122	261,554	200,906 3/	219,127 3/	249,887 3/	347,784 3/	290,068 3/
Other	212	319	206 3/	294 3/	352 3/	341 3/	400 3/
Total	259,700	276,148	212,140	232,080	265,610	364,080	306,830
South America	17,720	14,554	15,780	11,860	9,830	16,800	18,500
Asia	5,910	17,554	8,590	13,310	15,070	20,800	30,000
Africa	4,380	5,424	4,160	4,120	6,840	4,600	7,400

Table 32 (Continued)

COCOA: WORLD IMPORTS BY COUNTRY OF DESTINATION

Continent and Country	Average 1952-56	Average 1958-62	1958	1959	1960	1961	1962
Oceania							
Australia	8,373	11,199	8,346	10,324	13,040	15,941	8,346
New Zealand	2,533	3,088	2,347	2,837	3,328	3,069	3,859
Total	10,910	14,286	10,690	13,160	16,370	19,010	12,200
GRAND TOTAL	710,000	877,300	681,800	782,100	889,100	1,013,500	1,020,000

1/ Average 1958-61.   2/ Czechoslovakia 12,230.   3/ El Salvador.

Source: Cocoa Statistics, FAO, Rome.

Table 33

C O C O A

ECUADOR EXPORTS BY COUNTRY OF DESTINATION: 1952-62
(In 1,000 Pounds)

Destination	1952	1953	1954	1955	1956	1957	1958	1959²/	1960	1961	1962
North America											
Canada	-	-	-	-	-	-	-	77	626	115	399
United States	29,564	27,217	41,278	26,860	31,205	26,440	26,610	32,399	50,440	36,615	29,085
Total	29,564	27,217	41,278	26,860	31,205	26,440	26,610	32,476	51,066	36,730	29,484
Europe											
Belgium	2,760	2,287	2,390	2,250	2,472	5,306	1,863	2,138	3,130	3,098	3,905
Denmark	-	638	-	300	322	265	203	295	679	791	766
France	417	541	877	476	465	575	271	428	618	467	677
West Germany	3,799	3,423	4,108	3,995	7,202	6,113	4,711	6,034	7,794	8,400	9,517
Italy	4,034	2,936	1,888	2,694	3,281	2,447	3,172	3,688	3,900	3,902	4,076
Netherlands	157	1,194	1,104	1,715	1,859	1,572	1,548	2,690	3,238	4,271	6,120
Norway	-	27	9	-	-	-	-	154	60	162	125
Spain	-	-	-	-	-	-	-	-	4	-	-
Sweden	337	146	394	210	598	223	269	351	414	414	342
Switzerland	-	72	142	432	1,106	137	864	906	1,137	830	379
United Kingdom	948	3	1,190	-	-	-	-	165	664	138⁵/	334
Other	-	-	-	-	545¹/	313¹/	-	600³/	306⁶/	1,371	206⁶/
Total	12,452	11,267	12,102	12,072	17,850	16,951	12,901	17,449	21,944	23,844	26,261
South America											
Argentina	-	-	1,521	-	-	-	-	126	58	197	125
Bolivia	-	30	-	-	-	-	-	-	-	-	-
Chile	4	231	126	-	-	-	-	174	170	215	23
Colombia	11,283	9,920	10,528	14,317	16,222	15,774	9,094	12,330	5,901	7,885	8,779
Peru	-	-	11	-	-	-	-	-	-	-	-
Uruguay	-	-	-	-	-	-	-	29	22	-	-
Total	11,287	10,181	12,186	14,317	16,222	15,774	9,094	12,659	6,151	8,297	8,928
Asia and Oceania											
Australia	-	-	-	-	-	-	-	57	67	7	11
Israel	-	67	-	-	-	-	-	-	110	84	116
Japan	-	-	-	-	-	-	-	163	908	2,635	4,483
Other	-	-	-	-	-	-	-	42	38	22	13
Total	-	67	-	-	-	-	-	262	1,123	2,748	4,623
Africa	-	-	-	-	-	-	913	22	33	34	33
Not Specified	123	-	-	973	952	333	-	5	-	-	-
GRAND TOTAL	53,426	48,732	65,566	54,222	66,229	59,498	49,518	62,873	80,317	71,653	69,329

1/All to Czechoslovakia. 2/Revised. 3/Czechoslovakia and Finland. 4/Greece and Yugoslavia. 5/Poland, Greece,
Czechoslovakia and Finland. 6/Finland and Greece. Source: U.S. Department of Agriculture.

Table 34

C O C O A

ECUADOR EXPORTS: TOTAL AND TO THE U. S., BY VOLUME AND VALUE,
1952-62

	Volume (in 1,000 pounds)			Value (current US $ f.o.b.)	
Year	Total	To US	To US as % of total	Total (in million $)	Avg. price per pound (in dollars)
1952	53,426	29,564	55.3	17.0	.318
1953	48,732	27,217	55.8	15.6	.320
1954	65,566	41,278	62.9	34.0	.520
1955	54,220	26,860	49.5	19.0	.350
1956	66,229	31,205	47.2	17.8	.268
1957	59,498	26,440	44.4	18.7	.314
1958	49,518	26,610	53.7	20.7	.417
1959	62,873	32,399	51.5	21.8	.347
1960	80,317	50,440	62.8	21.6	.269
1961	71,653	36,615	51.1	15.6	.218
1962	69,329	29,564	42.6	15.7	.227

Source: Data for 1952-61 from U. S. Department of Commerce; for
1962 from Banco Central del Ecuador.

Table 35

C O C O A

UNITED STATES IMPORTS BY COUNTRY OF ORIGIN: 1957-62
(In Metric Tons)

Country of Origin	1957	1958	1959	1960	1961	1962
Latin America						
Brazil	49,869	46,257	44,590	60,420	49,887	17,420
Costa Rica	4,696	4,248	7,223	6,007	6,211	5,986
Cuba	1,682	847	953	660	-	-
Domincan Republic	23,358	23,352	20,556	26,202	10,702	18,468
ECUADOR	11,743	11,616	15,290	22,240	17,035	12,218
Haiti	1,971	1,764	2,358	1,174	783	544
L. W. and W. W. Islands	108	187	163	125	236	273
Mexico	6,764	3,946	4,380	2,391	4,230	10,433
Panama	2,543	2,307	3,548	3,006	2,954	2,561
Trinidad and Tobago	3,752	4,462	4,049	4,301	3,404	3,514
Venezuela	9,413	9,660	5,993	6,383	4,716	4,463
Other	692	1,759	2,767	3,098	1,296	1,586
Total	116,591	110,405	111,870	136,007	101,454	77,466
Africa						
Cameroon	8,312	5,493	4,951	4,722	8,652	5,557
Ghana	49,638	48,717	61,026	59,581	137,572	108,577
Ivory Coast-Togo	22,520	17,292	15,123	11,202	26,647	31,372
Nigeria	32,388	16,534	22,992	33,613	69,196	60,113
Portuguese Africa	965	640	1,027	633	3,359	1,745
Spanish Africa	200	-	45	1,900	350	-
Other	1,024	872	573	25	1,090	305
Total	115,047	89,548	105,737	111,676	246,866	207,669
Asia and Oceania	636	762	1,152	1,936	1,201	4,835
Europe	118	193	346	270	96	101
GRAND TOTAL	232,392	200,908	219,105	249,889	349,617	290,071

Source: U. S. Department of Agriculture.

Table 36

C O C O A

BELGIUM IMPORTS BY COUNTRY OF ORIGIN: 1957-61
(In Metric Tons)

Country of Origin	1957	1958	1959	1960	1961
Africa					
Cameroon	-	-	-	124	19
Congo (Leopoldville)[1]	1,991	1,374	1,321	1,983	2,200
Equatorial Africa[2]	-	-	40	54	-
Ghana	3,749	1,721	3,263	4,687	3,625
Ivory Coast	-	305	567	693	1,216
Nigeria	-	-	607	631	195
Portuguese Africa	-	-	32	50	46
Togo	-	-	175	694	1,607
Total	5,740	3,400	6,005	8,916	8,908
Latin America					
Brazil	-	-	558	1,129	1,185
ECUADOR	1,084	678	770	1,206	1,078
Fed. West Indies	497	435	1,138	1,270	977
Venezuela	1,321	1,004	946	1,255	1,193
Total	2,902	2,117	3,412	4,860	4,433
Asia and Oceania					
New Hebrides	-	-	5	-	-
Total	-	-	5	-	-
Europe					
Netherlands	448	323	298	497	599
Total	448	323	298	497	599
Not Specified	1,581	998	424	186	808
GRAND TOTAL	10,671	6,838	10,144	14,459	14,748

[1] Formerly Belgian Congo. [2] Includes Gabon, Congo (Brazzaville), and
Central African Republic.

Table 37

C O C O A

COLOMBIA IMPORTS BY COUNTRY OF ORIGIN,
Crop Years 1957/58-1961/62
(In Metric Tons)

	1957/58	1958/59	1959/60	1960/61	1961/62
Registered Imports From:					
Costa Rica	1,584	1,317	1,378	2,332	1,252
Panama	194	36	0	148	810
ECUADOR	4,057	5,674	2,252	5,972	5,021
Brazil	88	0	0	0	0
Philippines	68	0	0	0	0
Total	5,991	7,027	3,630	8,452	7,083
Contraband[1]	n.a.	n.a.	3,400	3,400	2,000
GRAND TOTAL	5,991	7,027	7,030	11,852	9,083

[1] These are estimates as reported to the source, by the Ministry of
Agriculture, in Bogota, Colombia.

Source: Foreign Agricultural Service Reports, U.S. Department of Agriculture.

Table 38

C O C O A

FRANCE IMPORTS BY COUNTRY OF ORIGIN: 1957-62
(In Metric Tons)

Country of Origin	1957	1958	1959	1960	1961	1962
Africa						
Cameroon	17,412	23,104	19,819	18,953	12,894	16,906
Congo (Leopoldville)[1]	-	-	-	35	119	70
Equatorial Africa[2]	295	517	519	501	572	756
Ghana	5,400	6,380	4,753	5,330	3,573	5,750
Ivory Coast	26,561	19,794	22,180	22,974	33,272	33,776
Malagasy Republic[3]	500	358	204	365	396	318
Nigeria	4,509	408	2,463	1,485	3,131	5,116
Portuguese Africa	659	514	115	114	69	43
Togo	2,336	3,122	4,640	4,216	3,294	4,619
Other	40	-	-	-	-	-
Total	57,712	54,197	54,693	53,973	57,320	67,354
Latin America						
Brazil	179	392	43	606	216	95
ECUADOR	275	157	190	344	229	298
Fed. West Indies	291	290	287	344	332	360
French West Indies	202	227	264	321	280	225
Venezuela	175	9	190	171	104	121
Other	-	-	-	18	-	-
Total	1,122	1,075	974	1,804	1,161	1,099
Asia and Oceania						
Ceylon	25	25	21	20	45	-
Indonesia	-	5	-	5	-	-
New Hebrides	637	660	423	749	388	448
Other	17	22	24	-	251	299
Total	679	712	468	774	684	747
Not Specified	46	9	93	116	13	25
GRAND TOTAL	59,559	55,993	56,228	56,667	59,178	69,225

[1] Formerly Belgian Congo. [2] Includes Gabon, Congo (Brazzaville), and Central African Republic. [3] Includes Comoros.

Source: U. S. Department of Agriculture.

351

Table 39

C O C O A

WEST GERMANY IMPORTS BY COUNTRY OF ORIGIN: 1957-62
(In Metric Tons)

Country of Origin	1957	1958	1959	1960	1961	1962
Africa						
Cameroon	6,481	5,089	5,409	9,347	8,347	11,919
Cameroon, West	675	404	35	766	574	-
Congo (Leopoldville)[1]/	967	1,017	923	937	707	877
Equatorial Africa[2]/	-	97	-	199	51	212
Ghana	53,361	46,303	49,971	52,262	60,195	68,095
Ivory Coast	4,488	3,978	4,654	5,452	6,677	5,704
Liberia	47	46	87	208	89	10
Malagasy Republic[3]/	-	-	-	-	-	5
Nigeria	12,281	8,735	17,615	19,873	23,650	27,884
Portuguese Africa	2,264	1,473	1,328	821	661	414
Spanish Africa	-	-	-	-	192	-
Togo	23	4/	34	439	550	675
Total	80,587	67,142	80,056	90,304	101,693	115,795
Latin America						
Brazil	21,991	17,600	17,249	16,007	15,677	11,901
Costa Rica	105	111	405	309	46	114
Dominican Republic	-	-	-	6	-	-
ECUADOR	2,624	2,033	2,679	2,759	3,377	4,604
Fed. West Indies	643	595	632	518	785	666
Haiti	10	-	-	-	-	-
Mexico	11	26	72	32	48	-
Surinam	-	-	11	108	21	189
Venezuela	1,622	1,401	1,474	1,454	1,608	1,347
Other	65	124	73	53	92	-
Total	27,071	21,890	22,595	21,246	21,654	18,821
Asia and Oceania						
Ceylon	10	7	46	54	23	-
Indonesia	230	304	262	269	168	104
New Guinea	13	58	215	729	152	-
New Hebrides	-	-	15	131	-	-
Western Samoa	479	363	505	517	-	-
Other	10	121	55	108	1,463	1,859
Total	742	853	1,098	1,808	1,806	1,963
Europe						
Italy	47	381	168	166	312	392
Total	47	381	168	166	312	392
Not Specified	2	6	3	5	10	9
GRAND TOTAL	108,449	90,272	103,920	113,529	125,475	136,980

1/Formerly Belgian Congo. 2/Includes Gabon, Congo (Brazzaville), and Central African Republic. 3/Includes Comoros. 4/Included with Ivory Coast.

Source: U. S. Department of Agriculture.

352

Table 40

C O C O A

ITALY IMPORTS BY COUNTRY OF ORIGIN: 1957-62
(In Metric Tons)

Country of Origin	1957	1958	1959	1960	1961	1962
Africa						
Cameroon	378	395	10	1,498	3,604	3,840
Cameroon, West	955	108	-	970	-	-
Congo (Leopoldville)[1]	9	22	1,140	10	2	-
Equatorial Africa[2]	2,222	14	13	-	-	-
Ghana	7,432	10,318	14,517	11,996	15,222	15,268
Ivory Coast	5,364	838	1,304	2,134	1,934	3,937
Liberia	92	-	-	-	-	-
Nigeria	6,127	4,848	5,017	7,151	10,133	8,414
Portuguese Africa	111	62	61	81	211	266
Sierra Leone	-	-	-	41	-	-
Togo	-	[3]	[3]	[3]	119	50
Other	198	48	17	58	-	-
Total	22,888	16,653	22,079	23,939	31,225	31,775
Latin America						
Brazil	2,611	2,523	1,708	1,532	1,635	1,496
Costa Rica	375	481	210	171	245	265
Dominican Republic	379	-	336	67	11	-
ECUADOR	1,208	1,261	1,289	1,414	1,692	1,924
Fed. West Indies	48	38	112	252	296	376
French West Indies	2	-	-	4	-	-
Haiti	4	17	54	-	-	-
Mexico	6	5	27	5	-	-
Venezuela	449	541	386	287	313	266
Other	20	52	20	10	-	-
Total	5,102	4,918	4,142	3,742	4,192	4,327
Asia and Oceania						
Ceylon	176	155	192	133	114	209
Indonesia	2	-	-	-	-	-
Other	18	30	12	153	97	26
Total	196	185	204	286	211	235
Europe						
France	8	-	-	22	-	-
Germany, West	96	161	3	-	-	-
Netherlands	-	100	8	13	5	-
United Kingdom	3	-	100	7	-	-
Other	10	47	15	18	-	-
Total	117	308	126	60	5	-
United States	-	1	4	9	-	-
Not Specified	-	-	-	-	375	466
GRAND TOTAL	28,303	22,065	26,555	28,036	36,008	36,803

[1]Formerly Belgian Congo. [2]Includes Gabon, Congo (Brazzaville), and Central African Republic. [3]Included with Ivory Coast.

Source: U. S. Department of Agriculture.

353

Table 41

C O C O A   B E A N S

JAPAN IMPORTS BY COUNTRY OF ORIGIN: 1957-61
(In Metric Tons)

Country of Origin	1957	1958	1959	1960	1961
Africa					
Cameroon	-	-	5	-	165
Equatorial Africa	-	-	79	303	45
Ghana	1,451	711	1,439	3,438	7,479
Ivory Coast	-	-	-	45	654
Nigeria	1,005	831	1,152	1,962	2,452
Other	15	-	47	51	116
Total	2,471	1,542	2,722	5,799	10,911
Latin America					
Brazil	2,586	437	784	973	1,071
Costa Rica	25	259	656	290	279
Dominican Rep.	6	233	526	91	-
ECUADOR	3	14	25	224	1,102
Guatemala	-	-	48	-	-
Mexico	6	254	225	153	513
Peru	16	15	110	-	-
Venezuela	506	1,404	1,737	492	318
Other	70	159	202	147	34
Total	3,218	2,775	4,313	2,370	3,317
Asia and Oceania					
Bismark Archipelago	42	160	356	629	210
Ceylon	156	612	713	579	870
Northeast N. Guinea	5	15	122	74	151
Other	9	227	5	56	125
Total	212	1,014	1,196	1,338	1,356
Other	160	104	43	113	10
TOTAL IMPORTS	6,061	5,435	8,274	9,620	15,594

Source: U. S. Department of Agriculture.

354

Table 42

C O C O A

NETHERLANDS IMPORTS BY COUNTRY OF ORIGIN: 1957-62
(In Metric Tons)

Country of Origin	1957	1958	1959	1960	1961	1962
Africa						
Cameroon	16,051	13,350	13,881	20,301	27,162	25,730
Cameroon, West	178	1,197	5,429	5,102	4,244	-
Congo (Leopoldville)[1]	2,194	2,058	1,343	1,418	2,261	2,028
Equatorial Africa[2]	608	156	336	235	324	940
Ghana	14,547	15,047	17,660	15,383	23,647	23,098
Ivory Coast	7,596	5,586	5,979	5,447	11,396	9,658
Liberia	474	565	492	643	607	894
Malagasy Republic[3]	-	19	-	-	-	-
Nigeria	17,166	7,506	17,593	17,195	18,673	23,499
Portuguese Africa	4,810	3,858	2,156	2,604	2,931	2,780
Sierra Leone	1,264	1,824	2,420	3,029	3,527	3,809
Spanish Africa	-	-	-	2,234	3,971	154
Togo	175	163	528	1,140	1,128	900
Other	-	-	-	-	-	36
Total	65,063	51,329	67,817	74,731	99,871	93,526
Latin America						
Brazil	7,495	6,304	5,352	5,999	4,979	4,499
Costa Rica	162	93	41	35	-	-
Dominican Republic	-	-	-	-	13	-
ECUADOR	221	112	174	163	382	444
Fed. West Indies	253	465	304	319	406	416
Haiti	-	25	39	32	119	-
Mexico	115	698	64	95	99	-
Surinam	153	147	283	507	550	1,193
Venezuela	186	126	97	116	209	139
Other	187	54	88	8	208	103
Total	8,772	8,024	6,442	7,274	6,965	6,794
Asia and Oceania						
Ceylon	145	114	48	55	27	14
Indonesia	61	112	58	18	22	4
New Guinea	-	-	14	80	200	95
Western Samoa	14	-	30	80	59	-
Other	-	6	-	60	100	111
Total	220	232	150	293	408	224
Europe						
Belgium	321	241	268	263	374	443
France	25	28	-	74	55	-
Germany, West	36	188	129	99	200	492
United Kingdom	448	1,262	313	463	551	1,056
Other	18	146	18	5	106	96
Total	848	1,865	728	904	1,286	2,087
United States	984	614	553	333	600	527
Not Specified	9	38	6	29	10	22
GRAND TOTAL	75,896	62,102	75,696	83,564	109,140	103,180

[1] Formerly Belgian Congo. [2] Includes Gabon, Congo (Brazzaville), and Central African
Republic. [3] Includes Comoros.

Source: U. S. Department of Agriculture.

355

Table 43

C O C O A

SWITZERLAND IMPORTS BY COUNTRY OF ORIGIN: 1958-62
(In Metric Tons)

Country of Origin	1958	1959	1960	1961	1962
Africa					
Cameroon	-	-	27	139	131
Ghana	4,317	7,121	8,431	10,648	6,211
Ivory Coast	124	-	118	990	792
Nigeria	557	1,410	2,040	1,055	1,505
Portuguese Africa	161	272	285	287	254
Togo	-	-	89	471	512
Other	82	111	91	55	20
Total	5,241	8,914	11,081	13,645	9,425
Latin America					
Brazil	589	616	1,428	960	699
ECUADOR	739	884	997	1,303	1,331
Fed. West Indies	268	323	220	297	421
Venezuela	865	1,216	1,469	1,732	1,388
Other	6	15	42	35	-
Total	2,467	3,054	4,156	4,312	3,839
Asia and Oceania	132	178	215	135	303
Not Specified	20	22	56[1/]	32	14[2/]
GRAND TOTAL	7,860	12,168	15,518	18,139	13,581

[1/] Includes 18 tons from the Netherlands. [2/] Includes 10 tons from the United States.

Source: U. S. Department of Agriculture, Foreign Agricultural Service.

Table 44

C O C O A

PRICES IN SELECTED COUNTRIES: 1952-62

(Cents per Pound[1/])

	United States (Spot New York) Bahia	United States Ghana	European Ports (nearest forward shipment c.i.f.) Good fermented Ghana	Belgium (c.i.f. Antwerp) Congo 1-A	France (exwhse. LeHavre) Ivory Coast	Italy (f.o.b. Milan) Sao Tome[2/]	Netherlands 5,000 kg. lots Amsterdam[3/]
1952	35.8	35.4	37.7	35.8	45.6	62.5	-
1953	34.9	37.1	36.0	34.8	43.5	58.9	-
1954	55.7	57.8	58.4	55.7	70.1	81.5	56.3
1955	36.2	37.4	37.7	36.4	43.8	73.7	35.9
1956	25.5	27.3	27.7	26.3	28.4	61.0	25.8
1957	30.5	30.6	30.0	29.0	32.1	57.5	29.2
1958	43.3	44.3	42.0	41.7	48.2	70.4	41.9
1959	35.4	36.6	34.1	33.8	39.1	63.3	33.9
1960	26.8	28.4	27.4	27.0	31.8	53.3	26.3
1961	22.4	22.6	21.9	21.0	24.9	46.2 [4/]	21.0
1962	21.3	21.0	20.6	20.2	24.3	45.7 [4/]	20.2 [5/]
Avg. 1953-1957	36.6	38.0	38.0	36.4	43.6	66.5	36.8 [3/]
Avg. 1958-1962	29.8	30.6	29.2	28.7	33.7	55.8	28.7

Price Indices (1957 = 100)

	Bahia	Ghana	Ghana	Congo 1-A	Ivory Coast	Sao Tome	Amsterdam
1952	117.4	115.7	125.7	123.4	142.0	108.7	-
1953	114.4	121.2	120.0	120.0	135.5	102.4	-
1954	182.6	188.9	194.6	192.1	218.4	141.7	192.8
1955	118.7	122.2	125.7	125.5	136.4	128.2	123.0
1956	83.6	89.2	92.3	90.7	88.5	106.1	88.4
1957	100.0	100.0	100.0	100.0	100.0	100.0	100.0
1958	142.0	144.8	140.0	143.8	150.1	122.4	143.5
1959	116.1	119.6	113.7	116.5	121.8	110.1	116.1
1960	87.9	92.8	91.3	93.1	99.1	92.7	90.1
1961	73.4	73.9	73.0	72.4	77.6	80.3	71.9
1962	69.8	68.6	68.7	69.6	75.7	79.5	69.2

1/Converted from source base of cents per kilograms. 2/Importers' selling price. 3/Miscellaneous qualities.
4/Average of 10 months. 5/Average of four years: 1954-1957.

Source: **F.A.O., Monthly Bulletin of Agricultural Economics and Statistics, Rome.**

Table 45

COCOA BEANS AND COCOA PRODUCTS

WORLD CONSUMPTION, TOTAL AND PER CAPITA, IN TERMS OF BEANS[1]: 1958-61

	Total Consumption (metric tons)				Per Capita Consumption[2] (kilograms)			
	1958	1959	1960	1961[2]	1958	1959	1960	1961[2]
I. IMPORTING COUNTRIES								
Europe, Western								
Austria	10,043	11,359	12,243	14,201	1.43	1.61	1.73	2.00
Belgium-Luxembourg	16,978	16,788	21,261	19,292	1.81	1.78	2.25	2.03
Denmark	5,153	4,881	6,671	7,691	1.14	1.07	1.46	1.66
France	49,933	46,549	52,864	58,038	1.12	1.03	1.16	1.26
Germany	94,073	98,735	112,074	122,054	1.73	1.80	2.02	2.17
Netherlands	21,250	21,536	22,619	29,755	1.90	1.90	1.97	2.56
Norway	3,796	3,989	4,646	5,944	1.08	1.12	1.30	1.64
Sweden	9,627	9,774	10,489	11,564	1.30	1.31	1.40	1.54
Switzerland	14,424	15,453	16,252	17,433	2.78	2.95	3.04	3.20
United Kingdom	95,649	83,973	94,836	102,007	1.85	1.62	1.81	1.93
Other	43,206	48,113	54,069	52,966	-	-	-	-
Total	364,132	361,150	408,024	447,000	1.14	1.12	1.25	1.36
Europe, Eastern	53,755	71,093	78,484	-	0.18	0.23	0.25	-
North and Central America								
Canada	27,064	27,826	28,112	30,000	1.59	1.60	1.57	1.64
United States	257,684	277,161	287,558	318,705	1.47	1.56	1.59	1.74
Other	1,254	1,406	1,554	387	-	-	-	-
Total	286,002	306,393	317,224	350,000	1.45	1.53	1.56	1.69
South America	10,987	6,294	7,044	8,000	0.36	0.20	0.22	0.25
Asia	13,002	14,975	19,220	26,000	0.02	0.02	0.03	0.04
Africa	8,463	7,611	9,244	9,500	0.07	0.06	0.08	0.08
Oceania								
Australia	12,386	13,511	14,406	16,000	1.26	1.34	1.40	1.52
New Zealand	2,858	3,746	4,191	4,500	1.25	1.61	1.77	1.87
Total	15,244	17,257	18,597	20,500	1.26	1.39	1.47	1.59
TOTAL IMPORTING COUNTRIES	751,585	784,773	857,837	945,000	0.48	0.49	0.53	0.57

Table 45 (Continued)

COCOA BEANS AND COCOA PRODUCTS: WORLD CONSUMPTION, TOTAL AND PER CAPITA, IN TERMS OF BEANS[1]

	Total Consumption (metric tons)				Per Capita Consumption (kilograms)			
	1958	1959	1960	1961[2]	1958	1959	1960	1961[2]
II. PRODUCING COUNTRIES								
Central America	14,033	15,283	16,062	17,000	0.29	0.32	0.31	0.32
South America								
Brazil	14,427	7,791	6,293	8,000	0.23	0.13	0.10	0.12
Colombia	18.001	21.580	20,400	21,000	1.33	1.56	1.44	1.45
Other	13,484	13,759	14,166	-	-	-	-	-
Total	45,912	43,130	40,809	43,500	0.46	0.42	0.39	0.40
Asia	5,577	5,534	6,296	6,400	0.04	0.04	0.05	0.05
Africa	679	823	910	1,100	0.01	0.01	0.01	0.02
Oceania	23	25	32	-	0.02	0.02	0.02	-
TOTAL PRODUCING COUNTRIES	66,224	64,795	64,109	68,000	0.19	0.18	0.17	0.18

1/ The following conversion factors were used in arriving at bean equivalent: cocoa butter, 1.33; cocoa paste, 1.25; cocoa powder and cake, 1.18; chocolate, 0.50; milk crumb, 0.154. 2/ Preliminary.

Source: FAO Cocoa Study Group.

Table 46

C O C O A   B U T T E R

INTERNATIONAL TRADE: 1957-61

(In Metric Tons)

	1957		1958		1959		1960		1961	
	Exports	Imports	Exports	Imports	Exports	Imports	Exports	Imports	Exports	Imports
Western Europe										
Austria	137	380	115	507	46	710	5	684	55	1,105
Belgium	60	4,358	81	4,260	23	4,095	64	4,808	121	5,022
Denmark	-	872	-	716	1	695	1	933	2	1,138
France	1,274	1,779	914	2,940	479	2,339	1,048	2,375	2,733	3,599
Ireland[1]	-	1,026	-	969	-	1,121	-	1,871	-	2,103
Italy	4,605	47	3,616	665	4,304	439	4,900	622	6,666	117
Netherlands[2]	27,223	2,590	23,325	1,845	27,342	3,933	32,647	5,383	36,068	4,323
Spain[2]	1,115	1	1,285	8	38	-	340	27	207	-
Sweden	232	1,907	209	1,671	285	1,400	339	1,862	330	2,320
Switzerland	51	5,918	4	5,344	-	5,925	19	6,386	-	7,715
United Kingdom	1,004	20,697	1,386	17,806	1,934	21,634	2,703	24,867	2,125	25,967
Other[3]	220	992	192	923	95	1,139	161	1,392	391	2,215
Total	35,970	40,570	31,130	37,650	34,550	43,430	42,230	51,210	48,700	55,620
North and Central America										
Canada	-	3,958	-	3,771	-	4,433	-	4,070	-	4,317
Dominican Republic[4]	38	-	68	-	96	-	841	-	3,380	-
Jamaica	1,028	-	679	-	491	-	615	-	487	-
United States[3]	458	6,094	339	4,044	530	3,909	67	6,367	228	8,018
Other[3]	435	-	240	-	589	1	366	-	108	-
Total	1,960	10,050	1,320	7,810	1,710	8,340	1,890	10,440	4,300	12,340
South America										
Brazil[1]	14,897	-	14,817	-	17,944	-	22,606	-	16,990	-
Other[2]	-	5	-	2	-	3	-	21	-	-
Total	14,900	10	14,820	-	17,940	-	22,610	20	16,990	-

360

Table 46 (Continued)

COCOA BUTTER: INTERNATIONAL TRADE

	1957		1958		1959		1960		1961	
	Exports	Imports	Exports	Imports	Exports	Imports	Exports	Imports	Exports	Imports
Asia										
Japan 1/	-	1,826	-	1,455	-	1,476	-	2,337	-	3,847
Other 3/	2	810	242	740	233	1,124	437	1,243	284	1,036
Total	-	2,640	240	2,200	230	2,600	440	3,580	280	5,000
Africa										
Cameroon	2,777	-	3,398	-	2,179	-	2,179	-	3,027	-
Ghana	86	-	103	-	597	-	68	-	1,344	-
South Africa	-	954	-	889	-	1,056	-	914	-	702
Other 3/	-	102	-	118	-	85	-	153	-	42
Total	2,900	1,020	3,500	970	2,780	1,140	2,250	1,060	4,370	800
Oceania										
Australia	-	1,651	-	1,729	-	1,749	-	1,698	-	2,635
New Zealand	-	353	-	456	-	613	-	713	-	748
Total	-	2,000	-	2,180	-	2,360	-	2,410	-	3,400
WORLD TOTAL	55,700	56,300	50,800	50,800	57,200	57,900	69,400	68,800	74,600	77,100

1/Includes paste. 2/Includes paste and powder. 3/Includes countries showing less than 1,000 tons, either in exports or imports. 4/Includes liquid cocoa.

Source: FAO, Cocoa Statistics; Volume 5, October, 1962.

Table 47

CHOCOLATE & CHOCOLATE PRODUCTS

INTERNATIONAL TRADE: 1957-61
(In Metric Tons)

	1957 Exports	1957 Imports	1958 Exports	1958 Imports	1959 Exports	1959 Imports	1960 Exports	1960 Imports	1961 Exports	1961 Imports
Western Europe										
Austria	237	395	242	446	266	879	314	939	454	1,509
Belgium	3,361	4,113	3,242	4,996	3,772	5,221	5,698	6,004	11,735	7,088
France	4,088	729	9,286	620	11,814	1,277	5,164	2,897	8,474	4,036
West Germany	1,786	8,070	2,192	12,695	2,962	16,236	3,419	19,604	3,787	23,065
Ireland 1/	35,140	14	36,462	8	39,126	38	39,886	56	41,137	76
Italy	831	269	863	283	1,045	384	1,228	584	1,819	509
Netherlands	9,705	1,709	9,391	1,670	10,769	2,054	20,271	3,264	19,302	7,942
Sweden	691	587	372	809	389	809	931	1,091	986	1,307
Switzerland 2/	7,837	224	8,564	47	8,551	55	9,416	309	10,585	713
United Kingdom 3/	16,796	36,319	16,812	37,122	15,607	39,207	17,292	40,595	17,138	40,628
Other 4/	653	1,494	660	1,638	1,179	1,849	617	2,099	769	2,768
Total	81,120	53,920	88,090	60,340	95,500	68,000	104,240	77,440	116,190	89,640
North and Central America										
Canada	59	6,565	77	7,847	108	9,226	178	10,995	490	10,382
Dominican Republic	8,100	-	7,792	-	8,557	-	8,794	-	10,398	-
United States	2,993	12,107	3,340	11,919	3,183	12,969	3,634	15,113	4,075	19,227
Other 4/	158	464	126	449	110	515	114	459	114	506
Total	11,310	19,120	11,340	20,220	11,960	22,710	12,800	27,000	15,100	30,200
South America	40	290	-	230	10	400	110	160	-	200
Asia										
Federation of Malaya	45	969	41	844	56	932	5	579	50	1,177
Japan	28	340	19	353	79	425	71	568	85	1,244
Other 4/	225	2,095	305	1,485	491	1,686	427	1,978	322	1,380
Total	300	3,400	360	2,680	620	3,040	500	3,120	600	3,500

Table 47 (Continued)

CHOCOLATE & CHOCOLATE PRODUCTS: INTERNATIONAL TRADE

	1957		1958		1959		1960		1961	
	Exports	Imports	Exports	Imports	Exports	Imports	Exports	Imports	Exports	Imports
Africa										
Algeria	1	2,541	-	2,740	-	2,467	1	2,733	-	-
South Africa	732	102	747	76	1,281	93	768	102	834	58
Other4/	165	2,356	141	2,298	103	2,111	112	1,700	68	1,213
Total	900	5,000	900	5,110	1,380	4,670	890	5,000	900	5,000
Oceania	20	250	30	100	30	60	40	150	40	160
WORLD TOTAL	93,700	82,000	100,700	88,700	109,500	98,900	118,500	112,900	132,800	128,700

1/Exports: Including milk crumb. 2/Exports: Including filled chocolate. 3/Imports: Including milk crumb.
4/Includes countries showing less than 1,000 tons of either exports or imports.

Source: FAO, Cocoa Statistics; Volume 5, October, 1962.

363

Table 48

C O F F E E

WORLD EXPORTS BY COUNTRY OF ORIGIN: 1957-62
(In 1,000 Bags[1]/)

Country of Origin	1957[2]/	1958	1959	1960	1961	1962[2]/
North America						
Costa Rica	492	771	712	766	835	902
Dominican Republic	361	429	362	481	335	487
El Salvador	1,270	1,399	1,345	1,178	1,431	1,478
Guatemala	1,038	1,205	1,385	1,329	1,255	1,552
Haiti	346	547	364	394	348	514
Honduras	168	189	255	258	210	266
Mexico	1,448	1,312	1,240	1,384	1,483	1,458
Nicaragua	367	382	273	361	349	338
South America						
Brazil	14,319	12,894	17,723	16,819	16,971	16,376
Colombia	4,824	5,441	6,413	5,938	5,651	6,562
ECUADOR	470	503	397	522	381	551
Peru	185	275	331	440	567	624
Venezuela	460	585	473	408	406	319
Other America	410	423	318	361	340	416
Total America	26,158	26,355	31,591	30,639	30,562	31,843
Africa						
Angola	1,267	1,317	1,483	1,454	1,976	2,620
Ethiopia	852	639	754	849	950	1,023
Kenya, Uganda, & Tanganyika	2,231	2,129	2,274	2,846	2,780	3,232
Malagasy Republic	803	797	632	670	651	700
Republic of Congo				878	555	600
Ruanda-Urundi				344	389	383
Spanish Africa	100	104	85	80	132	110
Cameroon	3/	3/	3/	508	591	750
Central African Republic	3/	3/	3/	99	121	130
Guinea	3/	175	240	240	200	200
Ivory Coast	3/	3/	3/	2,458	2,618	2,670
Togo	3/	3/	3/	73	171	175
Continental French Africa	2,291	2,330	2,489	-	-	-
Other	100	125	200	200	200	200
Total	8,760	8,772	9,686	10,699	11,334	12,793

Table 48 (Continued)

COFFEE: WORLD EXPORTS BY COUNTRY OF ORIGIN

Country of Origin	1957[2/]	1958	1959	1960	1961	1962[2/]
Asia and Oceania						
India	175	248	240	272	533	349
Indonesia	849	900	850	687	1,091	1,100
Yemen	90	80	70	69	80	80
Other	157	150	150	125	125	125
Total	1,271	1,378	1,310	1,153	1,829	1,654
GRAND TOTAL	36,189	36,505	42,587	42,491	43,725	46,290

[1/]Bags of 60 kilos (132.276 lbs.) each. [2/]Preliminary figures. [3/]Included in total for Continental French Africa.

Source: Pan American Coffee Bureau.

Table 49

C O F F E E

WORLD IMPORTS BY COUNTRY OF DESTINATION: 1957-62
(In 1,000 Bags[1/])

Country of Destination	1957[2/]	1958	1959	1960	1961	1962[2/]
Western Hemisphere						
United States	20,863	20,169	23,270	22,091	22,464	24,574
Canada	836	895	1,015	995	1,119	1,230
Argentina	584	672	315	460	582	495
Chile	83	91	107	92	88	129
Other	46	57	84	55	50	45
Total	22,412	21,884	24,791	23,693	24,303	26,473
Western Europe						
Germany, West	2,567	2,661	3,110	3,323	3,540	3,899
France	3,166	3,151	3,398	3,477	3,454	3,472
Italy	1,295	1,357	1,400	1,653	1,753	1,865
Netherlands	653	721	853	917	1,147	1,063
Belgium-Luxembourg	847	875	983	1,109	1,036	923
Total E. E. C.	(8,528)	8,765	9,744	10,479	10,930	11,222
Sweden	956	1,049	1,132	1,222	1,295	1,397
United Kingdom	762	741	883	920	978	1,155
Denmark	549	621	640	698	727	761
Finland	505	523	572	568	638	654
Norway	397	441	419	483	450	516
Switzerland	367	384	446	498	541	507
Spain	167	208	298	262	418	401
Austria	138	149	164	203	218	224
Portugal	144	179	175	350	210	204
Yugoslavia	71	64	99	153	143	171
Greece	92	116	124	127	132	146
Other	149[4/]	43	100	160	177	109
Total Other W. Europe	4,297	4,518	5,052	5,644	5,927	6,245
Eastern Europe						
U. S. S. R.	-	68	125	317	371	401
Germany, East	-	263	142	289	298	280
Czechoslovakia	105	90	160	85	175	181
Poland	-	27	130	65	89	112
Hungary	-	26	97	55	39	57
Other	-	25	25	64	10	35
Total	105[3/]	499	679	876	982	1,066
Total Europe	12,930	13,782	15,475	16,999	17,839	18,533

366

Table 49 (Continued)

COFFEE: WORLD IMPORTS BY COUNTRY OF DESTINATION

Country of Destination	1957[2/]	1958	1959	1960	1961	1962[2/]
Africa						
Algeria	455	455	498	491	428	456
South Africa	185	185	187	194	185	206
Sudan	133	73	133	106	154	131
Morocco	97	111	88	140	129	143
Other	111	196	163	215	200	165
Total	981	1,020	1,069	1,146	1,096	1,101
Asia and Oceania						
Japan	72	106	135	178	252	256
Australia	107	124	168	186	156	185
Other	320	228	256	371	303	384
Total	499	458	559	735	811	825
GRAND TOTAL	36,822	37,144	41,894	42,573	44,049	46,932

[1/] Bags of 60 kilos (132.276 lbs.) each. [2/] Preliminary. [3/] Imports by U. S. S. R., Hungary, and Poland included in "Other" Western Europe. [4/] Includes Eastern European imports.

Source: Pan American Coffee Bureau.

367

Table 50

C O F F E E

ECUADOR EXPORTS BY COUNTRY OF DESTINATION: 1952-62
(In 1,000 Bags[1])

Destination	1952	1953	1954	1955	1956	1957	1958	1959	1960	1961	1962
North America											
Canada	5.9	5.8	4.5	2.2	2.5	3.3	4.6	1.3	1.3	1.7	1.2
Panama	-	-	-	-	3.8	6.2	-	-	-	-	-
United States	165.7	232.1	253.8	259.1	240.2	307.6	366.0	247.3	320.5	193.2	373.2
Other	-	-	-	-	-	-	0.1	-	0.4	0.5	0.3
Total	171.6	237.9	258.3	261.3	246.5	317.1	370.7	248.6	322.2	195.4	374.7
Europe											
Belgium	19.9	4.9	8.5	3.9	3.7	1.9	1.3	0.2	6.8	2.3	1.8
Denmark	-	-	-	-	0.2	-	-	-	-	-	0.3
France	13.9	6.9	12.7	29.2	19.6	19.8	24.4	27.0	65.8	80.7	42.4
West Germany	4.1	9.3	5.5	9.7	34.6	32.8	15.9	11.7	37.0	37.9	53.6
Italy	87.1	12.5	15.4	29.8	41.6	67.5	53.2	61.8	50.5	45.2	43.0
Netherlands	4.4	6.8	12.1	5.7	12.7	6.2	2.2	15.2	16.7	14.9	15.9
Norway	-	-	0.1	-	-	-	-	-	0.6	0.2	0.6
Sweden	3.0	3.3	9.6	2.3	2.7	4.2	4.7	2.0	12.6	6.3	4.1
Switzerland	-	-	0.1	2.6	0.3	0.1	0.2	0.5	0.4	-	0.7
Trieste	30.7	10.3	14.1	10.0	12.8	-	-	-	-	-	-
United Kingdom	-	-	-	5.3	31.5	12.0	0.9	1.9	2.3	0.5	1.2
Other	-	1.6	0.9	8.8	0.4	0.1	9.8	11.0	2.8	2.1	2.8
Total	163.1	55.6	79.0	107.3	160.1	144.6	112.6	131.3	195.5	190.1	166.4
Asia											
Syria	2.4	5.8	4.3	2.7	0.3	2.1	0.6	-	-	-	-
Philippines	1.9	4.5	6.5	10.8	12.1	14.6	12.2	14.5	5.0	1.4	5.4
Other	-	0.4	0.1	-	2.2	0.9	0.1	-	0.7	0.4	-
Total	4.3	10.7	10.9	13.5	14.6	17.6	12.9	14.5	5.7	1.8	5.4
South America											
Chile	-	-	1.8	3.1	2.1	1.0	3.1	0.3	0.6	1.2	0.3
Other	-	0.5	-	-	2.5	-	-	-	-	0.9	-
Total	-	0.5	1.8	3.1	4.6	1.0	3.1	0.3	0.6	2.1	0.3
Africa	-	-	-	-	-	0.8	0.6	0.9	0.2	2.2	4.3
Not Specified	0.7	-	0.9	0.4	0.4	-	0.6	-	-	-	-
GRAND TOTAL	339.7	304.7	350.9	385.6	426.2	481.1	500.5	395.6	524.2	391.6	551.1

[1]/Bags of 132.276 pounds (60 kilos) each.

Source: U. S. Department of Agriculture, Foreign Agricultural Service; 1962 figures from Banco Central del Ecuador.

368

Table 51

C O F F E E

ECUADOR EXPORTS, TOTAL AND TO THE U. S., BY VOLUME AND VALUE,
1952-62

| | Volume (in 1,000 bags*) | | | Value (current U. S. $ f.o.b.) | |
Year	Total	To U. S.	To U. S. as % of total	Total (in million $)	Avg. price per pound (in dollars)
1952	340	166	48.8	20.2	.449
1953	311	232	74.6	18.9	.459
1954	351	259	73.8	27.6	.594
1955	384	256	66.7	23.1	.455
1956	426	240	56.3	29.7	.527
1957	481	308	64.0	29.3	.461
1958	500	366	73.2	25.8	.390
1959	396	247	62.4	17.4	.332
1960	524	321	61.3	21.8	.315
1961	381	191	50.1	14.3	.284
1962	551	373	67.7	20.9	.283

*Bags of 132.276 pounds each.

Source: Data for 1952-60 from U. S. Department of Agriculture;
1961 and 1962 figures from Banco Central del Ecuador.

Table 52

C O F F E E

UNITED STATES IMPORTS BY COUNTRY OF ORIGIN: 1957-62
(In 1,000 Bags[1]/)

Origin	1957	1958	1959	1960	1961[2]/	1962[3]/
North America						
Costa Rica	166	302	247	271	369	384
Cuba	124	91	34	-	-	-
Dominican Republic	296	381	308	403	263	418
El Salvador	676	724	621	446	583	843
Guatemala	830	882	988	798	949	967
Haiti	81	211	85	64	76	154
Honduras	118	148	146	332	144	160
Mexico	1,241	1,202	1,086	1,098	1,254	1,342
Nicaragua	239	247	154	170	225	190
Panama	-	8	19	16	6	-
Other	23	31	42	30	47	20
Total	3,794	4,227	3,730	3,628	3,916	4,478
South America						
Brazil	8,889	7,478	10,564	9,261	8,576	9,091
Colombia	4,054	4,245	4,902	4,254	4,078	4,332
ECUADOR	317	362	242	317	202	369
Peru	94	245	232	347	383	468
Venezuela	369	532	402	345	344	271
Other	2	21	28	75	43	35
Total	13,725	12,883	16,370	14,599	13,626	14,566
Africa						
Angola	797	699	742	802	1,024	1,481
British East Africa	767	766	730	934	1,246	1,413
Cameroon	23	11	8	35	71	124
Congo (Leopoldville)	518	513	813	645	593	499
Ethiopia	467	458	267	582	679	660
Ivory Coast	253	305	337	657	736	584
Malagasy Republic	255	155	33	83	114	165
Other	40	63	100	86	116	185
Total	3,120	2,970	3,030	3,824	4,579	5,111
Asia and Oceania						
India	7	7	6	8	48	12
Indonesia	93	21	13	19	138	301
Other	53	55	23	22	23	21
Total	153	83	42	49	209	334
Other Countries	-	-	-	-	2	1
GRAND TOTAL	20,792	20,163	23,172	22,100	22,332	24,490

[1]/Bags of 132.276 pounds (60 kilos) each. [2]/Revised. [3]/Preliminary.

Source: U. S. Department of Agriculture, Foreign Agricultural Service.

370

Table 53

C O F F E E

BELGIUM IMPORTS BY COUNTRY OF ORIGIN: 1957-62
(In 1,000 Bags[1/])

Country of Origin	1957	1958	1959	1960	1961	1962[2/]
Western Hemisphere						
Brazil	213.2	206.0	313.6	284.7	302.5	285.9
Colombia	54.2	75.0	102.6	103.5	98.8	82.2
El Salvador	20.6	15.1	14.1	11.8	13.4	13.7
Costa Rica	10.6	7.5	15.7	23.4	18.0	19.8
Guatemala	22.1	15.5	20.3	26.7	20.3	25.2
Mexico	8.2	2.9	2.1	4.5	2.5	4.0
ECUADOR	1.2	0.7	0.1	0.4	0.1	-
Nicaragua	8.5	7.2	9.8	13.0	18.9	12.0
Haiti	69.3	104.1	62.6	94.0	55.1	69.6
Peru	10.7	10.9	5.8	10.9	10.9	5.3
Other	11.4	17.4	61.0	74.3	45.0	36.3
Total	430.0	462.3	607.7	647.2	585.4	554.0
Africa						
Franc Zone	1.3	1.1	1.6	29.0	10.6	14.0
British East Africa	2.1	6.0	3.8	2.5	8.4	6.3
Portuguese Africa	68.5	56.6	34.2	32.5	40.1	78.4
Republic of the Congo	165.0	202.9	215.7	228.7	168.2	71.0
Malagasy	-	-	0.1	-	0.3	-
Ethiopia	0.6	0.2	0.1	0.1	0.4	0.2
Other	6.3	12.6	7.8	18.0	9.0	1.5
Total	243.8	279.4	263.3	309.8	237.0	171.4
Asia and Oceania						
Indonesia	66.8	56.7	31.8	28.6	51.6	67.6[3/]
India	14.3	12.4	9.3	9.2	20.1	8.8
Yemen	-	6.7	0.9	0.8	0.4	-
Other	25.0	-	21.5	32.0	44.5	3.2
Total	106.1	75.8	63.5	70.7	116.6	79.6
Other Countries	67.1	57.1	48.4	81.5	97.4	143.2
TOTAL IMPORTS	846.9	874.6	982.9	1,109.2	1,036.5	948.2

[1/]Bags of 132.276 lbs. (60 kilos) each. [2/]Preliminary. [3/]Includes imports from Malaya.

Source: Pan American Coffee Bureau.

371

Table 54

C O F F E E

FRANCE IMPORTS BY COUNTRY OF ORIGIN: 1957-62
(In 1,000 Bags[1/])

Country of Origin	1957	1958	1959	1960	1961	1962[2/]
Western Hemisphere						
Brazil	638.8	559.0	656.6	677.2	593.3	674.6
Colombia	13.9	14.3	13.3	12.3	24.9	27.0
El Salvador	2.0	0.7	4.1	0.6	0.3	0.6
Costa Rica	3.4	0.7	6.2	5.6	7.5	10.2
Guatemala	3.1	1.1	5.3	2.7	2.5	2.4
Mexico	3.2	0.5	0.1	2.2	1.6	4.8
ECUADOR	15.5	29.1	25.1	53.8	99.5	49.7
Nicaragua	0.1	-	1.4	2.9	1.3	2.0
Haiti	58.4	26.8	1.5	50.4	43.0	87.7
Peru	-	-	4.3	19.6	31.8	11.0
Other	2.7	3.0	23.5	21.8	13.9	19.8
Total	741.1	635.2	741.5	849.1	819.6	889.8
Africa						
Franc Zone	1,699.9	1,835.4	1,925.4	1,965.5	2,015.9	1,886.7
British East Africa	-	0.0	1.4	0.6	1.9	6.6
Portuguese Africa	2.7	1.3	0.5	5.9	3.7	24.2
Republic of the Congo	16.2	11.4	14.8	23.4	19.7	39.0
Malagasy Republic	539.9	602.7	536.9	560.6	497.9	507.3
Ethiopia	24.6	18.0	17.9	21.1	17.1	20.6
Other	0.4	-	0.0	0.1	1.5	20.1
Total	2,283.7	2,468.8	2,496.9	2,577.2	2,557.7	2,504.5
Asia and Oceania						
Indonesia	89.7	7.4	0.4	0.1	1.0	13.1[3]
India	0.5	0.0	4.0	7.5	25.8	7.0
Yemen	-	6.6	8.3	8.6	9.1	9.9
Other	50.8	32.7	27.7	26.1	40.6	43.1
Total	141.0	46.7	40.4	42.3	76.5	73.1
Other Countries	0.6	0.1	0.0	8.2	0.7	4.6
TOTAL IMPORTS	3,166.4	3.150.8	3.278.8	3,476.8	3,454.5	3,472.0

[1/]Bags of 132.276 lbs. (60 kilograms) each.   [2/]Preliminary.   [3/]Includes imports from Malay.

Source: Pan American Coffee Bureau.

372

Table 55

C O F F E E

WEST GERMANY IMPORTS BY COUNTRY OF ORIGIN: 1957-62
(In 1,000 Bags[1]/)

Country of Origin	1957	1958	1959	1960	1961	1962[2]/
Western Hemisphere						
Brazil	699.4	501.6	677.2	767.9	791.1	908.6
Colombia	252.6	370.2	531.1	586.4	619.0	773.9
Costa Rica	247.7	305.8	322.3	299.2	327.8	342.0
ECUADOR	40.8	21.7	10.8	20.6	33.8	43.3
El Salvador	433.6	522.1	530.7	607.9	628.9	691.9
Guatemala	123.9	166.1	257.1	269.8	280.8	283.5
Mexico	160.4	146.2	135.7	140.4	127.8	139.0
Peru	8.1	13.7	17.4	13.4	10.1	18.4
Haiti	4.2	5.2	1.8	3.9	1.5	3.3
Nicaragua	54.0	66.6	68.9	70.6	77.7	77.3
Other	91.0	82.8	72.7	62.1	53.4	80.7
Total	2,115.7	2,202.1	2,625.6	2,842.2	2,951.9	3,361.9
Africa						
Franc Zone	2.9	0.9	5.0	22.4	17.5	20.4
British East Africa	273.7	318.1	374.9	347.8	367.1	341.5
Portuguese Africa	22.5	11.9	15.5	23.7	41.9	79.0
Republic of the Congo	41.3	39.5	30.3	26.9	24.4	18.7
Malagasy	-	-	-	8.8	7.2	7.0
Ethiopia	1.0	1.8	3.9	7.1	9.3	13.8
Other	1.9	2.1	4.8	2.8	1.8	-
Total	343.2	374.4	434.4	439.5	469.2	480.4
Asia and Oceania						
India	14.2	69.0	34.5	27.1	105.1	37.1
Indonesia	93.4	14.8	10.6	12.4	10.5	11.0
Yemen	-	0.1	0.5	-	-	-
Other	1.5	0.7	4.1	1.0	1.8	0.1
Total	109.1	84.6	49.7	40.5	117.5	48.2
Other Countries	-	-	0.2	0.8	0.9	0.8
TOTAL IMPORTS	2,568.1	2,661.0	3,110.0	3,322.9	3,539.6	3,891.2

[1]/ Bags of 132.276 lbs. (60 kilos) each.   [2]/ Preliminary.

Source: Pan American Coffee Bureau.

Table 56

C O F F E E

ITALY IMPORTS BY COUNTRY OF ORIGIN: 1957-62
(In 1,000 Bags[1])

Country of Origin	1957	1958	1959	1960	1961	1962[2]
Western Hemisphere						
Brazil	303.8	331.3	506.8	658.2	660.0	721.1
Colombia	8.7	18.5	26.5	29.6	36.0	39.4
Costa Rica	6.6	16.9	22.2	22.7	24.9	27.0
ECUADOR	57.5	60.4	41.4	45.2	43.2	28.5
El Salvador	16.8	19.4	16.8	14.6	6.9	5.1
Guatemala	4.4	8.5	10.4	13.5	13.5	14.1
Mexico	1.6	2.2	-	-	2.4	4.2
Peru	16.5	22.2	24.5	24.5	40.5	33.6
Haiti	83.8	115.1	93.1	118.7	77.8	116.5
Nicaragua	3.8	7.7	10.3	-	10.4	10.5
Other	56.5	47.2	60.0	75.2	71.6	60.6
Total	559.8	649.3	812.0	1,002.2	987.2	1,060.6
Africa						
Franc Zone	16.6	14.9	17.6	106.6	144.7	196.6
British East Africa	38.4	63.0	49.9	21.5	21.0	15.5
Portuguese Africa	6.5	1.4	-	-	2.9	36.3
Republic of the Congo	164.8	210.0	214.7	210.8	269.0	244.3
Malagasy	-	-	-	16.8	10.3	10.5
Ethiopia	65.5	79.7	73.2	67.3	51.1	58.0
Other	3.2	14.3	18.1	-	10.9	2.2
Total	295.0	383.4	373.4	423.0	509.9	563.4
Asia and Oceania						
India	14.0	27.8	27.0	13.3	38.7	15.3
Indonesia	401.3	263.5	26.8	18.6	162.2	144.9
Yemen	-	18.2	13.3	8.4	12.9	-
Other	17.6	12.3	90.3	87.0	0.5	1.4
Total	432.9	321.8	157.3	127.3	214.2	161.6
Other Countries	7.6	1.6	57.6	100.7	41.9	29.7
TOTAL IMPORTS	1,295.4	1,356.1	1,400.3	1,653.2	1,753.3	1,815.5

[1] Bags of 132.276 lbs. (60 kilos) each.   [2] Preliminary.

Source: Pan American Coffee Bureau.

374

Table 57

C O F F E E

JAPAN IMPORTS BY COUNTRY OF ORIGIN: 1957-62
(In 1,000 Bags[1]/)

Country of Origin	1957	1958	1959	1960	1961	1962
Brazil	23.9	24.3	31.9	51.0	80.0	84.5
Colombia	7.2	11.5	27.3	41.5	52.5	41.6
Ethiopia	2.7	11.2	21.2	24.1	27.2	29.5
Uganda	1.7	1.8	7.4	17.6	20.8	13.2
Federation of Malaya	3.3	5.6	7.2	9.9	13.1	13.0
Indonesia	11.3	9.9	3.8	4.8	12.1	12.3
Portuguese West Africa	-	-	2.4	0.3	0.1	9.4
Malagasy Republic	-	1.4	0.4	0.5	5.8	3.9
Peru	1.2	1.1	2.5	4.0	3.1	3.3
Guatemala	0.3	0.7	2.6	3.8	3.7	3.0
Jamaica	1.0	0.9	1.7	2.0	3.6	2.8
Yemen	2.8	3.7	3.9	3.0	6.8	1.9
Other	36.0	34.1	23.1	15.9	23.3	37.3
TOTAL	91.4	106.2	135.4	178.4	252.1	255.7

[1]/ Bags of 60 kilos (132.276 lbs.).

Source: U. S. Department of Agriculture, Foreign Agricultural Service.

375

Table 58

C O F F E E

NETHERLANDS IMPORTS BY COUNTRY OF ORIGIN: 1957-62
(In 1,000 Bags[1]/)

Country of Origin	1957	1958	1959	1960	1961	1962[2]/
Western Hemisphere						
Brazil	149.4	132.6	253.8	223.6	286.3	290.6
Colombia	63.4	96.0	130.1	138.5	109.1	163.7
El Salvador	24.3	12.4	23.6	19.2	25.3	25.3
Costa Rica	3.9	4.2	3.5	10.4	20.3	25.5
Guatemala	18.2	22.5	26.6	31.8	24.2	29.9
Mexico	3.4	4.5	3.4	2.8	3.4	5.2
ECUADOR	4.0	0.3	2.7	7.0	7.8	5.2
Nicaragua	30.2	34.6	14.8	20.5	17.7	14.7
Haiti	1.1	6.0	1.0	2.6	1.9	4.6
Peru	0.3	2.1	2.0	6.2	12.6	11.2
Other	6.1	7.7	9.8	10.7	8.9	8.9
Total	304.3	322.9	471.3	473.3	517.5	584.8
Africa						
Franc Zone	0.7	-	0.8	7.8	7.5	7.1
British East Africa	8.6	18.6	9.4	27.6	35.4	36.5
Portuguese Africa	221.4	260.3	306.1	335.2	460.3	366.7
Republic of the Congo	7.1	6.0	1.0	0.8	0.4	1.2
Malagasy	0.2	-	0.2	0.4	0.3	0.1
Ethiopia	0.2	1.4	4.8	3.4	0.9	-
Other	1.5	2.5	4.3	9.7	4.4	4.1
Total	239.6	288.7	326.5	384.9	509.1	415.7
Asia and Oceania						
Indonesia	54.9	71.8	10.6	6.4	15.2	11.1
India	13.3	14.0	4.8	7.1	30.6	2.0
Yemen	-	9.6	-	-	-	-
Other	31.2	-	26.1	28.0	27.0	6.4
Total	99.4	95.4	41.4	41.5	72.7	19.5
Other Countries	9.7	14.3	13.9	17.3	47.4	34.3
TOTAL IMPORTS	653.0	721.2	853.0	917.0	1,146.6	1,054.2

[1]/ Bags of 132.276 lbs. (60 kilos) each.   [2]/ Preliminary.

Source: Pan American Coffee Bureau.

376

Table 59

C O F F E E

SWITZERLAND IMPORTS BY COUNTRY OF ORIGIN: 1957-62
(In 1,000 Bags[1]/)

Country of Origin	1957	1958	1959	1960	1961	1962[2]/
Western Hemisphere						
Brazil	92.5	88.2	160.3	125.4	129.8	143.0
Colombia	21.3	29.4	31.7	36.6	46.7	46.5
Costa Rica	26.1	22.7	33.8	45.2	45.8	40.2
ECUADOR	3.2	3.2	2.9	10.3	7.6	4.5
El Salvador	24.3	19.4	19.1	23.6	23.7	18.9
Guatemala	25.2	19.4	22.9	32.5	26.6	29.5
Haiti	18.5	32.6	17.4	24.5	25.0	30.7
Mexico	6.1	7.2	5.2	6.2	5.2	4.4
Nicaragua	3.9	2.4	2.8	6.4	6.8	4.2
Peru	1.2	2.7	1.2	3.6	4.5	3.1
Other	23.0	17.0	13.4	17.9	8.9	8.2
Total	245.4	244.3	310.8	332.2	330.7	333.2
Africa						
Franc Zone	10.8	12.8	21.3	24.8	19.8	15.3
British East Africa	33.2	39.2	51.4	53.4	50.1	40.8
Portuguese Africa	27.8	25.7	19.4	18.0	32.6	44.5
Republic of the Congo	20.0	23.1	23.8	30.5	28.3	29.0
Malagasy	-	-	-	14.7	12.3	5.8
Ethiopia	8.1	8.8	7.0	7.5	6.8	10.3
Other	0.1	0.1	1.2	5.7	2.8	-
Total	100.0	109.8	124.2	154.6	152.7	145.7
Asia and Oceania						
India	6.1	12.9	4.3	3.3	32.1	5.1
Indonesia	11.7	12.9	4.2	3.3	21.1	18.8
Yemen	-	4.1	2.3	3.3	2.1	-
Other	2.9	-	0.2	0.9	1.3	2.8
Total	20.7	29.9	11.0	10.8	56.7	26.7
Other Countries	0.8	-	-	0.2	0.1	1.2
TOTAL IMPORTS	366.9	384.0	446.0	497.7	540.6	506.7

[1]/Bags of 132.276 lbs. (60 kilos) each. [2]/Preliminary.

Source: Pan American Coffee Bureau.

377

Table 60

C O F F E E

PER CAPITA CONSUMPTION IN SELECTED COUNTRIES: 1957-62
(In Pounds per Year)

Country	1957	1958	1959	1960	1961	1962[1]
United States	15.7	15.9	15.9	15.8	15.8	15.9
Canada	6.9	7.1	7.7	7.4	8.1	8.7
Western Europe:						
Belgium-Luxembourg	12.0	12.3	14.0	15.5	14.6	12.8
Denmark	16.1	18.2	18.8	20.3	20.9	21.4
Finland	15.3	15.8	17.0	16.9	18.8	19.0
France	19.0	9.4	10.1	10.1	9.8	9.8
Germany, West	6.2	6.4	7.2	8.0	8.2	9.0
Italy	3.5	3.7	3.8	4.3	4.7	5.0
Netherlands	7.7	8.5	10.1	10.7	13.1	12.0
Norway	14.8	16.5	15.6	18.0	16.5	18.8
Sweden	17.1	18.7	20.1	21.7	22.8	24.3
United Kingdom	1.9	1.9	2.3	2.3	2.5	2.9

[1] Preliminary.

Source: Estimated by U.S.D.A., Foreign Agricultural Service, Sugar
and Tropical Products Division, from AMS and FAS/USDA data
and other official and trade sources; and Brazilian Coffee
Institute, Curso sôbre Economia Cafeeira, 1963.

378

Table 61

C O F F E E

U. S. CONSUMPTION ROASTED & SOLUBLE COFFEE: 1954-62
(In Thousands of 60-kilo Bags)

	Total volume roasted	Total consumption regular	Volume converted into soluble	Annual % Increase		% Increase over 1954	
				Regular	Soluble	Regular	Soluble
1954	17,601	15,549	2,052	-	-	-	-
1955	18,813	16,490	2,323	+ 6.1	+ 13.2	+ 6.1	+ 13.2
1956	20,263	17,123	3,140	+ 3.8	+ 35.2	+ 10.1	+ 53.0
1957	20,321	16,985	3,336	- 0.8	+ 6.2	+ 9.2	+ 62.6
1958	20,937	17,445	3,492	+ 2.7	+ 4.7	+ 12.2	+ 70.2
1959	21,698	17,954	3,744	+ 2.9	+ 7.2	+ 15.5	+ 82.5
1960	21,895	17,896	3,999	- 0.3	+ 6.8	+ 15.1	+ 94.9
1961	22,294	18,284	4,010	+ 2.2	+ 0.3	+ 17.6	+ 95.4
1962	22,677	18,595	4,082	+ 1.7	+ 1.8	+ 19.6	+ 98.9

Source: Brazilian Coffee Institute, Curso sôbre Economia Cafeeira, 1963.

Table 62

C O F F E E

PRICES IN SELECTED COUNTRIES: 1952-62
(Cents per Pound[1/])

| | United States (spot New York) | | Uganda | West Germany (c.i.f. Hamburg) | | Belgium (c.i.f. Antwerp) | France (ex-warehouse LeHavre) |
	Santos 4	Manizales		Santos extra	Kenya A	Congo Arabica	Ivory Coast robusta
1952	53.98	57.15	n.a.	55.34	n.a.	56.25	n.a.
1953	57.93	59.93	47.59	59.88	n.a.	58.97	n.a.
1954	79.71	80.09	57.86	82.10	85.73	75.30	55.34
1955	57.09	64.63	38.41	58.97	80.29	55.34	40.37
1956	58.01	73.99	33.59	61.24	89.81	67.13	38.10
1957	56.92	63.94	34.65	59.42	81.65	58.51	40.37
1958	48.40	52.34	38.10	53.07	70.76	47.17	41.73
1959	36.97	45.22	29.29	40.37	70.31	39.01	31.75
1960	36.60	44.89	20.65	38.56	70.31	n.a.	31.75
1961	36.01	43.62	18.92	37.65	68.04	n.a.	30.39
1962	34.02	40.82	n.a.	37.65	63.96	n.a.	30.84

Price Indices: 1957 = 100

	Santos 4	Manizales	Uganda	Santos extra	Kenya A	Congo Arabica	Ivory Coast robusta
1952	94.8	89.4	n.a.	93.1	n.a.	96.1	n.a.
1953	101.8	93.7	137.3	100.8	n.a.	100.8	n.a.
1954	140.1	125.3	167.0	138.2	105.0	128.7	137.1
1955	100.3	101.1	110.9	99.2	98.4	94.6	100.0
1956	101.9	115.7	96.9	103.1	110.0	114.7	94.4
1957	100.0	100.0	100.0	100.0	100.0	100.0	100.0
1958	85.0	81.9	110.0	89.3	86.7	80.6	103.4
1959	65.0	70.7	84.5	67.9	86.1	66.7	78.6
1960	64.3	70.2	59.6	64.9	86.1	n.a.	78.6
1961	63.3	68.2	54.6	63.4	83.3	n.a.	75.3
1962	59.8	63.8	n.a.	63.4	78.4	n.a.	76.4

[1/] Converted from source base of cents per kilograms.

Source: F. A. O., Monthly Bulletin of Agricultural Economics and Statistics, and Commodity Bulletin Series. No. 33.

Table 63

S O L U B L E   C O F F E E

WORLD IMPORTS OF GREEN COFFEE & CONSUMPTION OF SOLUBLE COFFEE: 1957-62
(Imports in Millions of 60-kilo Bags; Soluble in Green Coffee Equivalent)

Year	World imports green coffee	World consumption soluble coffee[1]	Annual increase soluble	% share soluble of total imports
1957	36,735	4,487	466	12.2
1958	37,144	4,745	258	12.8
1959	41,894	5,179	434	12.4
1960	42,573	5,594	415	13.1
1961	44,049	5,957	363	13.5
1962	46,937	6,367	410	13.6

[1]/Estimated. Excludes soluble coffee manufactured by
Latin American grain producers for domestic consumption.

Source: Brazilian Coffee Institute, Curso sôbre
Economia Cafeeira 1963.

Table 64

S O L U B L E   C O F F E E

U. S. IMPORTS, VOLUME AND VALUE; BY COUNTRY OF ORIGIN: 1958-62
(Volume in 1,000 Pounds; Value in Thousands of Dollars)

| | 1 9 5 8 | | 1 9 5 9 | | 1 9 6 0 | | 1 9 6 1 | | 1 9 6 2 | |
	Volume	Value	Volume	Value	Volume	Value	Volume	Value	Volume	Valu
Canada	2	4	-	-	-	-	-	-	216	21
El Salvador	1,995	5,662	2,110	4,793	2,062	4,097	1,493	2,566	38	5
Guatemala	283	627	1,198	2,463	2,047	3,405	503	839	145	20
Mexico	1,355	3,118	1,302	1,627	513	635	96	123	1,295	1,13
Nicaragua	-	-	-	-	-	-	1,324	1,834	2,313	3,13
Other	1	3	7	17	5	11	9	19	13	2
TOTAL	3,636	9,413	4,616	8,900	4,627	8,147	3,425	5,382	4,021	4,77

Source: Brazilian Coffee Institute, Curso sôbre Economia Cafeeira, 1963.

Table 65

S O L U B L E   C O F F E E

UNITED STATES IMPORTS: VOLUME, GREEN-COFFEE EQUIVALENT, VALUE, AND AVERAGE PRICE PER POUND:
1960-62

	El Salvador	Nicaragua	Guatemala	Mexico	Other	Total
1 9 6 0						
Volume (1,000 pounds)	2,062	--	2,047	513	5	4,627
Green coffee equivalent (60-kilo bags)	56,120	--	55,711	13,956	134	125,921
Value (thousands of dollars)	4,096	--	3,405	635	11	8,148
Average price per pound ($)	1.99	--	1.66	1.24	1/	
1 9 6 1						
Volume (1,000 pounds)	1,493	1,323	503	96	9	3,425
Green coffee equivalent (60-kilo bags)	40,646	36,033	13,678	2,609	258	93,224
Value (thousands of dollars)	2,566	1,834	839	123	19	5,381
Average price per pound ($)	1.72	1.39	1.67	1.29	2/	
1 9 6 2						
Volume (1,000 pounds)	38	2,313	145	1,295	229	4,021
Green coffee equivalent (60-kilo bags)	863	52,457	3,297	29,370	5,203	91,190
Value (thousands of dollars)	51	3,137	205	1,138	243	4,774
Average price per pound ($)	1.35	1.36	1.41	0.88	3/	

1/ Average price per pound imported from other sources (8 countries) varied from a low of $1.07 (Great
Britain) to a high of $5.45 (Spain). 2/ Average price per pound imported from other sources (6 countries)
varied from a low of $1.41 (Colombia) to a high of $2.62 (France). 3/ Average price per pound imported
from other sources (9 countries) varied from a low of $1.00 (Canada) to a high of $7.38 (Belgium).

Source: Pan American Coffee Bureau.

Table 66

S O L U B L E   C O F F E E

U. S. EXPORTS, VOLUME AND VALUE; BY COUNTRY OF DESTINATION: 1958-62
(Volume in 1,000 Pounds; Value in Thousands of Dollars)

	1958		1959		1960		1961		1962	
	Volume	Value	Volume	Value	Volume	Value	Volume	Value	Volume	Value
America										
Bermuda	24	71	38	101	45	104	45	113	46	114
Canada	3,804	8,062	4,238	7,505	4,622	7,134	3,301	4,921	3,018	3,918
Dutch West Indies	103	320	123	388	106	285	109	268	146	338
Other	54	152	70	166	107	239	118	258	118	242
Total	3,985	8,605	4,469	8,160	4,880	7,762	3,573	5,560	3,328	4,612
Europe										
Germany, West	94	216	146	238	163	244	351	510	375	442
Finland	-	-	35	91	109	282	216	532	209	463
Great Britain	1	1	713	1,182	387	440	905	1,062	1,639	1,829
Netherlands	109	201	593	906	148	218	150	221	87	160
Sweden	28	78	24	60	51	109	62	133	134	222
Other	17	49	45	91	45	80	56	95	95	135
Total	249	545	1,556	2,568	903	1,373	1,740	2,553	2,539	3,251
Africa, Asia, and Oceania										
Australia	-	-	1	2	440	729	547	878	1,004	1,601
Nansei and Nanpo Island	97	320	169	495	285	810	154	420	97	245
Japan	39	117	38	110	66	173	3,285	7,331	5,597	12,569
Singapore	2	3	3	4	9	15	15	33	98	212
Thailand	24	52	30	78	32	80	45	105	51	112
Other	84	225	74	171	176	339	164	400	199	443
Total	246	717	315	860	1,008	2,146	4,210	9,167	7,046	15,182
Other	-	-	-	-	8	16	18	46	67	149
WORLD TOTAL	4,479	9,867	6,337	11,589	6,796	11,296	9,542	17,325	12,980	23,197

Source: Brazilian Coffee Institute, Curso sôbre Economia Cafeeira, 1963.

384

Table 67

S O L U B L E   C O F F E E

U. S. TRADE, COMPARISON OF IMPORTS AND EXPORTS: 1956-62
(In Thousands of Soluble Pounds)

	Imports	Exports	Net Exports
1956	1,375	3,067	1,691
1957	3,309	4,807	1,498
1958	3,636	4,479	843
1959	4,616	6,337	1,721
1960	4,627	6,796	2,169
1961	3,425	9,542	6,117
1962	4,021	12,980	8,959

Percentage gain/loss over 1956

	Imports	Exports	Net Exports
1957	140.7	56.7	- 11.4
1958	164.4	46.0	- 50.1
1959	235.7	106.6	1.8
1960	236.5	121.4	27.9
1961	149.1	211.1	261.7
1962	192.4	323.2	429.8

Source: Pan American Coffee Bureau.

Table 68

S O L U B L E   C O F F E E

CANADA PRODUCTION AND IMPORTS: 1956-62
(In Thousands)

Year	Production[1]		Imports[2]		Domestic consumption[2]		
	bag equivalent[1]	soluble pounds	bag equivalent[1]	soluble pounds	bag equivalent[1]	soluble pounds	% increase over '56
1956	113	4,492	88	3,485	201	7,977	-
1957	151	6,207	119	4,890	271	11,096	39.1
1958	178	7,282	110	4,491	287	11,773	47.6
1959	210	8,881	108	4,585	319	13,466	68.8
1960	257	10,857	111	4,675	368	15,532	94.7
1961	307	13,550	76	3,368	384	16,917	112.1
1962	395	17,398	66	2,904	460	20,302	154.5

[1] 60-kilo bags of green coffee. [2] Over 90% imported from the United States each year.
[3] Negligible amounts of exports not accounted for.

Source: Brazilian Coffee Institute, Curso sôbre Economia Cafeeira, 1963.

386

Table 69

P A L M   K E R N E L S

EXPORTS FROM PRINCIPAL PRODUCING COUNTRIES,
Average 1950-54, Annual 1957-61
(In Short Tons[1]/)

Country of Origin	1950-54	1957	1958	1959	1960[2]/	1961[2]/
Africa						
Angola	12,261	13,906	15,141	8,293	5,711	11,259
Congo, Republic of the	92,893	33,540	42,711	43,312	22,597	13,999
Cameroun	25,125	15,362	14,292	24,877	16,866	16,049
French Equatorial Africa[3]/	9,418	8,016	8,730	7,772	8,486	9,247
Former French West Africa[4]/	86,147	86,846	109,090	99,931	115,496	95,110
Gambia	1,859	1,184	1,653	1,992	1,985	1,985
Ghana	6,442	7,787	8,902	3,198	3,416	1,980
Liberia	18,337	11,719	12,271	21,301	16,779	14,220
Nigeria	447,645[5]/	454,942	494,170	482,057	468,205	459,903
Portuguese Guinea	14,959[5]/	15,797	18,251	17,500	10,800	15,432
Sao Tome and Principe	6,444	4,950	4,794	4,173	4,902	4,500
Sierra Leone	80,580	59,323	61,162	64,434	61,068	66,705
Togo	10,659	8,080	13,290	8,903	15,632	12,280
Total	812,769	721,452	804,457	787,743	751,943	722,669
Asia						
Malaya	13,142	18,192	24,606	23,389	27,593	23,797
Indonesia	39,786	44,460	39,166	36,004	36,929	36,003
Total	52,928	62,652	63,772	59,393	64,552	59,800
TOTAL	865,697	784,104	868,229	847,136	816,465	782,469

[1]/2,000 pounds. [2]/Preliminary. [3]/Now the independent countries of Chad, Congo, Gabon, and the Central African Republic. [4]/Now the independent countries of Guinea, Mauritania, Senegal, Mali (Soudan), Ivory Coast, Niger, Upper Volta and Dahomey. [5]/Less than 5 years.

Source: U. S. Department of Agriculture, Foreign Agricultural Service.

Table 70

P A L M   K E R N E L S

IMPORTS INTO PRINCIPAL IMPORTING COUNTRIES,
Average 1950-54, Annual 1957-61
(In Short Tons[1]/)

Country	Average 1950-54	1957	1958	1959	1960[2]/	1961[2]/
United States	3/4/ 23	5/	5/	5/	5/	5/
Belgium-Luexmbourg	13,911	19,456	32,915	33,564	25,504	25,642
Denmark	19,349	14,547	28,677	24,569	18,278	12,765
France	122,256	122,714	119,208	90,512	104,758	90,996
West Germany	130,075	89,314	127,694	146,369	170,868	140,854
Netherlands	59,697	114,880	147,329	171,603	134,365	157,578
Poland	-	7,606	-	-	26,865	22,000
Portugal	19,613	29,771	30,419	26,615	18,989	16,771
United Kingdom	459,284	365,341	305,945	261,750	265,877	251,481
TOTAL	824,208	763,629	792,187	754,982	765,504	718,087

[1]/2,000 lbs. [2]/Preliminary. [3]/Includes palm nuts. [4]/1950-53 average. Not separately classified in 1954. [5]/Not separately classified.

Source: U. S. Department of Agriculture, Foreign Agricultural Service.

388

Table 71

P A L M   O I L

EXPORTS FROM PRINCIPAL PRODUCING COUNTRIES,
Average 1950-54, Annual 1957-61
(In Short Tons[1/])

Country of Origin	Average 1950-54	1957	1958	1959	1960[2/]	1961[2/]
Africa						
Angola	12,386	10,062	9,965	9,642	14,334	16,139
Congo, Republic of the	146,982	168,705	180,482	202,332	186,178	170,856
Cameroon	2,866	61	365	724	676	243
French Equatorial Africa[3/]	3,087	4,156	3,162	3,040	3,894	5,804
Former French West Africa[4/]	14,534	13,006	14,337	14,589	12,250	13,000
Ghana	376	-	-	-	-	-
Liberia	1,904	72	17	5/	17	-
Nigeria	201,420	186,469	190,968	205,707	205,367	184,343
Portuguese Guinea	873	696	513	664	700	700
Sao Tome and Principe	2,453	1,717	1,274	1,063	1,356	1,000
Sierra Leone	1,623	12	11	10	6	6
Togo	614	796	689	111	751	955
Total	389,118	385,752	401,783	437,882	425,529	393,046
Asia						
Malaya	54,111	67,504	89,124	86,654	106,892	105,455
Indonesia	138,226	142,135	145,104	113,695	119,602	129,694
Total	192,337	209,639	234,228	200,349	226,494	235,149
TOTAL	581,455	595,391	636,011	638,231	652,023	628,195

[1/]2,000 pounds. [2/]Preliminary. [3/]Now the independent countries of Congo, Chad, Gabon, and the Central African Republic. [4/]Now the independent countries of Guinea, Mauritania, Senegal, Mali (Soudan), Ivory Coast, Niger, Upper Volta, and Dahomey. [5/]Less than 0.5 ton. [6/]Partially estimated.

Source: U. S. Department of Agriculture, Foreign Agricultural Service.

389

Table 72

P A L M   O I L

IMPORTS INTO PRINCIPAL IMPORTING COUNTRIES,
Average 1950-54, Annual 1957-61
(In Short Tons[1/])

Country	Average 1950-54	1957	1958	1959	1960[2/]	1961[2/]
North America						
Canada[3/]	11,732	19,597	20,230	15,835	9,098	26,163
United States	31,070	9,320	21,506	15,658	23,409	28,004
Total	42,802	28,917	41,736	31,493	32,507	54,167
Europe						
Belgium-Luxembourg	44,777	44,930	41,985	42,780	46,760	46,867
Denmark	848	14,154	10,608	13,433	2,143	6,400
France	19,632	33,872	31,797	30,330	36,881	30,558
West Germany	79,075	85,639	82,117	78,100	80,049	85,691
Ireland	1,236	3,575	3,609	4,545	4,793	4,612
Italy	19,943	16,648	24,557	22,759	34,190	27,287
Netherlands	83,385	87,357	95,591	88,203	95,684	98,088
Portugal	9,376	12,283	11,343	10,684	17,279	16,228
Spain	3,503[4/]	5,607	5,890	4,635	260[4/]	254
Sweden	1,342	1,078	3,451	3,493	3,791	1,389
Switzerland[3/]	5,143	2,952	2,658	1,493[4/]	7,869[4/]	7,897[4/]
United Kingdom	251,641	212,980	204,135	217,062	194,973	180,172
Total	519,901	521,075	517,741	517,517	524,672	505,443
Africa, Republic of S. Africa	5,346[3/]	404	1,118	486	744	338
Asia, India	[5/]	20,607	20,478	30,965	38,152	34,660
TOTAL	568,049	571,003	581,073	580,461	596,075	594,608

[1/]2,000 pounds.   [2/]Preliminary.   [3/]Includes palm kernel oil.   [4/]Includes coconut oil.
[5/]Not separately classified.

Source: U. S. Department of Agriculture, Foreign Agricultural Service.

Table 73

PALM OIL & PALM-KERNEL OIL

UNITED STATES IMPORTS BY COUNTRY OF ORIGIN: 1957-62
(In 1,000 Pounds)

Country of Origin	1957	1958	1959	1960	1961	1962
PALM OIL						
Congo, Republic of the	264	3,268	1,391	4,227	30,018	16,112
Indonesia [1]	18,194	39,353	29,337	40,234	23,509	14,333
Other Countries [1]	181	391	588	2,357	2,480	5,083
TOTAL	18,640	43,013	31,315	46,818	56,007	35,529
Value ($1,000)	2,243	4,611	3,418	5,011	5,353	3,279
Unit value (¢/lb.)	12.03	10.71	10.91	10.70	9.55	9.22
PALM-KERNEL OIL						
United Kingdom	4,495	3,443	5,831	12,219	1,121	11,765
Edible	4,495	3,443	1,123	10,107	-	11,765
Inedible	-	-	4,708	2,112	1,121	-
Netherlands	775	2,918	17,699	16,462	12,402	16,045
Edible	775	2,918	15,186	13,938	10,639	15,273
Inedible	-	-	2,513	2,524	1,763	772
Congo, Republic of the	44,531	44,905	46,995	59,636	56,312	42,379
Edible	44,409	44,905	42,791	48,307	45,480	41,692
Inedible	122	-	4,204	11,329	10,832	687
Other Countries [2]	-	40	428	-	14,252	14,007
Edible	-	9	6	-	14,252	13,346
Inedible	-	31	422	-	-	661
TOTAL, Edible and Inedible	49,801	51,306	70,954	88,317	84,087	84,195
Total, Edible oil	49,679	51,275	59,107	72,352	70,371	82,075
Value ($1,000)	5,808	6,253	9,257	10,720	8,428	8,697
Unit value (¢/lb.)	11.69	12.19	15.66	14.81	11.97	10.59
Total, Inedible oil	122	31	11,847	15,965	13,716	2,120
Value ($1,000)	14	4	1,788	2,166	1,466	211
Unit value (¢/lb.)	11.49	12.00	15.09	13.56	10.68	9.96

[1] Principally Nigeria, Costa Rica, and Belgium. [2] Principally West Germany and Japan.

Source: U. S. Department of Commerce, Bureau of the Census.

Table 74

P I N E A P P L E   C A N N E D

EXPORTS FROM SPECIFIED COUNTRIES,
Average 1954-58 and Annual Marketing Years 1958-61
(1,000 Cases, 24/2½'s)

| Exporting Country | Average 1954-58 | 1958-59 | Marketing Years | | 1961-62 |
			1959-60	1960-61	
Australia	628.0	955.0	666.0	173.0	-
Cuba[1]/	485.9	471.6	-	-	-
Malaya[1]/	1,686.7	1,921.4	1,900.5	2,052.4	576.3
Mexico[1]/	694.7	916.6	566.8	810.8	858.1
Philippines[1]/	1,677.0	1,396.6	1,985.3	1,609.6	-
Puerto Rico	149.9	193.1	230.0	206.5	212.4
South Africa	905.6	1,363.0	2,342.7	2,173.0	-
Taiwan[1]/	912.0	1,363.9	1,790.3	1,865.2	2,850.0
United States	2,162.3	2,138.1	1,763.5	1,595.4	1,886.5
TOTAL	9,302.1	10,719.3	11,245.1	10,485.9	[2]/

[1]/Calendar year.   [2]/Unavailable.

Source: U. S. Department of Agriculture, Foreign Agricultural Service.

Table 75

P I N E A P P L E   C A N N E D

CANADA IMPORTS BY COUNTRY OF ORIGIN,
Average 1954-58 and Annual 1958-61
(1,000 Cases, 24/2½'s)

Country of Origin	Average 1954-58	Marketing Season			
		1958-59	1959-60	1960-61	1961-62[1]
United States	456.7	453.6	382.4	330.7	173.7
Mexico	167.6	186.5	103.0	106.2	68.9
Australia	82.3	150.2	160.7	116.5	45.0
Malaya	67.9	192.8	258.2	289.8	187.8
South Africa	5.7	13.8	57.6	130.0	61.0
Other	36.5	51.3	13.6	14.1	14.3
TOTAL	816.7	1,048.2	975.5	987.3	550.7

[1] Six months, July-December.

Source: U. S. Department of Agriculture, Foreign Agricultural Service.

Table 76

PINEAPPLE CANNED

DENMARK IMPORTS BY COUNTRY OF ORIGIN,
Average 1954-58 and Annual 1958-60
(1,000 Cases, 24/2½'s)

Country of Origin	Average 1954-58	Calendar Year			
		1958	1959	1960	1961[1]
United States	6.4	5.3	45.1	46.0	
United Kingdom	27.0	31.9	0.2	0.7	
Australia	0.2	-	8.1	14.0	
China	1.9	7.4	4.9	12.5	
Malaya and Singapore	1.2	1.7	11.5	55.3	
Taiwan	3.2	1.8	28.4	95.7	
South Africa	2.1	1.5	14.6	36.9	
Other	7.6	8.6	3.1	15.4	
TOTAL	49.6	58.2	115.9	276.5	

[1] Not available.

Source: U. S. Department of Agriculture, Foreign Agricultural
Service.

Table 77

P I N E A P P L E   C A N N E D

FRANCE IMPORTS BY COUNTRY OF ORIGIN,
Average 1954-58 and Annual 1958-61
(1,000 Cases, 24/2½'s)

| Country of Origin | Average 1954-58 | Calendar Year | | | |
		1958	1959	1960	1961
Martinique	164.7	223.9	436.5	486.5	472.1
West Africa, n.e.c.	71.5	114.5	149.3	192.3	197.0
Other	45.2[1]/	18.3	33.3	14.4	14.7
TOTAL	281.4	356.7	619.1	693.2	683.8

[1]/Includes 20,210 cases from China.   [2]/Includes 28,449 cases from New Guinea.

Source: U. S. Department of Agriculture, Foreign Agricultural Service.

Table 78

P I N E A P P L E   C A N N E D

WESTERN GERMANY IMPORTS BY COUNTRY OF ORIGIN,
Average 1954-58 and Annual 1958-61
(1,000 Cases, 24/2½'s)

Country of Origin	Average 1954-58	Marketing Season			
		1958-59	1959-60	1960-61	1961-62[1]
United States	744.5	724.6	716.3	571.5	800.5
Australia	5.6	10.4	104.6	3.7	-
Cuba	50.5	41.6	15.3	0.8	8.9
Kenya	5.7	9.0	48.2	11.4	31.9
Malaya and Singapore	89.9	104.1	176.8	116.1	163.8
Mexico	30.4	108.3	24.7	82.0	98.9
Philippines, Rep. of	30.6	24.5	54.1	235.6	216.8
Taiwan	476.0	975.7	1,014.5	815.8	630.9
South Africa	68.5	221.2	715.8	569.0	372.4
Other	8.2	7.5	7.7	48.5	26.9
TOTAL	1,509.9	2,226.9	2,878.0	2,454.4	2,351.0

[1] Nine months, July-March.

Source: U. S. Department of Agriculture, Foreign Agricultural Service.

Table 79

P I N E A P P L E   C A N N E D

JAPAN IMPORTS BY COUNTRY OF ORIGIN,
Average 1954-58 and Annual 1958-61
(1,000 Cases, 24/2½'s)

| Country of Origin | Average 1954-58 | Calendar Year | | | |
		1958	1959	1960	1961[1/]
Nansei and Nanpo Islands	45.5	143.2	401.6	607.5	-
Taiwan	191.3	297.4	359.0	209.8	-
Other	20.4	1.3	0.9	2.0	-
TOTAL	257.2	441.9	761.5	819.3	1,080.7

[1/] Country breakdown not available.

Source: U. S. Department of Agriculture, Foreign Agricultural Service.

Table 80

PINEAPPLE CANNED

NETHERLANDS IMPORTS BY COUNTRY OF ORIGIN,
Average 1954-58 and Annual 1958-61
(1,000 Cases, 24/2½'s)

		Marketing Season			
Country of Origin	Average 1954-58	1958-59	1959-60	1960-61	1961-62[1]
United States	63.8	41.7	55.6	122.3	112.2
Philippines, Rep. of	5.5	9.7	9.7	10.5	33.9
Trust Territories of Pacific Is. (U.S.)	65.8	75.2	59.4	-	-
Taiwan	5.8	28.9	113.9	94.1	112.0
Other	13.6	31.9	29.2	40.2	28.1
TOTAL	154.5	187.4	267.8	267.1	286.2

[1] Nine months, July-March.

Source: U. S. Department of Agriculture, Foreign Agricultural Service.

Table 81

P I N E A P P L E   C A N N E D

SWEDEN IMPORTS[1]/ BY COUNTRY OF ORIGIN,
Average 1954-58 and Annual 1958-61
(1,000 Cases, 24/2½'s)

Country of Origin	Average 1954-58	Calendar Year			
		1958	1959	1960	1961[2]/
United States	175.6	167.4	159.9	112.4	-
Australia	2.8	-	33.5	10.0	-
Philippines, Republic of	3.0	7.4	5.8	20.2	-
Taiwan	19.9	50.4	28.4	10.4	-
U. S. Oceania	37.4	53.7	-	-	-
Other	18.4	15.8	22.8	50.9	-
TOTAL	257.1	294.7	250.4	203.9	164.3

[1]/Prior to 1959 include grapefruit.   [2]/Breakdown not available.

Source: U. S. Department of Agriculture, Foreign Agricultural Service.

399

Table 82

P Y R E T H R U M [1]/

UNITED STATES IMPORTS BY COUNTRY OF ORIGIN: 1957-62

(Volume in Thousands of Pounds; Value in Thousands of Dollars)

Country of Origin	1957 Volume	1957 Value	1958 Volume	1958 Value	1959 Volume	1959 Value	1960 Volume	1960 Value	1961 Volume	1961 Value	1962 Volume	1962 Value
ECUADOR	337	83	477	151	512	167	470	301	349	480	291	465
Crude[2]/	337	83	477	151	511	159	446	139	294	86	238	56
Advanced[3]/	-	-	-	-	1	8	24	162	55	394	53	409
Congo [2]/	1,643	1,037	522	832	273	2,027	173	1,652	425	458	13	88
Crude[2]/	1,592	557	450	157	56	20	-	-	393	157	-	-
Advanced[3]/	51	480	72	675	217	2,007	173	1,652	32	301	13	88
British East Africa	3,529	1,404	3,719	2,529	713	2,963	1,147	3,772	3,816	5,395	2,117	4,203
Crude[2]/	3,497	1,105	3,569	1,306	403	141	784	314	3,393	1,355	1,749	698
Advanced[3]/	32	299	150	1,223	310	2,822	363	3,458	423	4,040	368	3,505
Other	96	31	241	301	46	138	45	153	40	51	85	22
Crude[2]/	91	7	210	41	22	2	27	6	36	9	74	18
Advanced[3]/	5	24	31	260	24	136	18	147	4	42	11	4
TOTAL IMPORTS	5,605	2,554	4,959	3,814	1,545	5,296	1,833	5,878	4,630	6,383	2,506	4,778
Crude	5,517	1,751	4,706	1,655	993	322	1,256	459	4,116	1,606	2,061	772
Advanced	88	803	253	2,159	552	4,974	577	5,419	514	4,777	445	4,006

[1]/ Crude and advanced pyrethrum have been added together primarily to show total value of imports of this commodity; weight figures should be considered separately because the two forms are not comparable. [2]/ Dried pyrethrum flowers. [3]/ Pyrethrum extract, diluted and undiluted. On the average 100 lbs. of pyrethrum flowers yields approximately 1.5 lbs. of pyrethrin concentrate.

Source: U. S. Department of Commerce, Bureau of the Census.

Table 83

R I C E[1]/

WORLD EXPORTS BY COUNTRY OF ORIGIN,
Average 1951-55, Annual 1957-61
(In Million Pounds)

Country of Origin	Average 1951-55	1957	1958	1959	1960	1961
Asia						
Burma	2,910	3,865	3,109	3,740	3,857	3,623
Cambodia	225	429	465	428	783	521
China, Mainland[2]/	630	1,085	2,774	3,750	2,804	850
Pakistan	291	5	4	183	145	261
Taiwan	210	319	431	353	77	143
Thailand	3,042	3,474	2,513	2,428	2,652	3,455
Vietnam	336	405	248	542	750	337
Other	175	300	240	217	415	51
Total	7,819	9,882	9,784	11,641	11,483	9,241
Western Hemisphere						
United States	1,389	1,731	1,305	1,554	2,198	1,841
Argentina	31	39	73	15	10	16
Brazil	151	1	114	22	1	332
British Guiana	84	85	40	126	142	195
ECUADOR	60	84	57	37	59	54
Uruguay	27	18	21	2	13	45
Other	77	44	52	69	48	111
Total	1,819	2,002	1,662	1,825	2,471	2,594
Europe						
Italy	493	316	404	341	289	480
Spain	98	141	214	62	64	205
Portugal	15	3/	25	3/	3/	3/
Other	61	130	162	108	96	41
Total	667	587	805	511	449	726
Africa						
Malagasay Republic	65	46	128	65	52	55
U.A.R.:Egypt	249	652	852	108	669	503
Other	38	44	31	26	34	21
Total	352	742	1,011	199	755	579
Australia	71	67	94	114	154	157
WORLD TOTAL	10,728	13,280	13,356	14,290	15,312	13,297

[1]/Milled equivalent. [2]/From returns of importing countries. [3]/Less than
500,000 pounds.

Source: U. S. Department of Agriculture, Foreign Agricultural Service.

Table 84

R I C E[1]/

WORLD IMPORTS INTO PRINCIPAL IMPORTING COUNTRIES,
Average 1951-55, Annual 1957-61
(In Million Pounds)

Country	Average 1951-55	1957	1958	1959	1960	1961
Ceylon	884	1,153	1,063	1,286	1,164	1,034
Hong Kong	478	690	841	779	817	868
India	1,168	1,760	902	698	1,568	884
Indonesia	905	1,242	2,150	2,072	2,256	2,466
Japan	2,438	765	1,114	611	385	278
Korea	246	445	15	7	2	1
Malaya	1,113	1,163	1,413	1,500	1,490	1,420
Pakistan	-	950	757	666	714	453
Philippine Republic	132	172	509	14	-	435
Arabian Peninsula	223	385	375	521	428	445
Cuba	470	422	426	380	314	380
Belgium-Luxemburg	83	140	114	172	165	119
France	125	196	132	187	196	139
West Germany	189	197	264	342	334	290
Netherlands	151	132	151	179	179	134
United Kingdom	164	186	190	188	209	228
Senegal-Sudan-Mauritania	137	247	166	298	182	242
Mauritius	106	137	155	128	134	148
Other	1,810	3,455	3,617	4,882	4,839	3,404
WORLD TOTAL	10,822	13,837	14,354	14,910	15,376	13,368

[1]/ Milled equivalent.

Source: U. S. Department of Agriculture, Foreign Agricultural Service.

Table 85

R I C E [1]

ECUADOR EXPORTS BY COUNTRY OF DESTINATION, 1952-62

(In Metric Tons)

Country of Destination	1952	1953	1954	1955	1956	1957	1958	1959	1960	1961	1962
Western Hemisphere											
Nicaragua	-	-	-	552	4,476	184	230	-	-	2,168	966
Costa Rica	-	-	-	7,900	3,248	3,490	1,733	3,938	-	-	-
Panama	2,028	457	1,460	2,722	1,302	716	25	-	-	4,183	3,684
Aruba and Curaçao	362	143	42	419	448	472	175	6	7	-	-
El Salvador	-	-	8,556	3,450	1,723	-	248	3	-	-	-
Colombia	-	-	-	-	-	10,000	-	-	-	10,083	-
Peru	46	-	-	-	-	20,046	46	10	14	-	-
Chile	339	-	62	682	-	-	-	75	-	-	-
Venezuela	-	644	-	-	-	-	23,235	12,891	20,968	4,569	-
Other[2]	2,859	3,041	75	5,130	500	2,602	37	-	5,796	-	-
Total	5,634	4,285	10,195	20,855	11,697	37,510	25,729	16,923	26,785	21,003	4,650
Other	51,549 [3]	38,195 [4]	500	44	-	461	-	-	-	4	-
TOTAL	57,183	42,480	10,695	20,899	11,697	37,971	25,729	16,923	26,785	21,007	4,650

[1] Milled equivalent. [2] Includes a number of other countries which have sporadically imported rice from Ecuador. Principal among these have been Cuba, Bolivia, Jamaica, Surinam, Puerto Rico, Canada, and Guatemala. [3] All to the Far East. [4] 28,453 tons to Japan and 9,737 tons to the Republic of South Africa.

Source: U. S. Department of Agriculture, Foreign Agricultural Service.

Table 86

R I C E

UNITED STATES IMPORTS BY COUNTRY OF ORIGIN: 1957-62

Country of Origin	1957	1958	1959	1960	1961	1962[1]
Cleaned or milled rice	lbs.	lbs.	lbs.	lbs.	lbs.	lbs.
Canada	-	-	-	-	400	4,000
Argentina	211,739	50,198	-	-	-	-
France	12,500	-	-	-	-	-
Spain	-	7,804	-	3,902	5,688	-
Italy	101,630	102,745	157,313	288,331	201,289	256,196
Iran	6,587	3,310	-	-	441	871
Thailand	152,637	101,718	71,658	-	-	-
Japan	-	-	-	15,000	2,500	-
TOTAL	485,093	265,775	228,971	307,233	210,318	261,067
Broken rice[2]	1,000	1,000	1,000	1,000	1,000	1,000
	lbs.	lbs.	lbs.	lbs.	lbs.	lbs.
Canada	6,607	-	306	3,864	4,032	-
Mexico	-	-	-	-	-	2,765
Argentina	-	-	-	-	-	99
Netherlands	6,342	4,723	5,153	3,806	1,352	5,040
Belgium	3,914	1,272	-	2,688	6,736	7,939
West Germany	5,037	5,707	10,369	51,372	1,120	5,043
Iran	-	-	-	2	-	-
Thailand	-	10	-	-	-	-
TOTAL	21,901	11,712	15,828	61,732	13,241	20,887

[1] The United States imported an additional 4,409 lbs. of uncleaned or brown rice (Schedule A No. 1051100) from Thailand in 1962. [2] Includes brewers' rice.

Source: U. S. Department of Commerce.

404

Table 87

N A T U R A L   R U B B E R

PRODUCTION, BY PRINCIPAL TERRITORIES:
Average 1952-56 and Annual 1957-62
(In Thousands of Long Tons)

Territory	Average 1952-56	1957	1958	1959	1960	1961	1962
Asia							
Malaya	592.0	637.5	662.9	697.8	708.4	736.7	751.9
Indonesia	722.6	684.5	685.2	693.5	629.8	671.4	658.6
Ceylon	95.7	98.2	100.2	91.7	97.3	96.0	102.4
Viet-Nam	57.2	68.6	70.5	74.2	75.4	77.9	77.2
Cambodia	24.7	31.2	33.1	33.9	36.5	39.3	40.9
Thailand	114.8	133.0	137.4	170.3	167.2	181.7	190.8
India	21.7	23.8	24.3	23.4	24.8	26.6	30.9
Sarawak	31.8	41.0	38.9	43.4	49.7	47.3	43.4
Other[1]	36.5	38.5	38.3	41.8	40.3	42.5	41.0
Total	1,697.0	1,756.3	1,790.8	1,870.0	1,829.4	1,919.4	1,937.1
Africa[1]	89.2	116.3	124.0	141.0	141.3	140.8	139.6
Latin America							
Brazil	23.9	24.0	20.3	21.1	22.7	22.4	21.3
Other[1]	7.2	6.0	6.0	7.0	7.0	7.0	7.0
Total	31.1	30.0	26.3	28.1	29.7	29.4	28.3
WORLD TOTAL[1]	1,826.5	1,902.5	1,940.0	2,040.0	2,000.0	2,090.0	2,105.0

[1] Estimated or partly estimated figures.

Source: Rubber Statistical Bulletin, Volume 17, Number 4; published by International Rubber Study Group, London.

405

Table 88

N A T U R A L   R U B B E R

NEW SUPPLY[1] INTO PRINCIPAL CONSUMING COUNTRIES: 1957-62
(In Thousands of Long Tons)

	1957	1958	1959	1960	1961	1962
United States	542.9	457.7	557.4	398.3	385.0	413.3
Canada	42.6	37.4	45.3	34.7	31.5	37.5[2]
Europe						
Czechoslovakia	43.1	47.8	41.7	61.4	56.5	18.0[2]
France	138.6	135.0	120.4	129.5	123.3	119.9
Germany, West	135.6	132.2	143.9	150.6	133.7	140.5
Italy	59.0	55.1	56.1	67.7	78.4	78.5
Netherlands	20.3	17.8	20.6	20.6	21.0[2]	20.6
Poland	31.7	31.5	31.8	33.9	41.0[2]	33.0[2]
Spain	27.1	23.6	21.5	22.1	22.4	31.6[2]
Sweden	21.7	21.5	21.3	22.4	19.9	22.5
United Kingdom[3]	215.4	147.7	166.4	137.5	153.0[2]	151.6
U.S.S.R.	120.5	236.0	221.0	174.5	363.8[2]	345.5[2]
Other[4]	104.1	110.7	107.8	122.4	101.5	107.4
Total	917.1	958.9	952.5	942.6	1,114.5	1,069.1
Africa						
South Africa	24.7	20.2	19.9	18.9	17.3	17.6
Other[2]	5.4	6.6	4.8	7.7	8.0	9.2
Total	30.1	26.8	24.7	26.6	25.3	26.8
Latin America						
Argentina	33.1	31.7	21.8	21.9	33.2	22.2[2]
Brazil	37.8	38.0	43.9	46.8	42.1	40.4
Other[2]	32.6	40.5	34.5	40.0	36.5	38.5
Total	103.5	110.2	100.2	108.7	111.8	101.1
Asia						
China[2]	56.8	92.3	108.8	119.8	83.3	107.0
India	33.4	36.2	37.9	47.4	47.9[2]	53.9
Japan	130.5	129.4	157.7	169.8	178.0[2]	188.8[2]
Other[2]	51.3	54.1	52.3	63.5	64.4	79.2
Total	272.0	312.0	356.7	400.5	373.6	428.9
Oceania						
Australia	34.0	34.8	37.8	36.7	28.3[2]	34.4[2]
New Zealand	6.4	6.6	5.7	6.0[2]	5.9[2]	5.1[2]
Total	40.4	41.4	43.5	42.7	34.2	39.5
WORLD TOTAL[2]	1,947.5	1,947.5	2,077.5	1,952.5	2,080.0	2,117.5

[1] For most countries the figures represent "net imports." [2] Estimated. [3] Not including deliveries from the Government stockpile, which began in October, 1959. [4] Includes all countries with imports less than 20,000 tons per year.

Source: Rubber Statistical Bulletin, Volume 17, Number 4, January, 1963. Published by International Rubber Study Group, London.

Table 89

N A T U R A L   R U B B E R

NET EXPORTS FROM PRINCIPAL TERRITORIES:
Average 1952-56 and Annual 1957-62
(In Thousands of Long Tons)

Territories	Average 1952-56	1957	1958	1959	1960	1961	1962
Asia							
Malaya	592.3	638.9	666.6[3/]	742.8	659.1	744.8[5/]	721.2
Indonesia	708.3	666.5	649.6[2/]	678.5	577.3	666.5[5/]	637.6
Ceylon	92.1[2/]	94.0	90.4	92.0	104.7	88.1	100.2
Viet-Nam	59.5[2/]	72.5	67.7	72.3	72.7	81.3	68.2
Cambodia	25.8[2/]	31.2	32.7	33.4	34.5	39.4	36.8
Thailand	114.8	133.0	137.4	170.3	167.2	181.7	190.8
Sarawak	31.8	41.0	38.5	43.9	50.0	46.9	43.8
Other[1/]	32.7	34.1	32.7	36.4	33.2	35.4	33.0
Total	1,657.3	1,711.2	1,715.6	1,869.6	1,698.7	1,884.1	1,831.6
Africa							
Liberia	36.8	38.2	42.3	42.4	41.8	42.6	43.4[1/]
Nigeria	25.8	39.5	41.1	53.2	58.5	54.9[1/]	57.4[1/]
Congo	22.9	33.8	34.5	39.5	35.0	35.0[1/]	35.0[1/]
Other	3.6	3.9	5.2	5.3	4.9	5.0	2.2[1/]
Total[1/]	89.0	115.3	123.0	140.0	140.3	140.8	138.0
Latin America[1/]	1.2	0.4	-	-	-	-	-
Oceania	3.3	3.7	4.5	4.4	4.1	4.4	4.6
WORLD TOTAL[1/]	1,742.5	1,830.0	1,875.0[4/]	2,015.0	1,842.5	2,030.0	1,975.0

[1/] Estimated or partly estimated figures.   [2/] Represents average for 1954-56: for previous
years only combined Viet-Nam-Cambodia figures available.   [3/] Indonesian export data for 1958
are incomplete.   [4/] Includes an allowance of 33.000 tons for not yet reported rubber.
[5/] Year-end adjustment provisionally pro-rated over reported monthly exports.

Source: Rubber Statistical Bulletin, Volume 17, Number 4; published by International
Rubber Study Group, London.

Table 90

S Y N T H E T I C   R U B B E R

PRODUCTION BY MAJOR PRODUCING COUNTRIES: 1957-61
(Thousands of Long Tons)

	1957	1958	1959	1960	1961
United States	1,118.2	1,054.6	1,379.7	1,436.4	1,404.0
Canada	132.1	135.0	100.7	159.7	164.5
Germany, West	11.6	22.7	48.1	79.8	85.6
United Kingdom	0.8	11.3	56.3	90.4	105.5
Italy[1]/	-	20.0	47.0	70.0	87.0
Other	-	-	8.2	48.0	133.5
TOTAL	1,262.7	1,242.5	1,640.0	1,885.0	1,980.0

1/Estimated, except for 1959. 2/Estimated, except for 1957.

Source: Rubber Statistical Bulletin, Volume 17, Number 4; published
         by International Rubber Study Group, London.

Table 91

SYNTHETIC RUBBER

EXPORTS BY MAJOR PRODUCING COUNTRIES: 1957-62
(In Thousands of Long Tons)

	1957	1958	1959	1960	1961	1962
United States	203.4	193.9	290.5	342.0	297.0[1]/	303.7[1]/
Canada	93.4	99.2	75.8	108.2	122.0[1]/	118.0[1]/
United Kingdom	#	0.7	6.7	19.7	21.4	27.7
Germany, West	2.6	4.9	11.8	21.1	18.3	24.4
Italy	-	0.6	24.3	36.4	45.2	40.7
Other	-	-	3.2	12.7[1]/	31.9	63.2
TOTAL	299.4	299.3	412.3	540.1	535.8	577.7[1]/

#Less than 50 tons. [1]/Estimated or partly estimated figures.

Source: Rubber Statistical Bulletin, Volume 17, Number 4; published
by International Rubber Study Group, London.

409

Table 92

NATURAL AND SYNTHETIC RUBBER[1]

CONSUMPTION BY PRINCIPAL CONSUMING COUNTRIES: 1957-62
(In Thousands of Long Tons)

	1957	1958	1959	1960	1961	1962
United States	1,464.6	1,364.4	1,627.8	1,558.3	1,529.5	1,701.5
Canada	88.4	83.8	101.5	91.0	94.4	107.8
United Kingdom	246.0	247.3	264.5	295.7	287.4	290.5
France	185.1	192.0	199.7	218.1	222.5	233.3
Germany, West	183.0	183.7	217.5	250.1	256.1	275.2
Netherlands	23.7	22.4	28.7	32.1	33.2	33.8
Eastern Europe[2]	227.9	356.0	342.5	333.7	519.8	458.3
Other Europe[2]	223.5	231.5	249.3	305.8	337.5	370.0
Australia	49.3	52.1	56.4	62.4	52.2	58.8
Brazil	39.3	44.1	53.8	59.5	59.2	66.7
India	34.8	38.0	43.0	51.7	57.0	61.2
Japan	143.3	144.7	190.9	226.5	259.8	294.2
China[2]	56.8	98.2	114.3	135.5	96.5	107.2
Others[2]	192.0	201.0	199.3	232.8	246.8	262.5
WORLD TOTAL[2]	3,157.5	3,260.0	3,690.0	3,852.5	4,050.0	4,322.5

[1] No account taken of synthetic rubber originating from Eastern Europe.   [2] Estimated.

Source: Rubber Statistical Bulletin, Volume 17, Number 4; published by International Rubber Study Group, London.

Table 93

S E S A M E   S E E D[1]

WORLD EXPORTS BY COUNTRY OF ORIGIN,
Average 1950-54, Annual 1956-60
(In Short Tons[2])

Country of Origin	Average 1950-54	1956	1957	1958	1959[3]	1960[3]
North America						
El Salvador	3,887	2,456	2,142	2,406[4]	1,853[4]	976[4]
Nicaragua	11,388	3,858	4,393	7,009	9,561	6,954[5]
Other	559	112	415	620	500	246
Total	15,834	6,426	6,950	10,035	11,914	8,176
Africa						
Angola	495	168	132	560	1,247	1,088
Congo, Republic of the	1,358	839	599	788	439	1,102
Egypt	325	7,611	7,152	1,637	435	263
Ethiopia[6]	11,281[7]	3,418	3,664	2,661	2,220	-
Former French West Africa[8]	607	1,545	1,689	2,558	2,561	193
Kenya	-	427	642	659	962	1,645
Uganda	116	96	542	620	474	403
Mozambique	1,842	55	4	2,021	871	902[9]
Nigeria	14,912	24,858	21,511	13,664	20,265	30,554
Sudan	12,102	33,811	45,188	32,936	49,309	61,729
Tanganyika	889	11,903	9,162	9,516	12,553	12,117
Other	287	526	1,220	4,075	1,562	1,190
Total	44,214	85,257	91,505	71,695	92,898	114,486[10]
Asia						
Cambodia, Laos, Vietnam	1,190	2,951	5,481	836	999	1,846[11]
China, Mainland[12]	32,055	9,149	4,000	6,000	6,000	8,000
Hong Kong	16,446	12,467	8,397	5,607	3,908	3,687
India	1,357	80	1	52	487	320
Indonesia	2,373	22	982	1,878	1,111	-
Iran[13]	2,721	2,905	599	550	-	-
Iraq	3,643	1,998	1,678	1,673	1,940	28[14]
Syria	1,080	514	1,241	64	1,241	331[15]
Thailand	1,499	8,588	3,309	3,152	3,295	3,171
Other	2,116	1,923	853	217	123	50
Total	64,480	40,597	26,541	20,029	19,704[10]	19,033[10]
Other Countries	1,269	604	57	597	1,643	1,473
TOTAL	125,797	132,884	125,053	102,356	126,159	143,168

[1] The bulk of world trade in sesame is in the form of seed; oil exports are practically negligible. [2] 2,000 lbs. [3] Preliminary. [4] U. S. imports. [5] January-June. [6] Year beginning December 11. [7] Includes large quantities of Niger seed. [8] Includes the independent countries of Dahomey, Ivory Coast, Guinea, Mauritania, Niger, Senegal, and Volta. [9] January-October. [10] Includes estimates for the above countries for which data are not available. [11] January-August. [12] Unofficial estimate. [13] Year beginning March 21. [14] January-March. [15] January-September.

Source: U. S. Department of Agriculture, Foreign Agricultural Service.

411

Table 94

S E S A M E   S E E D

IMPORTS INTO PRINCIPAL IMPORTING COUNTRIES,
Average 1950-54, Annual 1956-60
(In Short Tons[1]/)

Country	Average 1950-54	1956	1957	1958	1959[2]/	1960[2]/
North America						
United States	7,216	6,569	7,457	7,369	6,679	8,689
South America						
Venezuela	7,784	3,225	19,988	12,310	11,271	37,478
Europe						
Denmark	4,324	5,372	5,538	3,210	2,497	2,361
France	2,391	1,779	614	434	295	356
Italy	10,753	31,058	18,351	20,686	20,898	28,343
Netherlands	4,683	18	-	8	11	-
United Kingdom[3]/	14,297	4	9	12	-	-
Total	36,448	38,231	24,512	24,350	23,701	31,060
Africa						
Algeria	308	11,723	7,272	202	440	4,410
Egypt	1,749	8,508	8,829	7,021	8,581	6,972
Total	2,057	20,231	16,101	7,223	9,021	11,382
Asia						
Hong Kong	15,880	11,082	8,263	1,222	4,548	5,143
Japan	8,234	23,847	12,462	18,649	30,033	30,772
Lebanon	3,842	3,714	5,246	4,193	3,914	3,968
Malaya	3,516	2,551	3,302	3,680	3,847	3,102[4]/
Total	31,472	41,194	29,273	27,744	42,342	42,985
TOTAL	84,977	109,450	97,331	78,996	93,014	131,594

[1]/2,000 pounds.   [2]/Preliminary.   [3]/Less than 5 years.   [4]/January-September.

Source: U. S. Department of Agriculture, Foreign Agricultural Service.

412

Table 95

S E S A M E[1]

UNITED STATES IMPORTS BY COUNTRY OF ORIGIN: 1957-62
(In 1,000 Pounds)

Country of Origin	1957	1958	1959	1960	1961	1962
Western Hemisphere						
Guatemala	75	446	1	1,159	2,795	2,574
El Salvador	3,877	4,814	3,707	1,952	2,729	2,511
Nicaragua	7,664	8,831	8,831	13,260	14,658	10,969
Brazil	-	-	637	113	328	2,573
Other	344	82	16	9	106	729
Total	11,960	14,173	13,192	16,493	20,616	19,356
Europe	-	16	-	54	28	-
Africa	1,678	350	125	447	2,229	684
Asia	1,276	199	40	383	21	98
TOTAL	14,914	14,737	13,358	17,378	22,895	20,138
Value ($1,000)	2,376	2,379	1,911	2,494	2,975	2,879
Unit value (¢/lb.)	15.92	16.14	14.30	14.35	12.99	14.29

[1]Sesame seed. During the 6-year period, 1957-62, the U. S. imported a total of 5,785,123 lbs. of edible sesame oil valued at $1,457,108 principally from Denmark (74%) and Japan (23%). Less than 1,000 lbs. of inedible sesame oil was imported during this period.

Source: U. S. Department of Commerce, Bureau of the Census.

413

Table 96

S H R I M P

UNITED STATES IMPORTS BY COUNTRY OF ORIGIN: 1957-62
(In 1,000 Pounds)

Country of Origin	1957	1958	1959	1960	1961	1962
North America						
Canada	243	262	134	332	249	161
Mexico	47,907	56,098	68,654	73,583	79,181	77,665
Guatemala	-	39	182	257	743	2,298
El Salvador	66	1,130	1,836	6,697	8,093	7,156
Honduras	-	836	314	361	227	379
Nicaragua	1	278	213	266	803	1,971
Costa Rica	227	717	1,157	461	1,321	1,671
Panama	8,379	7,917	8,805	8,423	9,892	10,117
Other	686	634	439	379	81	220
Total	57,509	67,911	81,734	90,759	100,590	101,639
South America						
Colombia	487	891	1,898	2,174	1,873	2,207
Venezuela	137	122	370	344	2,469	6,341
British Guiana	-	-	967	3,568	3,506	4,129
Surinam	65	81	289	381	447	1,036
ECUADOR	3,867	4,437	4,712	4,192	4,684	5,121
Peru	626	486	280	256	358	387
Chile	45	164	328	739	537	629
Other	137	606	1,026	106	60	216
Total	5,365	6,787	9,870	11,759	13,933	20,066
Europe						
Norway	132	144	161	110	71	62
Denmark	20	46	197	81	112	85
Spain	22	229	192	225	446	502
Italy	60	268	185	-	30	-
Other	96	132	194	101	180	75
Total	330	819	928	517	839	723
Asia						
Iran	-	-	739	1,226	1,953	724
Kuwait	-	-	-	146	194	415
India	1,252	1,699	2,866	2,892	3,220	5,616
Pakistan	472	637	640	1,018	1,686	3,156
Korean Republic	58	128	170	93	171	1,756
Hong Kong	1,586	4,029	667	3	14	568
Japan	2,865	2,552	7,227	2,947	1,823	3,922
Other	21	19	119	235	158	516
Total	6,254	9,064	12,428	8,559	9,219	16,673
Africa						
Egypt	40	449	1,309	1,667	1,650	1,782
Other	-	1	-	1/	-	12
Total	40	450	1,309	1,668	1,650	1,794
Australia and Oceania	233	363	286	155	36	289
TOTAL	69,732	85,394	106,555	113,418	126,268	141,183

1/Less than 500 pounds.

Source: U.S. Department of Commerce

414

Table 97

S I S A L   A N D   H E N E Q U E N

UNITED STATES IMPORTS BY COUNTRY OF ORIGIN,
Average 1955-59, Annual 1960-62

Country of Origin	Quantity (in long tons)				Value (in dollars)			
	Average 1955-59	1960	1961	1962 2/	Average 1955-59	1960	1961	1962 2/
SISAL								
Haiti	27,748	15,850	12,555	9,042	4,765,563	3,082,927	2,272,824	1,754,454
Brazil	43,068	18,049	23,612	27,757	5,833,403	3,265,971	4,105,658	4,486,892
Other America	976	160	60	24	160,687	28,335	10,948	3,575
Europe	185	70	-	24	28,129	11,043	-	4,468
Angola Portuguese Guinea	1,790	1,419	4,488	1,344	296,578	261,200	959,445	214,063
Mozambique	6,654	7,906	8,635	9,467	1,190,863	1,570,215	2,036,466	1,992,621
Other Portuguese Africa	666	215	365	25	117,480	34,430	83,918	3,555
Tanganyika, Kenya & Uganda	18,903	24,301	18,661	27,128	2,878,871	4,878,360	3,757,227	5,157,410
Other Africa	301	466	680	1,148	52,134	91,004	159,873	221,977
Indonesia	6,352	2,769	2,818	1,714	1,037,257	494,921	391,991	222,640
Other Asia	279	563	641	243	65,595	120,478	250,482	36,169
TOTAL SISAL	106,922	71,768	72,515	77,916	16,426,560	13,838,884	14,028,832	14,097,824
HENEQUEN								
Cuba	1,269	186	-	-	196,784	20,618	-	-
El Salvador	17	75	-	-	3,086	10,404	-	-
Mexico	21,060	23,950	30,793	30,458	3,206,994	4,084,972	4,612,422	4,763,509
TOTAL HENEQUEN	22,346	24,211	30,793	30,458	3,406,864	4,115,994	4,612,422	4,763,509

1/2,240 lbs. 2/Preliminary. 3/Imports from Mexico, Cuba, and El Salvador include very little, if any, sisal, and their total roughly represents total henequen; imports from all other countries include little, if any, henequen, and their total roughly represents total sisal.

Source: U. S. Department of Agriculture, Foreign Agricultural Service.

Table 98

S U G A R   (Raw Value)[1]

WORLD PRODUCTION IN PRINCIPAL PRODUCING REGIONS AND COUNTRIES,
Average 1950-51 through 1954-55, Annual 1957-58 through 1962-63[2]
(In 1,000 Short Tons)

	Average 1950-51 thru 1954-55	1957-58	1958-59	1959-60	1960-61	1961-62	1962-63
North America							
Canada[3]	142	138	187	151	162	141	154
United States[4]	4,656	4,495	4,853	4,918	5,297	5,463	5,821
Mexico	900	1,315	1,460	1,731	1,591	1,649	1,791
Cuba	6,078	6,372	6,574	6,462	7,460	5,400	4,600
Dominican Republic	657	850	994	1,120	1,370	960	900
West Indies Federation	773	793	866	925	982	941	946
Other	449	587	662	675	772	873	849
Total	13,655	14,550	15,596	15,982	17,634	15,427	15,061
South America							
Argentina	773	767	1,185	1,041	914	754	841
Brazil	2,110	3,114	3,770	3,550	3,797	3,928	3,950
British Guiana	266	305	350	340	365	364	364
Colombia	231	247	292	335	390	385	444
ECUADOR	60	75	96	110	113	160	165
Peru	628	788	794	904	942	904	937
Venezuela	94	187	180	205	260	271	275
Other	61	138	162	145	188	216	233
Total	4,223	5,621	6,829	6,630	6,969	6,982	7,209
Western Europe[5]							
Austria	176	312	320	326	324	231	258
Belgium-Luxembourg	395	430	510	241	555	500	369
Denmark	351	404	431	271	365	233	221
France	1,549	1,733	1,725	1,162	3,006	1,878	1,648
Germany, West	1,252	1,745	2,064	1,533	2,155	1,585	1,779
Italy	828	950	1,264	1,550	1,078	1,033	1,047
Netherlands	457	437	629	550	782	645	587
Spain	392	398	514	598	567	649	650
Sweden	331	385	296	313	395	358	331
United Kingdom	764	694	879	943	1,082	926	851
Other	177	212	207	253	255	287	297
Total	6,672	7,700	8,839	7,740	10,564	8,325	8,038

Table 98 (Continued)

SUGAR: WORLD PRODUCTION IN PRINCIPAL PRODUCING REGIONS AND COUNTRIES

	Average 1950-51 thru 1954-55	1957-58	1958-59	1959-60	1960-61	1961-62	1962-63
Eastern Europe							
Czechoslovakia	803	970	1,018	791	1,132	1,025	937
Germany, East	826	940	942	874	970	808	728
Hungary	284	295	323	423	525	384	352
Poland	1,047	1,299	1,312	1,072	1,650	1,662	1,433
Other	389	659	597	852	937	831	852
Total	3,349	4,163	4,192	4,012	5,214	4,710	4,302
USSR (Europe and Asia)	3,010	5,800	6,800	6,300	6,600	7,300	7,200
Africa	1,955	2,685	2,807	2,949	2,623	2,993	3,143
Asia							
Turkey	205	393	419	599	771	518	461
China (Mainland)	293	700	520	650	630	-	-
China (Taiwan)	724	1,025	1,074	882	1,044	800	800
India	1,690	2,485	2,662	3,323	4,042	3,775	4,128
Indonesia	578	913	854	942	743	707	783
Japan	38	102	145	172	173	182	183
Philippines	1,190	1,371	1,512	1,529	1,563	1,668	1,739
Other	237	455	524	603	576	638	638
Total	4,955	7,444	7,710	8,700	9,542	8,588[1/]	9,032[7/]
Oceania[6/]	1,297	1,767	1,762	1,706	1,668	1,695	2,235
WORLD TOTAL	39,116	49,730	54,535	54,019	60,814	56,020	56,220

[1/]Centrifugal sugar (raw value), as distinguished from non-centrifugal, includes cane and beet sugar produced by the centrifugal process, which is the principal kind moving in international trade. [2/]Years shown are crop-harvesting years. For chronological arrangement here, all campaigns which begin not earlier than May of one year, nor later than April of the following year, are placed in the same crop-harvesting year. The entire season's production of each country is credited to the May/April year in which harvesting and sugar production began. [3/]All beet sugar. [4/]Includes continental U.S. production, the major part of which is beet sugar, and Hawaii, Puerto Rico, and Virgin Islands of the U.S., all of which is cane sugar. [5/]All beet sugar. [6/]Virtually all Australian production (cane). [7/]Includes estimates for non-reporting countries.

Source: U.S. Department of Agriculture, Economic Research Service.

417

Table 99

S U G A R (Raw Value)

INTERNATIONAL TRADE: 1957-61
(In 1,000 Short Tons)

	1957		1958		1959		1960		1961	
	Exports	Imports	Exports	Imports	Exports	Imports	Exports	Imports	Exports	Imports
North America										
Canada	1	691	1	735	1	762	4	630	9	760
United States	10	4,165	12	4,765	7	4,571	5	4,707	7	4,226
Mexico	109	5	195	#	169	#	520	#	733	#
Cuba	5,946	#	6,120	-	5,458	-	6,211	-	7,070	-
Dominican Republic	848	#	738	#	731	#	1,213	-	875	-
Other	1,036	35	951	32	1,082	26	1,215	71	1,352	21
Total	7,950	4,896	8,017	5,532	7,448	5,359	9,168	5,408	10,046	5,007
South America										
Brazil	456	-	844	-	688	-	852	-	821	-
British Guiana	286	#	336	#	286	#	346	#	340	#
Chile	0	192	0	251	0	223	0	160	-	193
ECUADOR	21	#	23	0	36	0	25	0	23	-
Peru	550	#	456	#	530	#	583	#	661	#
Venezuela	123	-	16	7	-	67	-	-	-	-
Other	111	182	7	229	24	146	156	157	162	82
Total	1,547	374	1,682	487	1,564	436	1,962	317	2,007	275
Western Europe										
Austria	#	59	#	27	#	11	#	1	#	12
Belgium-Luxembourg	89	62	124	59	128	74	132	145	128	4
Denmark	75	#	81	21	34	#	31	#	19	14
France	591	607	550	504	481	594	669	856	978	432
Germany, West	2	642	12	79	44	269	41	123	1	73
Italy	403	4	8	102	19	38	19	21	2	35
Netherlands	34	322	33	277	36	178	124	248	55	140
Norway	-	142	1	167	1	173	1	168	#	161
Sweden	2	40	#	62	#	97	#	59	#	38
United Kingdom	807	3,225	684	2,987	657	2,851	587	2,569	391	2,582
Other	12	766	6	963	4	815	3	750	18	849
Total	2,015	5,869	1,499	5,248	1,404	5,100	1,607	4,940	1,610	4,340

Table 99 (Continued)

SUGAR: INTERNATIONAL TRADE

	1957		1958		1959		1960		1961	
	Exports	Imports	Exports	Imports	Exports	Imports	Exports	Imports	Exports	Imports
Eastern Europe										
Czechoslovakia	110	-	460	-	433	-	378	-	479	6
Hungary	5	30	34	48	78	12	81	-	146	0
Poland	77	-	272	-	344	-	371	192	792	288
Other	69	132	248	200	465	109	288	218	295	309
Total	261	162	1,014	248	1,320	121	1,118	410	1,712	603
USSR (Europe & Asia)	222	572	245	440	242	390	289	1,893	1,048	3,965
Africa										
Algeria	#	258	#	249	#	248	#	266	1	248
Mauritius	639	-	574	-	560	0	353	-	565	-
Morocco	34	402	18	367	13	377	13	396	8	401
Other	629	763	739	824	654	854	766	759	902	651
Total	1,302	1,423	1,331	1,440	1,227	1,479	1,132	1,421	1,476	1,300
Asia										
India	200	18	46	2	21		20		305	0
Indonesia	159	#	96	#	43	#	38	#	0	#
Iran	-	266	-	294	-	287	-	298	-	425
Japan	6	1,231	11	1,348	22	1,341	29	1,409	16	1,508
Malaya	26	237	17	298	7	254	11	291	37	264
Philippines	917	-	1,011	#	1,124	#	1,164	#	1,325	-
Taiwan	959	-	931		815		1,007	#	732	#
Other	131	1,157	192	1,476	134	1,291	338	1,794	449	3,029
Total	2,398	2,909	2,304	3,418	2,166	3,173	2,607	3,792	2,864	5,226
Oceania	1,087	118	975	147	922	117	1,106	132	1,097	149
WORLD TOTAL	16,782	16,323	17,067	16,960	16,293	16,175	18,989	18,313	21,860	20,865

Less than 500 tons.

Source: U. S. Department of Agriculture, Economic Research Service.

419

Table 100

S U G A R

WORLD CONSUMPTION, TOTAL AND PER CAPITA, BY PRINCIPAL REGIONS AND COUNTRIES,
Prewar Average and Annual 1957-59
(Totals in 1,000 Metric Tons; Per Capita in Kilos)

Region and Country	Prewar Average		1957		1958		1959		% Increase 1959 over prewar	
	Total	p.c.	Total	p.c.	Total	p.c.	Total	p.c.	Total	p.c.
North America										
Canada	458.4	40.8	739.1	44.6	802.1	47.0	815.8	46.8	78.0	14.7
United States	6,029.0	47.0	7,923.3	46.3	8,265.8	47.0	8,404.9	47.1	39.4	0.2
Greenland	0.7	38.3	1.9	65.5	1.9	66.8	2.0	67.0	185.7	74.9
Total	6,488.1	46.5	8,664.3	46.1	9,069.8	47.0	9,222.7	47.0	42.1	1.1
Central America										
Mexico	277.6	15.1	971.2	30.9	942.4	31.0	979.2	31.2	252.7	106.6
Cuba	158.7	37.0	303.8	47.4	285.0	43.6	331.0	49.8	108.6	34.6
Other	192.3		533.7		566.9		587.9		205.7	
Total	628.6	16.6	1,808.7	29.6	1,794.3	28.9	1,898.1	30.3	202.0	82.5
South America										
Argentina	426.6	32.2	795.8	40.0	811.5	40.1	794.3	38.5	86.2	19.6
Brazil	649.1	17.1	2,070.8	33.8	2,450.2	39.1	2,426.7	37.8	273.9	121.1
Chile	123.1	25.8	200.0	28.1	213.8	29.3	220.8	29.6	79.4	14.7
Colombia	46.8	5.6	282.6	21.4	289.1	21.4	289.4	20.9	518.4	273.2
Peru	79.2	12.0	245.3	24.7	263.9	25.8	261.4	24.8	230.1	106.7
Venezuela	18.0	5.4	145.0	23.4	192.8	30.2	233.9	35.5	1199.4	557.4
Other	128.5		294.4		307.3		321.4		150.1	
Total	1,471.3	17.8	4,033.9	31.0	4,528.6	34.0	4,547.9	33.4	209.1	87.6
Western Europe										
Austria	179.0	26.5	269.0	38.4	283.0	40.3	271.1	38.5	51.5	45.3
Belgium-Luxembourg	252.7	29.3	304.1	32.7	288.3	30.8	289.2	30.7	14.4	4.8
Denmark	206.0	55.3	266.8	59.4	279.0	61.8	260.3	57.2	26.4	3.4
France	1,032.9	24.7	1,441.8	32.8	1,457.5	32.7	1,518.1	33.7	47.0	36.4
Germany, West	1,000.0	25.2	1,628.9	30.3	1,700.3	31.3	1,705.7	30.6	70.6	21.4
Italy	336.0	7.9	884.7	18.2	940.4	19.4	1,000.0	20.4	197.6	158.2
Netherlands	237.9	27.9	454.1	41.2	502.3	44.9	506.6	44.7	112.9	60.2
Spain	308.0	12.4	492.4	16.7	487.0	16.5	508.0	17.0	64.9	37.1
Sweden	308.7	49.3	339.8	46.1	347.4	46.9	353.4	47.4	14.5	-3.9
Switzerland	171.0	41.0	261.4	51.1	265.0	51.1	270.0	51.5	57.9	25.6
United Kingdom	2,308.0	49.0	2,985.6	58.0	2,728.0	52.8	2,979.0	57.3	29.1	16.9
Other	565.9		973.8		1,036.7		1,059.5		87.2	
Total	6,906.1	25.2	10,302.4	32.4	10,314.9	32.2	10,720.9	33.0	55.2	31.0

Table 100 (Continued)

SUGAR: WORLD CONSUMPTION, TOTAL AND PER CAPITA, BY PRINCIPAL REGIONS AND COUNTRIES

Region and Country	Prewar Average		1957		1958		1959		% Increase 1959 over prewar	
	Total	p.c.	Total	p.c.	Total	p.c.	Total	p.c.	Total	p.c.
Eastern Europe and USSR										
Czechoslovakia	404.0	26.6	496.0	37.1	511.0	37.9	524.7	38.7	29.9	45.5
Germany, East	700.0	25.2	568.0	32.4	568.0	32.7	562.0	32.5	-19.7	29.0
Hungary	100.9	11.2	270.0	27.4	267.0	27.0	279.0	28.0	176.5	150.0
Poland	380.8	11.8	815.0	28.8	891.3	31.0	939.1	32.1	146.6	172.0
Romania	111.8	5.8	190.0	10.7	220.0	12.2	240.0	13.1	114.7	125.9
USSR	1,923.2	11.2	4,777.0	23.5	5,245.0	25.3	5,858.0	27.8	204.6	148.2
Other	31.1		132.5		148.0		153.5		393.6	
Total	3,651.8	12.9	7,248.5	24.2	7,850.3	25.8	8,556.3	27.8	134.3	115.5
Near East Asia										
Iran	95.5	6.4	331.9	17.3	399.2	20.3	465.7	23.1	387.6	260.9
Iraq	40.0	10.3	160.0	24.7	170.0	25.8	180.0	25.9	350.0	151.5
Turkey	81.0	4.9	290.4	11.4	329.2	12.6	308.0	11.5	280.2	134.7
Other	93.3		286.9		321.8		356.4		282.0	
Total	309.8	4.9	1,059.2	12.4	1,220.2	13.8	1,310.1	14.5	322.9	195.9
Far East Asia										
India	975.0	3.2	2,193.0	5.6	2,255.0	5.7	2,297.0	-	135.6	-
Indonesia	308.0	4.6	665.0	7.8	704.8	8.1	729.3	8.1	136.8	76.1
Japan	866.4	12.3	1,159.0	12.8	1,255.0	13.7	1,321.0	14.2	52.5	15.4
Malaya and Singapore	110.3	22.5	215.0	24.6	235.2	26.1	242.7	25.9	120.0	15.1
Pakistan	200.0	3.1	210.0	2.5	221.0	2.6	221.0	2.5	10.5	-19.4
Philippines	116.5	7.7	274.0	13.4	313.3	13.9	287.6	15.9	146.9	106.5
Other	282.9		640.7		683.8		720.7		154.8	
Total	2,859.1	4.7	5,356.7	6.7	5,668.1	7.0	5,819.3	7.1	103.5	51.1
Africa										
Algeria	78.9	10.7	210.3	21.0	215.0	20.9	219.0	20.0	177.6	86.9
Egypt	140.0 1/	8.9 2/	306.9	12.8	328.0	13.2	330.0	13.0	135.7	46.1
Morocco	183.9 1/	25.1 2/	317.4	31.4	325.0	31.5	330.0	31.3	79.4	24.7
Union of South Africa	206.6	19.4	642.8	40.3	690.7	42.6	713.5	43.2	245.4	122.7
Other	211.5		828.7		962.3		1,048.9		395.9	
Total	820.9	5.0	2,306.1	10.1	2,521.0	10.6	2,641.4	10.7	221.8	114.0

Continued

Table 100 (Continued)

SUGAR: WORLD CONSUMPTION, TOTAL AND PER CAPITA, BY PRINCIPAL REGIONS AND COUNTRIES

Region and Country	Prewar Average		1957		1958		1959		% Increase 1959 over prewar	
	Total	p.c.	Total	p.c.	Total	p.c.	Total	p.c.	Total	p.c.
Oceania	464.0	43.3	678.9	45.0	696.8	45.3	713.3	44.8	53.7	3.5
China, Mongolia, and North Korea	470.0	1.0	950.0	1.5	1,000.0	1.5	1,300.0	1.8	176.6	80.0
WORLD TOTAL	24,114.7[3]	11.3	42,614.8[3]	15.3	44,823.8[3]	15.7	46,914.5[3]	16.1	94.5	42.0

[1] Addition of totals for former French and Spanish zones. [2] Average of totals for former French and Spanish zones.
[3] Adjusted totals.

Source: F. A. O., The World Sugar Economy in Figures: 1880-1959.

422

Table 101

S U G A R (Raw Value)

UNITED STATES IMPORTS BY COUNTRY OF ORIGIN: 1957-61
(In 1,000 Short Tons)

Country of Origin	1957	1958	1959	1960	1961	1962[1]
Latin American Republics						
Mexico	38	72	72	385	601	
Cuba	3,039	3,495	3,216	2,217	-	
Dominican Republic	69	75	130	425	367	
Peru	84	82	100	258	615	
Brazil	-	-	-	100	324	
Other	21	30	39	90	210[2]	
Total	3,251	3,755	3,557	3,476	2,118	
Other Countries						
British West Indies	-	-	-	68	190	
India	-	-	-	-	163	
Philippines	877	968	973	1,092	1,313	
Taiwan	4	-	-	10	164	
Other	4	9	9	42	272	
Total	885	977	982	1,212	2,102	
TOTAL IMPORTS	4,136	4,732	4,539	4,688	4,220	4,616

[1] Breakdown of imports by country of origin not yet available, as of July 5, 1963

SOURCE: U. S. Department of Agriculture, Foreign Agricultural Service

[2] Includes imports from Ecuador of 31,285 short tons.

Table 102

S U G A R (Raw Value)

JAPAN IMPORTS BY COUNTRY OF ORIGIN: 1957-61
(In Thousands of Metric Tons)

Country of Origin	1957	1958	1959	1960	1961
ECUADOR	-	19.6	15.6	10.2	15.0
Argentina	-	-	-	-	23.2
Cuba	513.8	516.7	389.8	205.7	325.5
Brazil	-	69.8	94.8	183.4	357.3
Dominican Republic	37.3	70.7	61.5	79.5	107.0
Peru	98.7	33.2	98.5	111.1	2.7
Formosa	315.1	312.4	364.0	451.9	351.3
Ryukyu	29.7	37.1	36.0	4.3	12.9
Australia	111.2	145.3	110.3	122.4	96.2
Other	54.5	15.7	37.4	61.4	27.4
TOTAL	1,160.3	1,120.5	1,207.9	1,229.9	1,318.5

Source: U. S. Department of Agriculture, Foreign Agricultural Service.

Table 103

T O B A C C O[1]

WORLD EXPORTS BY COUNTRY OF ORIGIN,
Average 1950-54 and 1955-59, Annual 1960-61
(In 1,000 Pounds)

Country of Origin	Average 1950-54	Average 1955-59	1960[2]	1961[2]
North America				
Canada	31,050	37,223	37,199	40,000[3]
United States	473,640	499,795	496,149	500,840
Honduras	3,803	3,325	2,953	3,880[3]
Mexico	555	955	2,911	2,985
Cuba	36,642	53,228	57,172	45,000[4]
Dominican Republic	29,763	27,389	33,496	38,000[3]
Other	271	274	78	52
Total	575,724	622,189	629,958	630,757
South America				
Argentina	973	3,084	5,059	6,634
Brazil	64,847	63,618	69,002	107,415
Colombia	9,315	11,059	14,023	19,163
Paraguay	7,267	5,692	13,490	13,004
Other	10	1,434	560	539
Total	82,412	84,887	102,134	146,755
Europe				
France	1,183	4,740	7,899	7,482
Greece	88,077	127,743	134,459	144,864
Italy	22,160	25,547	29,643	36,631
Yugoslavia	15,712	39,723	40,730	30,600[3]
Turkey	132,971	146,417	127,968	194,939
Other	4,182	6,846	4,948	5,802
Total	264,285	351,016	345,647	420,318
Africa				
Algeria	27,716	19,048	18,600	20,250[3]
Malagasy Republic	8,596	8,804	6,607	6,504
Rhodesia and Nyasaland	116,811	149,496	192,323	209,990
South Africa, Republic of	2,823	2,144	10,403	7,967
Other	4,938	6,494	6,148	7,830
Total	160,884	185,986	234,081	252,541
Asia				
India	84,405	92,265	89,748	108,000[3]
Indonesia	30,192	33,116	50,200	38,680
Japan	1,254	6,274	12,196	14,672
Philippines	19,281	22,192	27,700[4]	37,029
Other	9,444	15,450	12,118	11,907
Total	144,576	169,297	191,962	210,288
Oceania	1	181	73	142
Other Countries[5]	23,254	20,083	16,807	14,772
TOTAL	1,251,136	1,433,639	1,520,662	1,675,573

[1]Unmanufactured tobacco. [2]Preliminary. [3]Estimated from data for less than
one year. [4]Approximated from unofficial sources. [5]Re-exports from Denmark,
Netherlands, Norway, Portugal, United Kingdom, Aden, Malaya, and Hong Kong.

Source: U. S. Department of Agriculture, Foreign Agricultural Service.

425

Table 104

T O B A C C O[1]

WORLD IMPORTS,
Average 1950-54 and 1955-59, Annual 1960-61
(In 1,000 Pounds)

Country	Average 1950-54	Average 1955-59	1960 [2]	1961 [2]
North America[3]	114,094	144,901	176,013	184,586
South America	15,419	11,986	17,824	19,344
Europe				
Belgium-Luxembourg	48,717	54,264	64,532	66,427
France	69,912	73,042	58,504	79,050
West Germany	114,993	164,528	192,848	214,905
Netherlands	69,370	71,773	105,032[4]	95,583
Spain	48,270	47,419[4]	43,780[4]	48,900[4]
United Kingdom	302,358	319,435	364,607	345,398
Other	148,772	158,019	178,304	183,923
Total	802,392	888,480	1,007,607	1,034,186
Africa				
Algeria	9,856	15,009	15,664	14,150[5]
Morocco	4,997	4,876	4,525	5,000[6]
Tunisia	5,465	5,548	4,952	5,200[6]
U. A. R., Egypt	26,278	25,564	25,024	25,397
Canary Islands	1,240	6,108	9,500[6]	10,000[6]
Congo, Republic of the	6,554	9,869	1,500	3,200[6]
Nigeria	6,596	5,568	4,125	2,750[5]
South Africa, Republic of	2,989	8,489	5,072	4,145
Other	12,512	9,193	13,693	13,709
Total	76,487	90,224	84,055	83,551
Asia				
Aden	-	9,332	9,805	9,764
Cambodia	13,748	1,445	1,878	1,200
Hong Kong	11,470	9,531	10,476	13,030
Indonesia	13,484	15,430	1,272	3,364
Japan	11,810	11,816	14,997	25,177
Malaya	462	4,673	10,983	14,000
Pakistan	7,453	1,531	1,326	1,600
Philippines	22,374	8,238	650	46
Thailand	5,488	10,292	5,814	12,688
Vietnam	-	8,023	4,650[7]	5,000[5][7]
Other	10,067	10,471	8,842	10,773
Total	96,356	90,782	70,693	96,642
Oceania	37,678	49,796	37,646	37,889
TOTAL	1,142,426	1,276,169	1,393,838	1,456,198

[1] Unmanufactured tobacco. [2] Preliminary. [3] Imports into the United States account for 90% of total North American tobacco imports. [4] Includes Cueta. [5] Estimated from data for less than one year. [6] Approximated from unofficial sources. [7] Includes manufactured products.

Source: U. S. Department of Agriculture, Foreign Agricultural Service.

426

Table 105

T O B A C C O   A N D   T O B A C C O   P R O D U C T S

ECUADOR: ESTIMATED PRODUCTION AND CONSUMPTION,
Average 1935-39, 1951-55, Annual 1957-62
(In 1,000 Pounds)

	Average 1935-39	Average 1951-55	1957	1958	1959	1960	1961	1962
Tobacco								
Estimated Farm Production[1]	2,800	2,589	2,500	2,493	2,028	2,205	2,300	2,400
Tobacco Products								
Estimated Consumption, by Type								
Cigarettes								
Domestic	1,361	1,792	1,613	1,555	1,613	1,620	1,650	N.A.
Imported	25	677	1,100	927	1,085	1,025	1,000	N.A.
Total	1,386	2,469	2,713	2,482	2,698	2,645	2,650	N.A.
Cigars	825	153	250	260	270	300	305	N.A.
Other Tobacco Products	100	110	330	336	370	416	420	N.A.
Total	2,311	2,732	3,293	3,078	3,338	3,361	3,375	N.A.

1/Year of harvest.

Source: U. S. Department of Agriculture, Foreign Agricultural Service.

427

Table 106

T U N A [1]/

UNITED STATES IMPORTS BY COUNTRY OF ORIGIN: 1957-62

(In 1,000 Pounds)

Country of Origin	1957	1958	1959	1960	1961	1962
North America						
Canada	33.6	45.7	64.9	123.1	56.1	566.0
Mexico	413.8	3,583.0	5,128.6	4,061.5	3,495.5	4,228.4
Trinidad	-	-	6,540.3	7,168.0	11,516.1	15,411.4
Panama	-	-	1,112.6	661.4	-	-
Canal Zone	-	-	3,692.0	-	-	160.0
Other	-	83.7	93.0	660.0	-	-
Total	447.4	3,712.4	16,631.4	12,674.0	15,067.7	20,365.8
South America						
Venezuela	-	-	-	-	-	1,109.8
ECUADOR	460.9	1,340.2	9,159.9	9,508.2	6,945.4	11,686.3
Peru	23,581.0	28,562.4	53,695.0	40,711.7	6,682.7	31,781.2
Other	558.4	-	34.0	213.1	-	23.5
Total	24,600.3	29,902.6	62,888.9	50,433.0	13,628.1	44,600.8
Europe	-	-	20.0	-	-	550.9
Africa						
Canary Islands	-	-	-	546.5	-	5,292.5
Ethiopia	-	-	-	-	-	767.5
South Africa, Republic of	-	-	-	-	18.1	4,718.1
Ghana	-	-	-	550.0	4,488.0	156.7
British West Africa	-	-	-	12,487.3	19,237.8	16,914.5
Western Africa, n. e. c.	-	-	-	9,417.9	9,038.3	4,757.6
Total	-	-	-	23,001.7	32,782.2	32,606.9

Table 106 (Continued)

TUNA: UNITED STATES IMPORTS BY COUNTRY OF ORIGIN

Country of Origin	1957	1958	1959	1960	1961	1962
Asia						
Japan	114,229.4	159,164.6	151,374.8	135,063.3	117,280.7	150,729.6
Taiwan	-	274.3	1,324.4	1,245.3	1,024.1	1,656.5
Nansei and Nanpo Is.	-	139.5	435.7	-	251.0	1,881.4
British West Pacific Is.	-	4,765.0	3,232.5	10,419.1	15,908.0	17,469.3
Other	10.0	-	-	299.5	-	895.5
Total	114,239.4	164,343.4	156,367.4	147,027.2	134,463.8	172,632.3
Australia	-	-	2.7	1,512.7	1,185.8	1,708.8
TOTAL	139,287.0	197,958.4	235,910.5	234,648.7	197,127.7	272,465.4

1/ Albacore, yellow fin, big eye, blue fin, skipjack, and other tuna, fresh or frozen, not cooked. Prepared tuna loins and discs have been excluded because these items were not separately classified prior to January 1, 1960.

Source: U. S. Department of Commerce, Bureau of the Census.

429

Table 107

C A N N E D   T U N A[1]

UNITED STATES IMPORTS BY COUNTRY OF ORIGIN: 1957-62
(In 1,000 Pounds)

Country of Origin	1957	1958	1959	1960	1961	1962
Western Hemisphere						
ECUADOR	147	806	1,127	2,497	3,107	3,373
Peru	651	800	1,054	1,512	1,564	232
Other	21	-	819	31	-	1
Total	819	1,606	3,000	4,009	4,671	3,606
Europe						
Azores	450	553	387	266	252	1,635
Spain	139	489	4,406	1,747	691	137
Portugal	1,040	1,752	2,000	1,842	3,568	1,484
Italy	29	23	286	123	221	223
Other	9	49	67	224	553	50
Total	1,667	2,866	7,146	4,202	5,285	3,529
Africa						
Angola	168	743	924	617	1,508	1,716
Other	260	25	161	94	468	481
Total	428	768	1,085	711	1,976	2,197
Asia						
Japan	41,472	40,964	44,891	42,834	46,730	47,353
Other	2/	1	12	2/	2/	33
Total	41,472	40,965	44,903	42,834	46,730	47,386
TOTAL	44,386	46,204	56,134	51,755	58,662	56,718

[1] Includes tuna canned in oil and in brine. For each year shown tuna canned in brine accounted for 98 or 99 percent of total imports. [2] Less than 1,000 pounds.

Source: U. S. Department of Commerce, Bureau of the Census.

ABOUT THE AUTHOR

Ralph J. Watkins, a Vice President of Surveys & Research Corporation, has had a wide experience in directing research for industry and governments and as a teacher of economics and business administration on a number of university faculties.

In addition to the subject study, he has directed a number of the firm's major research projects, among them a continuing informational survey of scientific research and development in Communist China, for the National Science Foundation, and an evaluation of Mexico's steel requirements, for the Export-Import Bank. At present he is director of a regional economic development project in India, with emphasis upon transportation needs of the Calcutta area, financed by the World Bank.

Prior to joining SRC, Dr. Watkins was Director of Economic Studies, at the Brookings Institution; a Director of Research, at Dun & Bradstreet, Inc.; and a chief of various U. S. government offices. He served on the faculties of the University of Texas, Ohio State University, University of Pittsburgh, and Columbia University.

Dr. Watkins received his undergraduate degree in economics and business administration from the University of Texas and his graduate degrees from Columbia University.